ADHD and Education

Foundations, Characteristics, Methods, and Collaboration

Sydney S. Zentall
Purdue University

PEARSON
Merrill
Prentice Hall

Upper Saddle River, New Jersey
Columbus, Ohio

Library of Congress Cataloging-in-Publication Data

Zentall, Sydney S.
ADHD and education : foundations, characteristics, methods, and collaboration / Sydney S. Zentall.
p. cm.
Includes bibliographical references and indexes.
ISBN 0-13-098173-7
1. Attention-deficit-disordered children—Education. 2. Attention-deficit hyperactivity disorder—Treatment.
I. Title.
LC4713.2.Z47 2006
371.94—dc22 2005045817

Vice President and Executive Publisher: Jeffery W. Johnston
Senior Acquisitions Editor: Allyson P. Sharp
Editorial Assistant: Kathleen S. Burk
Senior Production Editor: Linda Hillis Bayma
Production Coordination: GGS Book Services, Atlantic Highlands
Design Coordinator: Diane C. Lorenzo
Cover Designer: Bryan Huber
Cover image: Super Stock
Production Manager: Laura Messerly
Director of Marketing: Ann Castel Davis
Marketing Manager: Autumn Purdy
Marketing Coordinator: Brian Mounts

This book was set in Garamond by GGS Book Services, Atlantic Highlands. It was printed and bound by R.R. Donnelley & Sons Company. The cover was printed by R.R. Donnelley & Sons Company.

Photo Credits: Photo on page 172 was taken by the author. All cartoons © Stephanie Funcheon.

Pearson Education Ltd.
Pearson Education Singapore Pte. Ltd.
Pearson Education Canada, Ltd.
Pearson Education—Japan
Pearson Education Australia Pty. Limited
Pearson Education North Asia Ltd.
Pearson Educación de Mexico, S.A. de C.V.
Pearson Education Malaysia Pte. Ltd.

PEARSON
Merrill
Prentice Hall

10 9 8 7 6 5 4 3
ISBN: 0-13-098173-7

Preface

ADHD is a major clinical and public health problem because of its prevalence and its disabling effects on children and adolescents (Wilens, Biederman, & Spencer, 2002). The disabling effects of ADHD are found primarily in school contexts.

Although a number of important books and scientific articles on ADHD have been written in medicine/psychiatry, psychology, and school psychology, books written by and targeting special or general educators are difficult to find. To this purpose and as a way to bring together more than 30 years of educational reading and research in ADHD, this text focuses on education and special education and the vital collaboration between these systems.

Professionals outside the educational field are concerned about what educators know about ADHD:

> Educators may lack knowledge about the current understanding of ADHD, hold misperceptions about ADHD, and continue to use traditional intervention approaches that are inconsistent with current knowledge. (Tannock & Martinussen, 2001, p. 21)

> [There is a] lack of research into the educational needs of children with mental health problems. This has resulted in classification of children into categories of exceptionality with very little guidance for those attempting to meet their needs. ADHD is a classic example of this problem. (Evans, 1995, p. 46)

Information that is needed by educators who daily instruct these children is difficult to find and typically is not evidence-based. General education is where students with ADHD spend the majority of their time, even when they also receive special education services (Reid, Vasa, Maag, & Wright, 1994). Perhaps this lack of scientific information disseminated into the field has contributed to lists of "practical suggestions." Fads and "how-to" lists are more prevalent in recently recognized areas of exceptionality, such as ADHD, where less educational research has been done. Education and special education were late to recognize children with ADHD, and for this reason few educational researchers have dedicated research to this area. Thus, a larger gap exists between educational research and educational practice than between, for example, school or clinical psychology and clinical practice.

A scarcity of information exists in most textbooks as well:

> Although most educational psychology and special education textbooks devote one chapter . . . most fail to provide the depth and detail necessary for classroom teachers to identify students with attention deficits and effectively meet their cognitive, academic, and affective needs. (Swartz & Martin, 1997, p. 164)

In fact, educators have had to turn to the fields of learning disabilities for answers to the academic problems of students with ADHD and have had to rely on medication and the field of emotional and behavioral disorders for the social and behavioral problems of these students. Although these related fields have provided some direction, important differences exist between students with ADHD and these populations in (a) the nature of their learning and behavioral difficulties and strengths, (b) contributors to these problems, and (c) interventions that are differentially beneficial for them. Thus, one purpose of this text is to provide educators with a body of knowledge about students with ADHD, separate from related areas in special education, and to explain how these students differ from students with learning disabilities and emotional and behavioral disorders. Those few texts that do emphasize ADHD and not related populations are written from a school psychology perspective, emphasizing diagnosis and assessment, and the behavioral/psychosocial methodologies presented in chapter 9.

ADHD and Education: Foundations, Characteristics, Methods, and Collaboration is based on the premise that educators are concerned professionals who are interested in distinguishing between what people think is true and what is the best scientific knowledge. In addition to this emphasis on evidence, the perspectives of individual educators, parents, and students are presented in this text. These participants can easily capture the true nature of both their difficulties and their strengths and often have a clear understanding of what has worked for them in the past. These different voices within each chapter are denoted with the following icons:

Chapter Objectives

Family Practices

Evidence-Based Practice or Principle

Student Practices

Teacher Strategies

Limitations

USES OF THIS TEXT

This text is relevant to instructors in higher education who organize instruction within the domains of (a) foundations, (b) characteristics, (c) methods, and (d) indirect methods of consultation and collaboration. Thus, this text can be used as a supplement to a course on mild disabilities, the inclusive classroom, characteristics, or methods. In categorical programs where ADHD is addressed in the field of learning disabilities or in educational methods in general education, chapters 6, 7, 10, and 11 are important; and where ADHD relates to the problems of children with behavioral disorders or classroom management in general education, chapters 4, 5, 8, and 9 are important.

Finally, this text is designed to be useful for in-service programs. In particular, I recommend the information and activities of functional assessment in chapter 4 and the richness of the methods chapters (8 through 12) as they relate to the learning and behavioral challenges of students with ADHD.

For each of these different purposes, the chapters can be rearranged (i.e., the instructor may decide to present information on inattention and learning and use only chapters 6, 7, 10, and 11). Although this reordering of chapters for specific purposes is part of the design of this text, I would strongly recommend that students read the brief section in chapter 1 related to the optimal stimulation theory. This section will help them understand why these children behave as they do, the rational and empirical basis for their behavior, and criteria for selecting interventions.

CHAPTER CONTENT

To provide a balanced perspective and different perspectives, most chapters include limitations and controversies. Some of the controversies are:

1. defining and labeling children with ADHD, producing possible stigma and a failure to capture the individual but also powerful knowledge and legal protections (chapters 2 and 3);
2. understanding students with ADHD as a group (causes and theories in chapter 1) as well as understanding the needs of individuals (through functional assessments in chapter 4);
3. recognizing problems and outcomes as well as the adaptive social/behavioral characteristics of each of the subtypes of ADHD—inattentive and hyperactive/impulsive subtypes (chapters 5 and 6);
4. recognizing the differences between the learning and academic problems of children with pure ADHD and those of children with ADHD plus co-occurring learning disabilities;
5. providing accommodations while examining questions about "enabling," independence, and fairness to other children;
6. providing interventions that immediately change the behavior or the biology of the child, producing a better fit and greater short-term success as

well as questions about issues of long-term compliance and outcomes (chapters 9 and 10); and

7. recognizing how to increase support for children with ADHD through understanding the perspectives and needs of their parents, teachers, and administrators (chapter 12).

Recurrent themes within this text are working collaboratively and expressing positive attitudes toward and expectations of students with ADHD (Bos, Nahmias, & Urban, 1999). Differences in social perspective are important to this field and perhaps essential to the nature of ADHD, as exemplified in a "Non Sequitur" cartoon by Wiley. It shows two characters, each sitting at an identical table but around the corner from one another. A gypsy-type woman sits with a statement written on her table: "All of Life's Questions Answered." Around the corner from her sits an individual with the statement written on his table that says, "All of Life's Answers Questioned."

ACKNOWLEDGMENTS

Thanks to Stephanie Funcheon, artist, whose cartoons and icons appear throughout this book.

The range of information in this text can be credited to my former doctoral students, who uncovered new areas to explore related to their own interests in ADHD. These former doctoral students are Avi Madan-Swain, Marty Meyer, Melissa Stormont, Arlene Hall, David Lee, Sandra Beyda Lorie, Suneeta Kercood, Janice Grskovic, Doreen Ferko, James Javorsky, Andres Vargas, and Deitra Kuester. I am also grateful to my graduate and undergraduate students, who made suggestions on early versions of these chapters, and to Heather Moody, who was resourceful in tracking references. I am most indebted to Thomas Zentall for his mentoring in research design and to Ron Langdon for his considerable support and suggestions.

I also thank the reviewers for their thoughtful commentary and helpful suggestions: Judy L. Bell, Furman University; Marion Boss, University of Toledo; Lynda Conover, Western Illinois University; Marilyn R. Eggers, La Sierra University; John D. Foshay, Central Connecticut State University; Michael P. Gallo, Minnesota State University, Moorehead; Mickie Mathes, Breman University; Thomas F. McLaughlin, Gonzaga University; Robert Michael, State University of New York, New Paltz; Darlos Mummert, Western Illinois University; and Phyllis M. Tappe, San Francisco State University.

Finally, this text would not have been possible without the administrators, counselors, teachers, parents, and children who allowed us into their schools, classrooms, homes, and lives, so that we might more fully understand ADHD. To all of these individuals and in support of students with ADHD, I dedicate this book.

Discover the Merrill Education Resources for Special Education Website

Technology is a constantly growing and changing aspect of our field that is creating a need for new content and resources. To address this emerging need, Merrill Education has developed an online learning environment for students, teachers, and professors alike to complement our products—the *Merrill Education Resources for Special Education* Website. This content-rich website provides additional resources specific to this book's topic and will help you—professors, classroom teachers, and students—augment your teaching, learning, and professional development.

Our goal is to build on and enhance what our products already offer. For this reason, the content for our user-friendly website is organized by topic and provides teachers, professors, and students with a variety of meaningful resources all in one location. With this website, we bring together the best of what Merrill has to offer: text resources, video clips, web links, tutorials, and a wide variety of information on topics of interest to general and special educators alike. Rich content, applications, and competencies further enhance the learning process.

The *Merrill Education Resources for Special Education* Website includes:

RESOURCES FOR THE PROFESSOR—

- The **Syllabus Manager**™, an online syllabus creation and management tool, enables instructors to create and revise their syllabus with an easy, step-by-step process. Students can access your syllabus and any changes you make during the course of your class from any computer with Internet access. To access this tailored syllabus, students will just need the URL of the website and the password assigned to the syllabus. By clicking on the date, the student can see a list of activities, assignments, and readings due for that particular class.
- In addition to the **Syllabus Manager**™ and its benefits listed above, professors also have access to all of the wonderful resources that students have access to on the site.

RESOURCES FOR THE STUDENT—

- Video clips specific to each topic, with questions to help you evaluate the content and make crucial theory-to-practice connections.
- Thought-provoking critical analysis questions that you can answer and turn in for evaluation or that can serve as basis for class discussions and lectures.
- Access to a wide variety of resources related to classroom strategies and methods, including lesson planning and classroom management.
- Information on all the most current relevant topics related to special and general education, including CEC and Praxis standards, IEPs, portfolios, and professional development.
- Extensive web resources and overviews on each topic addressed on the website.
- A message board with discussion starters where you can respond to class discussion topics, post questions and responses, or ask questions about assignments.
- A search feature to help access specific information quickly.

To take advantage of these and other resources, please visit the *Merrill Education Resources for Special Education* Website at

http://www.prenhall.com/zentall

Educator Learning Center:

An Invaluable Online Resource

Merrill Education and the Association for Supervision and Curriculum Development (ASCD) invite you to take advantage of a new online resource, one that provides access to the top research and proven strategies associated with ASCD and Merrill—the Educator Learning Center. At **www.educatorlearningcenter.com**, you will find resources that will enhance your students' understanding of course topics and of current educational issues in addition to being invaluable for further research.

HOW THE EDUCATOR LEARNING CENTER WILL HELP YOUR STUDENTS BECOME BETTER TEACHERS

With the combined resources of Merrill Education and ASCD, you and your students will find a wealth of tools and materials to better prepare them for the classroom.

Research

- More than 600 articles from the ASCD journal *Educational Leadership* discuss everyday issues faced by practicing teachers.
- A direct link on the site to Research Navigator™ gives students access to many of the leading education journals as well as extensive content detailing the research process.
- Excerpts from Merrill Education texts give your students insights on important topics of instructional methods, diverse populations, assessment, classroom management, technology, and refining classroom practice.

Classroom Practice

- Hundreds of lesson plans and teaching strategies are categorized by content area and age range.
- Case studies and classroom video footage provide virtual field experience for student reflection.
- Computer simulations and other electronic tools keep your students abreast of today's classrooms and current technologies.

LOOK INTO THE VALUE OF EDUCATOR LEARNING CENTER YOURSELF

A four-month subscription to Educator Learning Center is $25 but is **FREE** when packaged with any Merrill Education text. In order for your students to have access to this site, you must use this special value-pack ISBN number **WHEN** placing your textbook order with the bookstore: 0-13-220471-1. Your students will then receive a copy of the text packaged with a free ASCD pincode. To preview the value of this website to you and your students, please go to **www.educatorlearningcenter.com** and click on "Demo."

Brief Contents

Contents

Note: Every effort has been made to provide accurate and current Internet information in this book. However, the Internet and information posted on it are constantly changing so it is inevitable that some of the Internet addresses listed in the textbook will change.

PART *One*

Foundations

CHAPTER 1

Legal Issues

OBJECTIVES

- Name the two major laws that have influenced the area of ADHD.
- Explain how their specific provisions protect rights and provide guarantees of students with ADHD.

KEY TERMS

U.S. statutes
Individuals with Disabilities Educational Act Section 504
least restrictive environment
individualized education plan
free and appropriate public education
multidisciplinary team
manifest determination
Americans with Disabilities Act
504 plan
interim alternative educational setting
harassment
Office of Civil Rights

U.S. statutes or laws determine eligibility for services and have significantly altered the public education of students with disabilities. The source of these federal laws is the U.S. Constitution, mainly the Bill of Rights, which includes the 14th Amendment guaranteeing civil rights. These public laws are (a) the Individuals with Disabilities Educational Act (IDEA) and (b) Section 504 of the Vocational Rehabilitation Act of 1973. Each of these laws requires placement of a child with disabilities in a least restrictive environment (LRE), with IDEA requiring an individualized education plan (IEP) with specially designed instruction and related services and Section 504 requiring a plan of reasonable accommodations and related services.

IDEA

What legally protects the rights of children with disabilities?

Public Law (P.L.) 94-142, the Education for All Handicapped Children Act, was passed by Congress in August 1975, grandfathered by the antidiscrimination law *Brown v. Board of Education of Topeka Kansas* (1954), under which African Americans sought admission to public schools on a nonsegregated basis. Before 1975, there was no national legislation covering the evaluation and education of students with disabilities. Public Law 94-142 was later reinterpreted or reauthorized in 1990 as IDEA; additional provisions were added in 1997 and most recently in the IDEA Improvement Act of 2004 with provisions effective July 1, 2005. IDEA is the main federal law that provides for the education

of disabled youth ages 3 to 21 years and was extended downward from birth to 3 years by P.L. 99-457 amendments.

IDEA provides federal financial assistance so that state and local education agencies have additional funding for identified students. IDEA is the funding act for special education. The purpose of federal assistance is to support a free and appropriate public education (FAPE) for students with disabilities. A FAPE includes the rights of appropriate assessment and identification (i.e., protection against discriminatory assessment and the rights of due process of assessment, placement, and programming procedures) and appropriate education (i.e., a program designed to provide "educational benefits" and related services, if necessary, in order for the students to benefit from specially designed instruction).

If the parent disagrees with the school's evaluation and the hearing officer concurs, there is a provision for independent educational evaluation at district expense. Parents may also initiate due process procedures under IDEA and address the nonprovision of a FAPE. IDEA is enforced by the U.S. Office of Special Education Programs, and compliance is monitored by state departments of education.

IDEA delegates specific responsibilities to local school systems to locate and educate children with disabilities. If the school system has reason to suspect that the child has a disability (e.g., indicated by comments in the report card) but fails to act by referring the child for a comprehensive special education evaluation, they have failed in their obligation to find, evaluate (the "Child-Find Mandate"), and provide a FAPE for a child with a disability. House Resolution 1350 (2004) provided further clarification on this issue. That is, parents must have put into writing to school

NOTE
Due Process Rights of Children—Their Parents and Guardians

1. Receiving written notice of proposed change of placement 10 days in advance, with the right to contest that change within the 10-day period through a due process hearing
2. Parental access to school records
3. Confidentiality of assessment results
4. Informed consent (information about their rights and parental signature required) before initial evaluation can be conducted and before any placement can occur
5. A reevaluation at least every 3 years

personnel that their child needs special education services (with an exception of an illiterate parent or a parent with a disability). Clearly, school systems are not responsible for providing a FAPE when parents have refused evaluation for services or the child's evaluation failed to document a disability.

The plan for delivering special education and related services is called an IEP. A child is to be provided with an IEP if he or she is found to be eligible for special education services. An IEP is a legal document, and general education teachers must have a copy of and comply with it for those students in their classes who are receiving special education services. The IEP represents accountability; it defines the responsibilities of the school. The school is legally bound to provide only those adaptations or accommodations listed in the IEP. The IEP allows students to benefit from their available public educational programs and takes the responsibility for learning and places it within the educational system (specifically on the case conference committee) rather than blaming students with disabilities for their failure to learn.

General educators may not always be aware of the importance of compliance. In one legal case in a 1992 civil jury trial (*Doe v. Withers*, Civil Action No. 92-C-92: http://www.wrightslaw.com/law/caselaw/case_Doe_Withers_Complaint.html), a general education teacher refused to do oral testing with a child for whom oral testing was specified in thc IEP. The teacher was sued for failure to comply with the terms of the IEP. The outcome of that case was that this teacher had to pay $15,000, his own legal fees, and the legal fees for the complainants.

The IEP is developed by a multidisciplinary team including the child's parents, at least one special educator, at least one general educator or, where appropriate, (i.e., not required at a team meeting), a representative of the local educational agency (qualified to supervise or provide specialized designed instruction and knowledgeable about the general curriculum and resources), an individual who can interpret and provide implications for evaluation results at the discretion of the parent or agency, others who have knowledge or expertise regarding the child or related services, and, when appropriate, the student at the elementary, middle, and secondary levels (House Resolution [H.R.] 5, pp. 131–132). Reauthorization

H.R. 1350 (signed into law in 2004) modifies the requirements of team participation at team meetings. That is, if the parent so designates in writing, all members of the IEP team are not required to attend all or part of the IEP meetings where their input is unnecessary or has already been gathered and integrated into the written IEP document.

An IEP contains information about the child's current level of educational functioning, annual goals and objectives, a listing of special services to be provided (e.g., transportation, occupational therapy), projected start and review dates for services, and how the child's progress will be measured. Where progress is not being made, different materials or methods must be implemented. School systems often use goals that are based on their state standards.

Reauthorization H.R. 1350 (2004) also modifies the frequency of the IEP's reevaluation from 1 to 3 years and changes the evaluation focus to annual goals rather than objectives. Reevaluation may not occur more than once a year but must occur every 3 years unless otherwise ageed on by the parents and the local educational agency. With this change from yearly to multiyear IEPs, measurable annual goals must coincide with natural transition points for the child and a description of the process for review and revision of the multiyear IEP must be included. For example, a review would be conducted by the IEP team at each of the child's natural transition points (from preschool to elementary, elementary to middle school, and so on) and an annual review would be done to determine current progress toward annual goals with a provision for amendments to the IEP to help the child meet the annual goals. In turn, H.R. 1350 modifies reporting information to parents on the child's progress from specific objectives to reporting on progress toward the end-of-year goals (e.g., through the use of quarterly or other periodic reports, concurrent with use of report cards). H.R. 1350 further stipulates that the parent and local educational agency may agree to amend the IEP in writing when changes are indicated rather than convene an IEP meeting. On request, the parent will be provided with a revised copy of the IEP with the amendments incorporated.

Assistance and services are defined by what is required for students with disabilities to achieve parity with nondisabled peers. With reauthorization of IDEA in 2003, states must now report the number of children who are provided with accommodations—comparing their performance with the achievement of nondisabled students. With the reauthorization of IDEA in 2004, states must also have policies and procedures prohibiting schools from requiring a child to obtain prescription medications (specifically "psychotropic medications") as a condition of attending school or receiving services.

IDEA also requires the student to be educated in the least restrictive educational environment (LRE) with his or her nondisabled peers to the maximum extent possible. The case conference committee determines the LRE placement for the child, including consideration of the educational and social benefits available to this child in the general education classroom with supplemental services in comparison to the benefits available in special settings. Special classes, separate schooling, or the removal of students (restrictive educational environments) occurs only when it can be documented that learning cannot be satisfactorily achieved in the general education environment, even with supplementary aids and services.

The team also considers the degree to which the child's disruptiveness interferes with the education of students both with and without disabilities. When making that consideration, team members must keep in mind that average students in classrooms with students with disabilities had (a) achievement that was as good as the achievement of students in classes without students with disabilities (Salisbury, 1993), (b) more positive attitudes toward students with disabilities (California Research Institute, 1992), and (c) improved social and problem-solving skills and self-concept for both disabled and nondisabled groups (for a review, see *Executive Summary*, 1995, p. 5).

Placement decisions are written into the IEP as part of the individualized goals and objectives. The case conference committee can place a child with attention deficit hyperactivity disorder (ADHD) who was eligible for services under the other health impaired (OHI) category of IDEA, within other categorical settings (e.g., a learning disabilities classroom), or within a multicategorical resource setting. Because OHI does not have a teacher licensure or a funding weight attached to it, a student with ADHD could be placed with a teacher certified with any of the exceptionalities. Reauthorization H.R. 1350 (2004) lists requirements for special education teachers stipulating that the teacher must (a) hold at least a bachelor's degree, (b) have a special education certification in the state or passed the state teacher licensing exam, and (c) not be teaching on an emergency, temporary, or provisional basis.

If the setting selected is outside the general classroom, opportunities must exist for the student to interact with nondisabled peers to the maximum extent possible. Thus, when students with ADHD receive services in special education settings, they often receive general education with their peers in nonacademic subject areas (e.g., art, physical education).

In practice, students with inattentiveness but not hyperactivity are placed more often in learning disabilities classes, whereas students with hyperactivity are placed in classes for students with behavioral disorders (Barkley, DuPaul, & McMurray, 1990). Placement within these programs makes it essential that teachers who have categorical training understand the differences between students with ADHD and students with learning disabilities and/or emotional and behavioral disorders (see chapters 5 and 7). When parents of children with ADHD decide that the schools are not providing their children with an appropriate education, they can turn to the legal system to obtain appropriate services.

When services were not forthcoming, parents have placed their children into private schools, obtained outside services, and successfully sued to obtain a reimbursement of these costs. To these ends—and more typically to contribute to the planning of an IEP (see chapter 12)—parents may need to establish and maintain a record. (See "How to Keep Records" on page 8.)

NOTE
How to Keep Records

1. Obtain a complete set of records from the school.
2. In a three-ring binder, date and place all written reports, including the school's records, minutes of meetings, communications, and reports from the school, doctors, and diagnosticians. Keep a log of telephone calls (dates, times, persons, actions promised, and conclusions).
3. Make a second copy of this notebook to highlight information with which you agree or disagree or about which you have further questions. (Never loan your original or master copy except to legal representatives.)
4. Transcribe information (with its source and date) onto a summary sheet divided into columns for strengths and weaknesses for each academic area (see chapter 7) and social areas (see chapter 5). When the same observation is seen in the record, you can simply cite the new source and date. When contradictory information is noted, this is an area for questions.
5. Notification of formal action, such as a request for a hearing or filing of a complaint, must have copies sent by certified mail to the local superintendent, director of special education, principal, and school board president (Fowler, 1994).

SECTION 504

What are the foundational rights of all children within a public classroom?

Section 504 is a civil rights law that was first important in public school settings for those students needing physical access. Increased physical access (e.g., ramps, elevators, larger bathroom stalls) was undertaken in the 1970s, although work continues today (e.g., installing automatic doors). A more recent impact of Section 504 has been on obtaining access to the content of instructional programs. This focus of Section 504 became nationally recognized with the need for services for individuals with ADHD.

Schools, colleges and universities, and other educational institutions receiving federal funds must ensure equal educational opportunities for all students. This includes activities that are related to instruction and to educational and social opportunities, such as field trips, recess, or evaluation procedures. Thus, not allowing a student with ADHD (or with emotional and behavioral disorders) to go on a field trip because he runs in the hall is an instance of punishing the child for his disability. That is, the school cannot exclude children from educational or social opportunities as a way to punish them for behavior that is a manifestation of their disability any more than the judicial system can unreasonably punish someone who is legally insane, mentally deficient, or a juvenile. This is called manifest determination, that is, determining whether a behavior was a manifestation of a student's disability. Manifest determination has been revised (H.R. 1350) to determine whether the conduct was caused by or had a direct and substantial relationship to the child's disability or whether the conduct was the direct result of the local educational agency's failure to implement the IEP.

Manifest determination is based on Section 504 of the Rehabilitation Act of 1973 (P.L. 93-112). Section 504 provides the following:

> No otherwise qualified individual with a disability . . . shall, solely by reason of his disability, be excluded from the participation in, or denied the benefits of, or be subjected to discrimination under any program or activity receiving federal assistance. (29 U.S.C 794[a] CFR PART 104)

In this regard, Section 504 is only somewhat different from the Americans with Disabilities Act (ADA). That is, Title II of the ADA of 1990 guarantees equal educational opportunity but is not dependent on whether the institution is receiving federal funds (e.g., can be applied to parochial or charter schools). Title II provides the following:

> No qualified individual with a disability shall, by reason of such disability, be excluded from participation in or be denied the benefits of the services, program, or activities of the services, programs, or activities of a public entity, or be subjected to discrimination by any such entity. (42 U.S.C. 12132 CFR Part 35)

Section 504 also differs from IDEA in that it does not require a written IEP document. However, it does require a plan, although this plan need not be written. Because discrimination laws such as Section 504 allow for personal civil suits to be taken against school systems, a written record may still be important in demonstrating compliance with the nondiscrimination edicts of Section 504. This written record can be accomplished using functional assessment (see chapter 4).

It is recommended that those persons who are knowledgeable about the student (e.g., teachers, parents, administrators, counselors) convene and agree on a plan of services and accommodations that are "reasonable," meaning that the modification is not costly and does not harm the education of other students. The most common modification includes reducing the quantity of written work required while still assessing the student's attainment of the objectives (Reeve, Schrag, & Walker, 1994). Related services, if required by the disability, include transportation, speech, psychological assessment, occupational and physical therapy, and counseling.

Similar to IDEA, Section 504's regulations require that a child with a disability be served in a LRE with the use of supplementary aids and services to the maximum extent appropriate before placement in special education. The majority of students with ADHD are served in the general education classroom with a 504 plan (Reeves et al., 1994). However, students with 504 plans could be placed in special education resource rooms, for example, with related services.

The Office of Civil Rights is the enforcement agency for Section 504 and ensures that the educational institution is providing what is necessary for the student to benefit from education. Section 504 also requires districts with more than 15 paid employees to designate a 504 coordinator from among their employees. The 504 coordinator is responsible for assuring district compliance with Section 504 and providing a grievance procedure for parents, students, and employees. IDEA procedures may be used to implement Section 504 but are not required.

The Office of Civil Rights monitors school systems on a nonsystematic basis but more often in response to specific complaints from parents. There are sanctions for *not* being in compliance (i.e., losing federal monies that support other educational programs). However, Section 504 does *not* have a funding mechanism. It mandates services and reasonable accommodations but does not provide additional funds. It should be noted that H.R. 1350 authorizes local educational agencies to use up to 15% of IDEA funds for supportive services to help students who have not been identified with disabilities but who require additional academic and/or behavioral support to succeed in general education settings.

LEGAL LIMITATIONS

What are possible problems that should be anticipated?

In the context of public elementary and secondary education, both Section 504 and IDEA stipulate that children with disabilities will receive a FAPE. These statutes define the *boundaries* but not the *practices* themselves. The statutes are subject to interpretation (i.e., judicial decision) by the U.S. courts, for which there is a parallel system in each state. That is, states and even school districts will interpret these statutes differently. Thus, as school systems attempt to comply with these laws, the task can be compared to holding a greased pig. Not only is it moving, but it is also changing shape and color. There are even instances of misinterpretation. That is, the intent of funding under IDEA was to provide additional funding for students with disabilities. Thus, the expenditures should include comprehensive funds from general as well as special education (Executive Summary of the President's Commission on Excellence in Special Education, 2002).

Moreover, the laws are dramatically different from the way they were 30 years ago and even 2 years ago. The statutes contain the same original language, but the interpretation has developed and will continue to change (e.g., re-authorizations and reinterpretations). These advancements are due to additional legal interpretations of the regulations, which may have been undertaken because of new scientific knowledge or in response to pressure from parental advocacy and support groups (e.g., Children and Adults with Attention Deficit Disorders, http://www.chadd.org).

In addition, some modifications are unresolved, primarily because there are no funding provisions for implementation under Section 504. Fifteen percent of IDEA funds can now be used for students who do not have a disability (although this amounts to "taking from Peter to pay Paul"). Implementing modifications without additional funds is of concern to local districts (Reeve, et al., 1994) that attempt to provide low-cost modifications using local resources, such as volunteers, peers, and special education teachers, on a consultant basis. When costs become too great, students are often reconsidered for IDEA eligibility. Another limitation is the adequacy of procedures, specifically for Section 504, which provides fewer procedural safeguards than does IDEA. Section 504 references IDEA procedures as a way to meet its requirements, but it does not require these procedures.

Controversial issues related to IDEA (modified in 1997 and 2004) also relate to in-school and out-of-school suspensions and expulsions. (Some school systems do not define in-school suspensions to be exclusions from the classroom if excluded students were provided with classroom assignments.) This interpretation has not been assessed in the courts. Under IDEA of 1997, students with disabilities could be suspended for no more than 10 cumulative days in a school year unless a group of qualified persons determined that the behavior for which the student was suspended or expelled was unrelated to his or her disability (manifest determination). If the behavior was disability related (i.e., the child was unable to understand the consequences of or control the behavior), the school had to identify strategies to prevent a reoccurrence of that behavior by making modifications in the IEP rather than by excluding the child.

Even those students not currently eligible under IDEA could claim procedural safeguards under IDEA of 1997 if the school had knowledge or some indication that the student might have ADHD. For example, procedural safeguards would be granted if (a) the parent had at some time expressed written concern or requested an evaluation, (b) the teacher or other personnel had expressed concern to administrative personnel suggesting that the child might have a disability, or (c) the child's behavior or performance in school demonstrated a need for services. H.R. 1350 (2004) narrowed the conditions under which the local educational agency "should have known" the child had a disability. That is, parents must put into writing to school personnel that their child needs special education services unless the parent is illiterate or has a disability.

IDEA of 1997 provided that a request for evaluation must be expedited during the disciplinary 10-day period. With the latest IDEA reauthorizations in 2003 and 2004, the following simplifications were accepted (U.S. General Accounting Office, 2001):

NOTE
Rights of Students Who Are Suspended

1. Any child who violates a code of student conduct may be removed to an interim alternative educational setting (IEAS) for not more than 45 days or longer if required by state law for the particular violation. However, the school may consider "unique circumstances" on a case-by-case basis.
2. A child with a disability who "violates a code of student conduct policy" may be required to change placement to an IAES or another setting or be suspended for not more than 45 school days without a hearing officer. The team will consider a change of placement for a child with a disability, especially when a student has inflicted serious bodily injury on another person while at school, on school premises, or at a school function.
3. Students removed will continue to receive educational and behavioral intervention services; however, schools are not required to follow a student's IEP during suspension or expulsion.
4. If parents disagree with decisions regarding placement, punishment, or duration of punishment, they may request a hearing.

Some of these changes broaden the scope of exclusions and do not state that the student will return to the regular classroom at the end of the placement. For the 2004 reauthorizations, suspension for greater than 45 days (i.e., on the 46th day) are considered a change of placement, which requires due process. This protection is not offered under Section 504.

Although only IDEA deals with expulsions/suspensions, both federal laws require states and school districts to prevent and respond to harassment that has been directed to students and that is related to their disability. Harassment may take the form of physical conduct that is harmful, humiliating, or threatening; restrictive or excluding practices; name-calling; or graphic or written statements on student papers, on notes home, or on the chalkboard. Examples include an administrator or teacher who (a) repeatedly excludes a student from access to lunch, field trips, assemblies, recess, and/or extracurricular activities as punishment; (b) criticizes a student for using accommodations in class; or (c) allows other students to taunt or intimidate a student with a disability. These harassment clauses are little known in general or special education (http://www.ed.gov/about/offices/list/ocr/docs/disabharassltr.html).

SUMMARY

Section 504 and IDEA are related federal laws. Both require districts to provide notice and impartial hearings to parents or guardians with respect to (or for those who disagree with) the identification, evaluation, or placement of a student. (Written notice is not required under Section 504 but is considered good practice.) Both laws provide parents and students with grievance procedures and the right to review records, to participate in a hearing and be represented by counsel, and to due process at the local level. In addition, both laws (a) consider information from multiple sources, (b) determine eligibility using a group of persons knowledgeable about the child and the evaluation data, and (c) ensure that the child is educated with his or her nondisabled peers to the maximum extent appropriated (LRE).

NOTE
FORMER PRESIDENT FORD'S VISION

Before signing the Education for All Handicapped Children Act of 1975 (since reauthorized as the Individuals with Disabilities Education Act), President Ford expressed some concerns about the effect of the law. He worried that it would create new complexities and administrative challenges for public education. But ultimately it was hope and compassion that inspired him to sign the law. More than a quarter century later, we know that many of President Ford's concerns were realized. But we also know that IDEA has exceeded President Ford's greatest hopes. (Executive Summary of the President's Commission on Excellence in Special Education, 2002, p. 4).

DISCUSSION AND APPLICATION QUESTIONS

1. Under what conditions are children identified under Section 504 rather than IDEA?
2. Which law provides more written guarantees and procedural safeguards for children with ADHD?
3. What might the benefits of Section 504 be for a student with ADHD?
4. What is the name of the stage wherein the school system considers whether the child should be identified under Section 504 or IDEA?
5. What are the enforcing agencies for Section 504 and IDEA?
6. Teachers often express the concern that implementing a child's IEP will single the child out, and for this reason they do not comply with the IEP. What arguments would you make to them?

CHAPTER 2

Diagnostic Perspectives and Controversies

OBJECTIVES

- Understand that a set of questions exists that must be addressed in diagnosing a child.
- Know how diagnoses are guided by laws and by professional organizations.
- Summarize diagnostic controversies.

KEY TERMS

Diagnostic and Statistical Manual of Mental Disorders
subtypes of ADHD
other health impairments
major life activities
clinical versus community/school samples
conditional disorder
Child-Find Mandate
behavior rating scales
primacy of disorders
exclusion clauses
impairment
posttraumatic stress reactions
gender bias
functional requirements of society
invisible disabilities
SOAPP

Children with disabilities are those who have an inherent condition that so seriously affects their ability to learn that they need special education and related services. From this definition, we see that the primary symptoms of attention deficit hyperactivity disorder (ADHD) must be severe enough to produce significant loss of everyday social or academic functioning. Both the medical and the educational communities rely on specific criteria to identify children with disabilities. The laws that are applicable and that contribute significantly to the specifics of *educational* diagnosis are the Individuals with Disabilities Educational Act (IDEA) and Section 504.

The most widely accepted medical/clinical definition and assessment tool is the *Diagnostic and Statistical Manual of Mental Disorders (4th ed.) (DSM-IV-TR)* (American Psychiatric Association, 2000). The diagnosis of ADHD is determined by a set of *DSM-IV-TR* criteria that guide the identification of three subtypes of ADHD: (1) the hyperactive-impulsive type (ADHD-H; see chapter 5), (2) the inattentive type (ADHD-I; see chapter 6), and (3) the combined type (ADHD). It should be noted that there is only a 50% chance that an individual will fit neatly within only one *DSM* category; that is, co-occurring conditions are typically found, especially for children with ADHD (Kaplan, Dewey, Crawford, & Wilson, 2001) (See Figure 2.1).

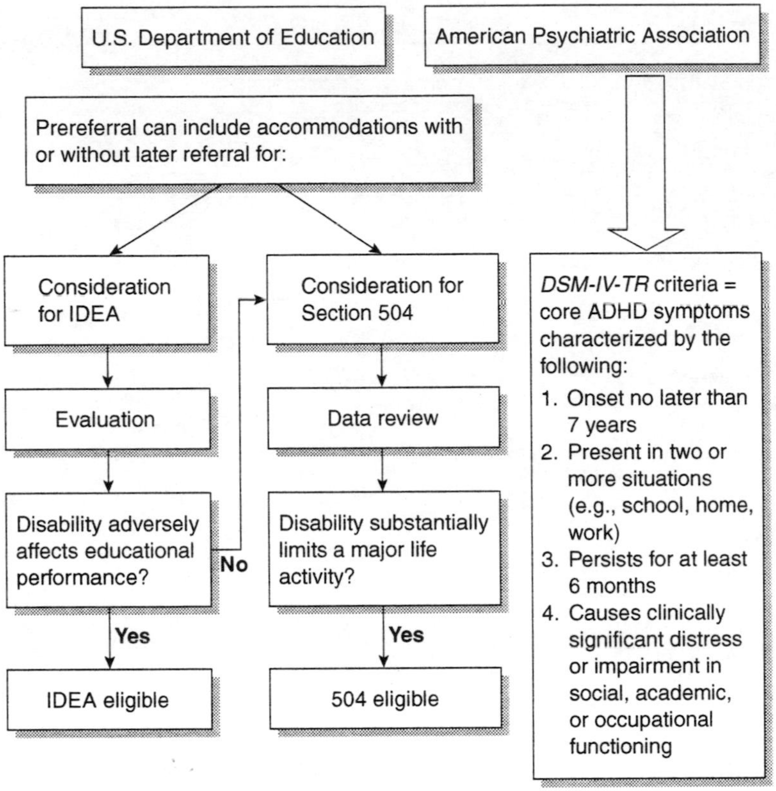

FIGURE 2.1
Identification of ADHD

IDEA DEFINES INDIVIDUALS WITH DISABILITIES

How are children defined educationally?

Children evaluated in accordance with procedures outlined in IDEA must have one or more specified physical or mental impairments and must need special education and related services (see Table 2.1).

Under IDEA, there is a difference between diagnosis and eligibility for services. If a child is diagnosed with a disability but can make educational progress in the general education classroom without services, that child is not covered by IDEA. Special education is needed only if a child has unique needs requiring specially designed instruction or services. Special education is eligibility for a *service*, not for a placement or diagnosis. For example, a child in a wheelchair does not necessarily require special services. Similarly, a child with ADHD may not need special services if he or she is provided with an active curriculum and extracurricular responsibilities.

TABLE 2.1 Comparisons Among Medical and Educational Diagnostic Systems

	American Psychiatric Association	U.S. Department of Education	
	***Diagnostic and Statistical Manual of Mental Disorders* (*DSM-IV-TR*, 2000)**	**IDEA**	**Section 504 of the Rehabilitation Act of 1973**
General purpose	Identification for the specific purposes of prevention, prediction, and treatment	Federal funding statute to 1. provide financial aid to help states support appropriate services for students with disabilities, 2. protect the rights of children and their parents, and 3. ensure the effectiveness of efforts to educate students.	• Broad civil rights law • Protects rights of individuals in federally funded programs or activities
Who is identified	Disorders usually diagnosed from infancy through adolescence: 1. mental retardation 2. learning 3. motor skills 4. communication 5. pervasive developmental 6. attention-deficit and disruptive behavior 7. feeding and eating 8. tic 9. elimination 10. other	Children ages 3–21 identified in specific categories: 1. deaf-blindness 2. hearing impairments 3. mental retardation 4. multiple disabilities 5. orthopedic impairments 6. other health impairments 7. emotional disturbance 8. specific learning disabilities 9. speech or language impairments 10. traumatic brain injury 11. visual impairments 12. autism 13. developmental delay	All individuals who meet the definition of one of the following: 1. has a disability that substantially limits one or more of life's major activities (e.g., learning) 2. has or had a disability 3. is regarded as having a disability Typical are those conditions that are (a) communicable (e.g., HIV), (b) medical (e.g., asthma, heart), (c) temporary (e.g., accidents), (d) behavioral (e.g., ADHD), (e) addictive (e.g., drug), etc.
Diagnosis and evaluation	Evaluations to assess the criteria listed in the *DSM*	• Full comprehensive evaluation is required after informed consent. The cost of assessment varies by state but is $1,000 to $2,000, with only about $400 of that money reimbursed. • Requires a reevaluation no more than once a year, unless parents and district agree otherwise, and	• A formal individual assessment is not required under Section 504. • Does not require consent from parent—only notice. • Evaluation draws from building-based team members who are knowledgeable about student, evaluation data, etc. and agree on a plan of services and accommodations.

(*Continued*)

TABLE 2.1 *(Continued)*

	Diagnostic and Statistical Manual of Mental Disorders (*DSM-IV-TR*, 2000)	IDEA	Section 504 of the Rehabilitation Act of 1973
		at least once every 3 years unless parent and district agree a reevaluation is unnecessary under the IDEA reauthorization 2003. • Can provide independent evaluation at schools' expense if guardian disagrees with school evaluation data and a hearing officer agrees. • Multidisciplinary team determines specific disability eligibility.	• Requires periodic reevaluations only for changes in placement. • No funding is provided for independent evaluation at school's expense.
Provides a free and appropriate education	Not applicable	• Requires a written IEP at no cost to parents. • Requires the provision of related services and a continuum of placements, including general education. • IEP changes allowed without reevaluation.	• A plan—not necessarily a written document. • Reasonable accommodations, such as an aide, counseling, medication monitoring. • IDEA services may fall within the domain of reasonable.
Funding	Not applicable	• Provides additional funding for eligible students.	• Provides no additional money besides what is available in general education. • IDEA money may now be used for Section 504 (i.e., up to 15% to support students in general educational settings, see H.R. 1350).
Procedural safeguards for families and for the child	Not applicable	• Requires notice to parent/guardian for identification, evaluation, and placement. IDEA delineates the required components of written notice. • Requires an IEP meeting for a change of placement.	• Requires notice to parent/guardian but not written notice unless there will be a review for significant placement changes. • Protects the parental right to inspect records, participate in a hearing, and be represented by counsel.

		• Requires informed consent for services under reauthorization of IDEA in 2003. The school district must seek informed consent from parents to provide services (separate from consent for evaluation). If consent to provide services is not given, the district "shall not" provide services, nor will the district be required to convene an IEP team meeting or develop an IEP.	
Grievance	Not applicable	• Individual complaints can be filed with the state department of education. • Enforced by the U.S. Office of Special Education Programs. • Requires the pursuit of an administrative hearing before seeking redress in the courts. • With reauthorization of IDEA in 2003, the two-tier system, where the initial hearing is at the local level, has been eliminated. The state will conduct due process hearings, with appeal directly to the court system.	• Individual family complaints can be filed with the U.S. Office of Civil Rights, which enforces Section 504. • An administrative hearing is not required before Office of Civil Rights or court actions are taken. • Compensatory damages allowed.
Settings and roles	Hospitals and clinics: clinical psychologists, psychiatrists, case managers, and family doctors	• School districts: school psychologists, educators, and multidisciplinary team members. • With IDEA reauthorization in 2003, a regular education teacher will not be required at the team meeting if no issues pertaining to the child's participation in general education are discussed. If the child has several general education teachers, all will not be required to attend a meeting.	School districts: school psychologists and educators

Data from *Comparisons Between Medical and Educational Diagnostic Systems* (adapted from Reeve, et al., 1994).

IDEA defines students with ADHD IDEA regulations state that the child is eligible for special education services under (a) a co-occurring category of disability (e.g., learning disabilities and emotional and behavioral disorders) or (b) on the basis of ADHD under the category of other health impairments. Children with other health impairments are defined as those who exhibit

> limited strength, vitality *or alertness*, due to chronic or acute health problems such as a heart condition, tuberculosis, rheumatic fever, nephritis, asthma, sickle cell anemia, hemophilia, epilepsy, lead poisoning, leukemia, or diabetes, to such a degree that it adversely affects a student's educational performance.

Whether a child is determined to have limited alertness will depend on the manifestation of the primary characteristics of ADHD (attention, impulsivity, and hyperactivity) in the classroom. However, for a child to be eligible for services, his or her limited "alertness" must adversely affect performance as determined by the school's evaluation team. Educational or functional impairment is defined operationally in the diagnostic steps later in this chapter.

About 25% to 50% of students with ADHD qualify for services, the majority being served within the categories of behavior disorders or learning disabilities. Still, a majority of their time is spent in general education settings (Bussing, Gary, Leon, & Garvan, 2002).

SECTION 504 DEFINES INDIVIDUALS WITH DISABILITIES

Can students remain in the general classroom and still get help?

Section 504 and its implementing regulations do not identify disabilities as IDEA does; there are no categories in Section 504. Instead, Section 504 functionally defines disability ("handicap" was the original language in the law) as "a physical or mental impairment that substantially limits one or more major life activities," including walking, seeing, hearing, speaking, sleeping, breathing, working, caring for oneself, performing manual tasks, and learning.

Under Section 504, students can also be considered disabled but not necessarily eligible for services if they have a "history of" (e.g., past record of a physical or mental impairment) or are "regarded as" having a disability. To be "regarded as" can include appearing crazy (making noises like an animal). Similarly, when parents called their son mentally retarded, even though he had an IQ of 75, he was "perceived" by the parents as having a disability. Overall, the definitions are open to interpretation by school systems (i.e., a group of persons who are knowledgeable about the child, the meaning of the evaluation data, and the services options).

Section 504 defines ADHD All students who are currently receiving special education under IDEA are automatically Section 504 students. That is, Section 504 is a broader civil rights statue that includes all students with disabilities. In addition, the wider scope of protection may grant eligibility for a student under Section 504 even though he or she is *not* considered disabled under IDEA.

Historically, the Office of Civil Rights attended to those students who failed to qualify for services under IDEA and ruled that ADHD was a Section 504 disability, with rights of assessment, individualized education, hearings, and all the rights of special education students.

ADHD does not have to overlap with other disabling conditions (e.g., learning disabilities, emotional and behavioral disorders) even though, in the past, students with ADHD were eligible for services only when they had a co-occurring disability. When IDEA was amended in 1990, there was a debate in Congress about whether to expand the disability categories. At that time, Congress specifically declined to include ADHD. Nevertheless, in response to a clear need and to many years of parental and professional advocacy, the Office of Special Education Programs in the Department of Education published a policy memorandum on September 16, 1991 that provided a reinterpretation of IDEA and Section 504 for children with ADHD. The policy memorandum outlined the official position that a child with ADHD may be eligible for educational services under Section 504 of the Vocational Rehabilitation Act (Public Law 93-112) if ADHD substantially limits his or her ability to learn (Davila, Williams, & MacDonald, 1991). Furthermore, if a student is found to have a disability under Section 504, he or she is still legally entitled to special education services if the team determines that any of these services is necessary.

THE DIAGNOSTIC AND STATISTICAL MANUAL DEFINES ADHD

How do psychologists and medical personnel define ADHD?

Diagnosis must document the severity of ADHD and its effects on functioning (i.e., impairment) and rule out or exclude other conditions (i.e., not pervasive developmental, schizophrenia, or other psychotic disorders) and not mental disorders (e.g., mood, anxiety, dissociative, personality).

Although individuals with ADHD must demonstrate symptoms prior to the age of 7, in practice many children are not identified until elementary or even high school. Late identification of these students could be due to (a) parent or teacher accommodations for students, (b) parental resistance to early identification, or (c) changes in context requirements, with greater expectations for attention and response inhibition during later elementary and high school.

Behavioral symptom information may be obtained from parents (or guardians) using open-ended questions, semistructured interviews, questionnaires, or rating scales. ADHD-specific rating scales have been shown to have a specificity greater

> **NOTE**
> ***DSM-IV-TR* Criteria Specify That Core Symptoms Must:**
>
> 1. have an onset no later than 7 years,
> 2. be present in two or more situations (e.g., school, home, work),
> 3. have persisted for at least 6 months to a degree that is maladaptive and inconsistent with developmental level, and
> 4. cause clinically significant distress or impairment in social, academic, or occupational functioning.

than 94% in studies differentiating children with ADHD from normal, age-matched community controls (American Academy of Pediatrics, 2001a). By contrast, global rating scales (assessing several types of behavioral disorders) have less than 86% sensitivity, and global clinical impressions are insufficient to diagnose ADHD. If the evaluation of a child suggests that the symptoms are insufficient to warrant a clinical diagnosis, the *DSM-IV-TR* suggests a diagnosis of ADHD–not otherwise specified.

Even with formal procedures such as these, there is *no* assessment protocol for comprehensively assessing ADHD (McKinney, Montague & Hocutt, 1993; National Institutes of Health, 2000). For example, medical and attentional tests have specificity less than 70% in differentiating children with ADHD from comparisons. Therefore, the diagnosis of ADHD does not require the use of any of these additional procedures.

PREVALENCE

How many children should we expect to identify?

ADHD is the most prevalent form of childhood disorder in the United States (National Institutes of Health, 2000). Some experts estimate that up to 2 million school-age students have ADHD (Bloomingdale, Swanson, Barkley, & Satterfield, 1991). Identified as ADHD are 44% of students receiving special education services (Bussing, Zima, Perwien, Belin, & Widawski, 1998). Additionally, 8% to 20% of school and community samples (e.g., Shaywitz & Shaywitz, 1988) would receive a diagnosis of ADHD, but only 3% to 7% of children manifest disorders severe enough to warrant services. That is, the prevalence drops when students must also show evidence of poor social or academic functioning.

In the general population, 9.2% (5.8% to 13.6%) of males and 2.9% (1.9% to 4.5%) of females are found to exhibit behaviors consistent with ADHD, with a ratio of about four boys to one girl (e.g., August, Realmuto, MacDonald, Nugent, & Crosby, 1996; Wolraich, Hannah, Baumgaertel, & Feurer, 1998; Wolraich, Hannah, Pinnock, Baumgaertel, & Brown, 1996). Within the total population of children identified as ADHD, the inattentive subtype represents about 27%, the pure ADHD-H group about 18%, and the combined (ADHD-H + ADHD-I) subtype 55%, ranging from 50% to 75% (McBurnett, 1995; Wilens, Biederman, & Spencer, 2002). These subtypes are discussed in chapters 5 and 6.

DIAGNOSTIC STEPS

What are the identification procedures?

Prior to an assessment of eligibility under IDEA and Section 504 comes a prereferral stage. With reauthorization of IDEA in 2004, individual states must now develop and implement

> comprehensive coordinated prereferral educational support services for students in grades K–12, with an emphasis on students in K–3. These children are not identified as children with disabilities but are identified as needing additional academic and behavioral support to succeed in a general education environment.

Districts may use not more than 15% of federal funds in combination with other funds for these purposes. Activities may include professional development.

If the child responds positively to the accommodations provided, it does not mean that the disorder was never present. ADHD is a conditional disorder that responds positively to optimal conditions in the general classroom. When these accommodations fail to address the significant difficulties experienced by the child, the school team (variously labeled the school assistance team, building assistance team, child study committee, and so on) convenes to generate more intensive accommodations for use within the classroom. If the child has sufficient difficulties to justify review by the committee, he or she is, by definition, 504 eligible (Reeve, et al., 1994).

Consideration for eligibility for special education services under IDEA will be undertaken when (a) the child's behavior is very difficult or is negatively affecting other students, (b) there are co-occurring behavioral and academic problems, and/or (c) when general accommodations, individual analysis, and individual programming have failed to produce sufficient change. If eligibility is first assessed under IDEA and the student fails to qualify under IDEA, he or she will be referred to a Section 504 committee. Sometimes the same members serve on both teams.

There are some important procedural implications of the policy memorandum for schools regarding the evaluation of ADHD for determining eligibility. These have been adapted from the CRS Report for Congress (1991).

Documentation is accomplished through six related steps (abbreviated from Zentall & Javorsky, 1995).

STEP 1: Document the primary characteristics of the disability. The first step involves documenting the severity of the primary characteristics of the disorder across the contexts of home and school. The most widely employed

NOTE
Policy Implications

1. Schools have an obligation to evaluate children with ADHD, as with any student with educational problems (Child-Find Mandate), if it is suspected that they need special education.
2. Schools will need to develop expertise on ADHD. This often requires in-service training. The evaluation team or case conference committee formed by the school to determine the effects of ADHD on educational performance must include at least one teacher or other specialist knowledgeable in the area of the suspected disability (ADHD).
3. Schools must document the extent to which the condition is pervasive across school and home and represents a substantial impairment in educational and/or social functioning. The individuals who can provide input into the diagnostic process are general educators, parents, clinicians, medical professionals, and the children themselves.
4. Schools can provide a licensed physician to make a medical diagnosis of ADHD, depending on state evaluation guidelines. School districts do not have to conduct a medical evaluation if the district believes there are other effective methods of determining eligibility. However, if the district *does* require a medical evaluation, it must be provided at no cost to the parents.

measures of ADHD are behavior rating scales. Such scales provide (a) normative data collected from parents and educators in both home and school contexts, (b) an assessment of both low- and high-frequency behavior, and (c) an inexpensive and relatively easy quantitative assessment of behavior. Numerous rating scales are available to provide reliable and valid diagnostic indicators of ADHD, often based on *DSM-IV-TR* criteria. With these criteria, students can be classified into one of two specific subtypes of ADHD (described in chapters 5 and 6).

Step 2: Document behavioral/social impairment. Brief classroom observations have three possible uses, providing documentation for the following:

1. The type and frequency/intensity of problem behavior.
2. An assessment of the effectiveness of intervention through an assessment of behavioral change, i.e., pre versus post intervention (see chapters 8 to 11).
3. A determination of the effects of disability on social behavior to document impairment. Classroom observations tend to correlate highly with academic productivity and with teachers' ratings of ADHD (DuPaul, 1991).

Observation is less costly in time and training when only a few clearly defined types of behavior are observed and recorded. Behavior that characterizes students with ADHD in the classroom as well as at home includes the following.

NOTE
Home and Classroom Activity Indicators

1. Activity—off chair/up and down, talk/noisemaking
2. Inattention—changes in the focus of play or free-time activities, visual off task, verbal off task (e.g., off the subject)
3. Social impulsivity—disrupt, interrupt
4. Social negativity
   - *Verbal*—disagree/argue/command/verbal statement
   - *Physical*—negative physical contact with another or noncompliance or nonperformance of a request or an assigned task (Zentall, 1985a)

This behavior has been converted to a data collection procedure (see Table 2.2).

TABLE 2.2 Coding Time Intervals

Child A:	1	2	3	4	5	6	7	8	9	10	11	12	13	14	15
Up/down, noise															
Change focus															
Disrupt/interrupt															
Social negative															
Child B:	1	2	3	4	5	6	7	8	9	10	11	12	13	14	15
Up/down, noise															
Change focus															
Disrupt/interrupt															
Social negative															

	Totals *Child A*	*Child B*
Up/down, noise/activity	Activity /15	/15
Change focus/inattention	Inattention /15	/15
Disrupt/interrupt/impulsivity	Social impulsivity /15	/15
Social negative	Social negative /15	/15
	Child A /60	Child B /60

Note. The intervals are defined as 1 to 15. The observer needs to select time units of 1 to 4 minutes per interval. (If 4 minutes, then total time observed = 1 hour; if 2 minutes, then total time = 30 minutes; and if 1 minute, then total time = 15 minutes.)

When recording these types of behavior, a comparison is available in the same setting using an average student who is the same gender, mental age, race, and socioeconomic status (see Zentall, 1980). Each student would be observed for 5 minutes in an alternating order; for example, watch John for 5 minutes, watch Peter for 5 minutes, watch John again, and so on.

Diagnostic practices require a stable estimate of the frequency of behavior. For this reason, observations should be repeated across days and settings and range from 10 to 30 minutes (DuPaul & Stoner, 1994). A minimum of three observations (more if there is variability) of 15 minutes should be observed.

A significant social impairment is said to occur when there is a difference in the quantity of behavior observed between a child with ADHD and his or her classmates. A 10% difference is often used (e.g., off task observed for average boys = 23%, ADHD = 33%, and clinic-referred boys with ADHD = 37% [Jones, Loney, Weissenburger, & Fleischmann, 1975]). Qualitative indicators of social impairment can be documented using Tables 5.1 and 5.2 in chapter 5.

Step 3: Document educational impairment. Academic products (e.g., independent work, homework samples) can be used to document significant educational impairment. The possible types of everyday classroom performance include the following:

NOTE
Performance (SOAPP) Indicators

1. *Start*, **S**: time taken to start a task or comply with a directive)
2. *Organization*, **O**: ratings of organization of written work, desks, or lockers
3. *Accuracy*, **A**: percentage of work that is accurate
4. *Persistence*, **P**: time sustaining work effort
5. *Production*, **P**: percentage of work turned in or completed (Zentall & Javorsky, 1995)

The acronym is SOAPP, and one or more of these indicators may be used to document the effects of disability on performance. The most common indicator that schools use is production, wherein students complete only a portion of their assigned work. The academic problems of students with ADHD are assessed by a discrepancy between IQ potential and their academic productivity not between aptitude and achievement tests (see Cohen, Riccio, & Gonzalez, 1994). A percentage (e.g., 10%) of difference from an average comparison student could be used to indicate the effects of ADHD on educational performance.

STEP 4: Determine co-occurring disabilities. A fourth step involves determining if there are co-occurring disabilities. Typically, students with ADHD have secondary emotional outcomes of aggression, coexisting oppositional defiant disorder, conduct disorder, depression, or anxiety (see chapter 5). Anxiety can change the typical nature of activity from variable to repetitive (e.g., repeated topics of conversation or behavioral tics, twitches, habits, or rituals). These repetitive behaviors may also occur when psychostimulant dosage is too high (see chapter 9).

STEP 5: Determine primacy among co-occurring disabilities. A fifth step involves determining the primacy of disorders, where there may be several co-occurring disorders. As with most definitions, there are exclusion clauses. *DSM-IV-TR* required that the observed behavioral patterns should not be better accounted for by a diagnosis of a mood disorder, anxiety disorder, dissociative disorder, or personality disorder. A diagnosis of ADHD cannot occur with chronic schizophrenia or other psychotic disorders. If aggressive behavior or emotional disorders pre-date the characteristics of ADHD, then these disorders may be primary. Therefore, it may be important to determine the age of onset of aggression, anxiety, or depression with respect to ADHD.

STEP 6: Exclude reactions to physical and psychological events. A final, related step requires that the behavioral pattern observed should not be a temporary condition related to a child's abreaction to external events. Children with an abrupt onset to their disorder may be exhibiting posttraumatic stress reactions (e.g., acting out) in response to (a) family events (e.g., parental divorce, death of a family member or close acquaintance); (b) physical, sexual, or emotional abuse or neglect; (c) environmental disruption (e.g., a change in residence or in school); or (d) natural or man-made disasters. Except in a small percentage of allergy-prone children, diet is not chronically associated with ADHD. This has been established for some time in the literature (e.g., Barkley, 1997a). However, where students have allergies to specific foods, or parents held a belief that their child was sensitive to artificial food colors, eliminating these items can reduce parent-perceived behavioral difficulties (Schab & Trinh, 2004).

How does a parent or a teacher get a child evaluated for ADHD?

A request for evaluation may be made by a parent, an educator, a principal, or an 18-year-old student. This initial request must be made in writing and given to the principal or to the local school district. (See "Family Practices" example on page 28.)

To provide input to this process of determining eligibility, it will be important for parents to be prepared with their child's developmental records, a statement by a physician, medical records, copies of important information from the child's school files, and a list of questions and ideas about how to make the child's education more successful. These materials should be provided to the school before the case conference meeting. Even with this written record, the referral process can be overwhelming

FAMILY PRACTICES
We Are Applying for Services: Under the Category "Other Health Impaired"

Principal,

I am seeking services for my child, Jack Smith, under the category of "Other Health Impaired" of IDEA. Jack has chronic alertness problems due to his ADHD, as diagnosed by his family pediatrician in [month/year].

I realize you have 60 days to put together a case conference and decide on Jack's eligibility for services. Please keep us informed about how to proceed. We are available for conferences at these times:

Sincerely,
Mr. & Mrs. Smith

and intimidating for most parents. For this reason, parents may wish to identify an advocate to accompany them (e.g., professional, parent advocate, relative, friend).

If the child is a preschooler, he or she may be eligible for services under Part B of IDEA. In this case, a parent may wish to contact the state department of education or local educational agency to find out about accessing services and an evaluation under Part B.

It is also possible that parents refuse evaluation for assessment of disability. In these cases—and as stipulated by House Resolution (H.R.) 1350—the local educational agency cannot request a dispute hearing to override a parent's refusal to consent to special education and related services. Under these conditions, the local educational agency is not responsible to provide a free and appropriate public education.

DIAGNOSTIC LIMITATIONS

A number of difficulties exist in the initial identification and labeling of children. For example, there is no evidence to support the criterion that children with ADHD must show symptoms prior to 7 years of age (Barkley & Biederman, 1997). In addition, the types of behavior assessed appear to be more effective in identifying boys than girls, and parent ratings may be more sensitive to oppositional defiant disorder than to ADHD-H.

Teachers were able to discriminate between girls with and without ADHD, but few of the identified girls were receiving services (Grskovic & Zentall, 2005). In fact, for those girls who teachers identified as having severe ADHD, only one-third were receiving special education services. Teachers may fail to refer because (a) available services in the schools seem inappropriate for girls, with enrollments up to 90% male (Caseau, Luckasson, & Kroth, 1994); (b) girls' behavior does not fit the typical

Big Foot Loch Ness Girls with ADHD

manifestation of hyperactivity; or (c) girls appear to be responsive to teachers' attempts to manage their behavior in the classroom (for a review, see Grskovic & Zentall, 2005). Gender bias could also influence teacher identification of ADHD. For example, Greenblatt (1994) asked 57 elementary and middle school teachers and counselors to evaluate case studies of children described with the characteristics of ADHD (e.g., hyperactive, fidgety, uncooperative, inattentive, difficulty following through). Teachers assessed only 27% of the girl cases to have ADHD but identified boys in 72% of the identical cases. Future research is needed to examine the information that teachers use to make decisions about level of impairment and the need for services for girls with ADHD.

Prior to the reauthorization of IDEA in 1991, students with ADHD qualified for services only when they had a co-occurring disability (e.g., learning disability). Now IDEA recognizes individuals with a primary diagnosis of ADHD, but, unlike *DSM,* IDEA is less supportive of identifying co-occurring disabilities (Stahl & Clarizio, 1999). It is perhaps for this reason that some children have a series of disability labels. Other issues relate to the identification of impairment and how much is enough to meet IDEA standards under the other health impaired eligibility criteria (e.g., in an interpretation of "limited alertness" [Reeve et al., 1994]).

At a more general level, the current legal system often emphasizes procedures (e.g., compliance and paperwork) over results. Qualifying for special education becomes the end point rather than a process leading to effective instruction (Executive Summary of the President's Commission on Excellence in Special Education, 2002). This can mean that at-risk preschool children do not get help early enough to treat co-occurring conditions, such as oppositional defiant disorder. In other words, the model can be one of failure rather than prevention, more often for children with behavioral problems. That is, H.R. 1350 now modifies the definition of learning disability—no longer requiring a significant discrepancy between achievement and intellectual ability—and uses the child's positive response to evidence-based practices as diagnostic. Thus, children with early reading disability can now receive phonemic awareness training early enough to prevent long-term failure.

DIAGNOSTIC CONTROVERSIES

Is ADHD a disability or a social construct?

Isn't "ADHD" a socially constructed term used for energetic children who lack appropriate social behavior, which could be explained by lax parenting? Although questions about the validity of a disability are rarely found in reference to severe disabilities, they are often asked about the "invisible disabilities" (i.e., where children do not look different or are not easily assessed as being different from their peers). Those of us who have been in the field of special education remember similar concerns voiced about learning disabilities:

> The field quickly fell into a position where those who were alleged moderates claimed that 2–3% of the children had a significant learning disability; some claimed the condition to be a mere hoax, whereas others saw the prevalence to be well above 50%. (Senf, 1986, p. 28)

Today, "learning disability" is more accepted in elementary and middle/high schools but still with less acceptance in higher education (Shea, 1994). These levels of acceptance are probably less for the more recent field of ADHD.

Validity questions may simply reflect the difficulties inherent in the identification of any new disability, especially when there has been a change in societal requirements. For example, when literacy became important for learning in American society, "learning disability" came into focus as a disability category. For students with ADHD, it may have been the sedentary style of teaching literacy that contributed to the identification of this category. As specific traits become important in our increasingly complex world, accommodating for the impairment of functioning in these traits also becomes necessary.

Additional questions about the validity of a disability are fueled by evidence regarding the inconsistent number of children diagnosed and the variability of conditions and tasks that occasion their problems. Thomas Armstrong (1995a), a former special education teacher and author of the book *The Myth of the ADD Child*, has addressed the apparent nonconstancy of identifying conditions. He writes, "Why, for example, does identification of ADD vary so widely from one social context to another?" (Armstrong, 1995b, p. 33). He continues, "Unlike other medical disorders, such as diabetes or pneumonia, this is a disorder that pops up in one setting only to disappear in another" (Armstrong, 1996, p. 425). For example, performance differences are not found during tasks that are self-paced and self-selected, with strong rewards or novelty, nor are they recognized by all persons or role sources (parents, teachers, physicians) (Armstrong, 1995b). Furthermore, children with ADHD often know what to do when asked, tested, or given a limited number of choices even though they fail to enact what they know in a free setting.

There are many reasons to explain good functioning of children with ADHD in specific contexts and with certain tasks. Students with ADHD can actually outperform their peers under some novelty conditions and on some measures (see chapters 8 and 10). Inattention contributes to variability (Piek et al., 2004), although impulsivity could also be a factor. Finally, many children with ADHD have adaptive functioning, have learned to successfully channel their behavior, or have great competency (often in nonschool activities) even though unsuccessful in school (Rueda, Gallego, & Moll, 2000).

In addition, many adults with ADHD are successful. This may be due to the fact that certain professions have the necessary supports (e.g., administrative assistants, accountants, computer operators), job-inherent accommodations (e.g., frequent traveling), or a need for the personal qualities of ADHD (e.g., spontaneity, extroversion, energy, humor, synthesis skills, entrepreneurship, risk taking, multitasking). Similar long-term successes have been reported for individuals with apparent learning disabilities (e.g., Thomas Edison, Albert Einstein).

Because definitional practices have been subjected to so much controversy, the field has overly focused on accurate diagnosis. Labels can produce negative expectations and lead to an emphasis on problem characteristics, disorder subtypes, and expectations of impaired functioning. Being labeled or singled out may lock an individual into a deviant role regardless of appropriate behavior. Deviance based on stigma occurs when children internalize the negative reactions and statements of others and then behave in line with those expectations (e.g., using their disability as an excuse).

A balanced perspective is needed with respect to labeling. Children with ADHD have chronic functional impairment in some settings, with some tasks or task conditions, and at specific points in time. A child is like an artistic composition, which is defined as much by positive as by negative spaces—by light as much as by dark. This balanced perspective may not be appreciated by parents and clinicians who work with children, often at older ages, who have been referred to clinics for severe, multiple disorders and whose problems are relatively intractable and involve other societal institutions (e.g., the legal system).

A second criticism related to labeling is that "the diagnosis of ADHD does not provide clinicians with sufficient information to determine specific interventions" (DuPaul & Ervin, 1996, p. 601). In other words, does the label help us know what to do in the classroom? I would argue that the label gives educators an evidence-based direction for intervention planning (see chapters 8 to 11), and functional assessment (see chapter 4) provides additional individual assessment data, leading to intervention strategies. Without labeling and without functional assessment, educators would need to rely on a trial-and-error approach to intervention.

For students with ADHD and their families as well, the label has a powerful advocacy role, as stated by this mother:

FAMILY PRACTICES
Labeling and Empowerment

I can only speak for myself and the parents and teachers I know well. We are all thankful that the labeling occurs. Until our child was diagnosed, we had no idea if anything could be done to help him. . . . I am thankful for the diagnosis, and I would guess that the vast majority of parents agree with me. Knowledge is power. (Dr. Joan Hart, personal communication, 1995)

According to Maag and Reid (1996), most of the available research related to these labels is clinical/medical, with a focus on psychopharmacology or diagnosis, and therefore is not useful for education. Clearly, we need more educational research on students with ADHD. Maag and Reid (1996) would further argue that "accommodations for ADHD children in the general education classroom are similar to those recommended for other children at risk" (p. 38). In other words, students with ADHD will respond like other students with mild disabilities. What is critically missing in this statement is the understanding that students with ADHD do *not* respond in the same way as other children to many classroom conditions and variables (e.g., reinforcement [Tripp & Alsop, 1999] and stimulation [Zentall, 1995]). Thus, the label *is* educationally important.

SUMMARY

Diagnostic Procedures Summary. The primary characteristics of ADHD can contribute to impairment in school performance and in social performance. To document impairment, educators must assess and document behavioral outcomes (social, personal, classroom performance, and achievement). This assessment is first made with behavior. (See "Note" example on page 33.)

An assessment of a student using *DSM* criteria provides information relevant to many of these steps. Generally, *DSM* provides a normative framework for understanding groups of children with ADHD. It answers specific questions (yes/no) about the extent to which the child has co-occurring conditions and whether a child is or is not ADHD while documenting (a) specific types of behavior that the student is exhibiting, (b) the severity and pervasiveness of this behavior, and (c) the educational and social impairment outcomes of this behavior.

Diagnostic Summary. Students with ADHD can receive services related to their disability in one of three ways: (1) when they meet criteria for another disability under IDEA (e.g., learning disability); (2) when they meet IDEA's category of

NOTE

BEHAVIORAL SEVERITY INDICATORS

1. Frequency and intensity of behavior is measured by
   a. behavioral ratings (relative to norms [see step 1]) or
   b. observation (a 10% difference from an average child [see step 2])
2. Number of contexts affected (home, school, neighborhood, or school play [see step 1]) and the settings within each context (small group, large group, transition, independent, and so on)
3. Number and type of co-occurring emotional or behavioral disorders (see step 6)
4. Number and type of academic problems: lower-level skills (reading recognition, math computation, spelling, and handwriting) and higher-level skills (reading comprehension, math problem solving, social studies, science, and written language)
5. Number of indices of classroom performance (SOAPP, as described in step 3) and as they differ in percentage from an average child of the same gender, mental age, and race

"other health impairments," where ADHD adversely affects educational or social performance; and (3) when ADHD limits a major life activity under Section 504. Students who do not qualify under IDEA may qualify under Section 504.

For an educational diagnosis, a multidisciplinary team must be involved to determine eligibility (i.e., whether ADHD has an adverse impact on learning or socialization using criteria from both Section 504 and IDEA). A student medically treated for ADHD whose behavior or classroom performance improves on the basis of this medical treatment most likely will still need to have his or her educational services continued. That is, parents have argued successfully that medical treatment was needed to obtain "appropriate education" and that continued appropriate education was still necessary at school expense (Reeve et al., 1994). However, a medical diagnosis using *DSM-IV-TR* is insufficient in the educational diagnosis of ADHD.

In conclusion, not all legal questions have been answered in the diagnosis of individuals with ADHD. We do know, however, that the disorder is best diagnosed on the basis of the intensity, persistence, and clustering of characteristics rather than on the presence or absence of specific characteristics. When quantitative differences between students with and without ADHD are sufficient, a qualitative difference in functioning usually exists.

Diagnostic Controversies Summary. ADHD, like most disabilities, is identified by a failure to meet specific functional requirements of society (literacy, attending, or teamwork) as these requirements are translated into today's classrooms. Variability of behavior and performance is to be expected in children with mild disabilities. We no longer question the medical diagnosis of visual impairment. This impairment can change the functioning of a student from good vision to legal blindness in a matter of seconds, depending on lighting conditions or the size of print. Too much or too little lighting can also "blind" normally sighted individuals. The difference is that children with visual impairments are more sensitive to changes in these conditions, and it is these conditions that allow us to identify this disability.

Until the physical conditions that determine the expression of ADHD are more generally known, we should expect questions to be raised regarding the validity of the diagnosis as well as negative expectations about the label. However, even when labels are not used, reputation effects can be easily established by behavior. That is, when half the pairs of children were told that their work partner would be a child who disrupted the class, talked when he or she was not supposed to, did not sit still, and acted silly, children (and especially younger children) were less likely to see positive task or social performance in their partners than when no expectations were set (Harris, Milich, Johnston, & Hoover, 1990). Furthermore, those students who were expected to show characteristics of ADHD found the peer task to be more difficult than those children whose partners had no expectations. In other words, even without labels, behavioral patterns create expectations about future behavior.

Given the controversies about labeling children (stigma and negative expectations), perhaps a reasonable path is available for educators that involves understanding how the label can be educationally relevant (see chapters 8 to 11). It is equally important to understand specific behavior and how that behavior functions (appropriately or inappropriately) for individual children in specific settings (see chapter 4).

DISCUSSION AND APPLICATION QUESTIONS

1. Is the school required to diagnose a medical or psychological condition in a student with possible ADHD?
2. Can a school district tell a parent that they do not test for ADHD?
3. What are the pros and cons of labeling children with ADHD?
4. Is a student who meets IDEA eligibility also covered by Section 504 regulations?
5. Why is ADHD considered a health impairment, and where in the definition of "other health impairment" is it addressed?
6. Is an outside medical or psychological diagnosis of ADHD sufficient for IDEA eligibility?
7. Is an outside medical or psychological diagnosis of ADHD sufficient grounds for a school system to begin the process of determining Section 504 or IDEA eligibility?
8. What do you say when teachers complain that they do not want to follow the IEP because it will single out the child, something that is particularly important *not* to do at the middle and high school levels?

9. Talk-outs versus on-task talking and work production were the types of data collected on a student. The results indicated that the student was talking out more in subject areas (math and science) where talking was not encouraged while producing more and talking more on task in subjects where talking was encouraged (e.g., English and social studies). What specific recommendations might you suggest?
10. Analyze the following plan for the degree to which it conforms to the intent of Section 504. Keep in mind the following questions:
    a. Is there an acknowledgment of disability?
    b. Is there a listing of his problems and strengths?
    c. Were there any accommodations presented to allow him to be on a level playing field with his peers? Do we know who might be responsible for accommodations?
    d. What might be some appropriate accommodations for him?
    e. Do we know how he responded to earlier attempts?
    f. Does it indicate the conditions under which he will be rewarded?
    g. Can we determine whether Pete is improving?
    h. Did the team have a member who was knowledgeable about ADHD?
    i. Is it possible that this child is being punished on the basis of his disability?

FAMILY PRACTICES
Mother's Plea

At the end of fifth grade, we finally figured out that our son, now 13, had ADD. For 13 long years, we thought that he was just a disobedient child that didn't listen. It was a relief to find out that there was a reason that our very capable son was *not* making straight As and sitting quietly. We realized why he probably was not good at sports and keeping friends—and why he teases other children. He has trouble respecting authority and low self-esteem.

The reason I am writing is because we need help in figuring out the best way to educate an ADD [attention-deficit disorder] child. You were quoted as saying, "Individuals with ADD don't function well in regimens that stress passive, slower-rate, and repetitive learning." But the school system doesn't see it that way. Our son has a behavior contract that requires him to sit still, be quiet, and perform like everyone else. They will let him finish homework he can't find in the office—but in general I don't see any desire to change their ways. In a way their attitude is, if he's on Ritalin, he should be able to perform.

In closing, we are looking for ways to fight for and help our son. He's very bright but is making low grades. Teachers generally don't like him, and he hates school. He has very low self-esteem and is depressed. We have started seeing a clinical psychologist to help him with his depression and anger, but I don't yet see a "light" at the end of the tunnel. My husband, who also has a Ph.D., feels he had ADD as a youth. I am enclosing this behavior plan. I don't know if you will even be able to respond but wondered if this type of plan is what will help an ADD kid.

PETE'S PLAN

I. Pete will follow the rules and procedures of Y Middle School's discipline policy. He will display appropriate classroom behavior allowing for his education benefit and the education benefit of others. Pete will display appropriate behavior in the building, at any school-sanctioned activity on or off school grounds, or on the school bus. If Pete continues to be disruptive three more times and violates his behavior plan, he will be declared habitually disruptive.

II. The following inappropriate behavior will not be tolerated:
- Disrupting class; use of inappropriate language; or rude, disrespectful, and discourteous behavior toward peers and staff
- Unexcused absences
- Unexcused tardies
- Incomplete homework assignments and being unprepared for class
- Other offenses as defined by school board policy
- Inappropriate drawings or comments or a negative attitude

III. Action taken over the past year:
- Seat change
- Verbally reprimanded in class
- Private conference with student
- Team conference with parent
- Conferences with the school counselor
- Phone calls home
- Discipline referrals
- Warnings
- Time-out in hall
- Lunch detention
- Saturday school
- Out-of-school suspension

IV. Positives
- Very bright
- Good math skills
- Intuitive
- Good comprehension and discussion skills

V. Goals
- Pete will focus on his academics.
- Pete will maintain one homework folder.
- Pete will be more positive in interacting with his peers.
- Pete will need to attend all classes and not be late.
- Pete will take/accept responsibility for his actions.
- Pete will follow all classroom and school rules.
- Pete will come to class prepared.
- Pete will complete homework assignments.
- Pete will work on organizational skills.

Pete's Plan (*Continued*)

VI. Consequences
- One warning for behavior
- If homework is incomplete or poorly done, Pete will be sent to the office to complete the work. He may return to class when work is finished.
- Time-out in hall—5 minutes maximum
- Time-out in office for the remainder of the hour
- More than two time-outs weekly will result in Saturday school.
- Out-of-school suspension

VII. Positive rewards:
- Candy
- Sodas
- Computer time

CHAPTER 3

Etiologies and Theoretical Perspectives

OBJECTIVES

- Understand the probable causes of ADHD.
- Recognize theories and models that explain why the behavior presents itself with this specific set of symptoms and outcomes.

KEY TERMS

etiologies
post hoc
neurotransmitter
exogenous
prefrontal cortex
essential fatty acids
theory
descriptive models
primary characteristics
secondary characteristics
response impulsivity
working memory
arousal
trait
state
optimal stimulation theory
functional theories

This chapter presents information on the possible causes (etiologies) of attention deficit hyperactivity disorder (ADHD) and discusses models and theories explaining the pattern of behavior. Even though etiologies do not always help us educationally, theory is important in that regard because it helps us understand symptoms and determine which interventions should be useful.

As we might expect, ADHD appears to be multiply determined, with both genetic and environmental causes. Etiologies that are primarily genetic suggest inborn abnormalities in the structure or chemistry of the brain or in children's inherent abilities or temperaments. In addition, environmental factors can change biological functioning, including disease, trauma, and other health conditions. Finally, the way ADHD is expressed may represent responses learned within the social, family, and classroom contexts. In other words, at least some expression of ADHD can be learned (see Figure 3.1).

ETIOLOGICAL FACTORS

What causes ADHD?

Although we may know the cause of ADHD for a specific child (e.g., an accident), we cannot prove what causes ADHD for the population more generally. That is, for etiologies of genetics or brain damage, it is not possible to (a) damage parts of the brain and directly assess these effects or (b) randomly assign individuals to genetic backgrounds to see

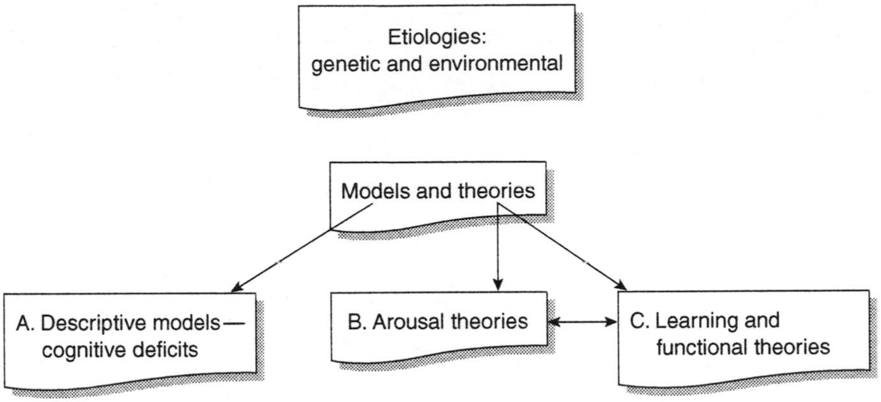

FIGURE 3.1 Etiologies and Theories of ADHD

which genes result in ADHD. If we were able to do this type of deterministic research, as is done in the hard sciences with animals or plants, we would have greater certainty related to etiologies. However, in the social sciences, we do research that suggests the probability of certain factors. The data reported are often post hoc (after-the-fact) examinations of brain structures or genes that are associated with individuals with ADHD.

Genetic factors

Relatives of boys and girls with ADHD have significantly higher rates of ADHD than relatives of students without ADHD (Faraone et al., 1992). Biederman, Faraone, Keenan, Knee, and Tsuang (1991) reported that 28.6% of biological parents of children with hyperactivity also had a history of hyperactivity.

Overall, about 80% of the differences in activity, inattention, and impulsivity between people with and without ADHD can be explained by genetic factors. The high end of this range may be explained by individuals with both ADHD-H and ADHD-I (the combined type), who have a higher probability of inheriting ADHD (as high as .92 to .98 [Willcutt, Pennington, & DeFries, 2000]). In fact, the probability of inheriting activity level is greater than that of inheriting IQ (.55) or of height (.81) (Willerman, 1973).

In addition, at the genetic level, some evidence suggests an association between certain genes and ADHD (DAT1 and DRD4 [Jensen, 2001]). Individuals with ADHD have a longer-than-normal D4 gene, which makes the nerve cell less sensitive to dopamine, a neurotransmitter that conveys signals from one neuron to another. This gene has a well-known association to sensation- or novelty-seeking behavior as well as excitability and impulsiveness (for a review, see LaHoste et al., 1996). Most genetic traits continue because they have provided some advantage to the species (i.e., to survival). Heterogeneity alone has some advantage to the species by allowing more individuals to survive changing environmental conditions (Calabi, 1997).

Even though there is greater genetic correspondence for identical twins to have ADHD (about 80%) than fraternal twins (about 30% same sex [Gillis, Gilger, Pennington, & DeFries, 1992; LaHoste et al., 1996]), about 30% to 50% of identical twins do *not both* manifest ADHD (Goodman & Stevenson, 1989; Johnston & Mash, 2001; LaHoste et al., 1996). This indicates that "biology shapes our impulses and aptitudes, but it doesn't act alone. There is always a context and always room for resistance" (Begley, 1995). In other words, external factors remain an important factor in etiology.

Exogenous factors

Exogenous (external) factors, such as maternal smoking, complications during birth or pregnancy, high levels of lead ingestion, accounted for another 20% to 30% of the causes of ADHD (Pennington, 1991). These prenatal or postnatal insults to the child's biological system can account for ADHD in about one in five children with ADHD. Specifically, for maternal smoking, 22% of mothers of children with ADHD smoked a pack of cigarettes per day during at least 3 months of pregnancy in contrast to only 8% of mothers of non-ADHD children (Milberger et al., 2002). (It is also possible that these mothers were also ADHD, thus contributing to the association.)

Structural (Neuroanatomical) factors

Considerable evidence exists of differences in the structure or size of the brain as possible determinants of ADHD. Brain structure differences could be inherited or externally altered through brain damage. Researchers have speculated about which areas of the brain may be especially vulnerable to insult. Pennington (1991) suggested that areas of the brain that have evolved most recently in the history of the human species would be more likely to be affected by genetic and environmental variation. These are (a) the prefrontal cortex, which is involved in planning, response inhibition, selective attention or visual search, maintenance of attention, self-monitoring, recognition memory, and even creativity, and (b) the left-hemisphere language functions, which are involved in phonological processing (Pennington, 1991; Pennington & Ozonoff, 1996). The left-hemisphere dysfunctions have been found in association with language-learning disabilities and dyslexia (Shaywitz & Shaywitz, 1991). See "Evidence-Based Practices" example on page 42.

Maturational factors

Developmental models focus on the unfolding of a child's biological nature over time. From a developmental perspective, we could expect children to eventually grow out of this disorder. Developmental changes take place in activity and attention (see chapters 5 and 6). However, the major symptoms of ADHD persisted into adulthood in 33% of an adult ADHD study sample (see Pennington, 1991) and in 67% of children with a childhood diagnosis (Barkley, 1997a, 1997b; Barkley, Fischer, Edelbrock, & Smallish, 1990). In addition, physiological data (event-related

EVIDENCE-BASED PRACTICES
ASSESSMENT OF BRAIN DIFFERENCES

Cortical activity in the prefrontal region of the brain has been assessed using a quantitative electroencephalographic procedure (QEEG), a technique that assesses electrical activity (Monastra et al., 1999). This technique alone showed that 86% of the individuals who had been diagnosed with ADHD using the conventional diagnostic procedures were also classified as ADHD and that 98% of those who did not have ADHD were classified non-ADHD. However, in this study, no disordered comparison group was used for differential diagnosis.

Other types of measures (positron emission tomography [PET] scans, electroencephalograms [EEGs], and magnetic resonance imaging [MRI]) have been used to visualize brain differences. PET images reveal biochemical changes in the tissues of the body. For individuals with ADHD, PET scans reveal evidence of reduced whole-brain glucose utilization (Zametkin et al., 1990 [but see Zametkin et al., 1993, for a failure to replicate]) and low cerebral blood flow (Lou, Henricksen, & Bruhn, 1989; Lou, Henricksen, Bruhn, & Borner, 1984). Some of the latter work, however, failed to control for age or co-occurring disabilities. Thus, additional study of the blood flow in the brain and its use of glucose are needed.

The EEG is a neurophysiologic technique that assesses voltage signals of the brain. EEGs have been used to find increased slow-wave activity primarily in the frontal regions and decreased beta activity in the temporal areas. Such findings "would indicate possible decreased cortical arousal in these children in those areas of the brain frequently associated with executive control and language" (Riccio, Hynd, Cohen, & Gonzalez, 1993, p. 120).

More recent evidence for students with ADHD has been reported using MRI, scans of which have revealed that typical children have slightly larger right frontal lobes (3% to 4% larger total brain sizes) and more symmetrical lobes than children with ADHD (Barry, Lyman, & Klinger, 2002; Castellanos et al., 2002). However, the size differences *cannot* be used to diagnose ADHD because the differences were calculated using group averages and do not necessarily apply to individual cases.

potentials) do not support maturational differences between students with and without ADHD (Callaway, Halliday, & Naylor, 1983).

Even so, there appears to be behavioral evidence suggesting that children with ADHD are developmentally immature. For example, the behavioral and emotional responses of students with ADHD are similar to responses of younger children (e.g., Moon, Zentall, Grskovic, Hall, & Stormont, 2001). In addition, deficiencies in basic skills have been documented for these children that improve over time (e.g., fine motor skills, math accuracy [Zentall, 1990; Zentall, Moon, Hall, & Grskovic, 2001]).

Some ecological/developmental models emphasize the fit between the child's skills and the requirements of the context (e.g., of family, school, culture). Behavioral differences are attributed to the child's inability to regulate behavior in line with new developmental or cultural tasks. Preschool and young elementary students must learn to conform to behavioral expectations (see chapter 5), and older elementary students learn to conform to academic (attentional) demands of increasingly difficult tasks (see chapters 6 and 7), whereas students in high school are practicing more complex social skills (requiring response inhibition) in preparation for the vocational and relational tasks of young adulthood (see chapters 5 and 12). Perhaps for this reason, gross motor hyperactivity characterizes preschool- and elementary-age students, which becomes restlessness and inattentiveness during later elementary and middle school years and social disorders in high school.

Neurochemical factors

Evidence of differences exists also in the neurochemistry of individuals with ADHD. It is generally accepted that the neurotransmitters dopamine and norepinephrine are involved in ADHD (for a review, see Riccio et al., 1993). What has been suggested is that dopamine may be deficient in the prefrontal synapses, or connection points between cells (Goldman-Rakic, 1992; Pliszka, McCracken, & Maas, 1996). The role of neurotransmitters is further supported by evidence that psychostimulants (e.g., Ritalin) increase the availability of the neurotransmitter dopamine at the synapses.

Nutritional determinants

Whereas much of the previously mentioned research involves a post hoc examination of biogenetics, a deterministic understanding can be made of nutrition. That is, it is possible to randomly assign individuals to placebo versus real (additive) diets. Findings from this research indicate that a subgroup of children with hyperactivity, perhaps as few as 3% to 5%, may be sensitive to food dyes or sugar; typically, these are preschoolers (for a review, see Barkley, 1997a; Whalen, 1989). Eliminating artificial food colors has been demonstrated to decrease parent (not teacher) ratings of behavioral difficulties. (For a meta-analysis review, see Schab & Trinh, 2004.) One study of food additives and sugar found a slight decrease in activity with no performance effects, while another study found an association between sugar intake and aggressiveness/restlessness in children with hyperactivity, with the opposite pattern observed for controls (for a review, see Leibowitz, 1991).

Although the evidence to date does not support placing children on restrictive diets, some evidence (Stevens et al., 1995) suggests gains from supplementing diets with essential fatty acids for those children with ADHD who had deficiencies (i.e., improvements over placebo on sustained attention, parent ratings of conduct, and teacher ratings of inattention). About 40% of children with ADHD in contrast to about 10% of comparison children had deficiencies in essential fatty acids. When children with reading disability and ADHD (not assessed for their level of deficiencies) were supplemented with a combination of omega-3 and -6 fatty acids, reductions in a wider range of ADHD symptoms were found (psychosomatic problems, cognitive problems, anxiety, attention problems, hyperactivity, and a global index measuring a broad range of behavior problems) over placebo conditions (Richardson & Puri, 2002).

DESCRIPTIVE AND THEORETICAL EXPLANATIONS

Why do these children behave with this pattern of characteristics?

Although knowing the causes of ADHD can help prevent and, in some cases, medically remediate ADHD, it does not help educators. Differences in brain structure, genetic makeup, or development may "cause" ADHD, but it does not tell us how children learn or respond to different classroom conditions. Theory provides this information.

Without theory, educators rely on "how-to" lists. These practices have a "stop-gap," or piecemeal, value but do not increase our understanding of the factors that control the manifestations of ADHD. Perhaps the difference in these positions is reflected in a debate between Poincare and Eysenck. Poincare said, "Science is built up with facts, as a house with stones." Eysenck said, "But a collection of facts is no more a science than a heap of stones is a house." Theory provides the foundation of a house.

Defining theory

Criteria Used to Define a Theory

1. Under what conditions will students with ADHD differ from similar peers in behavior or in performance?
2. Under which conditions will students with ADHD *not* differ from their age-mates?
3. Does the underlying cause predict and explain behavior and performance problems without additional constructs or circular logic?
4. Can treatments be predicted from this theory?

Related to the first criterion, most theories list a number of ways students with ADHD differ from their peers. However, theories need to tell us when children with ADHD should perform and behave as well as their peers of the same age, IQ, and gender. As stated in the field of learning disabilities (LD), "cumulative research of LD and non-LD children becomes almost redundant since the former children invariably give inferior performances, compared to non-LD children" (Wong, 1979, 1986, pp. 18–19).

Defining the conditions under which performance and behavior should be "normal" also reduces the likelihood of being overly inclusive, or circular. A theory is circular when it attempts to use the symptoms of a disability (e.g., hyperactivity, impulsivity, inattention, academic underachievement, social problems) as an explanation.

Descriptive models are "almost impossible to validate empirically because the diagnosis depends on the symptoms and vice versa" (Goodman & Poillion, 1992, p. 53). Circular models, such as the "Note" example on p. 45, could be useful in diagnosis, but they are not true theories. In the history of the field of ADHD, several descriptive models have emphasized one or another of the three primary symptoms of ADHD. Hyperactivity was described as the main cause initially and then attention (hence the label change from hyperactivity disorder to attention disorder). Current models emphasize impulsivity (response inhibition disorder). The early reasoning was that if activity problems occur first and inattention and impulsivity occur later, then activity was the first cause. This was supported behaviorally by Schaefer and Bayley (1963), who reported that the greater the activity at age 1, the greater the

NOTE

MODELS (BUT NOT THEORIES) DEFINE A DISABILITY BY ITS SYMPTOMS

Q: Why does Johnny fail to pay attention, complete his work, stay in his seat, and so forth?
A: Because he has an attention deficit disorder.
Q: How do you know he has ADD?
A: Because he doesn't pay attention, complete his work, stay in his seat, and so on. (Goodman & Poillion, 1992, p. 53).

inattentiveness at age 12, and by Gathercole and Pickering (2000), who reported that inattentiveness in kindergarten predicted reading underachievement in fifth grade even after controlling for IQ.

In the models presented next, there is an emphasis on one primary characteristic (core variable) that affects multiple areas of functioning that are secondary features of the disorder (Rapport, 2001).

Types of theories and models

Cognitive descriptive models Cognitive models describe differences in a primary characteristic (e.g., attention, impulsivity) of children with ADHD. Two models are well known in the field of ADHD. Douglas (1972) emphasized attention as the important primary characteristic of ADHD. More recently, Barkley (1997b) has gained recognition for his emphasis on response inhibition (impulsivity). Both Douglas and Barkley have added similar layers of cognitive and/or motivational factors (e.g., deficits in the reward system, working memory, arousal, metacognitive language factors) to more fully account for the differences observed in these children.

Douglas's inattention model. Douglas's model of ADHD has evolved over time. In 1972, she described the primary deficit of ADHD as the failure to invest, organize, or sustain attention and effort (and poor impulse control) (see Figure 3.2). From deficits in attention and impulse control, secondary features were failure to use language for self-control, academic underachievement, and poor social, behavioral, and morality performance. The main components of her treatment model were described as "stop, look, and listen." "Stop" was directed at the impulsivity characteristic, and "look and listen" were directed toward focusing attention. More generally, the use of language (rules, self-questioning, and verbal strategy rehearsal) was seen as a way to help children focus and maintain attention in order to internalize standards. These techniques were best implemented by therapists and consultants. In 1979, with evidence suggesting arousal deficits and the positive effects of increased

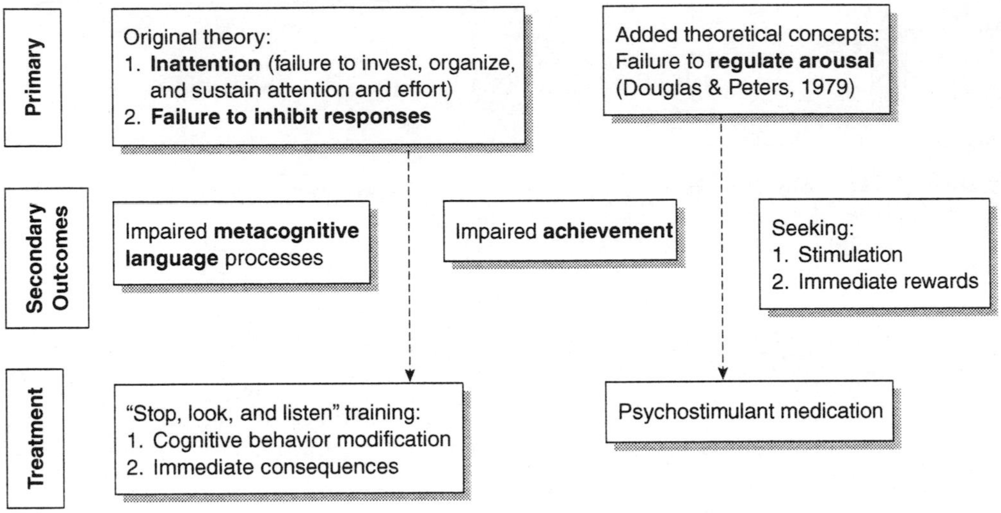

FIGURE 3.2 Douglas

stimulation, Douglas added the additional construct of arousal or need for immediate reinforcement and stimulation. This model must still be considered descriptive, as was similarly concluded by Barkley (1997b).

This descriptive model is not a testable theory. For example, it predicts disorder in any task or setting that requires attention or impulse control. However, most human behavior requires attention and response inhibition, so this model is overly inclusive and cannot specify conditions under which the symptoms of ADHD would be reduced. For this reason, the central constructs of inattention and response inhibition, which are both symptoms and outcomes, fail to be specific enough to provide a clear understanding of ADHD.

However, this model has been very useful in defining attentional problems and in examining some interventions that use cognitive, language-based methods for attention training (cognitive behavior modification [see chapter 9]). Furthermore, the impairments in Douglas' model are internally consistent with the treatments

NOTE
Douglas' Model Is Descriptive, Not Predictive

Q: Why does Johnny fail to complete his work, stay in his seat, and so forth?
A: Because he has poor attention and poor response inhibition.
Q: How do you know inattention is the major problem?
A: Because he performs poorly on most classroom and laboratory measures of attention and impulsivity.

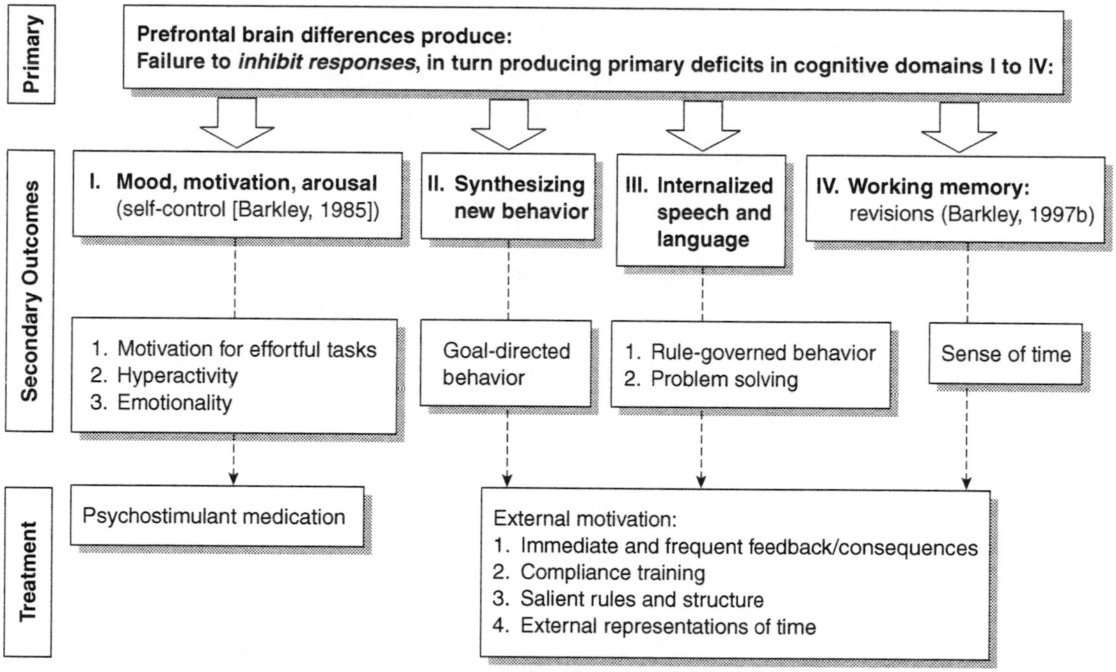

FIGURE 3.3 Barkley

proposed—improving attention by training children to "look and listen" and reducing impulsivity by training children to "stop."

Barkley's inhibition model. Barkley has presented his most elaborate model for ADHD (but not ADHD-I) (see Figure 3.3) with the cause located in the prefrontal region of the brain (Barkley, 1997b, 1998a). According to Barkley, problems in the prefrontal area contribute to response impulsivity (i.e., a failure to inhibit strong responses, to stop or interrupt an ongoing response, and to inhibit competing responses during periods of delay). In other words, there is an emphasis on the failure to stop activity (inhibition of action) rather than on understanding factors that contribute to excessive action. In this model, failure to inhibit contributes to three basic cognitive deficits, called executive functioning deficits:

1. Lack of internally regulated mood, motivation, and arousal (self-control)
2. Failure to analyze and synthesize new behavior (reconstitution)
3. Failure to internalize speech and poor working memory

These cognitive executive deficits further explain impairments in working memory (the inability to hold information in mind for the purposes of reordering, planning, reconsidering, and so on), contributing to difficulties with time (e.g., waiting for rewards that are delayed). Barkley has explained that children with ADHD are unable to bridge the time gap between a response and a reward because of poorer working memory and an inability to self-regulate distal events. In other words, executive motor disinhibition leads to "a cascade of downstream problems" (Nigg, 2001, p. 583).

However, questions have been raised about this model and whether it forms a cohesive, testable theory:

> Although the effects of these processes on working memory, self-regulation of affect, motivation and arousal, the internalization of language, and the reconstitution of behavior are very well elaborated, the theoretical status of the construct "behavioral inhibition" remains ambiguous. (Slusarek, Velling, Bunk, & Eggers, 2001, p. 356)

Similarly, Nigg (2001) stated that "support for the process details of that model is post hoc" (p. 583).

Logically, from Figure 3.3, children with ADHD should differ from their peers under conditions when behavioral inhibition is required, such as (a) a *time lag* between events and their consequences (e.g., temptations, delayed rewards) and (b) requirements to rely on *past* (recalled) motivation or internalized language (e.g., strategies). However, most human behavior requires delay, and the model cannot explain problems observed in a number of contexts when no language, working memory, or withholding of responses are required (Borger et al., 1999; van der Meere, Shalev, Borger & Gross-Tsur, 1995), including the greater activity observed during sleep and infancy for these children (Porrino et al., 1983), or the fact that children with autism also show these executive function impairments (e.g., Pennington & Ozonoff, 1996).

The descriptive model in Figure 3.3 bypasses theoretical concepts and connects impairments to current treatments for ADHD. Barkley specifically suggests the following:

1. Beginning medication earlier and requiring longer compliance, presumably to address difficulties with response inhibition
2. Using immediate consequences, presumably to avoid working memory requirements

Similar treatments were proposed by Douglas. However, the question is not whether the treatments of medication and immediate consequences work. Theoretically, if students with ADHD fail to inhibit responding, then treatments to increase delay should be useful. However, no evidence shows that imposing delay time helps these children perform better on their tasks (e.g., Sonuga-Barke, Williams, Hall, & Saxton, 1996). Thus, interventions that suggest increased processing time for students with ADHD are unfounded unless these students also have learning disabilities or additional time is needed for their handwriting.

In sum, the major problem is that this model is also untestable because it uses a major *symptom* of the disability (failure to withhold responding—response disinhibition or impulsivity) to explain other symptoms and to predict treatment. This is

Barkley's Model Is Descriptive but Not Predictive

Q: Why does Johnny fail to complete his work, stay in his seat, and so forth?
A: Because he has abnormalities in prefrontal brain structures that produce poor response inhibition leading to four primary executive deficits.
Q: How do you know prefrontal brain structures and associated impairments are the major problem?
A: Because he performs poorly on most classroom and laboratory measures requiring response inhibition or that involve the executive functions, such as working memory.
Q: Well, how do you treat ADHD?
A: We treat it with stimulant medication to strengthen those prefrontal cortex functions and thereby improve children's ability to inhibit responses.

like saying that reading disability is caused by an inability to recognize words (decode) or understand the meaning of words (encode). Reading disability is not caused by performing poorly on measures of decoding and encoding; reading disability *is* performing poorly (i.e., a description of the disability).

In contrast, a theory-based approach to reading identifies the underlying difficulties (e.g., with the phonological processes). Phonological processes are not part of the original diagnosis of reading disability. Although this construct (phonological processes) may not be the only theoretical explanation, it *is* testable (i.e., intervening with phonological skills and examining their effects).

Arousal or activation theories Activity, attention, and response inhibition are symptoms of ADHD that may be consistently related to an underlying construct, namely, arousal. Arousal is the physiological activation state of the child, which has *trait* and *state* qualities. Inherent trait differences (e.g., behavior observed even during infancy and sleep [Porrino et al., 1983]) and differences in the immediate state of that child exist, depending on setting conditions. Arousal cannot be directly observed, but it can be assessed by psychophysiological measures. In addition, contextual novelty, in the form of stimulating tasks and conditions, is observable, and children's responses should indicate a higher state of internal arousal.

Three theoretical orientations, discussed in the following sections, are related to the child's level of arousal (effective stimulation).

Overarousal model. One of the earliest educational models for students with ADHD used overarousal as the construct (Strauss & Lehtinen, 1947). This theory was rationally based on the behavioral similarities between brain-injured war veterans and students with hyperactivity. Strauss's theory was referred to as a "stimulus reduction" theory, taken from its treatment implications. Because the model had clear predictions and because stimulation (arousal) was defined as an underlying construct, it was possible to examine it scientifically. In other words, it was testable. However, the accumulation of evidence has failed to find support for overarousal (for a review, see Zentall, 1975; Zentall & Zentall, 1983).

Zentall's optimal stimulation theory (underarousal theory). The optimal stimulation theory was originally presented as a general explanation for the activity of all organisms. Hebb (1955) and Leuba (1955), for example, suggested that the brain needs stimulation to maintain its integrity and functioning. Effective performance depended both on the stimulation available in the setting and the time period and on what was provided internally by child factors, such as fatigue, hormonal levels, and drugs. When external and internally provided stimulation were not optimal, children regulated their own stimulation by changes in activity, their approach to or avoidance of stimulation, and their attentional responses. The optimal stimulation theory was first applied to students with ADHD in 1975 (Zentall, 1975). The following information specifies responses by children with ADHD when they are insufficiently stimulated and provides the basis for making predictions when conducting research on the optimal stimulation theory.

NOTE

BEHAVIOR TO OPTIMIZE STIMULATION

1. Activity
   a. Increased activity, which can be seen in talkativeness or restlessness
   b. Increased variability (nonrepetitiveness) of active responses
   c. Increased risk-taking behavior
   d. Decreased delay time between responses (difficulty waiting and impulsivity), which is seen
      i. socially as interrupting, blurting-out responses, disrupting, and bossiness;
      ii. academically as poor planning and lack of organization; and
      iii. nonadaptively as increased accidents.
2. Attention
   a. Length: a short span of attention that looks like decreased persistence, off task, and change seeking
   b. Selective focus on or attentional preferences for
      i. *external novelty*, seen as failure to attend to internal representations, such as strategies, values, subtle feelings, thoughts;
      ii. *cognitive novelty*, seen in stimulating reading material, thoughts or interests; and
      iii. *emotionally intense experiences*, such as
         - illegal activities
         - seeking emotional or aggressive reactions from others (i.e., a provocateur)

However, when children with ADHD have sufficient stimulation or active responses available, for example, such behavior will be less.

Cognitive effects that exist are secondary to the level of arousal. That is, attention, response preparation, motor inhibition, and the ability to allocate effort to a task at hand are dependent on sufficient arousal (Banaschewski et al., 2003; Sergeant, 2000).

Physiological researchers were the first to hypothesize underarousal for students with ADHD but thought that students with ADHD were continually underaroused (understimulated) and overactive (Rosenthal, 1973). Later evidence indicated that children with ADHD were not overactive in all settings (see chapter 5) and were physiologically underreactive only in response to some stimulus conditions (often showing smaller magnitude and delayed physiological orienting responses [Callaway et al., 1983; Rosenthal & Allen, 1978; Satterfield, Schell, Nicholas, Satterfield, & Freese, 1990]). Also in support of underarousal (understimulation or stimulus deficiency) was evidence that (a) individuals who were experimentally placed into sensory deprivation environments looked and acted like children with ADHD (i.e., an analogous state to ADHD) and that (b) when individuals were required to exercise, the effects of sensory deprivation were reduced (for a review, see Zentall, 1975; Zentall & Zentall, 1983).

Students with ADHD were described as needing more stimulation than their peers (Zentall, 1975) or as physiologically demonstrating suboptimal regulation of arousal (Banaschewski et al., 2003; Brandeis et al., 2002). Each of us may need more stimulation in some settings, as reflected in the following statement: "Anyone—even we professionals—can become hyperactive or distractible when forced to sit through a boring lecture or two" (Smelter, Rasch, Fleming, Nazos & Baranowski, 1996, p. 431). However, even in these stimulus-reduced settings, individuals with ADHD will need additional stimulation earlier than others. Students with ADHD have been described as the "canaries" in the mines. Canaries were set into cages in mines and used as a signal (i.e., by dying) to warn miners that insufficient oxygen was present.

Similarly, students with ADHD are more sensitive to a loss of stimulation. Their lack of tolerance for conditions of low stimulation is similar to genetically determined differences in IQ or in height. The basis of these genetic differences could be attributed to the gene DRD4. That is, DRD4 has been found in association with novelty-seeking behavior ("a well-defined psychological trait characterized by exploratory behavior, excitability, and impulsivity" [Jensen, 2001, p. 121]).

An examination of Figure 3.4 isolates the "primary" theoretical construct as difficulty maintaining an optimal level of stimulation, especially in low-stimulation tasks or situations. Although the original optimal stimulation theory suggested that activity was the means of self-regulating stimulation, we have added alternative ways that individuals can produce stimulation for themselves. These include more frequent shifts in attention, thought, or topics of conversation as well as seeking social or emotional stimulation (e.g., "risky" experiences, aggression [Meyer & Zentall, 1995; Shaw & Brown, 1999]). "Any risk-taking, exciting or illegal behavior is adrenaline producing" (Streett, 1995, p. 25). It is also possible to seek cognitive

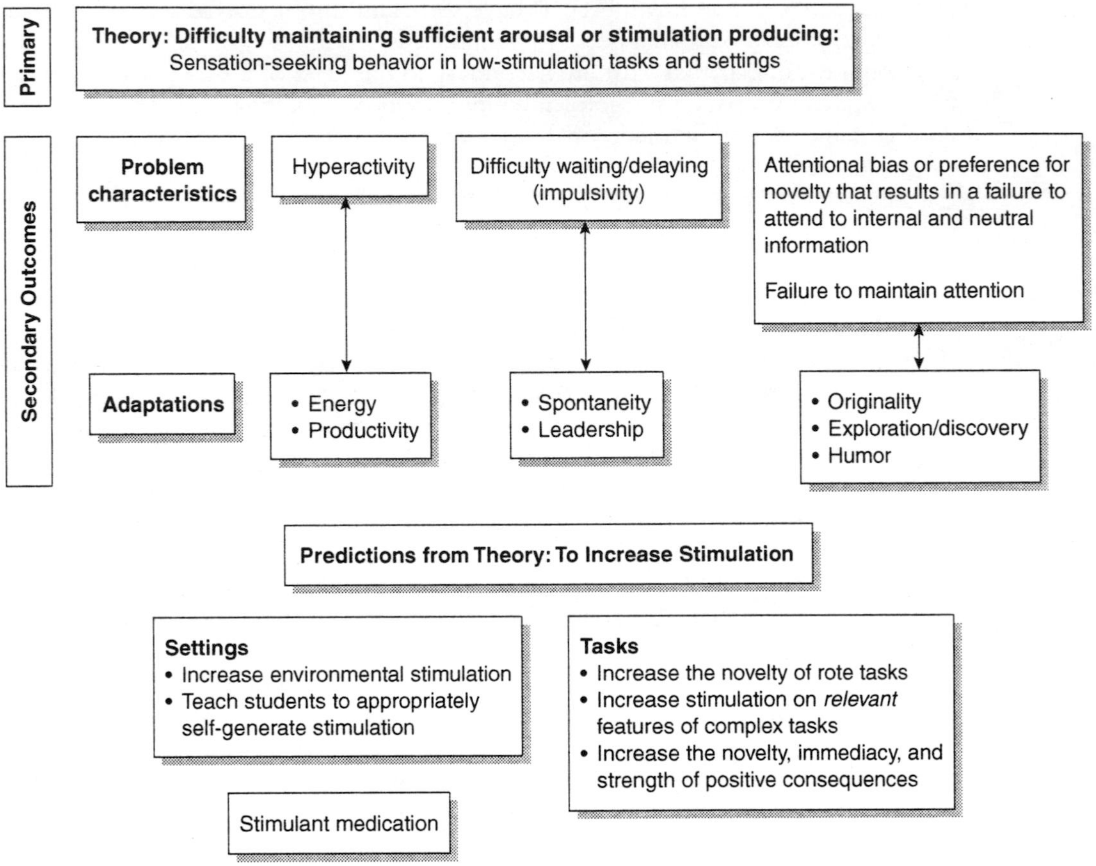

FIGURE 3.4 Zentall

stimulation through daydreaming, thought, or creative activities (Zentall, Moon et al., 2001).

The "secondary outcomes," or specific ways that children with ADHD attempt to increase stimulation, can lead to problem or adaptive behavior (see "Adaptation characteristics" in Figure 3.4). Problem outcomes can be seen, for example, when children *fail* to ignore unimportant features/events or associated ideas. Attentional preferences for stimulating events can also lead to responding overly emotionally and to specific behavior, such as procrastination, which functions by providing enough stimulation or arousal so that the individual is able to complete a low-preference task at "the last minute." Simulation-seeking behavior can also be adaptive (e.g., increased energy, productivity, originality, spontaneity; see Figure 3.4 and chapters 5 and 6).

NOTE

OPTIMAL STIMULATION THEORY OF ADHD CAN MAKE PREDICTIONS

Q: Why does Johnny fail to complete his work, stay in his seat, and so forth?
A: Because he has a greater need for stimulation than his peers.
Q: How do you know understimulation or underarousal is the major problem?
A: Because he attends poorly and behaves inappropriately under reduced stimulation conditions in comparison to environmental and task conditions of greater novelty.
Q: Well, how do you treat ADHD?
A: We treat it by asking teachers to provide additional task and environmental stimulation and by teaching Johnny how to self-generate stimulation in appropriate ways.

Because students with ADHD are more readily understimulated, they should more readily attend to, be reinforced by, and therefore learn from stimulation, especially if it is observable (salient), immediate, and intense (e.g., emotional, loud, visually or concretely represented). For this reason, educators need to increase the novelty and strength of positive consequences and of features of rote tasks, especially during later performance when effective stimulation is low. However, using stimulation within a complex task is somewhat trickier because stimulation can guide attention into relevant or irrelevant places, depending on its location. For example, when color stimulation is added randomly to complex tasks, students with ADHD may attend to nonessential features while disregarding neutral but essential task, social, or environmental features (see chapter 6). For this reason, stimulation must be placed by the child or by the teacher on relevant parts of tasks (e.g., the operation sign in mathematics). In sum, optimal stimulation theory can make educationally meaningful predictions and provide evidence in support of predictions.

Failure to regulate arousal. Douglas (1972) could be the first to suggest that individuals with ADHD may have difficulty with conditions that are too low and too high in stimulation. She hypothesized that individuals with ADHD failed to regulate arousal to meet task or situational demands and had a tendency to seek stimulation and immediate reinforcement (Douglas, 1985; Douglas & Peters, 1979; see also Sergeant, 2000; van der Meere & Stemerkink, 1999). These children were thought to be overreactive to high stimulation and underreactive to low levels of task stimulation. In other words, a smaller window of optimal arousal may exist for individuals with ADHD. In fact, documentation shows overarousal in children with ADHD when they also have oppositional defiant disorder or conduct disorder (i.e., a greater increase in arousal and retaliation in response to provocation than for students with only ADHD [Waschbusch et al., 2002]).

However, most findings document underarousal, which could be explained by the fact that most research has been conducted with boring attention tasks or in familiar classroom contexts. Anecdotally, we have observed that students with ADHD can respond with greater excitement to the stimulation they receive. A large amount of unstructured stimulation, to which they are unaccustomed, may easily tip them into a state of overarousal. During these occasions, students with ADHD can respond as if they were starved and in the presence of a great feast—stuffing food into their mouths as if there were no future. Further evidence for this failure to regulate arousal theory may be forthcoming.

Learning theories The assumption underlying behavioral theory (learning and social learning theories) is that children simply have not learned appropriate behavior or have learned inappropriate behavior from the environment. An individual acquires knowledge from the environment, such as "rules, skills, strategies, beliefs and attitudes" (Schunk, 1996, p. 102). Social cognitive theory states that learning may occur simply by watching others (Bandura, 1969), or it may occur through direct experiences with individuals or groups. Deviance, then, can result from people's interactions with other individuals or groups who have different or deviant values, behavior, or motivations (Traub & Little, 1994, p. 185).

Treatments predicted from these learning theories suggest that children can relearn appropriate behavior when appropriate models and consistent and immediate feedback are provided. Learning theory has particular explanatory power for behavior, such as aggression, and is further described in chapters 5 and 9.

Functional theories Functional theories also address the learning of behavior. However, behavior that is learned depends not only on adult and peer models and consequences but also on the specific needs or purposes of the child in those contexts. That is, it is within specific cultures, contexts, and settings that the behavior of a child derives its meaning. Chapter 4 examines functional theory in greater detail and describes its importance in individual assessment and intervention.

Sociological functionalism states even more broadly that both deviant and socially acceptable behavior exist because they serve some societal or family purpose. Recent sociological concepts of deviance state that deviance is an unavoidable clash between students' attempts to control their own activities and adults' attempts to maintain theirs. School deviance in this sense represents not willful resistance but rather an attempt to create alternative scenes under student control. Sociological functionalism could explain the significant relationship between deviant school behavior and susceptibility to boredom in adolescent students (Wasson, 1981).

SUMMARY

In this chapter, possible causes of ADHD were presented with considerable support found for a genetically based etiology of ADHD. That is, genetics can contribute to differences in the structure and in the neurochemistry of the brain.

These inherent child differences can interact with external factors (e.g., nutrition, learning, contextual requirements) to produce identified ADHD. Etiologies are important to our understanding, but they do not guide educational intervention.

Explanatory models were then presented. Models have been used in a description of problems and can be important in assessment and diagnosis. Overlap between the explanatory models of both Douglas and Barkley include the constructs of cognition (e.g., deficits in executive functioning, including working memory, metacognition, internalized language) and deficits in motivation or the reward system. These models review important information related to the attention and impulsivity of these students and tell us that these children have specific problems in attention (looking and listening) and/or in impulsivity (stopping, inhibition, planning, and time). However, these models do not tell us the conditions or variables in the classroom that contribute to or optimize the behavior and attention of these children.

Arousal theory (optimal stimulation theory) provides a basis for predicting and for intervening. With this theory, behavior and performance do not reflect deficit mental capacities (i.e., a deficit-based model). That is, optimal stimulation theory attributes biological functionality to the behavior of children, suggesting that students with ADHD attempt to regulate stimulation through novelty-seeking behavior. These predictions are empirically supported by the demonstrated benefits of environmental and task stimulation as well as by the parallel benefits of psychostimulant medication.

Even though optimal stimulation theory provides both explanatory and predictive power, important contributions have been made by other models and theories. For example, children develop different ways to create stimulation for themselves (explained by learning theory [see chapter 9]), mediated by their cognitive abilities/disabilities and learning contexts (e.g., that are explained by the ecological theory [see chapters 5 and 12]). It is also evident that at times these children are overstimulated (e.g., from a high dose of medication or stress), and this is explained by overarousal. For this reason, many of these models and theories are important and will reappear in chapters when relevant to the information presented.

DISCUSSION AND APPLICATION QUESTIONS

1. What are the similarities and differences in educational treatments derived from the following models and theories:
   a. Douglas's "stop-look-listen"
   b. Barkley's failure to inhibit
   c. Zentall's optimal stimulation
2. Why is it so much easier to know what causes diseases in plants than it is to know what causes disorders in humans?

3. Why does knowing the etiology of a disability not necessarily help us know what to do educationally?
4. What is the probable theoretical approach being used in the treatment of ADHD for Pete (see chapter 2, page 36)?

PART *Two*

Characteristics

CHAPTER 4

Functional Assessment of Individuals

OBJECTIVES

- Describe ways to obtain samples of behavior to analyze.
- List payoffs (get and avoid) that explain some of the purposes of the behavior of individuals with ADHD.
- List typical antecedents of off-task or disruptive behavior.

KEY TERMS

functional assessment
critical incident log
antecedents
consequences
get payoffs
avoid payoffs
multiple functions of behavior
replacement behavior
goals targeting the child
goals targeting the setting or task
high-priority behavior
"baby-step" objectives

This chapter identifies the purposes of individual student behavior through functional assessment. Because the method of functional assessment presented here is simple, it can be used by parents as well as by general and special educators and other specialists (e.g., school psychologists, behavioral consultants, clinicians). This chapter addresses several decision-making steps based on informal data collected from a log of classroom incidents.

WHY DOES DISRUPTIVE BEHAVIOR OCCUR?

Functional assessment contributes to an understanding of an individual's behavior, i.e., its usefulness in meeting specific needs (see Figure 4.1, page 60). Increased interest in functional assessment came about after the 1997 Amendments to the Individuals with Disabilities Educational Act (IDEA). Mandates required school personnel to conduct functional assessments to guide intervention plans, also called behavior intervention plans, especially when expulsion or dismissal of a student was a possibility (Ervin et al., 2001). Functional assessment is critical in determining appropriate interventions (positive behavioral support) for individual children.

Functional assessment is descriptive of the child within specific settings and thus contributes to the school's approach to intervention (Zentall & Javorsky, 1995). That is, once we understand how the behavior serves the child in that context (i.e., the function of the behavior), we can (a) teach the child to substitute more appropriate types of behavior with the same purpose or (b) change the setting to alter that behavior. The "Teaching Strategies" example on pages 60 and 61 is an educator's narrative.

NOTE
Functional Assessment Is Needed

1. when a student is not progressing academically or socially as expected,
2. when there is disagreement between home and school about the behavior of the child,
3. when assessing the success of specific accommodations,
4. after suspension when considering alternative placements,
5. in preparation for a team meeting about a child and in writing behavior intervention plans for specific disruptive behavior, or
6. when a child has been placed on psychostimulant medication and a reassessment of behavior is needed.

FIGURE 4.1
Functional Assessment Steps

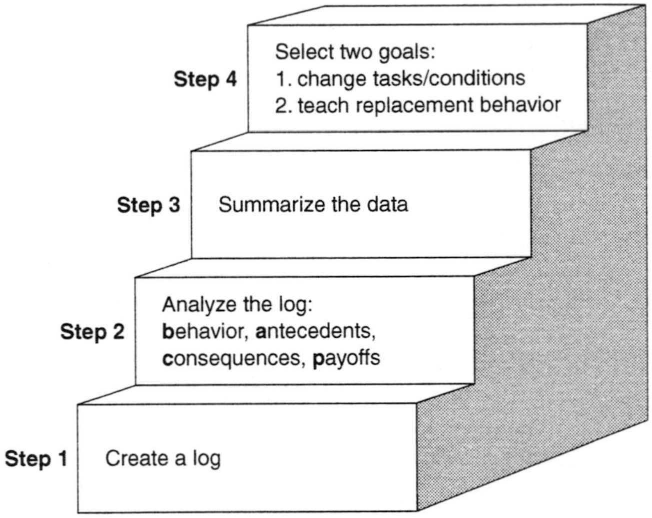

TEACHING STRATEGIES
Functional Assessment of A.J.

A functional assessment was conducted to determine the relationship between one of our student's challenging behaviors and events in the environment. It was hoped that results would allow us to develop an intervention that would reduce the problem behavior. The target student was A.J., a 10-year-old boy with a learning disability and attention-deficit hyperactivity disorder (ADHD). The respondents were the general education teacher and the special education teacher. The setting was a fifth-grade inclusion classroom with 12 general education students and 12 students with special needs.

TEACHING STRATEGIES *(Continued)*

A.J.'s Log

We began keeping a log to determine when and how often a target behavior occurred—the student systematically used a pencil to punch holes in his assignment papers. It was soon evident from observation and from comments made by A.J. that the setting events for the behavior extended beyond the classroom environment. We observed that the student often entered the classroom in the morning exhibiting an angry mood. We learned from information supplied by A.J. that he often missed the bus and that his mother drove him to school. They argued on the way. Further observation of A.J. showed that he avoided going to his desk in the morning and beginning his daily oral language assignment. It was only after repeated requests by the teachers that he finally went to his desk, and then he would begin to punch holes in his paper with a pencil. When given another paper, he would repeat the procedure. This behavior extended to other subject areas and assignment papers but with much less frequency. It was not observed during group instruction.

We graphed the information from the log and found that the target behavior clustered around the 8:30–9:00 time slot (see Table 4.1), that is, when A.J. arrived at school and had to begin his assignment. The behavior occurred at other times but more randomly and much less frequently. Based on this information, we developed our intervention to be used in the 8:30–9:00 time period.

TABLE 4.1 A.J.'s Paper Punching
■ Behavior was observed □ Behavior was not observed

Activity	Time	Day 1	Day 2	Day 3	Day 4	Day 5	Day 6	Day 7	Day 8	Day 9
Daily oral language	8:30–9:00	■	■	■		■	■	■		■
Reading group	9:00–9:50									
Independent	9:50–									
Math	10:00–									
Independent	10:50–									
Writing	11:00–11:30	■						■		
Lunch and recess	11:30–									
Silent reading	12:15–									
Science	12:30–						■			
Social studies	1:15–2:30			■						
Recess	2:30–2:50									

The approach described in the "Student Practices" example on page 62 differs from a more traditional behavior modification approach. That is, a behavioral approach for a child who walks around the room or who punches holes in his paper would be to provide consequences to reinforce him for sitting in his seat or punish him

STUDENT PRACTICES
A.J.'s Behavioral Analysis and Intervention

Our intervention was twofold. First, we simplified the language assignment to ensure moderate success. Second, when A.J. entered the classroom each morning, one of the teachers greeted him at the door and engaged in small talk while touching him lightly on the shoulder or arm. We then asked him to do a small job before he started his language assignment. When he returned, the rest of the class was working quietly on their assignments, and A.J. was directed to his desk.

The intervention appeared to show results by the third day and increased steadily. Mondays were always off, and we believe they were controlled by setting events that happened over the weekend. By Tuesday of the second week, we were getting daily results and even smiles in the classroom. He was expecting to be greeted and seemed to look forward to it. The little jobs seemed to help him settle down, and returning to a quiet classroom made it easier to get him on task. Success with the modified assignments was helpful in getting him to finish his work. Overall, we were pleased with the results of this intervention and would use it again.

Our last step and contrasting treatment was to drop the intervention and introduce a consequence. We began the following Monday by not greeting A.J. at the door or giving him a job to do. We returned him to the regular curriculum assignment. We reminded the class in general that not finishing assignments would result in detention during recess. This was a consequence of not finishing in-class assignments. When we changed to using consequences, we selected a consequence aversive enough that A.J. would not exhibit the behavior.

Since Mondays were always off, we felt that it did not point to a failure of the consequence to work. We did not see a return of the behavior on the first Tuesday but postulate that he may not have yet become aware that things had changed. By Wednesday, we saw a return of the behavior, and as A.J. perceived that he was being "punished," it worsened. By the second week, we saw the behavior every day except Friday, but that may have been because we only had school a half day and A.J. came to school in a good mood. We were not pleased with these results and felt that taking recess away from a child with ADHD was detrimental.

It is our conclusion that identifying antecedents to problem behavior and developing an intervention was a more effective strategy than using consequences. We would use this intervention again, and, in fact, we have begun greeting all our students each morning. We have found that this makes them feel special and more a part of the classroom. It has proven to be a good way to start the morning.

Above all, we found that by collaborating to identify and define problems, we have become a more effective team, and our students have gained from it.

when he punched holes in his paper. In contrast, functional assessment would make the task/setting easier or more interesting so that the child would not avoid the task.

A number of professionals have speculated that without a functional assessment, educators would be more likely to rely on punishing and restrictive procedures (for a review, see Arndorfer, Miltenberger, Woster, Rortvedt, & Gaffaney, 1994). Functional assessment is a counterweight to our psychological tendency to blame the students rather than the requirements of the environment (Jones & Nisbett, 1971).

Our reactive responses to misbehavior may be due to our assumptions about the consistency/inconsistency of behavior (i.e., motivational deficits, willful obstinance, or lack of skill on the student's or teacher's part). Adults observe that their children are able to perform or "behave" sometimes. However, variability typifies young students and students with disabilities more than their peers (e.g., Slusarek, Velling,

Bunk, & Eggers, 2001; Zentall, 1990). The situational nature of behavior and performance has little to do with motivation. Children rarely decide to underachieve, although they may hide their poor skills or avoid failure by reducing their efforts.

To overcome our notions of "shoulds" and that the child "could if he or she tried," we must analyze setting conditions. Functional assessment helps parents and professionals gain perspective on patterns between behavior (actions) and setting events. Students with inconsistent behavior and performance will typically perform well and behave optimally in some but not all situations.

A number of studies examining the efficacy of functional assessment have been conducted with students with developmental delay (for a review, see Ervin et al., 2001). Promising findings from the use of functional assessments with students with ADHD are also reported (Broussard & Northup, 1995; Ervin, DuPaul, Kern & Friman, 1998; Lewis & Sugai, 1996a; Northup et al., 1995; Umbreit, 1995). This work is presented in chapters 9 and 11.

STEPS IN CONDUCTING A FUNCTIONAL ASSESSMENT

Example with steps

The following log of Travis was written by a general educator who had no instruction. Her original data and our analysis are supported by additional information about each of the steps that follows in this example. Without this information, none of my college students have been able to explain the behavioral difficulties of Travis beyond assigning a possible diagnosis or suggesting treatments. Some of these college students could see that the child's disruptive behavior might be attention seeking or task avoidance, but these students did not know how to translate these understandings into interventions.

STEP 1: Create a log.

STUDENT PRACTICES
CRITICAL INCIDENT LOG FOR TROUBLEMAKING TRAVIS: AGE 7

November 12

1. Needs to be asked three times to join me for a writing conference. (Finally comes when I count to five) Brandon (2), Jesse (1)
2. Does not follow directions to cut out writing pyramid.
3. Is told to finish pyramid first and then work on spelling. He says, "Do I have to do it first?" I said he did, and he continues to do spelling.
4. Causes a disturbance by wrapping a string around his finger and cutting off the circulation.
5. After numbering off for groups, he goes to the wrong group.
6. When finally in correct group, he begins writing on the chalkboard.
7. Runs over to get the room sachet to smell instead of being seated ready for reading.
8. Travis has to be asked to get in his own seat during reading class. (This happens often)

(*Continued*)

STUDENT PRACTICES *(Continued)*

9. Sticks pencil in his shoe instead of paying attention during reading.
   11:15 a.m.: Stopped and had a conference over the above items. How do you feel about seeing so many items? Travis said, "Sad."
10. Playing on computer when it was in the middle of a program for someone else. (Warned of this before)
11. 12:15 p.m.: Travis spit in the cafeteria and got in trouble with Mrs. R.
12. In math groups when picking up, Travis was throwing chalk erasers.

November 13

1. 8:30: Travis disobeys Mrs. S.'s rule about not cutting through the gym. (She has reminded him) She gives him 25 sentences.
2. Stepped on a cracker (ran over and jumped on it) in the lunchroom and had to sweep it up.
3. In math groups, he kept unplugging other students' earphone jacks. He was asked to leave.
   Pretty good day. Got a treat!

November 14

1. Threw a wad of paper at Michael.
2. Not listening to discussions.
3. Not listening to discussions.
4. Not listening to directions.
5. Kicked, threw, and jumped on Derrick at recess.

November 15

1. Everyone is quietly taking the objective test in their spelling books when I notice Travis at the table working on his reading picture.
2. Travis urinated in the bushes at noon recess.
3. Travis threw a pencil on the floor at reading.

November 19

1. Travis is having difficulty concentrating.
   (I had him clean out his desk. We put an empty desk at the front of a row. This is where Travis is to work. He is to only have one piece of paper, one pencil, and the book for the subject we are working on.)
2. Travis is playing with his pen and makes the spring pop out, and it hits someone.
3. 9:05–9:45: Some kind of trouble in art class. He is assigned by Mrs. B. an escort to bring him back from art.
4. 1:15: He is angered in math groups and throws a whole set of flash cards.
5. 1:45: He is reminded to settle and work on writing a story.

November 20

1. Travis is getting behind on his work. He took a late note home for English and spelling last night. He felt ill last night so is making up work at recess. (2 days late) He is caught up by noon.
2. Travis becomes frustrated during morning indoor recess. He throws a bowling ball at Jesse and makes a red mark near his eye.
3. He gets in trouble in music and has to sit in another chair. He then tears off the sole of his shoe.
4. Threw a shoe at indoor recess.
5. Must circle his name during math for talking and does it so lightly, it may not be noticed.
6. Runs and trips Michael in the hall coming back from R. class.

November 21

1. Travis runs and slides several times in a mud hole at recess.
2. Travis chased and jumped on Jackie's back in the mud. She was very upset and hurt.

Just from making a **critical incident log**, this educator understood Travis better and wrote the following intervention: "Travis is not allowed to go outside for recess. He has a sign up sheet for buddies to stay in and play checkers etc. He runs on the playground a couple of laps to get some exercise. This works well. He is learning to make friends one on one and does not hurt anyone on the playground. He also has a better day when he isn't in trouble because of recess behavior." Even though the teacher has learned critical things about Travis without formally analyzing him (i.e., that recess is a reoccurring trigger setting, Travis needs to develop friendships in a more contained environment, and that he needs exercise), additional points are analyzed next, including the goal of getting Travis back outside in the playground.

STEP 2: Analyze the log. Place the collected information for Travis into the categories shown in Table 4.2.

TABLE 4.2 Travis' BACP Chart

Behavior Observed	Antecedent	Consequence	Payoffs
1–3: Asked three times to come to a writing conference.	Writing conference	Teacher negative	Get self-determination (stay with preferred spelling task)
Did not follow directions to cut out writing pyramid but continued doing spelling	Fine motor task	?*	Avoid failure in fine motor tasks
1–4: Not listening to directions or discussions	Listening tasks	?	Avoid boredom or difficulty of task
Goes to the wrong group	Listening task	?	?
Writing on chalkboard	Group academic task	?	Get self-determination
Out of seat (often?)	Seated independent task	Teacher attention	Get activity stimulation
Working on his reading picture	Spelling test	?	Get self-determination and avoid spelling test
Urinated in the bushes	Recess	?	Get self-determination
Talking	Math	Asked to put name on board and he writes it lightly	Get stimulation from talking and avoid punishment
Threw a ball at Jesse and made a red mark near his eye	Recess		Get kinesthetic and social-emotional stimulation
Ran and tripped Michael	Transition		Get kinesthetic and social-emotional stimulation
Chased and jumped on Derrick	Recess		Get kinesthetic and social-emotional stimulation
Unplugs earphones	Math groups		Get social-emotional stimulation

(Continued)

TABLE 4.2 (*Continued*)

Behavior observed	**Antecedent**	**Consequences**	**Payoffs**
Ran and slid into mud hole	Recess		Get kinesthetic stimulation
Throwing things (flash cards, chalk erasers, paper wads, pencil, shoe)	Transitions to groups, math groups, reading		Get kinesthetic and social-emotional stimulation
Jumps on cracker	Cafeteria		Get kinesthetic stimulation
Runs over and smells room sachet	Reading, independent activity		Get novelty stimulation
Spit in the cafeteria	Cafeteria		Get kinesthetic and social-emotional stimulation
Sticks pencil in his shoe	Reading		Get kinesthetic and stimulation and avoid failure or reading
Wrapping a string around his finger	?		Get kinesthetic stimulation
Playing on computer during another's time	?		Get self-determination
Playing with pen and it hits another child	?	Peer response?	Get kinesthetic and social-emotional stimulation

Note. Much information was not obtained since the teacher (a) did not tell us how she responded to Travis, (b) did not know what caused his problems in art and music, and (c) often did not describe the setting in her log. Furthermore, this teacher did not chart any positive behavior that could inform us of his potential. Even without this information, much can be gained from this log.

STEP 3: Summarize the data.

1. Organize the previously mentioned antecedents into BACP categories by cutting and repasting from the log into a template given in Tables 4.3 to 4.5. (Note that at times, two or more payoffs may be operating for any one behavioral incident.)
2. Chart the payoff data using a graphing program.
   a. Get stimulation (social-emotional, novelty, and activity) and get self-determination are represented within settings (academics, recess, and listening) as a percentage of the total instances of problem behavior (see Figure 4.2).

TABLE 4.3 Setting 1: Recess, Transitions, Cafeteria (Unstructured)

Threw a ball at Jesse and made a red mark near his eye	Recess	Peer anger/attention	Get kinesthetic and social-emotional stimulation	1
Ran and tripped Michael	Transition	?	Get kinesthetic and social-emotional stimulation	1
Chased and jumped on Derrick	Recess	?	Get kinesthetic and social-emotional stimulation	1
Ran and slid into mud hole	Recess	?	Get kinesthetic stimulation	1
Jumps on cracker	Cafeteria	Activity	Get kinesthetic stimulation	1
Urinated in the bushes	Recess	?	Get self-determination	1

TABLE 4.4 Setting 2: Academic and Transition to Academic Settings

Throwing things (flash cards, chalk erasers, paper wads, pencil, shoe)	Transitions to or during academics	Activity	Get kinesthetic and social-emotional pencil, stimulation	5
Unplugs earphones	Math groups	?	Get social-emotional stimulation	1
Talking	Math	Asked to put name on board and writes name lightly	Get social stimulation from talking and avoid punishment	1
Working on his reading picture	Spelling test	?	Get self-determination and avoid spelling test	1
Writing on chalkboard	Group academic task?	?	Get self-determination	
Sticks pencil in his shoe	Reading	?	Get kinesthetic and stimulation and avoid failure or reading	
Runs over and smells room sachet	Reading, independent activity	Smell	Get novelty stimulation	1
Playing on computer during another's time	?	?	Get self-determination	1
Playing with pen so that it hits another	?	?	Get kinesthetic and social-emotional stimulation	1

TABLE 4.5 Setting 3: Listening and Discussion Tasks

1–3: Asked three times to come to a writing conference.	Writing conference	Teacher negative	Get self-determination (stay with preferred spelling task) 3
Did not follow directions to cut out writing pyramid but continued doing spelling.	Fine motor task	?*	Avoid failure in fine motor tasks 1
1–4: Not listening to directions or discussions	Listening tasks	?	Avoid difficulty of task 4
Goes to the wrong group	Listening task	?	?

b. Avoid failure is represented similarly but as a negative number converted to a percentage.

These are the data:

Recess

Get social-emotional stimulation = 3 of 36 total instances

Get kinesthetic or activity stimulation = 5 of 36

Get self-determination = 1 of 36

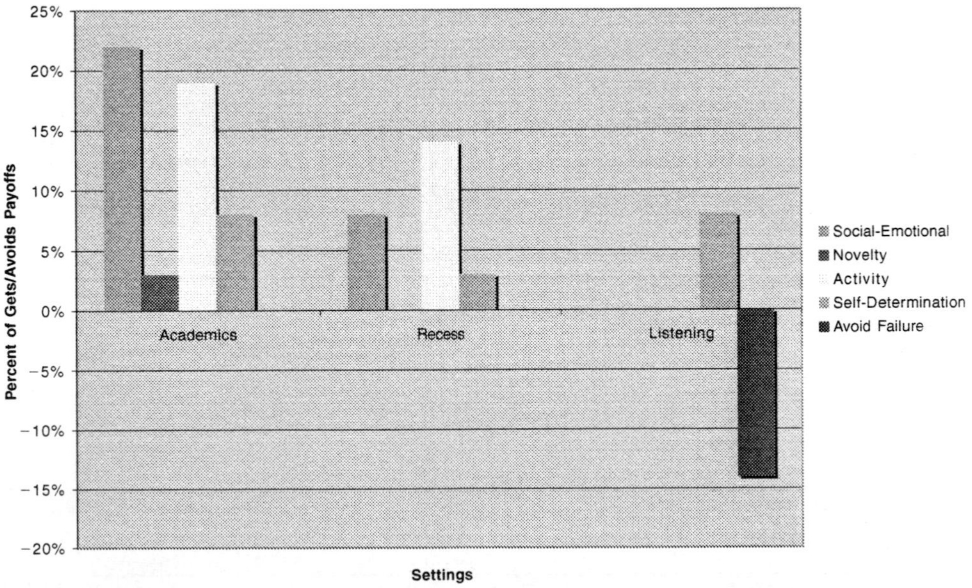

FIGURE 4.2
Travis' Functional Assessment

Academic
- Get social or emotional stimulation = 8 of 36
- Get novelty stimulation = 1 of 36
- Get kinesthetic or activity stimulation = 7 of 36
- Get self-determination = 3 of 36

Listening Tasks
- Get self-determination = 3 of 36
- Avoid failure = 5 of 36

3. List the consequences of behavior into those teacher responses that appear to be effective or ineffective.

   Effective Strategies
   1. one-on-one/personal attention
   2. classroom and task structure
   3. restitution (fixing things)

   Ineffective Teacher Strategies
   1. lectures
   2. reviewing bad behavior
   3. writing sentences
4. List high-frequency payoffs. These can be listed (as percentages of the total) or ranked.

   Travis

   1st: Get peer and social emotional (negative) attention

   2nd: Get kinesthetic stimulation, such as throwing items/physical activity

   3rd: Get sensory experiences

   4th: Get self-determination of staying with a preferred task and/or avoiding tasks that he isn't skilled with or doesn't like.

STEP 4: Select at least two goals. One goal should change the tasks or setting conditions to make it easier for the child to get needed payoffs (accommodations made by the teacher, such as providing peer tutoring for children with high relatedness needs), and a second goal should identify replacement behavior for the child (interventions that teach the child more appropriate ways to get relatedness, such as teaching the child how to ask questions or how to offer services rather than physically disrupting others' activities).

It may be necessary to write small incremental steps for teaching the child replacement behavior and include steps that fade structure and move the child toward independent functioning. In other words, the second type of goal should move Travis toward acceptable playground behavior.

Finally, it is important to realize that Travis may have difficulty understanding or sustaining attention to directions or classroom discussions, and this may contribute

TABLE 4.6a Goals That Require the Teacher to Change a Setting Variable (Accommodations)

Goals That Involve the Teacher Changing the Setting or Tasks

Goal 1: The teacher will provide opportunities for Travis to successfully engage in physical activities with his peers.

- Step 1: The teacher will assign one peer to play with Travis during indoor recess.
- Step 2: The teacher will assign two peers to play with Travis during indoor recess.
- Step 3: The teacher will assign Travis an active job helping younger children at outdoor recess and supervise this activity.
- Step 4: The teacher will ask for volunteers to describe how they could include other children into games and how they handle frustrating situations on the playground.

TABLE 4.6b Goals That Involve Teaching Replacement Behavior and That Require Travis to Change (Interventions)

Goal 1: Travis will demonstrate appropriate physical routines with his peers, using what he enjoys:

physical contact
social attention
throwing things
spelling activities

and incentives or tasks that have worked with him:

one on one—peer
structure
laps
smells
restitution (sweeping up)

- Step 1: The class will engage in a throwing game and a positive physical contact game to play at recess, using Michael as the peer tutor.
- Step 2: Travis will perform roles or jobs in relation to these games.
- Step 3: Travis will be assigned as a spelling tutor, with reversible roles.

Goal 2: Travis will make transitions while acquiring appropriate social attention from others.

- Step 1: Travis will deliver notes and materials to classmates within the classroom
- Step 2: Travis will leave from and return to a small-group activity during the performance of certain roles and responsibilities.
- Step 3: Travis will transition between classes and earn extra time to do laps in the gym with a peer.

to his problems during group learning activities. In fact, he may have also have (a) handwriting difficulties, indicated by problems when asked to cut or write and take spelling tests, and (b) problems in reading. These areas need follow-up assessments.

DESCRIPTION OF STEPS

Creating a critical incident log

A critical incident log is a selective recording of some behavioral incidents of both problem behavior and appropriate behavior within specific settings. (Recording positive incidents is important to provide insight into the factors that may provide normalization of behavior or performance.)

In general, logs can vary in length from several paragraphs to several pages and from several days to weeks, depending on the frequency of the behavior or observations. Teachers make brief written entries in a log or dictate entries into a tape recorder. Logs can also be made from recollected experiences or from video records. Logs are significantly correlated with educator ratings of students with ADHD and even with logs written by parents (see Rapoport & Benoit, 1975).

Alternatively, a functional assessment can be conducted using an informal interview with a teacher or parent. Both interview and observation of a child produced similar results (for a review, see Arndorfer et al., 1994). Aggression especially should be documented by interviewing teachers or parents. This protects children's safety as victims and victimizers. When logs are based on interviews, Dunlap et al. (1993) recommend that questions include (a) the conditions under which the behavior occurs and (b) the conditions under which the behavior rarely or never occurs. Additional data can be gathered from a portfolio or from written records. Positive instances should also be listed.

Analyzing the critical incident log

Once you have a critical incident log, you can begin an analysis of behavior, antecedents, consequences, and payoffs. Some observers turn a piece of paper in the long (or landscape) position and create their log in four columns, as shown in Table 4.7.

Behavior Behavior must be observable. Examples are writing, walking, talking, hitting, and sitting because they can be observed and measured. Volunteering does not describe a specific behavior; a student could volunteer in many ways. A better

TABLE 4.7 BACP Analysis Template

Behavior observed (what behavior)	Antecedents (when, where, types of tasks and activities, persons, instructional groups, etc.)	Consequences Observed (what happens)	Payoffs (to what purposes)
1.			
2.			
3.			

description would be to define the volunteering action as "raised his hand" or "asked to help." Acts of the environment on a person are not behaviors. For example, a person may walk in the rain (a behavior), but "getting wet" or "being blown over" by the wind are not actions—they are consequences of environmental actions. When identifying behavior, avoid (a) value judgments that often describe actions (e.g., acted badly, behaved well) (b) states of a person (e.g., being hungry, anxious, angry), and (c) predispositions to behave in certain ways (e.g., honest, suggestible). None of these can be observed without more specifics. (See question 7 in the "Discussion and Application Questions" section at the end of this chapter.)

Antecedents Antecedents can increase or decrease a behavior, especially if the antecedent has led to reinforcement or punishment in the past. The classic example is Pavlov's dogs. When the bell rang (antecedent), the dog salivated (behavior) because in the past the dog was given food (consequence) when the bell rang (antecedent). More generally, antecedents are defined as the type of task or setting that occurs just prior to or at the same time as the behavior. The antecedent can be people, places, things, or time periods. Examples include transition from one subject to another, a teacher's request or expectation for task performance, instructions, recess time, students or adults in the setting, the behavior of other students, subject area,

TABLE 4.8 Some Types of Settings

	Alone	Social	Transitional
1. Bus, field trips			
2. Playground/recess, lunch, hallway			
3. Home—TV, homework, play, meals			
4. Away from home—shopping, church, friends' homes, other			
5. Classroom during which subjects?			
• Reading, listening tasks (lecture, discussion), language, social studies			
• Science, math			
• Music, art			
• Gym, transitions			
6. Task settings			
• Worksheets, routines, or review			
• Commands/requests			
• New material			
• Independent or long-term projects			
• Responses (spoken, written)			
• Waiting (turn taking)			
7. Time periods (starting or finishing tasks, the day)			

method of presenting the subject, method of asking students to respond to the task, and length of and type of task. Some examples are listed in Table 4.8 and form some of the categories to consider in filling out the steps previously described.

Some students are sensitive to certain types of antecedent conditions. The following is a partial list of common triggers for children with different exceptionalities.

NOTE

Students with ADHD

Behavior difficulties will increase when

- the task is effortful in its length, repetitiveness, and nonmeaningfulness;
- little opportunity exists for movement or choice;
- few opportunities exist for active involvement in learning
- many students and only one teacher are present, and learning is large-group teacher directed;
- little supervision, feedback, or positive reinforcement takes place; and
- periods of transition exist with little structure (for a review, see Zentall, 1993, 1995).

Students with ADHD Plus Aggression

Aggression occurs primarily

- when entering new groups,
- when resources are scarce or information is needed,
- during low structure,
- during difficult tasks,
- when little flexibility exists,
- when few adults and much activity are present,
- when no apparent way to escape tasks or social demands is available, and
- when a peer group values "toughness."

Students with ADHD Plus Learning Disabilities

Task avoidance behavior, such as off-task behavior, occurs primarily when

- presented with a task that is within the student's area of specific learning disability (e.g., with reading requirements, mathematical calculations);
- presented with any kind of auditory input, such as listening tasks, group discussion, social interactions (in these contexts the child may be more likely to actively refuse, avoid, or act disruptively);
- presented with complex visual input, such as copying from the board or from dictionary to paper, art tasks using collage (with such tasks, the child may take a long time to produce work); and
- asked to respond in certain ways (e.g., fine motor handwriting or talking) (with such response requirements, the child may avoid or become negative and noncompliant).

(*Continued*)

NOTE *(Continued)*

Students with ADHD and Giftedness

Off-task or disruptive behavior is observed primarily when

- tasks are too easy;
- teachers believe that if the child can't do the easy work, he or she can't do the challenging work; and
- tasks involve a lot of rote lower-level skills.

Students with ADHD and Developmental Disabilities

Disruptive behavior and poor performance occur primarily

- during difficult, complex, higher-level tasks that require problem solving, analysis, synthesis, or reasoning abilities.

Students with ADHD and Anxiety

Avoidance, inflexible, or repetitive behavior occurs

- when entering new groups,
- in the presence of a lot of activity and confusion,
- during difficult or unstructured (ambiguous) tasks,
- when it is noisy, and
- when unpredictable activities that have not been scheduled are provided or changes in a schedule have been made.

Consequences What happens in response? Observable consequences are social reactions to the behavior of the child or what the child has actually gotten. Examples of observable payoffs include getting an object, a peer laughing, a teacher ignoring, verbal reprimands, joining a group, staying with a preferred task, or avoiding a task. These consequences immediately follow a behavior and are often teachers' responses.

Psychobiological payoffs What is the function of the behavior? This is the essence of the analysis. Payoffs that relate to a child's psychological and biological needs are psychobiological "payoffs" (Zentall & Javorsky, 1995). For example, crying is an unpleasant behavior that communicates to caretakers that an infant has a need. Adults attempt to escape from the crying by attending to the baby's needs. Crying changes as the individual matures; it becomes whining and complaining as the child ages and begins to communicate psychologically based needs rather than only physiologically based ones. At each age, crying, whining, and complaining are directed to achieving help from others.

Payoffs are not directly observable but rather are "educated guesses" about the goals of behavior. Rather than simply judging the behavior as appropriate or inappropriate, functional assessment encourages educators to understand behavioral intent. Such payoffs are discussed as social goals in chapter 5 as they specifically relate to children with ADHD.

All behavior, no matter how inappropriate it may seem, has a purpose. Usually, several functions are operating. For example, walking is important in getting us from place to place, but it also provides us with additional kinesthetic stimulation. Similarly, talking allows us to get attention from others (e.g., a feeling of relatedness), but it also provides us with two other possible outcomes: stimulation (kinesthetic, auditory, and cognitive) and mastery of our social environments by communicating our feelings, opinions, and needs to others.

The psychological needs described here are get competence, relatedness, and self-determination (autonomy), which were developed through repeated analysis of children's behavior. However, these three needs have simlarly been described as fundamental psychological needs in a book on motivation by Deci and Ryan (1985). The biological need I have added is the need for stimulation. Also added are the needs to avoid (e.g., persons, experiences, and events). Many of these are reciprocal of a "get need" (e.g., get stimulation and avoid boredom or get competence and avoid failure, as indicated by the double-pointed arrows in Table 4.9).

Get payoffs demonstrate the student's attempt to achieve satisfaction of a need. Each of these needs is normal. For example, most of us have a need to relate to others. What makes these payoffs difficult is not the need itself but rather the intensity of the need or the inappropriate manner in which the child attempts to meet the need (Zentall & Javorsky, 1995). For example, a student may repeatedly fall out of his or her seat (acting as the class clown and disrupting the lesson) in an attempt to get peer attention.

Not only do differences exist in the goals of individual children, but children with specific disabilities may have some similar goals or needs as well. For example, the get payoffs for students with ADHD often involve getting more stimulation—sometimes in the form of excitement—and may be reflected in the characters Piglet and Pooh from the stories by A. A. Milne.

Who Is Hyperactive—Pooh or Piglet?

"When you wake up in the morning, Pooh," said Piglet at last, "what's the first thing you say to yourself?"

"What's for breakfast?" said Pooh. "What do *you* say, Piglet?"

"I say, I wonder what's going to happen exciting *today*?" said Piglet.

Pooh nodded thoughtfully.

"It's the same thing," he said. (B. Hoff, *The Tao of Pooh*, p. xi)

Avoid payoffs provide escape. Students will avoid (a) adults who frequently exert pressure and control (use of threats, guilt, or fear) or deliver negative feedback

TABLE 4.9 Psychobiological Payoffs

Get Payoffs		Avoid Payoffs
Get competence (mastery or achievement) by: 1. Talking about or demonstrating accomplishments or interests in reading, math, special projects, attending after-school clubs 2. Directly asking for help or making statements such as, "I don't get this." 3. Creating or collecting objects, stories, or tokens of accomplishments 4. Reading by subvocalizing (whispering or reading out loud) to get the additional auditory input.	↔	Avoid possible social punishment or failure by: 1. Blaming others, making excuses, lying 2. Avoiding nonpreferred or disability-specific a. subject areas (e.g., math), b. response requirements (e.g., handwriting, talking), or c. input modalities, such as: listening and group contexts; embedded visual contexts: such as copying tasks and calendar time.
Get relatedness from: 1. Peer attention, stimulation, or interaction 2. Adults' attention, stimulation, or interaction	↔	Avoid social experiences and possible rejection or exclusion from: 1. Peers 2. Adults
Get self-determination by: 1. Controlling (provoke, choose, boss, lead) 2. Continuing an activity or task that is preferred 3. Maintaining independent action, opinion, or feelings (argue, debate)	↔	Avoid lack of control or lack of predictability by: 1. Resisting new social situations 2. Resisting specific tasks (e.g., difficult, independent, non-preferred)
Get stimulation from: 1. Emotional stimulation (intense or negative social reactions—shock, anger, disgust, disruption) 2. Activity or kinesthetic stimulation (physical contact) 3. Sensory and tangible stimulation (sights, plays with objects, tastes/food, smells, sounds) 4. Change or novelty (fun, excitement, play, risks, unusual projects, topics of conversation, activities) 5. Cognitive stimulation (thinking, daydreaming, creating)	↔	Avoid boredom on the following types of tasks: 1. Routine, review, or practice tasks 2. Repetitive activities 3. Familiar settings
		Avoid pain or possible physical harm of the following types: 1. Physical pain 2. Dangerous situations

Note. Sometimes children avoid tasks, pain, or possible social failure by getting self-determination or control.

or unpredictable responses and (b) events and tasks that lead to repeated failure or boredom or that are unpredictable or uncontrollable (Adelman & Taylor, 1990). That is, most children will stop making efforts when the situation is associated with a history of punishment. For example, in competitive classrooms, where few children are winners, many students attempt to avoid feelings of failure by not trying (Ames & Ames, 1984).

Avoid payoffs may be found more often in students with higher levels of anxiety and past failure (e.g., students with learning problems or histories of abuse). When students with ADHD also have co-occurring learning disabilities, they may resort to avoid payoffs when their tasks are too difficult. For example, two students with ADHD who were also academically behind by several years were disruptive and off task during difficult math tasks but not during easy math tasks (DePaepe, Shores, Jack, & Denny, 1996).

Some researchers speculate that the primary behavioral purpose for students with ADHD is an avoidance of effortful tasks (e.g., independent seat work or household chores [DuPaul & Ervin, 1996]). However, what underlies most of these activities is not the "effort" but rather low stimulation (rote practice tasks and repetitive physical tasks). Effort is required to persist on activities that are repetitive and highly familiar. Thus, a more accurate description is an avoidance of boredom that can co-occur with seeking stimulation from some alternative activity, as concluded by DuPaul and Ervin (1996).

Remember that a behavior often has several functions (i.e., for 23% of participants assessed [Ervin et al., 2001]). Teacher attention (get adult relatedness) was the get payoff that teachers most frequently identified for students with disabilities and was the second payoff most often selected by teachers for average peers (Ervin et al., 2001). (Interestingly, attempting to get teachers' attention was cited by teachers as one of three factors most often related to classroom disruptive behavior [Broussard & Northup, 1995].) Researchers, however, identified avoiding or escaping task demands as the most frequently occurring payoff for students with disabilities (44%) compared to their peers (3%) (Ervin et al., 2001). The implications of these findings are that teachers need to examine the task conditions that produce attention-seeking behavior.

Not only can one behavior have multiple payoffs for one student, but the same behavior may have different payoffs for different students. In a study of off-task behavior, each of four adolescent boys with ADHD and oppositional defiant disorder was off task for different reasons (i.e., to avoid task, to get teacher and peer attention, or to get tangible objects [Ervin et al., 1998]). A more dramatic example is a student who fights with peers on the bus in an attempt to "deal with" a specific peer (avoid social punishnment), find a seat on a bus (get competence), or wait for a bus (get emotional stimulation and avoid boredom). Although behavior is the same (i.e., fighting), as is the general setting (i.e., bus), fighting functions differently in each case. Thus, the child needs a different, more appropriate way to get what is needed (e.g., how to wait, interact with a difficult peer, or get competence/ safety).

FIGURE 4.3
Travis' Frequency of Payoffs within Antecedent Settings

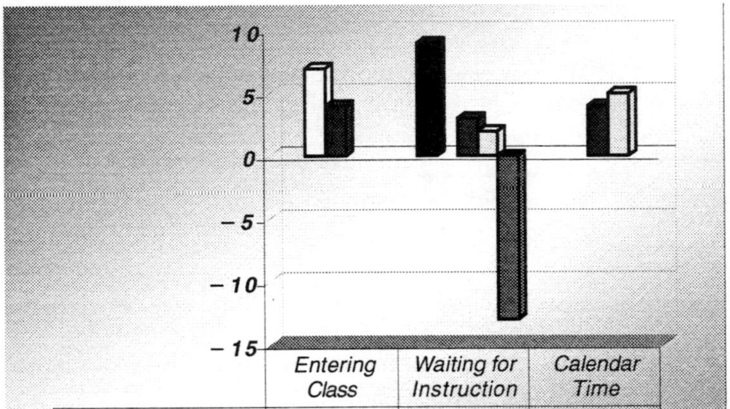

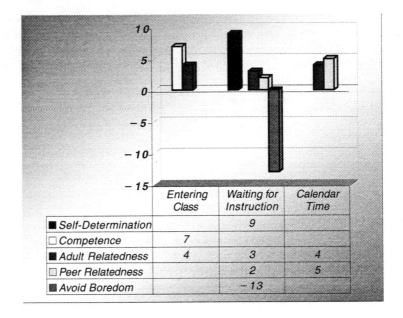

	Entering Class	Waiting for Instruction	Calendar Time
■ Self-Determination		9	
□ Competence	7		
■ Adult Relatedness	4	3	4
□ Peer Relatedness		2	5
■ Avoid Boredom		−13	

Typically, it is the context that tells us which need is operating. For this reason, summarizing payoff data by setting on a graph is useful, especially when teachers chart the "gets" in the positive part and the "avoids" in the negative part of a bar graph (see Figure 4.3).

In the example shown in Figure 4.3, all the get payoffs are in the positive direction, and all the avoid payoffs are entered into the graphing program as negative numbers. From this simple graph, it can be seen that the antecedent "Waiting for Instruction" is the primary antecedent, or trigger, for this preschool child's behavior, who attempts to avoid boredom while waiting by getting attention from peers and the teacher (social relatedness) and self-determination (in this case, by bossing others).

Selecting goals

Goals are of two types—those that involve making changes (a) in the setting or task (see chapter 8) and (b) in the student (see chapter 9). Typically, altering a task or setting allows positive events to occur naturally, thus evening up the odds for that child. For example, providing shorter assignments is an accommodation for a shorter attention span. This accommodation allows a child to now earn opportunities for computer time. In addition, using a tape recorder, a computer, or a note taker with duplicating paper avoids note taking so that he or she can focus on the information in the lecture.

It is easier in the long run to alter setting and task factors than to try to directly reduce the child's behavior. Although stopping disruptive behavior may be our first concern, it is only an in-the-moment fix because it will resurface again under a similar set of circumstances. In contrast, if the task is more engaging and the child is able to get his or her needs for competency met, disruptive behavior will be unnecessary in the long run, and learning will occur.

Perhaps we feel that changing others should be easier. However, some of us attempt to make lasting changes in our own behavior (e.g., losing weight, talking more or talking less, being assertive) and have realized how difficult this is. We fail to realize that if behavioral change is difficult for us when we are motivated, it will be even more difficult for a child. Thus, making changes in the setting or task will be easier in the long run.

TEACHING STRATEGIES
STORM'N NORMAN

When a high school student stormed out of his classroom before the bell rang, his teacher tried reprimanding and sending the child to see the principal. However, when I interviewed the teacher about the conditions prior to his leaving, she said that he had completed his work and did not have alternative tasks or activities. Norman found it overly frustrating to wait, but the teacher did not want to provide additional activities for him because she would have to do it for everyone. However, with this statement, the teacher indicated to us that this accommodation would be useful for more than just one student.

Even though we might side with Norman in this example, it is true that Norman needs to learn appropriate ways to ask for accommodations, to be excused, and so on. In this example, we would expect the teacher to provide some accommodations for wait time and for Norman to learn appropriate ways to ask for filler activities.

In general, we need to help children learn appropriate ways to achieve the same payoffs as the original behavior (*replacement behavior*). If children need to feel in control in order to have predictability in their lives, instruct them in appropriate ways of taking initiative (e.g., how to disagree without being disagreeable). Because replacement behavior serves the same function as the original behavior, it typically builds on a child's strengths and competencies. Table 4.10 presents examples of replacement behavior.

When asking for a change in students' behavior, we must ask ourselves how long, how often, and in which settings we need the child to demonstrate these changes. Exact compliance may be important in some situations but for short periods

TABLE 4.10 Replacement Behavior

Behavior That Gets	Possible Replacement Behavior
1. Brags of times sent to principal's office	Reports to class on real record setters—student picks several events to report to class weekly
2. Monopolizes conversation	Teach how to ask questions and how to stay on topic (e.g., using roleplay)
3. Talks a lot and disturbs others	Place with peers at a table; allow student to be a peer tutor or school reporter (interview; write newsletter)
4. Wanders in class	Job: room arranger, messenger
5. Grabs another student's toy	Plan active tasks (calculators, portable computers)
6. Class clown	Class drawings, poetry, or writings designed to be humorous

Behavior That Avoids	Possible Replacement Behavior
1. Complains and won't start a long project	Ask child to be a consultant to a small group (he or she has the information needed by the group to make decisions)
2. Won't go to the playground	Structure a safe supervised activity with one buddy on the playground
3. Won't ask teacher for help	Student to decide on order of tasks—easy to hard
4. Lies, hides, withdraws	Take away punishment and blame and look for positive parts of behavior

of time (e.g., manners). Children need to know their importance (e.g., for safety or impression management when meeting people, a job interview, interacting with adults). Teaching children to change their behavior for other people's "comfort" is a delicate balance and requires careful consideration. Carl Jung once said, "If there is anything we wish to change in the child, we should first examine it and see whether it is not something that could be better changed in ourselves." When we do decide to ask for behavioral change in the child, we need to focus on priority behavior. For example, goals for the student should encourage active engagement, such as (a) academic routines to help students begin and organize their work, (b) social routines to enter new situations or to deal effectively with other students who interrupt their ongoing activities, and (c) behavior that involves cognitive engagement and active responding.

Behavior that simply looks good on the outside can be deceptive. The child may look like he or she is attending, but the child's mind could be miles away. Furthermore, the child may actually attend better when moving or when "playing."

TEACHING STRATEGIES
THE "PRICE" OF PEACE AND LEARNING WAS A COLLAPSIBLE RULER

An undergraduate student teacher was observing in a classroom and noticed how well a teenager with ADHD attended to his reading when he could also "play with" a small collapsible ruler. When the "master" teacher took away his ruler, *he* spent the remainder of the period disrupting students around him, and *she* spent the remainder of her time yelling at him.

In asking for change, small improvements should be expected. That is, "baby-step" objectives need to be written toward each goal (shaping). Adults could help a child make baby steps by starting with easier or interesting tasks. For example, for the goal of walking, a short-term step for a toddler would be to encourage the child to stand for longer and longer periods of time. Students initially need support, such as prompts or lists, greater supervision, more feedback/rewards, and higher structure (e.g., with a paraprofessional, a buddy, a taped reminder, a checklist). In the example of walking, parents typically hold the child's hands as he or she attempts to make wobbly steps or uses a "walker." For a parent to enable the goal of walking independently, he or she would provide a room with furniture so that the child could hold on to objects.

Success is more probable when the child is involved in selecting his or her own behavior to change. We may be teaching helplessness if we say the child has no responsibility for the problem or for the solution. Children have some responsibility for finding more effective ways of getting what they want. This is particularly important for children with disabilities because, more than their classmates, they need to negotiate their differences with others throughout life. However, we cannot change the basic nature of children, and individual differences last a lifetime.

Other children also need to learn to take some responsibility. Teachers often ask students with learning differences to be considerate of other students' learning. Maybe some of these average students get teacher attention by complaining about the behavior of students with disabilities. If tattletales need teacher approval, allow them to get it in different ways. But even if that behavior does disrupt the learning of some average students, the average children who are complaining must assume at least some responsibility for this situation. Where can they place themselves in the classroom to avoid disruptions and distraction?

LIMITATIONS OF FUNCTIONAL ASSESSMENT

Neither the diagnostic approach, which identifies children from the characteristics of the group, nor the functional assessment approach, which identifies payoffs at the individual level, will fit all needs. A diagnostic label never captures the individual expression of that disorder, and functional assessment has problems, primarily in implementation: (a) functional relationships can change as the individual ages, (b) the relationships are always our best guesses (probabilities rather than certainties), (c) functional assessment may be less useful for high-intensity but low-frequency types of behavior (Ervin et al., 2001), and (d) over half the number of teachers surveyed identified distal factors (e.g., home environmental factors, such as dysfunctional families, economic status, truancy) as major contributors (Frank, Sanchez-LaCay, & Fernandez, 2000). Distal factors do predict dropout and delinquency (Walker & Sprague, 1999), but we have little control over such factors.

For those of us who work directly with teachers, we see that it can be difficult to redirect their attention away from distal explanations to proximal explanations (e.g., response to specific types of tasks, psychological needs, or biogenetically based behavior, such as vocal tics, a need for activity, a lack of skill). In defense, educators cannot always observe antecedent conditions (e.g., events prior to class, internal physiological states), even though some of these events are more likely to be within their control than distal events.

SUMMARY

Functional assessment guides the development of intervention plans for individual children. It provides information related to the immediate conditions that set the occasion for specific behavior. There are several tasks necessary in the development of a functional assessment. A log of incidents of behavioral problems and of appropriate behavior and the context of that behavior is needed. Logs can be made from observations, recollected experiences, audiotapes, video records, or interviews. Data need to be collected for at least three observations in several settings and time periods.

DISCUSSION AND APPLICATION QUESTIONS

1. Which would you say is easier—working with a child who has more get payoffs or more avoid payoffs? Why?
2. Which is a better goal and why?
   a. Look at me when I am talking
   b. Tell me in your own words what I have been saying.
3. What is a socially desirable replacement behavior that provides a similar payoff to what a student would get from being bossy?
4. What would be an accommodation for a child with bossiness in small-group settings?

EVIDENCE-BASED PRACTICES
GOOD ANALYSIS BUT INTERVENTIONS LACKING

A single-subject study found that Corey, an 8-year-old boy with ADHD, was disruptive to escape a task and to get peer attention.

Appropriately, Corey was instructed on how to ask for task breaks. The instructional staff also assigned him (a) to a work area away from his peers and (b) to groups that did not have any of his friends (Umbreit, 1995).

5. How do you handle a child who likes to be in control? That is, he will do 9 of 10 problems or follow 4 of 5 steps. He always does a little bit less so that he is in control.
6. In the above evidence-based practice, the interventions were successful in reducing disruptive behavior. Which child needs were not addressed in this study and which, therefore, could resurface?
7. Identify Behavior
   In the Student Practices box on page 84 check off those items that represent observable behavior and not value judgments, consequences of actions, states, or dispositions of people.
8. Identify Payoffs
   Here are some bits of behavior to analyze for their payoffs. Can you identify the payoffs for John and Jackie?
   a. John likes to move a lot. During study time, he got up and walked around the room. The teacher ignored him, but his body felt good when he moved. In the future, when it is study time and the teacher will ignore him, it is likely that John will get up and walk around the room again because __________ is a payoff for him.
   b. Jackie feels uncomfortable in social situations. She is afraid she will say something she will regret. When it is time to go to a party, she gets into a fight with her sister. Because of the fight, Jackie's mom says she cannot go to the party. The payoff for Jackie's aggressive action was the ___________ of the social situation that she found unpleasant.
9. Do the goal steps for Travis address his need for self-determination? If so, how?
10. In addition to normative assessments, how would you get additional internal information about Travis' possible fine motor problems or reading difficulties?

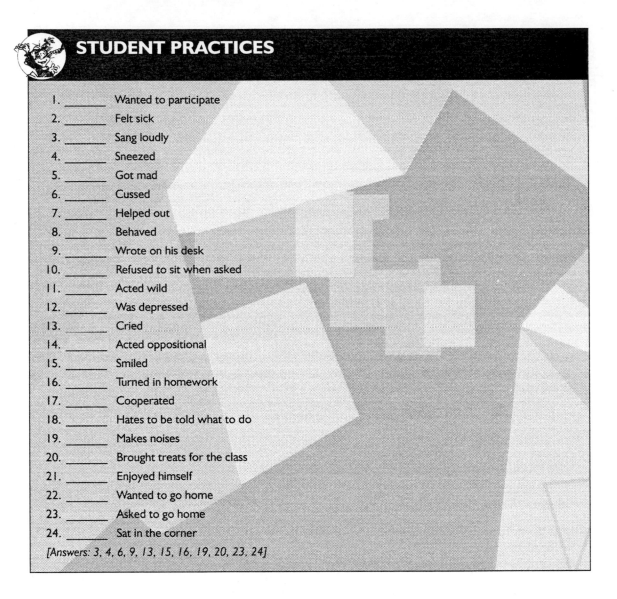

STUDENT PRACTICES

1. _______ Wanted to participate
2. _______ Felt sick
3. _______ Sang loudly
4. _______ Sneezed
5. _______ Got mad
6. _______ Cussed
7. _______ Helped out
8. _______ Behaved
9. _______ Wrote on his desk
10. _______ Refused to sit when asked
11. _______ Acted wild
12. _______ Was depressed
13. _______ Cried
14. _______ Acted oppositional
15. _______ Smiled
16. _______ Turned in homework
17. _______ Cooperated
18. _______ Hates to be told what to do
19. _______ Makes noises
20. _______ Brought treats for the class
21. _______ Enjoyed himself
22. _______ Wanted to go home
23. _______ Asked to go home
24. _______ Sat in the corner

[Answers: 3, 4, 6, 9, 13, 15, 16, 19, 20, 23, 24]

Notes About Critical Incident Logs or Anecdotes

A. Read and reflect on the cases before class so you can provide a carefully considered discussion. You should be prepared to provide evidence from the case data that supports your interpretation. There is no one correct answer for any case study underlying the differing interpretations of cases. Relate cases to other children that students have hade experience with.

B. Remember that most educators see behavior as functioning to get attention, and for many children this may be the case. However there are many ways to get attention. So ask yourself, "Why has the child picked this way?" "What else is she or he getting from this behavior?"

C. Put your responses on a dry-erase board to show the instructor and the class. Then discuss differences in answers in class.

CHAPTER 5

ADHD-Hyperactive/ Impulsive Subtype (ADHD-H)

OBJECTIVES

- Identify the ADHD-H subtype and the
  (a) characteristics that are required for identification and
  (b) informal problems and positive characteristics that you see in classrooms.

KEY TERMS

directionality of activity
variable activity
repetitive verbal activity
developmental tasks (preschool, elementary, middle, and high school)
delay aversion
verbal impulsivity
routines
multiple choice
social goal of participation
social goal of self-determination
goal of stimulation
social goals of competence
emotional reactivity
conditions that bring out aggression
gender differences in aggression
oppositional defiant disorder
conduct disorder
contagion effects
compensate

Children identified as the hyperactive-impulsive subtype (ADHD-H) represent about 18% of the total population, whereas about 55% of the total population fall into the combined subtype (ADHD-H plus ADHD-Inattentive subtypes) (Wilens, Biederman, & Spencer, 2002).

IDENTIFICATION

Activity is considered a better marker in the identification of ADHD than is inattention (Porrino et al., 1983), perhaps because problems in attention can be found in most childhood disorders (e.g., in children with learning disabilities, 53% had attention deficits, but only 13% had hyperactivity [Zentall, 1990]).

Formal screening for ADHD-H subtype requires parent and/or teacher ratings on six characteristics of hyperactivity and three characteristics of impulsivity, as specified in the *Diagnostic and Statistical Manual of Mental Disorders* (4th ed.) (*DSM-IV-TR* [American Psychiatric Association, 2000]). The child must display six of the following symptoms often and fewer than six inattention symptoms. (See "Note" on page 88.)

WHAT IS THE NATURE OF ACTIVITY?

Easily recognized in students with ADHD is excessive motor activity. This may explain why ADHD-H is identified around first grade—earlier than the inattentive subtype, ADHD-I (McBurnett, 1995; Nigg, 2001).

NOTE
DSM-IV-TR Checklist for Hyperactivity/Impulsivity

Hyperactivity:

1. Fidgets with hands or feet or squirms in seat
2. Leaves seat in classroom or in other situations in which remaining seated is expected
3. Runs about or climbs excessively in situations where it is inappropriate (in adolescents or adults it may be limited to subjective feelings of restlessness)
4. Has difficulty playing or engaging in leisure activities quietly
5. Is "on the go" or often acts as if "driven by a motor"
6. Talks excessively

Impulsivity:

7. Blurts out answers to questions before the questions have been completed
8. Has difficulty waiting in lines or awaiting turns in games or group situations
9. Interrupts or intrudes on others (e.g., blurts into conversations or games) (American Psychiatric Association, 2000)

Students with ADHD-H are easily recognized in preschool, kindergarten, and first grade when the developmental task in school is inhibiting activity.

Anecdotal reports indicate that preschoolers with ADHD get "kicked out" of preschool more often and have greater difficulty with routines, settling down for naps, and sitting still during story time. At home, preschool children were more likely than peers and older children with ADHD to display excessive activity cross situationally (Stormont & Zentall, 1999; Zentall, 1984) and to have more accidents.

During the elementary years, boys with ADHD still moved their heads twice as often, moved their bodies three times more often, and moved over four times greater an area than comparisons (Teicher, Ito, Glod, & Barber, 1996). Additionally, they spent more time out of their seats, especially over time in a setting (Schweitzer & Sulzer-Azaroff, 1995). However, gross motor activity (e.g., standing, climbing)

EVIDENCE-BASED PRACTICES
Preschoolers with ADHD Act Differently from Their Peers

1. Spent less time in their seats
2. Moved more and tilted their seats more during listening tasks
3. Talked more and were more dysfluent (using more exclamations, interruptions, and commands) during transitions and in listening tasks and were more disruptive and aggressive in play (Alessandri, 1992; Zentall, 1986a)

declines with age (Dienske, de Jonge, & Sanders-Woudstra, 1985; Hart, Lahey, Loeber, Applegate, & Frick, 1995). Thus, for elementary-age students with ADHD, the main developmental task is focusing and maintaining attention (i.e., ADHD-Inattentive subtype [see chapter 6]). The developmental tasks for adolescents and young adults are social interactions, which are addressed later in this chapter.

In general, activity is useful in providing mobility. Secondarily, activity functions by altering incoming stimulation through the following:

1. Movement toward or away from sources of stimulation (approach or avoidance)
2. Increasing or decreasing the repetitiveness of activity (variability)

The directionality of the activity of students with ADHD is typically approach and variable rather than avoidance and repetitive. Repetitive activity is very different in nature from variable activity, and these two types of activity typically do not occur together (i.e., they are negatively correlated [Dienske et al., 1985]). Excessive variable activity that characterizes students with ADHD is manifested across the contexts of home, school, and clinic and across settings defined as free and restrictive play, social and nonsocial, and sleep and awake and during a variety of tasks (Malone & Swanson, 1993; Zentall, 1985a, 1995). Even so, students with ADHD are able to reduce their activity in specific settings. For example, they can reduce activity during indoor free play relative to their greater activity expressed during outdoor free play (Porrino et al., 1983).

Activity can also be verbal; verbal activity increases with age (Dienski et al., 1985). Youth with ADHD were noisier and talked more than their peers (a) in classroom settings, (b) in task settings with adult examiners, (c) with peer partners, and (d) even in solitary play or task settings, especially over time (Schweitzer & Sulzer-Azaroff, 1995; Zentall, 1988). Students with ADHD spontaneously talk in order to describe and enhance aspects of their tasks and to guide their own immediate responding (e.g., by repeating cues, commenting on the materials, verbalizing their choices [Zentall, Gohs, & Culatta, 1983]).

The frequency of starting conversations and the number of words used typically were associated with high levels of motor hyperactivity (Dienske et al., 1985; Zentall et al., 1983). Thus, talking and moving are related forms of hyperactivity, even though some children talk more and some move more. Surprisingly, students with ADHD talk less than their classmates when they are individually asked to talk (i.e., to tell stories) or when asked to respond to requests or questions (Zentall, 1988). (These findings are discussed further in chapter 7.)

Boys and girls with ADHD have gender-specific types of activity (Abikoff et al., 2002). Boys with ADHD had more gross motor movements than typical boys and than girls with ADHD (Abikoff et al., 2002). Girls with ADHD-H were not different from their female peers in large motor activities, such as running and climbing or getting out of seats in the classroom (McBurnett, 1995). However, more than their peers, girls with ADHD rated themselves and were rated by parents as busier with small motor activities, such as foot shaking, doodling, twirling their hair, chewing their fingernails, and as talking too loudly or too much (Grskovic & Zentall, 2005; but see Abikoff at al., 2002, who reported no differences but coded fewer types of behavior).

Developmental changes also play a role in the expression of girls' activity and impulsivity. That is, girls with ADHD exhibited hyperactive motor behavior that was sufficient to identify them in preschool, but they no longer demonstrated this behavior sufficiently to differentiate them from their peers by 6 to 10 years of age (Battle & Lacey, 1972; Huessy & Howell, 1988). (For purposes of diagnosis and for an assessment of interventions, the quantity of specific types of activity can be assessed in relation to a matched pair using the procedure described in Table 2.2 in chapter 2.)

In contrast to the previously mentioned variable types of activity, repetitive motor activity (tics) and verbal activity (phrases or topics seen in Tourette's syndrome and obsessive-compulsive disorder) may become apparent when using high levels of psychostimulant medication or when anxiety/depression develops as an overlay (Singer et al., 1995; Zentall & Zentall, 1983).

WHAT IS THE NATURE OF IMPULSIVITY?

Impulsivity is another core characteristic of ADHD that is associated with high levels of activity. Impulsivity has been described as delay aversion (Sonuga-Barke, Williams, Hall, & Saxton, 1996; Sonuga-Barke, de Houwer, de Ruiter, Ajzenstzen, & Holland, 2004). The punishing qualities of delay can be explained by the fact that delay requires stopping action or activity.

Educators view impulsivity as acting or blurting out a statement too soon in response to an external cue or internal event (e.g., a thought). Impulsivity can also be seen as "colorful" language (e.g., exclamations, swearing [Zentall, 1988]). Problems are often noted in social settings where the child grabs materials or interrupts others. Children with ADHD experience impulsivity as an overriding sense of impatience.

STUDENT PRACTICES
PETER'S UNDERSTANDINGS

I am 12 years old and I have ADHD, which basically means I'm more aggressive than others.

I have very unique qualities, such as I am able to speak out to say what I feel. I like to write letters; I wrote to the President twice and got two letters back and a picture of him.I want to be a lawyer when I grow up, but I think I started too early, because I got in trouble a lot last year for arguing.

I like to get to the bottom of things. I try to understand everything. And I have quicker reactions; I just automatically say something I am thinking. I'm not letting people that call me names get to me right now, because I have a lot more life to go through. I handle a lot of rejection. . .

I like to travel, play soccer, basketball; I like games and puzzles. I hope to go to Yale when I get to college . . . I'm not very patient. Well that's me (Sorrento, 1994).

In school, boys with ADHD disrupted the work of peers and teachers more than girls, whereas girls with ADHD solicited teachers' attention more than typical girls (Abikoff et al., 2002). Perhaps this is why teachers of girls with ADHD do not report impulsiveness (de Haas & Young, 1984), even though girls with ADHD self-reported (as their parents also reported for them) more interrupting, swearing, changing of topics, and saying things before thinking than comparison girls (Grskovic & Zentall, 2005).

Interrupting is not simply a failure to inhibit; interrupting increases participation in conversations (i.e., gets verbal activity stimulation) and reduces time listening to others (i.e., avoids boredom). For example, Sonuga-Barke, Houlberg, & Hall (1994) reported that students with ADHD performed fast and inaccurately when fast responding reduced time on task. In other words, fast responding may represent a preference for shorter tasks rather than an inability to inhibit. Students with ADHD appear to "grab and run" (Rapport, Tucker, DuPaul, Merlo, & Stoner, 1986), preferring minimal frustration and performing better with shorter experiences and more frequent, smaller rewards.

WHAT ARE THE OUTCOMES OF ADHD-H?

Academic outcomes

Motor activity has no direct academic outcomes. This could explain why students with ADHD-H have no greater incidence of academic difficulties than their peers (Chabildas, Pennington, & Willcutt, 2001; McBurnett, 1995). Even so, teachers do not always understand that activity per se does not disrupt learning.

Motor activity can have educational consequences only if the student must continuously divert energy away from learning to sitting still (behavioral inhibition). However, activity can have effects on children's ability to establish educational routines. Students with ADHD avoid repeating activity patterns that are necessary to the development of daily routines (e.g., for homework). Students with ADHD recognized that they did not have routine locations for books when returning home from school, lost things at school (including homework, even after doing it), and failed to complete tasks (Zentall, Harper, & Stormont-Spurgin, 1993). Even Charlie, a 54-year-old man with ADHD, stated, "I don't have any bad habits, because I don't have any habits."

FAMILY PRACTICES
SITTING ON HIS FEET AND STILL LEARNING

I could never understand why each year in conferences or on my child's report cards, teachers would tell me that my son sits on his feet. Every year: "Do you know that your child sits on his feet at his desk?" Somehow I could not see the relevance of this to his learning. (Grskovic, personal communication, 2001.)

EVIDENCE-BASED PRACTICES
FAILURE TO WAIT PRODUCES:

1. Poorer performance on multiple-choice tests because multiple choice requires attending to multiple items prior to making a response (Hoy, Weiss, Minde, & Cohen, 1978)
2. Poorer organization because good organization requires delay while categorizing objects
3. Poorer planning skills because planning requires holding back overt responses while making covert responses (thought)
4. Skipping directions and not asking for help or for additional cues because this requires waiting before beginning (Whalen, Henker, Collins, McAuliffe, & Vaux, 1979)

The educational outcomes of impulsivity are found primarily in tasks with delays, especially when tasks are unclear, ambiguous, detailed, or have several alternatives. Students with ADHD typically examine fewer alternatives and tend to select the first or most salient item in an array (Whalen, 1989). They fail to wait long enough to consider alternative information, consequences, or responses, leading to more task and social errors.

However, students with ADHD do ask as many task-related questions of a playmate and for as much information from an examiner when there are no delays (e.g., one-on-one interactions) (Madan-Swain & Zentall, 1990; Zentall & Gohs, 1984) and may request more feedback from their mothers (Campbell, Endman, & Bernfeld, 1977). Thus, these students are willing to ask for additional information as long as little interpersonal or instructional delay occurs.

Social outcomes

Social outcomes are often assessed through ratings. Peers rated children with ADHD as undesirable schoolwork partners and less desirable friends although not necessarily undesirable play partners (Grenell, Glass, & Katz, 1987; Mrug, Hoza, & Gerdes, 2001). Parents rated their children with ADHD-C more often as ignored, disliked, less liked, and as having lower social preference scores than did comparison parents or parents of children with ADHD-I (Maedgen & Carlson, 2000). When social functioning was defined as scores from an interview with mothers plus behavioral ratings discrepant from full-scale IQ potential, 22% of children and adolescents with ADHD qualified as socially disabled (Greene et al., 1996). These socially disabled students also had higher rates of depression and conduct disorder.

Friendship is another measure of social functioning. Thirty percent of the mothers of teenagers with ADHD reported that their boys had no steady friends (Hechtman, Weiss, & Perlman, 1980). When children with ADHD were also aggressive, about 60% to 76% of them had no friends in class (Mrug et al., 2001).

Poor social outcomes appear to be even greater for girls with ADHD, especially over a 5-week summer session (Battle & Lacey, 1972; Gaub & Carlson, 1997). For girls, these interpersonal difficulties may lead to greater problematic outcomes (e.g., risk for alcohol and drug abuse, early sexual activity, and adolescent pregnancy; for a review, see Grskovic & Zentall, 2005).

Behavior that contributes to the social failure of children with ADHD-H

The social responses of children with ADHD-H and the combined subtype were generally seen as less friendly, effective, and relationship enhancing and more negative and assertive (Grenell et al., 1987) and have been described by teachers as less considerate and more hostile/aggressive and more likely to end in fights and unpopularity than for students with ADHD-I (Lahey & Carlson, 1991; Margalit & Almougy, 1991; Plizska, 1989).

Even preschoolers who were disliked were observed to disagree, argue, and reject their peers' ideas more and exhibit fewer play-extending statements and more directives (Ladd, Price, & Hart, 1988). Specific behavior that may contribute to being disliked in elementary students with ADHD was assessed in the following study:

EVIDENCE-BASED PRACTICES
CHILDREN WITH ADHD

Purpose 1. How does the behavior of elementary children with ADHD who are liked differ from the behavior of children with ADHD who are disliked?

Participants. 25 children with ADHD (H) and comparison (C)
- Dyads (children in pairs):
- 10 pairs (a liked child with ADHD [LH] + a comparison [C-LH])
- 15 pairs (a disliked child with ADHD [DH] + a comparison [C-DH])
- 7 pairs of Cs with other Cs
- Equivalent in age, IQ, grade
  - LH and DH equivalent in: hyperactivity ratings
  - Not equivalent in: attentional ratings
    - play sociometrics
    - ITPA grammatical closure

Design. 2 group × 2 acceptance status × 2 conditions

Task. Block building in dyads

Conditions. High-structure task with instructions of what to build
Low-structure task with open instructions

(Continued)

EVIDENCE-BASED PRACTICES *(Continued)*

Results of Pairs (With and Without an ADHD Partner)

1. Group × acceptance status
   a. Positive questions DH pairs fewer than LH and Cs pairs
   b. Nontask questions DH pairs more than LH and Cs
2. Group × gender simple effects:
   a. Positive requests:
      Hboys fewer than Cboys
   b. Positive rough play:
      Hgirls less than Cgirls
3. Group × likeability (positive rough play)

Summary

1. Boys with ADHD made fewer positive requests than comparisons.
2. Girls with ADHD demonstrated less positive rough play than comparison girls.
3. Disliked boys with ADHD showed less positive rough play than liked boys with ADHD.
4. Pairs of children, when one partner was ADHD and disliked, were less positive with each other verbally and more off task physically and verbally.

Implications. Training children how to make positive requests and engage in positive rough play in social interactions may be important for both boys and girls with ADHD, especially for those who are disliked by others (Madan-Swain & Zentall, 1990).

Aggressive behavior is also a major contributor to peer rejection. Research with preschool children shows that aggressive and defiant behavior emerges developmentally at about 3 years (Campbell, 1990; Tremblay, 2000) but for only 4% to 10% for average children (Strain, Cooke, & Apolloni, 1976). However, aggression is learned by 45% to 70% of students with ADHD (Loney, 1987; Meyer & Zentall, 1995) at rates that are 90% higher than their peers and stable across situation, informant, and time (Prinz, Connor, & Wilson, 1981). Aggression is also reported to be the primary reason that children with hyperactivity are placed in special education classes for the emotionally and behaviorally disordered (Loney, 1987) and appears to be the major contributor to peer difficulties (for a review, see Landau, Milich, & Diener, 1998).

Specific conditions bring out aggression. For example, the more emotionally intense the child, the more likely is aggression, and emotional intensity and/or aggression combine to increase the likelihood of unfair outcomes and a discontinuation of social interaction (Laursen & Hartup, 1989). Other conditions include the type of activity. While engaged in social play with one or more other children, preschoolers with ADHD plus aggression had low percentages of aggression (.02 to .03) (Stormont, Zentall, Beyda, Javorsky, Belfiore, 2000). However, rates were markedly higher (.39 to.47) in preschoolers while (a) seeking entry into an activity and (b) when others interfered with the child's ongoing activity (Stormont et al., 2000). Learning to do something else while waiting for something a child wants and learning to use language to convince others may be important behavioral targets for preschool children to protect them from chronic aggression (Tremblay, 2000).

Gender differences exist in the expression of aggression as well. Boys with ADHD showed more total aggression than girls with ADHD, while girls did not differ from typical girls in observed verbal and physical aggression (Abikoff et al., 2002). The disruptive and aggressive behavior of girls with ADHD was about half the rate of boys with ADHD. However, indirect and relational types of aggression (e.g., gossiping, manipulating, "icing"), which are more typical female expressions of aggression, were not assessed in this study.

EVIDENCE-BASED PRACTICES
How Students with ADHD Learn Aggression

1. The consequences of aggression are usually strong social reactions (e.g., yelling), which are reinforcing for children with ADHD (see chapters 6 and 9).
2. Students with ADHD selectively focus attention to intense, loud, animated events (Cotugno, 1987) (see chapter 6).
3. Aggressive behavior is interesting or stimulating to watch and therefore to copy, especially if family models show aggression (see chapter 12). Peers who are active, aggressive, disruptive, and "fun to be with" often serve as the friends of and models for children with ADHD-H (Mrug et al., 2001; Whalen, 1989).
4. Individuals with ADHD have more intense emotional responses to the pleasant and unpleasant events in their daily lives and greater difficulty regulating their emotional responses to these events (see chapter 6).
5. Students with ADHD may be attracted to the emotional highs produced by speed, danger, sex, and drugs. For example, the rate of accidents increases, especially for adolescents with co-occurring oppositional defiance disorder or conduct disorder (e.g., greater involvement in car crashes as drivers, to incur greater damage to their vehicle, to be at fault, and to have more bodily injuries associated with crashes [Barkley, Guevremont, Anastopoulos, DuPaul, & Shelton, 1993; Whalen, 1989]). For teens with licenses, 46% of teens with ADHD had been involved in accidents compared to 33% of their peers (Barkley, DuPaul, & McMurray, 1990) even though they were not deficient in knowledge of driving safety or accident prevention (Barkley, 1997a).
6. Students with ADHD fail to attend internally to identify their own feelings and needs and therefore are more likely to respond only when feelings are strong. In addition, they may see responsibility as lying outside of themselves (i.e., to blame others for frustration and social failure [see Mrug et al., 2001, and chapter 6 for attentional bias).
7. Children with high levels of motor activity (typically boys) attempt to repair or enhance their lower self-view with "competence" in delinquent activity (for a review, see Pisecco, Wristers, Swank, Silva, & Baker, 2001).
8. Their behavior has the social character of aggression because of its invasion of others' space, even though the initial intention may not be aggressive, as indicated in the "Family's Observation" on page 96.

TEACHER'S OBSERVATION
TROUBLEMAKER TYPE

He tends to hang around the trouble-maker type. The kids who are also very active and athletic, stimulating. He tends to attract the other kids who are more domineering, like he is (Moon et al., 2001, p. 229).

FAMILY'S OBSERVATION
TOO MUCH TOUCHING

He's always had trouble with that [keeping his hands to himself] . . . not so much that he's wanting to hurt anybody, its just like he has to have this tactile thing. You know, he's just got to touch you or whatever. And most children don't want him doing that (Moon et al., 2001, p. 227).

The contribution of problem solving and social goals

Some of the social difficulties these children experience could also be due to problem-solving errors. For example, students with ADHD less frequently than their peers identified the nature of social problems involving authority (e.g., teacher held class after lunch bell) or social failure (child sat alone) but could identify peer block or frustration (peer cut in front of the lunch line) (Zentall, Javarsky, & Cassady et al., 2001). In addition, children with ADHD plus aggression recalled fewer social cues (Moore, Hughes, & Robinson, 1992), and children with ADHD provided fewer socially appropriate solutions, especially for resolving conflict, maintaining relationships, and joining and sharing (Grenell et al., 1987; Milch-Reich, Campbell, Pelham, Connelly, & Geva, 1999; Zentall, Javorsky, & Cassady, 2001). These areas would be appropriate targets for behavioral intervention plans.

Although this body of work did not report problems for initiating friendships, girls apparently have more difficulty making friends than girls without ADHD (Blachman & Hinshaw, 2002).

Some of the social interaction difficulties could also be due to the goals of students with ADHD and their lack of knowing how to achieve these goals. Students with ADHD-H clearly need more active responding, and for this reason they experience delays as being longer. That is, a sense of time is determined by the amount of attention allocated to its passage (Zakay, 1992). When activity fills that time, less attention is allocated to the passing of time, so time will be experienced as shorter. When time is passively observed with "nothing to do," elementary and adolescent students with ADHD typically perceive lengths of time to be longer

STUDENT PRACTICES
IMPULSIVITY: THE HATING-TO-WAIT SYMPTOM

Don was sent to the office because he was in a fight with another student. He yelled at her, called her names, and threatened to beat her up.

When questioned why he acted that way, he responded that she was taking too long putting away the recess balls, and he was tired of waiting for her (Zentall et al., 2001).

than IQ-matched peers even though they were as good as their IQ-matched peers in estimating past experiences of time (e.g., for recess, getting dressed, sleeping; for a review and data, Barkley et al., 1997a; Barkley, Edwards, Laneri, Fletcher, & Metevia, 2001; Grskovic, Zentall, & Stormont-Spurgin, 1995). When children experience the length of time as longer when waiting with nothing to do, they may be more likely to respond with disruptive or aggressive responses. (See "Student Practices" above.)

Children with ADHD also appear to have strong needs for social participation or social stimulation. Findings indicate that as early as 15 months, full-term infants (later identified in the fifth grade as ADHD) were observed to allocate a greater number of attentional "episodes" to persons than typical infants (Cherkes-Julkowski, 1998). Mothers saw their infants at 30 months as highly competent, perhaps because of such active social engagement. "Viewing the videotapes of the children in this study confirmed their enthusiastic involvement. The children with ADD were hardly ever non-engaged. Mothers were likely to see these children as curious, alert, exploratory, and charming" (Cherkes-Julkowski, 1998, p. 304). Whalen (1989) also cited evidence for these children having an "apparently strong and enduring interest in being with other people" (p. 145).

However, an intense need for social contact in the absence of skills to meet these needs may produce frustration and long-term impairment for elementary-age students. (See "Teaching Strategies" below.)

DuPaul and Ervin (1996) also concluded that a major function for the behavior of these children was to get adult and peer attention (negative or positive). Attempts to achieve relatedness goals and disappointment with their own failures at these

TEACHING STRATEGIES
OVERREACTIONS TO SOCIAL ATTENTION

When somebody does give him their full attention, he just goes crazy . . . real animated, squirrely sounds . . . being silly") (Moon, Zentall, Grskovic, Hall, & Stormont, 2001, p. 225.

attempts may alter the status of these children over time. That is, at the elementary level, mothers of boys with ADHD had lower expectancies for their child's behavior than mothers of matched comparisons (Sonuga-Barke & Goldfoot, 1995), and by adolescence, students with ADHD reported more time spent alone, fewer interpersonal interactions, and less confidence and rated their peer, sibling, and adult relationships as negative and unsatisfactory (Dumas, 1998; Waddell, 1984). At this age, they described themselves by what they were *not* ("I'm not smart; I'm not friendly"). Social withdrawal may be a consequence of peer exclusion (Ladd, 1999). These students had not learned how to achieve their social goals of participation and specifically how to maintain social relationships or friendships—a task critical to learn during preschool.

Students with ADHD also seek power and dominance (self-determination or control [see chapter 4]) and excitement and disruption (social/emotional stimulation) (for data and review, see Melnick & Hinshaw, 1996). The combined subtype (ADHD-C), compared to the inattentive subtype, rated themselves and were rated by their teachers and parents (Carlson, Booth, Shin, & Canu, 2002) as competitive and ego involved—with goals of competence and the social display of that competence—more than were IQ-matched children with ADHD-I or typical peers (Carlson et al., 2002). Not only was the inattentive group less competitive and more passive than typical children or students with ADHD-C (Maedgen & Carlson, 2000), but they were also more motivated to please the teacher and make good grades. Students with ADHD-I also relied somewhat more on external academic motivations than on their own internalized curiosities or interests (Carlson et al., 2002).

In contrast, children with ADHD plus aggression self-reported more goals related to getting into trouble and having fun and fewer goals related to being fair than did children with low aggression (Melnick & Hinshaw, 1996). Children who engaged in more school misbehavior than their peers were also higher in stimulus-seeking behavior (Wasson, 1980).

In summary, it appears that students with ADHD-H and the combined subtype have primary goals of getting relatedness (social stimulation), being in control, being seen as competent by their peers, and having fun and experiencing excitement—often through "stirring up trouble."

However, when aggression accompanied ADHD, similar goals were related to needing fun, but "stirring up trouble" changed into "getting into trouble," and fewer goals were related to being fair.

STUDENT PRACTICES
WEIRDEST ONE

I've spread some of my weirdness over on two of my friends. Sometimes my wackiness will prove fun, and . . . . Well, I'm the weirdest one. Actually, I'm the only one weird (Moon et al., 2001, p. 222).

HOW DO OTHERS RESPOND?

The degree to which peers must alter their own behavioral style to deal with children with ADHD may predict rejection. Children with ADHD were described by their peers as noisy, bossy, bothersome, causing trouble, cruel to children and rude to teachers, and getting mad when they do not get their way (for a review, see Mrug et al., 2001). In response to children with ADHD, peers (a) retreat from aggression, ignoring, being less responsive to and less talkative, and communicating less efficiently with their partners, and (b) increase activity and off-task, negative, and commanding/controlling responses (Madan-Swain & Zentall, 1990; Fischer, Barkley, Edelbrock, & Smallish, 1990; Stormont-Spurgin & Zentall, 1995). The following study provides evidence of the "contagion" effects when working with a partner who is ADHD (liked and disliked).

EVIDENCE-BASED PRACTICES
THE PARTNERS OF CHILDREN WITH ADHD
(See data from this study and Purpose 1, presented earlier)

Purpose 2. How do typical peers respond to the behavior of both liked and disliked children with ADHD?
Findings related to the partners of liked hyperactive (LH), disliked hyperactive (DH), and comparison (C) children

- 10 normal play partners of LH
- 15 normal play partners of DH
- 7 normal play partners of 7 normal children

A. Partners of both liked and disliked children with ADHD showed
   fewer positive requests than partners of C,
   fewer positive statements than partners of C, and
   more ignoring than with partners of C.

B. Partners of disliked children with ADHD showed
   fewer positive questions than partners of LH and C,
   less talk than with partners of C,
   more negative commands of others than partners of C,
   more negative statements than with partners of C,
   more negative sharing than with partners of C,
   more play alone/nonshare than with partners of C, and
   more activity than with partners of C.

Normal Partners Summary

1. If average children have partners who are ADHD (liked and disliked), they become less positive verbally and ignore their partners more.
2. If average children have partners who are both ADHD and disliked, they retreat—becoming less talkative, more solitary, and more negative than when with peers who are ADHD and liked.

Implications. Training typical children in how to interact with children with ADHD is important (see chapter 8 and Madan-Swain & Zentall, 1990).

Contagion may be even greater when siblings are their partners. That is, siblings exhibited as much negative play behavior as children with ADHD (about two times more than normal sibling dyads when supervised and four times more when not supervised [Mash & Johnston, 1983]).

Elementary and secondary educators reported on questionnaires that they were less concerned about these types of peer relations (e.g., resolving conflicts, initiating or maintaining positive interactions, recognizing moods in others, following through on group decisions) than just about any other classroom adaptation factor (Kauffman, Lloyd, & McGee, 1989). What educators may not know or feel responsible for is evidence that early peer rejection is the single most powerful predictor of later social adjustment (for a review, see Madan-Swain & Zentall, 1990).

In sum, significant social impairment can be identified not only for the child with ADHD but also by the similar responses of peers and siblings. Social impairment can be observed with relationship criteria (items 1 to 3 in Table 5.1; see also Culbertson & Silovsky, 1996, pp. 205–206).

Children with ADHD can also radically modify the behavior of their parents. In response to such grocery store episodes parents become more negative and directive and less positive and responsive (see chapter 12). This directive adult style in response to nonmedicated children is made more normal when the children are taking psychostimulant medication (for a review, see Culbertson & Silovsky, 1996; Wells, 2001). Overall, these findings indicate that the negative and controlling responses of parents are brought out by the difficult behavior of their children. Even so, directive parenting may limit opportunities for children with ADHD to learn how to direct, control, and maintain their own interactions (MacDonald & Parke, 1984).

Teachers also become more controlling and intense in their interactions with children with ADHD. For example, 74% of preschool teachers' statements consisted of verbal reprimands and task redirections (Alessandri, 1992). Furthermore, when teachers of elementary school students become more negative, it spreads to other

TABLE 5.1 Indicators of Social Impairment with Peers and Siblings

	Child with ADHD	Sibling	Peers
1. Social isolation or diminished involvement in home or school activities			NA
2. Impaired communication patterns (low rates of positive and high rates of negative and controlling statements)			
3. Passive, solitary, ignoring, and retreating interactions			
4. Child feels devalued or has a low self-esteem because of neglect, criticism, rejection, or isolation		NA	NA
5. Siblings' devaluation of him or herself and of accomplishments	NA		NA

Note. NA = not applicable.

FAMILY PRACTICES
He Embarrasses Me in Public

I don't like the way he embarrasses me in public. The way he runs through the stores. I mean as old as he is, he'll run through stores. If you try to stop him he screams like I'm killing him. So everybody looks at you like you are abusive.

So I was in the grocery store and walking by the frozen food locker and there he was in the locker! I had to take him out of the freezer, the ice freezer, with the bags of ice and doors that hook. . . . Because he said—he got too hot, so he was cooling off (unpublished data from Zentall, Moon et al., 2001).

children in the same environment. That is, typical children who shared classrooms with children with ADHD also received more negative teacher attention than typical children in control classrooms (Campbell, Endman & Bernfeld, 1977).

Thus, relational impairment can also be assessed using the adult markers outlined in Table 5.2 (see also Culbertson & Silovsky, 1996, pp. 205–206; Greene, 1996, p. 212):

TABLE 5.2 Indicators of Adult-Child Social Impairment

	Adults	
	Parents	**Teachers**
1. Inappropriate limits or expectations for achievement or for behavior		
2. Impaired adult–child communication patterns (e.g., vague, inconsistent)		
3. Low satisfaction or frustration expressed in working with the child		
4. Inappropriate control management style (rigid, overly controlled, overly structured or overly permissive, lack of involvement, or absent)		
5. Inadvertently attending to inappropriate behavior		
6. Chronic conflict over homework, assignments, or behavior		

COMMON CO-OCCURRING CONDITIONS OF STUDENTS WITH ADHD-H

Oppositional defiant disorder and conduct disorder

Oppositional defiant disorder and conduct disorder have the highest rates of co-occurrence with ADHD (Banaschewski et al., 2003), although these rates are higher for children with ADHD-C than for those with ADHD-H (McBurnett, 1995). Approximately 35% of children with ADHD have oppositional defiant disorder (Kuhne, Schachar, & Tannock, 1997)—68% of teenagers have oppositional defiant disorder, and 39% have conduct disorder (Barkley, Anastopoulos, Guevremont, &

Fletcher, 1991). However, girls with ADHD have fewer conduct problems than do boys (de Haas & Young, 1984).

ADHD usually precedes oppositional defiant disorder, with an average age of identification at about 4 years and identification of conduct disorder follows at about 6 years (Barkley et al., 1990). However, it is unlikely that oppositional defiant disorder is a developmentally early form of conduct disorder because about 75% of children with the former never developed the latter (50% retained the diagnosis of oppositional defiant disorder, and 25% remitted [August, Realmuto, Joyce, & Hektner, 1999]). In addition, conduct disorder can occur without prior oppositional defiant disorder, and it differs in specific acts (e.g., Loeber, Burke, Lahey, Winters, & Zera, 2000).

Low economic status; serious forms of oppositional defiant disorder behavior, such as physical aggression, fighting, and parental inconsistent discipline; lack of supervision; and substance abuse predict a child's progression to conduct disorder (Green, Keenan, & Lahey, Loeber, 1995). ADHD-H (but not inattention) also increased the risk of conduct disorder by almost six times.

Teens with a persistent disorder often show multiple disorders in adolescence, including depression and its association with conduct disorder (Stahl & Clarizio, 1999). The co-occurrence of ADHD with conduct disorder (about 12% of community samples) or with oppositional defiant disorder or aggression has been well established as more serious disorders (more physical aggression, antisocial activity, persistence of ADHD, negative social outcomes, and higher rates of social rejection as well as more academic problems) than either ADHD or conduct disorder separately (Culbertson & Silovsky, 1996; Stahl & Clarizio, 1999; Stormont-Spurgin & Zentall, 1996).

Noncompliance is the typical complaint of parents of children with oppositional defiant disorder. It is probable that high levels of activity bring out frequent "stop" or "no" commands from parents, with reciprocal "no" statements volleyed back from these children. That is, higher scores on ADHD-H ratings predict higher oppositional defiant disorder scores several years later (Burns & Walsh, 2002). Over time, the "no" statements become a challenge, as depicted in a cartoon "Non Sequitur" by Wiley. This cartoon shows a middle-age couple standing on a curb next to a sign that reads, "Absolutely NO Machete Juggling." The caption describes what the man replies in response to this sign: "Suddenly I have an urge to juggle machetes."

NOTE
Symptoms of Oppositional Defiant Disorder

1. "Angry or resentful" and "deliberately annoys people" at least four times per week
2. "Touchy or easily annoyed," "loses temper," "argues with adults," and "defies or refuses adults' requests" at least twice per week
3. "Spiteful or vindictive" and "blames others for his or her mistakes" at least once in the past 3 months (American Psychiatric Association, 1994)

TABLE 5.3 Oppositional Defiant Disorder In-Class Behavioral Rates

40%	On task
22%	Talked at inappropriate times
15%	Argued with the teacher
10%	Refused teacher requests
10%	Annoyed other students
3%	Blamed others for mistakes

Source: Mike Hardebeck (personal communication, 2001).

Table 5.3 shows analysis of child behavior in which rates of behavior were observed for a child with oppositional defiant disorder, ADHD, and learning disabilities.

SUCCESSFUL ADAPTATIONS

The success of some individuals with ADHD can help us understand how behavior can be redirected positively. For example, the potential adaptation of hyperactivity is energy, productivity, enthusiasm, and "liveliness," recognized by Brian's camp counselor in Figure 5.1.

Successful children with ADHD channel their considerable energy into sports or positive play. Family members describe individuals who have learned to appropriately

Certificate of Recognition
Brian D
is awarded this certificate of Notable Accomplishment in Recognition of
Liveliness
This 7 day of August,
Signed

FIGURE 5.1

channel activity as "busy." Even within the popular press, we can find examples of adaptations:

FAMILY PRACTICES
Cognitively Active First Grader

Our son, Brian, 7, is extremely active. He's constantly busy, whether indoors or out. His room is always cluttered with projects of every size and description. When one is finished, he displays it proudly for a while, then tears it apart and uses the parts to build something else. He can't seem to just sit down and be still for any length of time. For example, he rarely watches an entire television program. About midway through, he'll get an idea and jump up and run into his room or outside to get started on it.

Brian is bright and makes good grades, but his teachers tell us that he's disorganized and somewhat forgetful. With other children, he tends to be bossy, which sometimes causes problems in his relationships with them. When he gets excited about something he has seen or done, which is often, he tends to monopolize the conversation. We've been wondering whether he might be hyperactive? (submitted to the *Indianapolis Star* for the column "Parenting" by John Rosemond).

Unfortunately, Rosemond responded to this parent by stating that Brian was just cognitively active and that any child who could finish projects could not be hyperactive. He said that hyperactivity "tends to be random and purposeless, rather than goal-oriented" behavior.

Such interpretations are outdated. Behavior exhibited by students with ADHD is purposeful, as previously addressed in chapter 4. These children do finish projects and attend for long periods of time to projects and activities that are within their interests and skill levels. Even children with average intelligence can learn to channel their need for active responding into creative expressions in art and design, storytelling, and computer expertise (Zentall, 1988; Zentall, Moon et al., 2001).

Children with ADHD plus giftedness have more talents than children without giftedness. Brian is similar to children with co-occurring giftedness and ADHD, who are high energy, focused, directed, and intense (Zentall, Moon et al., 2001). Brian has been able to succeed in school by virtue of his energy, intelligence, and creativity, which may compensate sufficiently for his disorganization and bossiness. Clearly, he could use help redirecting his bossiness into leadership and in learning some organizational skills.

Parents also observed positive social qualities in their children with ADHD, including the following: friendly, helpful, an outgoing nature, funny, enthusiastic, emotionally expressive, does not hold a grudge, and children who share and care (i.e., motivation and desire to please). Parents of young boys with ADHD reported that their children were happy most of the time, with only some school-related emotional adjustment difficulties (Moon et al., 2001).

Henker and Whalen (1989) called for research on "resilient hyperactivity." They proposed that some children with ADHD (i.e., those with high social or cognitive intelligence) escape detection because they channel "their ardor and unconventionality into high-energy productivity" (p. 218). Additional positive characteristics listed were zest, indefatigability, and "certain facets of intensity." A teacher described a "successful" child with ADHD as one who finished his own assignments and then went to help others with their work.

Active involvement in sports also seems to help individuals with ADHD (Zentall, Moon et al., 2001). Basketball, swimming, and soccer appear to be favorites. The positive effects were noted indirectly by one teacher:

TEACHING STRATEGIES
ADHD Becomes Invisible When the Child Is Involved in Athletics

I don't think there's hyperactivity. I don't see that at all. But he's in so many athletic activities, I don't know (unpublished data from Moon et al., 2001).

More recently, Michael Phelps won six gold medals and two bronzes in 17 swimming races in 7 days at the 2004 Summer Olympics in Greece. "Hard to believe, all this from a kid with attention-deficit/hyperactivity disorder, a kid whose mother was once told by a teacher, 'Debbie, he will never be able to focus on a *thing* in his life'" (Reilly, 2004, p. 110).

The importance of having one friend has also been identified as an important protective factor:

TEACHING STRATEGIES
The Importance of One Friend

Teacher A: "I worry about him a great deal . . . just because of the lack of really at least one really good friend. . . ."

Teacher B: "He's got a friend in class now, a new friend, and he asked me the other day: 'next week could I get a seat beside M?' And so that's a very good sign. That's really neat" (unpublished data from Moon et al., 2001).

Girls with ADHD also have a number of successful adaptations. Since interpersonal relationships are closely related to the self-esteem of girls, appropriate social functioning may be a protective factor (Grskovic & Zentall, 2005). For the self-esteem of girls with symptoms of ADHD, active involvement with friends, organizations, and activities in general education settings (prosocial factor) was protective. In addition, girls with ADHD (fifth through eighth grades) may be receptive to interventions to help them regulate their faster pace and their intense social and emotional style because they (a) were aware that they were more likely to react with strong feelings than either girls with learning disabilities or typical peers and (b) knew the difference

NOTE
A DULL LIFE?

Late arriving for his flight, this man was amusing, charming, and full of stories about how much trouble he had making his flight. After recounting several stories of haplessness, he said, "I keep trying to lead a dull life, and everyone else keeps trying to make it exciting."

between inappropriate, stimulating behavior (e.g., swearing, breaking rules, stirring up trouble) and more appropriate active social involvement.

Finally, evidence exists that many individuals with ADHD become successful adults. Rapid responding can be channeled into adult leadership, spontaneity, and even comedy (e.g., Robin Williams or Bob Gallagher).

SUMMARY

Children with the hyperactive/impulsive subtype can be easily recognized by their gross motor activity and disruptiveness (mostly boys), small motor movements and verbal impulsivity (mostly girls), talkativeness (initiating conversations, commentary, or swearing/exclamations), and rapid or impulsive responding. The social outcomes for activity and difficulty waiting are seen in difficulties establishing routines, asking for help, planning, organizing, initially responding to tasks or tests with multiple choices, and judging the passage of time when there are long, inactive delays. Children with impulsivity (combined subtype) and girls with ADHD appear to be at greater social risk.

The evidence of social impairment can be found early in the negative and controlling behavioral reactions of peers and adults in response to these students with ADHD. Later it is seen in their decreased likability and fewer friendships. The impairment becomes pervasive during adolescence, especially for children with co-occurring disruptive and aggressive behavioral disorders, such as oppositional defiant disorder and conduct disorder.

Children with ADHD learn aggression more readily than their peers because they attend to emotional and aggressive cues and models and because their own aggressive behavior produces strong, socially reinforcing responses from others (stimulating consequences, such as anger, yelling). Aggression occurs most often when young children with ADHD want entry into an activity or want to protect their ongoing activities. Perhaps these situations are difficult for children with ADHD because they have fewer spontaneous solutions for waiting, handling conflicts, and maintaining relationships, especially when given their high need for participation, active responding, fun, and control (social goals).

In spite of the breadth of social outcomes and impairments that are possible from hyperactivity, impulsivity, and aggression, a number of successful adaptations exist for this behavioral style. These adaptations typically involve the channeling of activity and energy into sports, hobbies and projects, and computers. For girls with ADHD, involvement with friends, organizations, and school-related activities is adaptive. For both genders, the redeeming personality variables are energy (vs. hyperactivity), enthusiasm, spontaneity (vs. impulsivity), and seeking fun (vs. stirring up or getting into trouble).

DISCUSSION AND APPLICATION QUESTIONS

1. Activity, impulsivity, and inattention are the three primary characteristics of ADHD. Design an acronym, a mnemonic, or a picture to help you to remember them.
2. All behavior is purposeful. But *are we* always aware of the purpose of our own behavior? Give an example. How would you cut through the secondary outcomes to improve achievement and positive school adjustment?
3. Many students with ADHD find strong emotional responses rewarding and may seek negative attention. Here is an example:

STUDENT PRACTICES
ADHD MOTTO

"It's got to be fun! If it's not fun, it's got to be moving! If it's not moving, and I'm not moving, maybe I can make it mad."

Imagine you are working with a student with ADHD who can really push your buttons. You try to ignore him, but eventually you can't take it any more and blow up and yell at him. Knowing this child likes a strong emotional response, how can you constructively use that knowledge to reinforce appropriate behavior?

4. How does a student with ADHD-I seek stimulation differently from students with only ADHD-H?
5. Write a short scene that demonstrates the social problems an impulsive child with ADHD might have during an in-class small-group activity.
6. As a group, draw a continuum to represent the biologically based variation in needs for stimulation. Place a very nervous child on the left who is followed by couch potato and a very active or talkative student on the right. Each member of the group can place him or herself on the continuum. Discuss the ways you differ.

CHAPTER 6

ADHD-Inattentive Subtype (ADHD-I)

OBJECTIVES

- Recognize the characteristics that are required in the identification of ADHD-Inattentive subtype.
- Identify the informal problems and positive characteristics that you see in your classrooms.

KEY TERMS

skill or cognitive deficits
performance deficits
attentional style
selective inattention
habituation
sustained inattention
vigilance tasks
low stimulus intensity
attentional bias
anger-biased
change-seeking behavior
self-generated stimulation

One of the most common childhood school problems is inattention (Carrol, Bain, & Houghton, 1994). Using a community- or school-based sample, 1.3% of 7-year-old children showed inattentiveness (2% showed hyperactivity, and 1.7% showed combined features) (Warner-Rogers, Taylor, Taylor, & Sandberg, 2000). Even at this early age, clear differences in verbal IQ and reading were also noted compared to peers. Thus, it is not surprising that inattention has been associated with significant school failure (Gathercole & Pickering, 2000) and is observed in almost every type of child with mild disabilities (Krupski, 1980).

IDENTIFICATION OF THE ADHD INATTENTIVE SUBTYPE, ADHD-I

Because inattention is a marker for many mild disabilities, determining the correct diagnosis can be a challenge. However, an analysis of specific tasks and conditions that occasion inattention provides a basis for differential diagnosis (see Figure 6.1).

Skill or cognitive deficits

Skill deficits can be diagnosed in students with learning disabilities by their consistent avoidance of subject areas (e.g., math, reading) in their specific domain of deficit (McGee & Share, 1988). For example, when early reading requires sounding out new words (phonetic analysis), children with dyslexia may attempt to avoid these reading recognition tasks with inattentive or disruptive responses (e.g., getting sent out of class whenever oral reading is required). Also indicative of specific learning disabilities is a consistent pattern of errors, performance anxiety, or a

FIGURE 6.1
Differential Diagnosis After Analysis of Specific Conditions

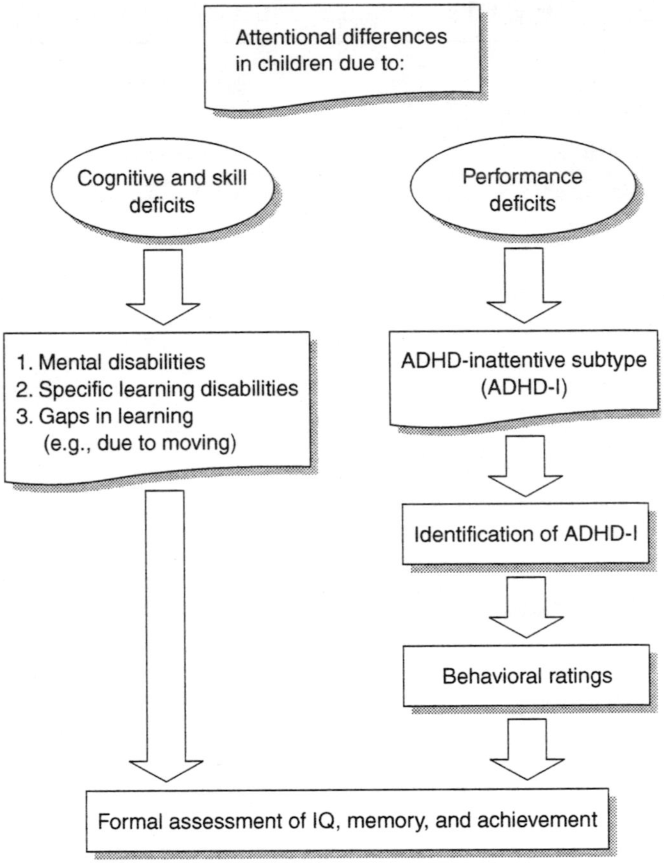

clear preference for type of task (e.g., visual tasks over listening tasks). However, teachers report that children with learning disabilities are more willing to be redirected back to their materials than are students with ADHD, even though redirection to the same tasks does not typically help these students learn (for a review, see Dykman, Ackerman, & Oglesby, 1979).

Differently, children with mild mental disabilities may appear inattentive when asked to demonstrate their story understanding (e.g., to write a new ending for a story), to transfer their learning from prior experience to a new task, or to process information that is beyond their reduced attentional capacity (Carter & Swanson, 1995). Children with giftedness who have advanced abilities will avoid tasks that do not challenge them.

Skill deficits can also be found in children with gaps in learning experiences, such as having missed school because of frequent relocations, sickness, or poor instruction. Children with hearing impairments will evidence attentional problems during oral discussions and transitions but less often during computer class or seat work, whereas children with visual impairments could show the reverse pattern. Sometimes poor performance is due to the response requirements of the task. For example, some children may appear inattentive or disruptive when they are attempting to use a pencil in contrast to using a computer keyboard or when verbally responding.

Once assessment and accommodations have been made for skill or learning deficits (specific learning disabilities, IQ differences, sensory/motor impairments, or experiential learning factors), performance-related problems due to inattention can be assessed.

Performance deficits

Only when the task is of moderate skill difficulty can we expect a child to pay attention. Thus, addressing task difficulty is an initial priority because "paying" attention is investing energy into a task where successful completion is possible. If the child *can* perform the task but still has problems attending or considerable variability exists in performance, then the problem probably lies in the attentional style of the child. Children with ADHD are described as having performance or production deficits demonstrated by inconsistent use of skills. These are students with ADHD-I.

Children identified as the pure inattentive subtype represent over a quarter of all students with ADHD (Wilens, Biederman, & Spencer, 2002). Screening for ADHD-I requires parent or teacher ratings on six of the following attention-related characteristics (as specified by the *Diagnostic and Statistical Manual of Mental Disorders*, 4th ed. [*DSM-IV-TR*]; American Psychiatric Association, 2000) but fewer than six ADHD-H symptoms, described in chapter 5 (unless the child is defined with combined subtype, ADHD-C, which requires six symptoms of inattention and six of hyperactivity/impulsivity):

NOTE

***DSM-IV-TR* CHECKLIST FOR INATTENTION**

1. Is often easily distracted by extraneous stimuli
2. Often fails to give close attention to details or makes careless mistakes in schoolwork, work, or other activities
3. Often does not seem to listen to what is being said to him or her
4. Often has difficulty organizing tasks and activities
5. Often loses things necessary for tasks or activities (e.g., school assignments, pencils, books, tools, or toys)
6. Often has difficulty sustaining attention in tasks and play activities
7. Often does not follow through on instructions and fails to finish schoolwork, chores, or duties in the workplace (not due to oppositional behavior or failure to understand instructions)
8. Often avoids or strongly dislikes tasks (such as schoolwork or homework) that require mental effort
9. Often forgetful in daily activities (American Psychiatric Association, 2000).

The combined subtype represents over half of students with ADHD (Wilens et al., 2002) and does not differ from ADHD-I in rated attention when controlling for age, gender, race, and economic background (Edelbrock, Costello, & Kessler, 1984). An additional subgroup was included to address cases with mild impairment, called ADHD–not otherwise specified.

ADHD-I DIFFERS FROM THE HYPERACTIVITY/ IMPULSIVITY SUBTYPE AND FROM STUDENTS WITH LEARNING DISABILITIES

ADHD-I can be differentiated from ADHD-H using the presence of hyperactivity and conduct difficulties (see chapter 5). However, it is more difficult to differentiate ADHD-I from learning disabilities because both involve inattentive symptomology and learning problems (Chhabildas, Pennington, & Willcutt, 2001), and many children have both disorders. That is, from a quarter to half of students with ADHD-H and ADHD-I have learning disabilities (Barkley, 1990; Lambert & Sandoval, 1980; Shelton & Barkley, 1994). Children with combined ADHD and learning disabilities may be more severely involved as indicated by lower verbal IQ than for those with learning disabilities alone (Halperin, Gittelman, Klein, & Rudel, 1984).

WHAT ARE THE OUTCOMES OF ADHD-I?

Children with ADHD-I are not disruptive, as observed by this general educator:

TEACHING STRATEGIES
HE JUST TENDS TO DAYDREAM A LOT

He's not a child really that disturbs other children as far as he doesn't run around the room or necessarily talk a lot or anything. He just tends to daydream a lot and just be in another world. So it's not that he's disturbing to other children (unpublished data from Zentall, Moon et al., 2001).

Teachers and parents perceive the ADHD-I group (and the learning disabilities group) as better able to inhibit responses than the ADHD-H group and as exhibiting behavior that was less problematic and less likely to have a codiagnosis of conduct disorder (20% vs. 41%, respectively [Lahey & Carlson, 1991; Warner-Rogers et al., 2000]).

Rates of co-occurring diagnoses in girls with both subtypes of ADHD

	Conduct Disorders	Oppositional Defiant Disorder	Anxiety	Depression
ADHD-Combined subtype	27%	71%	31%	10%
ADHD-Inattentive subtype	11%	47%	19%	4%
Typical Children	0%	7%	3%	0%

Source: Hinshaw (2002)

Even though there are fewer conduct problems in ADHD-I and these children suffer less peer rejection (Dumas, 1998), unpopularity still exists because of their greater shyness and social withdrawal (for a review, see Morgan, Hynd, Riccio, & Hall, 1996). Additional evidence suggests higher rates of anxiety and depression (Lahey & Carlson, 1991; Plizska, 1989; but see Morgan et al., 1996). The academic outcomes of ADHD-I are addressed in chapter 7.

TYPES OF INATTENTION

Whereas behavioral style is defined by the practice of certain types of behavior, attentional style is defined by a preference for and repeated attention to certain kinds of stimuli. The attentional symptoms of children with ADHD-I and combined ADHD can be grouped into problems in selective and sustained attention. Selective and sustained inattention are bound in a time relationship: selective attention problems are typically demonstrated early in task performance, whereas sustained attention errors generally occur later.

Selective inattention

Items 1 to 4 (see page 111, *DSM-IV-TR* checklist) could be used to screen for problems in selective attention. Selective inattention indicates difficulty regulating attention within academic and social tasks. Relevant information includes teachers' instructions; peer task-related talk; students' thoughts, feelings, and strategies; and specific attributes of tasks or contexts (e.g., sequence, structure, organization). Almost all new, complex, or unstructured academic and social tasks have selective attention requirements.

A second component involves ignoring "irrelevant" information (Cooley & Morris, 1990). Irrelevant interferences can be perceptual (e.g., what we see or hear), ideational (intruding thoughts), or motor events. The degree to which a child can ignore irrelevant information requires maintaining focus and is seen in reduced response variability.

Increased age and experience can reduce the selectivity requirements of a task. For this reason, young children have more problems with selective attention. As children gain experience with different types of tasks and task formatting, tasks lose their selectivity requirements. Children also experience problems with attentional selectivity when they are preoccupied with needs for (a) safety/security, (b) competence, or (c) relationships with adults, siblings, and peers.

An optimal amount of arousal is required for maintaining an attentional focus and reducing response variability (Cooley & Morris, 1990). Sometimes this arousal is provided by the meaningfulness and stimulation inherent within the task (how novel or personally meaningful or habitual the information is, such as one's own name or whether the irrelevant is in the same modality as the relevant). Sometimes the level of arousal is dependent on children's different needs for stimulation (i.e., due to over- or undersensitivity to the stimulation available in their tasks and environments). These students will differentially attend to or avoid stimulation. For example, the selective attention of children with autism or Asperger's syndrome is directed to objects of low stimulus intensity (e.g., "sameness" or detailed, familiar stimuli) (for a review, see Zentall & Zentall, 1983).

In contrast, children with ADHD are less sensitive to stimulation or have a greater need for change (novel stimulation [Zentall, 1993, 1995; Zentall & Zentall, 1983]; see also the optimal stimulation theory in chapter 3). For this reason, they are more likely than their peers to pay attention to what is brighter, bigger, more intense, more colorful, louder, or moving (Copeland & Wisniewski, 1981; Radosh & Gittelman, 1981; Zentall, 1988, 1989a). They may even become overexcited in the presence of stimulation, especially boys during group games (Berry, Shaywitz, & Shaywitz, 1985). The attention of students with ADHD appears to function by taking in the maximum amount of stimulation available.

Thus, students with ADHD do not have an attentional deficit; rather, they have an attentional bias or preference for novelty. Their preference for novelty is due to their rapid habituation (physiological adaptation [Allen, 1986]) or underreactions to stimuli, often showing smaller, delayed, orienting responses (Satterfield, Schell, Nicholas, Satterfield, & Freese, 1990).

Because of this attraction to stimulation, added irrelevant detail or information that overlaps (shares the same space, sensory features, or content) with important features of the task will disrupt the performance for these children more than for their peers (Rosenthal & Allen, 1980; Zentall, Zentall & Barack, 1978; Zentall, Zentall, & Booth, 1978).

EVIDENCE-BASED PRACTICES
Distractors Can Be "Distracting" for Students with ADHD When:

1. There are IQ differences between groups (van der Meere & Sergeant, 1988).
2. The task is selectively more difficult for students with ADHD (e.g., perceptual tasks involving conflicting shapes, such as a triangle, next to words that are to be read, such as "square" [Leung & Connolly, 1996]). That is, "when task demands were increased, ADD children then exhibited a deficit in selective attention" (Milich & Lorch, 1994, p. 179). In fact, when a task is selectively more difficult for students with any disability, "distractors" will produce greater disruption (Harvey, Weintraub, & Neale, 1984).
3. Interesting cartoons and toys are placed within the context of listening tasks (i.e., it decreased the recall of causal connections even though students with ADHD recalled just as many facts [see the research by Lorch and colleagues reviewed by Zentall et al., 2001]).
4. Interesting cartoons were presented on a monitor next to a second monitor with math facts (i.e., when the child could attend to one but not both monitors, children with ADHD choose the more stimulating alternative [Lee & Zentall, 2002]).
5. Interferences are added within delay intervals in long tasks (see chapter 7).

(Continued)

EVIDENCE-BASED PRACTICES *(Continued)*

6. Detail and description are added within a listening comprehension task (e.g., Shroyer & Zentall, 1986).
7. Conversations overlap thought and make thinking more difficult, especially when the task is unfamiliar or complex or the children are young, have skill deficits, or little experience with the task (Edmonds & Smith, 1985).
   a. Even small changes in loudness can make a difference. For example, second-grade students with ADHD made more performance errors (but not achievement-matched classmates) during high 70-decibel classroom conversational noise than in low noise (64 decibels) when working on an unfamiliar alphabet-sequencing task (Zentall & Shaw, 1980).

Even on these rare occasions when distractors do mask the task and produce negative effects, "the present study suggests that their influence fades away rapidly with repeated trials" of a task (Schweitzer & Sulzer-Azaroff, 1995, p. 683).

In contrast, when students with ADHD looked at distal (nonoverlapping) "distractions" more than their peers, no performance loss was observed. Thus, looking is not harmful and can actually produce better performance from children with ADHD than for their classmates when the tasks are not difficult (Milich & Lorch, 1994, p. 179; Tannock, Purvis, & Schachar, 1993). The following represents several examples:

EVIDENCE-BASED PRACTICES
"DISTRACTORS" ARE NOT DISTRACTING WHEN THEY ARE:

1. gadgets added during
   a. complex math and
   b. easy or boring tasks
2. cartoons presented
   a. during a video game
3. noises added
   a. during familiar visual tasks
4. combinations of telephones ringing, calculator noises, lights, and oscilloscope patterns added
   a. during reading performance (Bremer & Stern, 1976; Carrol et al., 1994; Lawrence et al., 2002; Milich & Lorch, 1994; Steinkamp, 1980).

In sum, most types of immediate performance are not made worse by gadgets, lights, or noises. Only conversations overlapping language tasks (e.g., reading) and adjacent cartoons can contribute to poorer performance, but even here performance will not be disrupted when the child is performing an interesting task.

Social/Emotional outcomes and impairment Selective inattention can have indirect effects that produce impairment. Preferences for what is bright, loud, or intense can greatly reduce accuracy when "reading" (a) feedback from the self (e.g., standards, thoughts, strategies, values, subtle feelings, experiential histories, intentions or expectations) and (b) external information and subtle cues available in interpersonal contexts.

In "reading" others, children with ADHD were less accurate than their peers when asked to match a brief story to pictures of emotional facial expressions (Singh et al., 1998). However, they were not biased in recognizing types of emotions. In other words, their pattern of errors and of correctly identified emotions was similar to the pattern of average children but different from the anger-biased pattern of children with conduct problems (Cadesky, 2000; Singh et al., 1998). Conclusions were that an inconsistent pattern of errors represented a failure to consistently attend to affect cues. They are also more likely to make negative (but not hostile) interpretations when the social cues are unclear. That is, they have more negative reactions (play more negatively with neutral toys) and predict fewer long-term positive social outcomes than their peers (Madan-Swain & Zentall, 1990; Zentall et al., 2001). This pattern of reactions and expectations could be based on their history of negative experiences. That is, boys, girls, and adults with ADHD report more failure and more negative events in their lives (Hoza, Pelham, Milich, Pillow, & McBride, 1993; Rucklidge & Tannock, 2001; Vitaro, Tremblay, Gagnon, & Pelletier, 1994; Weiss & Hechtman, 1993). A lack of awareness of their own feelings and intentions could also explain their tendency to (a) blame others for frustration and social failure (for a review, see Mrug, Hoza, & Gerdes, 2001), (b) use excuses, and (c) feel disconnected from the outcomes of their behavior.

NOTE
Disconnected at 20 Years of Age

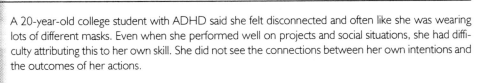

A 20-year-old college student with ADHD said she felt disconnected and often like she was wearing lots of different masks. Even when she performed well on projects and social situations, she had difficulty attributing this to her own skill. She did not see the connections between her own intentions and the outcomes of her actions.

In addition to consistent differences in "reading" social and personal cues, students with ADHD also have greater difficulty regulating responses to their own emotional states. For example, teens with ADHD were rated by their parents as having more emotional adjustment problems (Barkley, Anastopoulos, Guevremont, & Fletcher, 1991), and children who were ADHD and gifted were rated as more emotionally immature than boys with only ADHD (Moon, Zentall, Grskovic, Hall, & Stormont, 2001). Teachers and parents and even the children themselves report that they overreact to the good and bad events in their daily lives (Abikoff et al., 2002; Eisenberg et al., 1997; Grskovic & Zentall, 2005; Moon et al., 2001). For example, the highest score on parents' ratings of their girls was found on girls' unregulated emotions or stubbornness, moodiness, and reactiveness. Girls' self-ratings on a similar factor (feels angry or guilty or worries and responds loudly with their family and friends) yielded their second-highest self-rating. One item within that factor ("more likely than other girls to react with strong feelings") stood alone in separating elementary-age girls with ADHD from peer groups of girls with and without learning disabilities (Grskovic & Zentall, 2005).

Similarly, adolescents reported fewer feelings of alertness, happiness, and well-being and more negative emotionality than their peers (anger was experienced 40% of the time and anxiety about half the time, as well as stress and sadness [Whalen, 2001]). Adolescent girls with ADHD also self-reported that negative events had a greater effect on them than comparison girls or than boys with ADHD (Rucklidge & Tannock, 2001). Thus, these children, especially girls, overreact to positive and negative events.

TEACHING STRATEGIES
HE GETS SO UPSET ABOUT THEM

Most of the time he is legitimate in getting frustrated about something. At recess if it's a game of soccer and somebody does something wrong, even though it's only a game it's major to him. So some things are legit that he gets upset about, but he gets so upset about them it's inappropriate (unpublished data from Moon et al., 2001).

Similarly, children with learning disabilities (75% of whom experience social problems [Kavale & Forness, 1996]) overreact to both social rejection and acceptance. When responding to unfriendly contacts, children with learning disabilities, especially girls, were more likely to make negative self-judgments (Settle & Milich, 1999). In response to friendly contacts, they were more likely than typical children to make positive self-judgments. It has also been reported that children with aggression who have a history as both victim and perpetuator more often report that others were hostile or intending to cause them harm when cues were ambiguous (Dodge, Price, Bachorowski, & Newman, 1990; Moore, Hughes, & Robinson, 1992). Expecting negative outcomes may protect children from further disappointment, but it can also produce depression by reducing the number of good experiences and positive opportunities available.

In summary, intense, negative, and variable emotional reactions are magnified during adolescence. However, no evidence of significant impairment associated with this emotionality exists. For example, girls from school-based samples do not have more anxiety or mood disorders (Grskovic & Zentall, 2005; Hinshaw, 2002), even though about 25% of children with ADHD from clinical samples do have anxiety disorders (Gaub & Carlson, 1997; Rucklidge & Tannock, 2001).

Academic impairment as an outcome of selective inattention Academic disabilities are more strongly related to symptoms of inattention than to symptoms of hyperactivity/impulsivity (Willcutt & Pennington, 2000). For example, many learning tasks require children to attend to detail for periods of time. Thus, preferences for what is bright, loud, or intense can replace attention to details in academic tasks. Less attention will be directed to feedback and to small, detailed, and informational cues (Copeland and Weissbrod, 1983; Cunningham, Siegel, & Offord, 1985; Meyer & Zentall, 1995; Tant & Douglas, 1982; Zentall & Gohs, 1984).

Selective attention difficulties may also contribute to impairments in organization (i.e., attending to subtle structure). Specific difficulties reported by elementary-age children with ADHD were in locating completed homework, books, and school materials (Zentall, Harper, & Stormont-Spurgin, 1993). One adolescent compared her experiences to those of someone who must feel her way around darkened spaces, learning only by bumping into things—where everyone else had a flashlight and fewer bruises. Children who are disorganized may also be slower in finding objects, producing work, or logically sequencing verbal or written responses. Observers rated students with hyperactivity as having lower desktop neatness scores, and the students themselves recognized problems in personal neatness (Atkins, Pelham, & Licht, 1989; Zentall et al., 1993). Educators described the following frustrations:

TEACHING STRATEGIES
HE *NEVER* HAS THE SUPPLIES HE NEEDS

He usually isn't in line when he is supposed to, not ready when he is supposed to be, he doesn't have the things he needs. I mean he never has the supplies he needs. Never can find a pencil, never can find a pen, never . . .

But I think a lot of this is just Jake. . . . Orderliness and that kind of [thing] is not important to him. You know . . . his desk is a pig pen all the time. You know, we have to clean it about two times a week. He's a saver . . . he throws nothing away. He can't find anything . . . and he assures me that his room is like this too. And I'm sure it is. And that's just the way he seems to be (Zentall et al., 2001, p. 504).

Some of the difficulties in organizing may be due to the number of objects, ideas, or perceptions that children with ADHD attempt to "hold" while gathering stimulation.

Sustained inattention

For preschoolers, the number of activity or toy changes (short span of attention) is a behavioral indicator that predicts ADHD symptoms in 6- to 8-year-olds. A parent of a preschool child with ADHD called her son "bug." When asked why, she said, "Because he lights for a short time, like a mosquito, and sometimes he bites."

Even though the ability to sustain attention increases with age, individuals with ADHD, regardless of age, still lag behind their peers in their ability to maintain attention (e.g., the duration of sitting [Dienske, de Jonge, & Sandars-Woudstra, 1985]). Thus, at the secondary level, students are off task visually, especially during academic tasks

EVIDENCE-BASED PRACTICES
Preschoolers Can Be Very Short

Preschoolers with ADHD more than their peers

1. shifted activities (i.e., were more often engaged in activities 20 seconds or fewer and in fewer activities 2 minutes or more);
2. engaged in sensory play with objects, sights, and sounds;
3. batted at rather than interacted with toys;
4. played alone during free and teacher-directed play; and
5. engaged in fewer peer conversations (Alessandri, 1992; Carlson, Jacobvitz, & Sroufe, 1995; Zentall, 1983, 1986a).

By the elementary years, children with ADHD continued to change their activities and topics of conversation more often than their peers:

Motor and Verbal Activity Changes: A Sign of Inattention in ADHD

1. More getting up and down or changing activities during homework or solitary play
2. More visual off task during copying and familiar seat-work tasks
3. Less sustained joint play in a peer context (Madan-Swain & Zentall, 1990; for a review, see Zentall, 1984)
4. More topic changes and verbal off task during social play (Madan-Swain & Zentall, 1990)

STUDENT PRACTICES

Sara has a *gameboy* in her room and her parents are Mark and Sue and uh, there is a bad bully messing with me at school. His name is Chris. Something funny happened today at school, well . . . (unpublished data from Zentall, Moon et al., 2001).

(e.g., during multiplication and word problems [Zentall, 1990]), and adults with ADHD make more changes of vocation, residence, and schools attended than comparisons (Barkley, Fischer, Edelbrock, & Smallish, 1990; Hartsough & Lambert, 1982).

In addition to these observations of change-seeking behavior, sustained inattention is documented by increased errors or variability at the end of performance. However, all children with mild disabilities will have some difficulty maintaining attention to tasks that have been difficult for them. Their greater initial effort leaves them less able to sustain effort. Thus, young children and children with ADHD and co-occurring learning disabilities will have greater difficulty sustaining attention to new or complex tasks.

In contrast, children with ADHD, without additional learning disabilities, have difficulty sustaining attention to long, rote/repetitive, uninteresting, or nonactive tasks. Thus, their attentional "deficit" occurs with increased task length, familiarity, and repetitiveness. While performing these types of tasks, students with ADHD look around or change their attentional focus more often than their peers, especially during later performance (Zentall, 1985b, 1986b; Zentall & Zentall, 1976; Zentall, Falkenberg, & Smith, 1985). Poor sustained attention can be inferred from error scores on vigilance types of tasks that require a response to an infrequent signal (e.g., the letter "X") within a sequence of hundreds of nonrelevant letters. Children with attentional problems have fast and inaccurate responding and more off-task behavior over time than their peers as well as high performance variability on these tasks (Borger et al., 1999; Neuringer, 2002; Zentall, 1986b). Errors on this task are not due to skill deficits because they make more errors as the length of the task increases, with slow task pacing, and when there is little or no reward or adult supervision (van der Meere & Stemerkink, 1999). Poor performance on rote vigilance tasks is related to observations of classroom inattention but not to IQ (Borger et al., 1999; Kupietz & Richardsom, 1978). In addition to repetitive experimental tasks, slower addition facts are typical of children with ADHD and similary indicate problems in sustained attention (Zentall, 1990; Zentall & Smith, 1993).

Social and academic outcomes of sustained inattention Frequent changes in the focus of play, in directed thought, and in conversational topics (i.e., irrelevant and off-task comments) have social consequences. Clearly, the relevance and coherence of what children say is important to social acceptance. Conversational quality may contribute even more to the acceptance of girls with ADHD-I, 62% of whom were rejected or avoided by their elementary-level peers compared to only 9% of comparison girls (Gaub & Carlson, 1997).

Because it is more difficult for students with ADHD to attend over time, especially to repetitive tasks, they are more likely to (a) rush through assignments and make careless errors, (b) show more messiness each time a task must be rewritten, (c) get bored more quickly than their peers, and (d) show more activity and related behavioral problems (Shroyer & Zentall, 1986).

Inattention during the performance of rote academic tasks is also associated with increased activity and impulsive responding, especially during later performance (Zentall, 1985, 1986b; Zentall & Zentall, 1976; Zentall et al., 1985). See "Teaching Strategies" page 121.

Specific impairments in homework One typical academic problem related to poor sustained attention is homework production. Perhaps it is the repetitive nature of homework assignments that contributes to the dislike of homework by students with ADHD. That is, over half of homework assignments are unfinished classwork and another quarter are practice tasks, with small percentages in preparation for upcoming assignments (Zentall & Goldstein, 1999).

In particular, students with ADHD complain about "a pile of homework" as well as long-term projects that typically require homework (Zentall, Moon, et al., 2001). Children experiencing problems completing homework often find themselves spending more time and energy discovering ways to avoid homework than in doing

TEACHING STRATEGIES
HIGH SCHOOL FINAL EXAMS FOR A STUDENT WITH ADHD PLUS READING DISABILITIES

Now Justin had already been in the resource room to have a 100-question final in English read to him earlier that day. It wasn't easy, but I did manage to keep him on task . . . . Around 1:00 p.m., Justin walked into my room again with a 187-question final in Earth and Space. At this point it was apparent that he was worn out and not at all happy. . . . Well, I started reading the final, and he stopped me close to the middle of the final. He looked at me and said, "Ms. Y, I only have two brain cells left right now, and I just want you to know that they are fighting over which one of them is going to survive. I'm just not sure that the surviving brain cell is going to be able to handle the rest of this final." I just looked at him, and we started laughing hysterically because it was such a true statement. (Deb Yocum, personal communication, 2000).

it (Zentall & Goldstein, 1999). Even gifted students with ADHD were described by their teachers either as not doing homework or as working hard at school to avoid taking it home. "He absolutely hates homework so he works very hard at not having homework" (Zentall, Moon et al., 2001, p. 507). Selective attention problems can also contribute to homework difficulties when students fail to get assignments, understand their directions, or organize an approach.

SUCCESSFUL ADAPTATIONS

Gains can be derived from attentional preference for novelty, seeking change, and a wide focus of attention, as stated here:

NOTE

It is interesting to speculate about the possible advantages of the hyperactive child's style of processing information. Many of life's tasks are relatively simple, and in these situations, the tendency to take a broader view and to process more information than is necessary may serve some adaptive functions, perhaps increasing a hyperactive child's tolerance for performing a monotonous but necessary job, or even facilitating creative responding (Whalen, 1989, p. 140).

In other words, an adaptive potential to this attentional style may exist. For example, preferences for computers and software games are often observed in these children. Some researchers think these preferences are stimulus–response behavior (i.e., lower levels of some video games involve only target-and-shoot responses). However, at higher levels, some games involve sports strategies, and adventure games at the next level require considerable problem solving (Jeff Moon, personal communication,

2003). Children with ADHD do not differ from their matched peers on the target games or on the adventure games when both age and verbal IQ were statistically controlled (Lawrence et al., 2002). Under self-paced high-feedback conditions of video games, they were able to function normally. Persistence in these activities could be explained by evidence that video games release dopamine, which temporarily increases arousal and may facilitate cognitive control functions (Lawrence et al., 2002).

Although children with ADHD more often complain (e.g., when tasks are "boring" or "stupid") and are less willing to repeat a previous activity, they also show more curiosity and ask more questions of their examiners (Whalen, 1989). In fact, some children with ADHD have spontaneous and often humorous topics of conversation or perspectives and unique and intense interests. Hollowell and Ratey (1995) suggested that tolerance for chaos and ambiguity contributes to the development of creativity in this population.

For storytelling tasks, students with ADHD told more creative stories (i.e., with novel themes and plots) than did comparison students (Zentall, 1988) and preferred neutral toys, such as blocks and Legos, over toys or games with specific purposes or rules. Neutral objects can be re-created into new forms, allowing these children to sustain attention to objects for longer periods of time. Related research by Shaw and Brown (1999) reported that boys with ADHD who had IQ scores of 115 or higher used more nonverbal information during problem solving and scored higher on a test of creative thinking than did boys with similar IQ scores but without ADHD. In other words, behavioral variability may provide some advantage for children with ADHD when novel responses and divergent thinking are of value. Creativity has similarly been observed by the children, their parents, and their teachers (Zentall & Stormont-Spurgin, 1995; Zentall, Moon et al., 2001).

Attraction to novelty can also produce strong interests and preferences that may be auditory based (e.g., listening to or composing stories, plays, or music) or visually based (e.g., drawings or collections of shells, rocks, insects, baseball cards). More noticeable interests and talents will be seen in children with ADHD and giftedness, but even individuals with pure ADHD may have a greater number and variety of interests.

Sometimes positive attributes of children are recognized only when the learning context changes. That is, they appear to be "sleepers" who awaken when they are given specific projects, assignments, or more flexible learning conditions. Many of

NOTE
A University Student's Multiple Interests

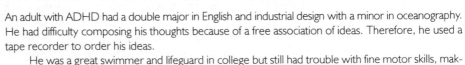

An adult with ADHD had a double major in English and industrial design with a minor in oceanography. He had difficulty composing his thoughts because of a free association of ideas. Therefore, he used a tape recorder to order his ideas.

He was a great swimmer and lifeguard in college but still had trouble with fine motor skills, making his handwriting difficult to read.

these children do better in college than in high school because of the choices available (e.g., majors, classes, living conditions, peers). The problem with school for many students with ADHD is that they must be proficient in all subjects, with all teachers, and in all homework. However, choices can alter these requirements, especially for adults with ADHD who can control the length of time on task by interchanging tasks or work environments and by employing assistants or selecting occupations that provide optimal working conditions.

NOTE

ADHD AND NEUROSURGERY

Fred Epstein, M.D. . . . [is a] pioneering 62-year-old neurosurgeon, one of the few in the world who operate on the treacherous tumors of a child's brain, areas once thought inoperable. More than a quarter of his patients lack medical coverage, Epstein says, so he does those surgeries for free. . . . Epstein, founder and director of the Institute of Neurology and Neurosurgery at Beth Israel Medical Center in Manhattan . . . hardly looked like brain surgeon material. "I fidgeted, had trouble concentrating. Nowadays it's called attention deficit disorder, but in those days everyone thought I was just stupid" (Holzwarth, 2001).

Finally, changes of culture can also contribute to a more positive frame when looking at individuals with ADHD:

NOTE

A TRAIN RIDE HALFWAY ACROSS INDIA

During the monsoon season of 1993, I took a 12-hour train ride halfway across India to visit an obscure town near the Bay of Bengal. In the train compartment with me were several Indian businessmen and a physician; we had plenty of time to talk as the countryside flew by from sunrise to sunset.

Curious about how the Indians viewed ADD, I asked, "Are you familiar with the personality type where people seem to crave stimulation but have a hard time staying with any one thing? Their attention hops from one thing to the next, but never seems to settle down."

"Ah, we know this type well," one of the men said, the other two nodding in agreement.

"What do you call it?" I asked.

"Very holy," he said. "These are old souls, near the end of their karmic cycle." Again the other three nodded in agreement, perhaps a bit more vigorously in response to my startled look.

"When the soul is very close to the end of its thousands of incarnations, it must take a few lifetimes and do many, many, things, to clean up the little threads left over from previous lifetimes. We have great respect for such individuals, although their lives may be difficult."

"In America we consider this a psychiatric disorder," I said. All three looked startled, and then laughed (Hartmann, 1998, pp. 19–20).

SUMMARY

ADHD-I subtype is screened for possible identification through the use of parent and teacher ratings on a set of attentional items from a *DSM-IV-TR* checklist. Attentional problems "caused" by skill-related problems (e.g., learning disabilities) will differ from ADHD-I subtype by consistently showing inattention in their specific academic deficits (e.g., reading, listening). However, students with learning disabilities should perform adequately when they understand and know how to make task-appropriate responses. In contrast, the types of problems that students with ADHD will demonstrate are variability in responding and failing to produce even when there is no accompanying learning disability or skill deficit. They demonstrate selective and sustained attentional problems.

Selective inattention or attentional bias to novelty indicates difficulty initially regulating attention to relevant academic, social, and personal cues. Students may have difficulty locating what is important, especially when important information is subtle or ambiguous or when the task field is complex or has other irrelevant but attractive actions or features. Problems are related to the highly reinforcing nature of stimulation. That is, the greater pull of added task novelty is due to the fact that students with ADHD need and prefer stimulation. Even so, at older age levels and with additional task practice, children with ADHD can learn to better identify and respond to relevant cues.

The impairments produced by selective inattention can be recognized as a disorganized approach to new or complex tasks, contexts, or social requirements. The performance of students with ADHD-I will be disrupted more than that of comparisons only when novel colors, movements, or shapes overlap visual information within the task or when conversations overlap with the thinking required for processing task information. Most types of novelty placed in the distant environment (e.g., gadgets, noise, lights, color, shapes) will not disrupt performance. Children with ADHD will choose to look at visual novelty in the environment and then look back to their tasks without a loss in performance and sometimes with increased effort. Only appealing cartoons can reduce timed or rote performance, but even here it will not disrupt performance on an engaging task or activity.

Selective attention to novelty is also associated with insufficient attention allocated to aspects of the self, such as thinking, feeling, or previously learned standards or strategies. This can be recognized as reliance on external cues and feedback, attributing responsibility to others, and an overly emotional response to life events (i.e., recognizing feelings only when they become intense).

In contrast to selective inattention, problems in sustained attention generally occur at the end of task performance or when similar tasks are presented to children day after day. When tasks are overly familiar, long, or repetitive, students with attention deficits refocus their attention away from the task and toward what is novel or intense in their internal or external environment. Because it is more difficult for them to remain alert under conditions of decreasing novelty, students with ADHD rush through assignments and make more careless errors or change their focus of attention, topic of conversation, or behavioral activity more than their classmates. Furthermore, when stimulation is not available in the environment and the task is long, familiar, or nonmeaningful, students with ADHD will attempt to self-generate stimulation through inappropriate activity, disruptiveness, or talking (see chapter 5). Clearly, less novelty exists over time after repeated exposure to practice tasks (e.g., math facts, handwriting).

However, in areas of interest and personal meaningfulness or with active responses available, children with ADHD can sustain attention for long periods of time. Furthermore, a number of children with ADHD-I are creative and successful and have multiple or a few intense interests.

DISCUSSION AND APPLICATION QUESTIONS

1. How can you tell for a particular child whether a task requires sustaining attention or more complex selective attention?
2. Students with ADHD are attracted to novelty the way bees are attracted to flowers. Similar analogies would be that students with ADHD are attracted to novelty the same way that
   a. women are attracted to signs that say "Sale,"
   b. men are attracted to car lots,
   c. young children are attracted to a carnival, and
   d. grandmas are attracted to bingo games

   What are additional analogies for attentional biases? (question from Janice Grskovic, 1999).
3. Print out a copy of a Web page and, using your knowledge of attentional variables, improve the Web format. Prepare a report for the class that you can share on the overhead projector.
4. Select good and bad examples of home pages from the Web or lessons from children's texts and bring them to class for presentation and discussion.

CHAPTER 7

Learning Problems and Co-Occurring Learning Disabilities

OBJECTIVES

- Make a distinction between the learning disabilities of children with ADHD plus learning disabilities and the learning problems that characterize students with pure ADHD.
- Recognize that IQ is an independent factor. That is, the lower IQ of *some* children with ADHD is unrelated to true learning differences, and the higher IQ of some students with ADHD and giftedness can prevent us from recognizing this subgroup.

KEY TERMS

perceptual
memory
working memory
problem solving
divergent thinking
learning disabilities
reading disability
verbal learning
basic skill areas
spoken language
selective listening
pragmatics
semantics
phonological analysis
dyscalculia
academic self-concept
biased outcome expectations

"*Is ADHD a learning disorder?" This was an educator's question who then proceeded to answer* her own question with the following observation: "Children with ADHD, in my experience have average intelligence and thus have the capacity to know and to perform adequately." Similarly, the American Academy of Pediatrics (1994) stated, "ADHD is not a learning disability, but a behavioral problem" (p. 2). The response to these assertions is "yes" and "no" and is addressed in this chapter through an examination of the perceptual, memory, and IQ processing abilities of students with ADHD as well as what we know about their academic performance and how they see themselves as learners. The graphic presented in Figure 7.1 represents the developmental progression of learning abilities as they are manifested initially in spoken language and later in written language.

It is a challenge to accurately assess the learning potential of children with ADHD, primarily because their behavioral and attentional style can alter an assessment of their learning abilities. For example, if children have difficulty focusing on critical features in tests or sustaining attention to lengthy tests, it could be difficult for them to demonstrate their understanding of a subject. Furthermore, if they have difficulty withholding responses, they will also have difficulty carefully (a) reading or listening to instructions, (b) asking for help, (c) considering alternative responses, (d) planning appropriately within a time frame, or (e) previewing all possible answers on multiple-choice tests. For example, it has been documented that children with ADHD perform worse

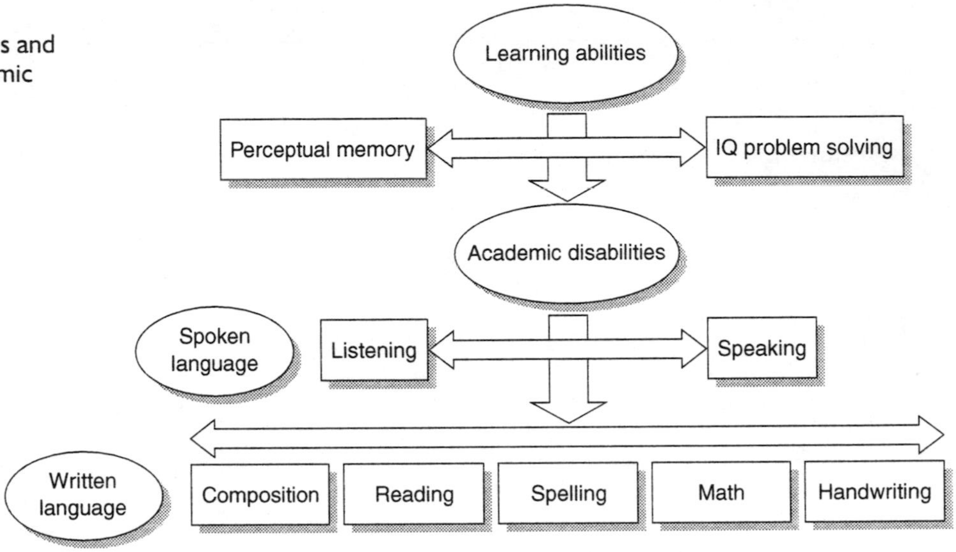

FIGURE 7.1
Learning Abilities and Potential Academic Disabilities

than their peers when a five-response multiple-choice format was used but not with two choices (Hoy, Weiss, Minde, & Cohen, 1978).

In addition, some factors could optimize test performance. For example, the novelty of both individual and group-administered tests could produce better performance than would be seen in routine classroom tasks. Individual testing could produce even better performance than group-administered achievement because of the one-on-one presence of an adult (social stimulation), typically without the requirements of reading, waiting, or following group-administered directions.

With these test-limiting factors in mind, the first section of this chapter addresses the learning-process skills of students with ADHD followed by their academic performance.

LEARNING PROCESSES: PERCEPTUAL

Do these students have perceptual problems?

Children with ADHD can perform tasks requiring perception of the whole (Gestalt closure) and can search pictures for global information or themes (Kalff et al., 2002; Karatekin & Asarnow, 1999; Pennington & Ozonoff, 1996). However, in these same studies, performance requiring visual analysis of detailed stimuli (e.g., the Embedded Figures Test) was worse. Similarly, the visual fixations on these detailed pictures were shorter than those of peers. Children with ADHD also respond faster initially to stimuli than do their peers (for a review of physiological data, see Banaschewski et al., 2003). Thus, they have difficulties with perceptual details, which require a slow, careful analysis. These problems are related to selective inattention. (See Chapter 6.)

MEMORY

Can these students remember what they have been taught?

Verbal IQ and memory deficits are more characteristic of students with reading disabilities than of matched ADHD groups without reading deficits (McGee, Williams, Moffitt, & Anderson, 1989; Willcutt et al., 2001). What is difficult for students with ADHD are the attentional requirements of holding verbal information in mind, especially over time when interferences occur (e.g., of new information or a motor task to perform) or information must be organized, categorized, or associated with other information. The problem of interferences is demonstrated when we attempt to follow students with ADHD to the zoo:

EVIDENCE-BASED PRACTICES
CAN STUDENTS WITH ADHD FIND THEIR WAY AROUND THE ZOO?

Purpose. To determine whether children with ADHD would demonstrate difficulties with working memory and show behavioral inhibition deficits in real-life types of tasks.

Participants. Fifty-seven boys with ADHD (20 inattentive and 37 combined subtypes) and 57 without ADHD matched in performance IQ and age.

Task. Students were required to walk as fast as possible along a path with a series of checkpoints and complete a number of tasks related to touching or looking at objects. Boys walked two routes in a random order that differed in length (maximum 15 minutes) around a zoo and that varied in the number of distracting animal exhibits and numbers of checkpoints. They were given verbal instructions with photographs showing routes.

Findings. Children with ADHD (both subtypes) made more deviations from their routes and took more time than their peers. Route complexity/length had more negative effects on students with ADHD.

Educational Implications. Students with ADHD will have more difficulty holding in mind the goal of completing a task when many steps and many attractive interferences exist along the way, especially when the task is long (Lawrence et al., 2002).

Evidence Basis for Memory

Initial storage into memory. Specifically for children with ADHD, relevant information appears to be initially understood (encoded) and is equivalent to the memory performance of typical peers (Benezra & Douglas, 1988; Higginbotham & Bartling, 1993; Webster, Hall, Brown, & Bolen, 1996; Kaplan, Crawford, Dewey, & Fisher, 2000; Pennington & Ozonoff, 1996). Once this information is stored in long-term memory, it can be retrieved.

Memory after delay and with interference. Only when verbal interference occurs prior to storage will memory differences between children with ADHD (without learning or reading disabilities) and their classmates be found (Kaplan, Dewey, Crawford, & Fisher, 1999). Kaplan et al. (2000) proposed that poorer performance on certain types of memory tests (working memory) probably reflects attentional deficits (also see Chang et al., 1999).

Students with ADHD have difficulty sustaining attention over time delays, especially when interference occurs (such as an additional task) or organization is required. In other words, the current data support attentional problems more than memory deficits (Dewey, Kaplan, Crawford, & Fisher, 1998). Delay time with interference is difficult

(Continued)

EVIDENCE-BASED PRACTICES *(Continued)*

because new, irrelevant information will be attended to and have a higher activation and recall level than older, relevant information (Kimberg, D'Esposito, & Farah, 1997). For example, no group differences were found on tasks that involved repeating numbers; however, when the 5- to 6-year-old children listened to a series of items to be recalled and then performed a second task of pointing out the pictures in the correct order that had previously been named, it was more difficult for them than for their peers (Kalff et al., 2002). In addition, children with ADHD recalled less information than comparisons with interference (dropping a book, someone walking in the room, or a combination) but only in the delayed recall of spoken sentences, not in the immediate recall condition (Higginbotham & Bartling, 1993).

Children with ADHD perform less accurately on tasks that involve delays

a. when attempting to recall verbal items in a specific order with verbal interference (Kataria, Hall, Wong, & Keys, 1992; Webster et al., 1996),
b. on an immediate recall task that also required memory updating (i.e., the recall of only the recent items in the proper order [Roodenrys, Koloski, & Grainger, 2001]), and
c. even when the task involved word recognition rather than recall and cues were available (Cutting, Koth, Mahone, and Denckla, 2003).

However, they did not perform poorly with a visual format, which provided more opportunities to review cues (Chaang et al., 1999).

Memory strategies. Children with ADHD relied on simple rote rehearsal for a free-recall task rather than categorizing information and recalled fewer items than their peers, although in practice they spent less time rehearsing information (Chaang et al., 1999; O'Neill & Douglas, 1996).

The fact that they do not generate effective ordering strategies could be attributed to the attentional requirements for generating categories. (Failure to use meaningful verbal categories to aid recall may be specific to boys with ADHD and not girls [Cutting et al., 2003].) When information was already categorized, children with ADHD recalled as many words as their peers and differed only on an uncategorized list (Voelker, Carter, Sprague, Gdowski, & Lachar, 1989).

The question presented by O'Neill and Douglas (1996) about whether students with ADHD lack memory skills or attentional skills would be answered as the latter. However, the relationship between these two is complex, and a middle ground seems to exist between the two, described as "working memory." Some believe that this would be better termed "working attention" (Sergeant, Geurts, Huijbregts, Scheres, & Oosterlaan, 2003) because it involves manipulating and organizing information. Recent evidence indicates that working memory deficits are associated with language impairment and are not found in spatial working memory nor are they characteristic of students without language impairment (Jonsdottir, Bouma, Sergeant, & Scherder, 2005).

INTELLIGENCE (IQ, COGNITIVE ABILITIES, AND APTITUDE)

Are children with ADHD as intelligent and as innovative as their peers?

When we look at measured IQ, individual children with ADHD fall across the full spectrum of IQ. However, research that uses samples drawn from clinics often report lower IQ. For example, Barkley (1991) reviewed evidence to indicate that students with ADHD were about 7 to 15 points below comparison samples on standardized IQ tests, including samples of siblings. Barkley (1995) concluded that hyperactive-impulsive behavior has an "inherent association" with diminished verbal IQ while also noting that these scores may reflect test-taking attentional difficulties. Barkley (1998) clarified his position by stating that students with ADHD can run the gamut from gifted to mental retardation but that cognitive problems were primary features of ADHD.

Others (e.g., Leung et al., 1996) have concluded that lower IQ and academic deficits may be a consequence of ADHD rather than a core feature. The fact that lowered IQ may be an outcome explains lower scores documented in later but not earlier grade levels (Leung & Connolly, 1998). A well-controlled study further demonstrated that the distribution of IQ for students with ADHD was not different from normals (Kaplan et al., 2000).

In sum, when differences in IQ are found, they are most likely due to the selection of more severe cases of children from clinical samples (Light & DeFries, 1995), with some evidence suggesting that the IQ of children with ADHD decreases as they age (Loney, 1974). When children with ADHD have been referred for special education services, it has been associated with poor classroom achievement but not typically with low IQ (Fischer, Barkley, Edelbrock, & Smallish, 1990). In contrast, non-ADHD students who received services had both lower achievement *and* lower IQ than students who were not receiving such services.

Because so many possible outcomes could result just from IQ differences, it is important to control IQ and examine the essential performance and behavioral differences of students with ADHD (Felton, Wood, Brown, & Campbell, 1987). In addition to statistically equating groups in IQ, students could be divided into subtypes using IQ and achievement to determine how these factors influence the expression of the disability. Bonafina, Newcorn, McKay, Koda, and Halperin (2000) have identified four subtypes to assess: (a) ADHD with average intelligence and reading ability, (b) ADHD with average intelligence but with reading disability, (c) ADHD with high intelligence, and (d) ADHD with low achievement and low intelligence.

Even when IQ is diminished in some students with ADHD, these differences in IQ do not define ADHD. Findings of normal and above-average IQ in any of these students indicates that IQ is an independent factor. Where decreased intelligence is observed, it represents only one type of contextual intelligence (i.e., failure to adapt to their current school environment) and their lack of control in being able to select a more optimal environment (Sternberg, 1985). When students with ADHD attempt to use the third type of contextual intelligence (i.e., to shape their present environment to better fit their skills, interests, and values [Sternberg, 1985]), it causes disruption. For example, when students with ADHD were placed in settings with delays, they more frequently "dived under the table that held the apparatus, danced while watching their reflection in the observation window, and twirled their chairs. Typical children, however, sat in their chairs waiting for each trial to begin" (Schweitzer & Sulzer-Azaroff, 1995, p. 682).

Executive dysfunction and problem solving Attentional factors also influence the interrelated concepts of intelligence, problem solving, and "executive dysfunction." Executive dysfunctions are defined as planning and sequencing complex behavior, paying attention to several components at once, grasping the gist of a complex situation, resisting distraction and interference, inhibiting inappropriate responses, and sustaining behavioral output for relatively prolonged periods (Stuss & Benson, 1984). However, when executive functions were operationally defined by performance on specific tasks and statistical controls were used for age and IQ, executive deficiencies no longer characterized students with ADHD (Scheres et al., 2004).

Intelligence can also be defined as performance on problem-solving tasks. We have documented that cooperative groups with a member who was ADHD solved more problems correctly than groups with only typical children (Zentall, Kuester, & Craig, 2005). Where poor problem-solving occurs, it may be due to attentional or working memory difficulties. This could explain findings that children with ADHD (a) spent less time in problem solving, especially when there were several possible solutions or responses (Cohen, Weiss, & Minde, 1972), and (b) used less efficient questions and strategies than comparison children with reading disabilities (matched on age and verbal IQ [Tant & Douglas, 1982]). In turn, failure of working memory could be explained by insufficient arousal (e.g., the optimal stimulation theory). Increased arousal can fuel three different areas: (a) cognitive input functions, such as attention; (b) processing functions, such as memory or problem solving; and (c) motor control output processes, such as planning and inhibition of responses (Aylward, Gordon, & Verhulst, 1997).

In the absence of working memory requirements or when arousal is optimal, the evidence also indicates that students with ADHD can show originality and innovation that are superior to their peers. Students with ADHD used more novel nonverbal strategies than their peers to avoid hazardous consequences in a problem-solving video game task (Lawrence et al., 2002). Shaw and Brown (1999) reported that students with ADHD demonstrated more creative performance after watching an arousing video (high-speed car chase scenes) relative to a nonarousing video. Early research has also documented "remarkable divergent thinking" within some children with ADHD who outwitted the computer and who used a row-by-row strategy for searching to reduce memory demands (Dykman, Ackerman, & Oglesby, 1979).

ACHIEVEMENT AND CO-OCCURRING LEARNING DISABILITIES

As many as 80% of students with ADHD face academic problems (Cantwell & Baker, 1991), while 30% fail to achieve to a level predicted by their IQ (Barry, Lyman, & Klinger, 2002). Learning disabilities have been defined as achievement that is lower than would be predicted from IQ potential, usually accompanied by inadequate perceptual or memory abilities. Formal assessment can provide data on achievement (e.g., in reading or understanding language) in relation to potential or aptitude (IQ test scores). Thus, a child with a reading disability demonstrates lower reading achievement than would be expected given his or her IQ. Some children have co-occurring learning disabilities in several areas. Note that H.R. 1350 no longer requires a significant discrepancy between achievement and intellectual ability and that it uses the child's positive response to evidence-based practices as diagnostic. This definition awaits further interpretation.

The major type of learning disability—deficits in verbal learning—will result in problems in a broad range of language systems (e.g., spoken language, spelling, reading). In addition, many students have deficits in nonverbal learning or visual learning disabilities and more frequently have problems with math and social learning. In both types of learning disabilities, deficits are in the basic skill areas (e.g., reading recognition, math calculations). However, failure to develop basic skills can impact higher-level skills (reading comprehension and math problem solving) unless the child develops compensatory strategies (e.g., using context clues in reading).

Specific learning disabilities are quite prevalent in students with ADHD (see Figure 7.2 based on a review by Mayes, Calhoun, & Crowell, 2000). Learning disabilities in this population were found at higher incidence rates than would be expected in the general population, shown with smaller bars in math and reading (based on Geary, 1993; Lindsay, Tomazic, Levine, & Accardo, 1999; Passolunghi & Siegel, 2004; Willcutt et al., 2001).

Subtype differences indicate that both ADHD-H and ADHD-I groups performed worse than typical peers on reading, spelling, and math subtests even when IQ was controlled (Barry et al., 2002; Marshall, Hynd, Handwerk, & Hall, 1997). Additional academic comparisons between the two subtypes are difficult to make because children with ADHD-I may need to demonstrate more school performance problems for teachers to refer them in the absence of clear behavioral markers. Perhaps this bias in referral contributes to the findings that 72% of children with ADHD-I were

FIGURE 7.2

Prevalence of Specific Learning Disabilities Within Typical and ADHD Samples

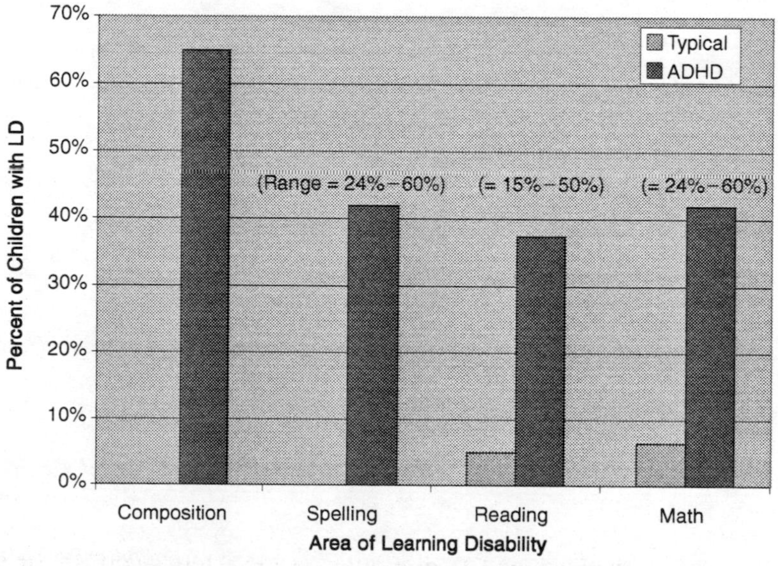

retained in grade for 1 year, while only 17% of ADHD students were similarly retained (Lahey, Applegate, & McBurnett, 1994). Although rates for girls are more evenly distributed (ADHD-I 20.5%, ADHD-C 14.1%, Comparisons 3.4% [Hinshaw, 1992]). Overall, few achievement differences between the two subtypes were found when IQ was controlled. Only poorer math calculation performance was found for the ADHD-I group and a greater probability of having a co-occurring learning disability than for students with ADHD-H (Marshall et al., 1997).

When a high rate of academic problems is found in children with both subtypes, it could be attributed to co-occurring learning disabilities that were present in 70% of clinical children with ADHD (Mayes et al., 2000). In addition, when chidren with ADHD pay insufficient attention during the presentation of information, it can contribute to gaps in learning. Children with learning disabilities plus ADHD have more severe learning problems than children with only learning disabilities and more severe attention problems than those with only ADHD (Mayes et al., 2000).

SPOKEN LANGUAGE ACHIEVEMENT

The data in Figure 7.3 report a significant number of language disorders (light bars) and speech disorders (dark bars) in community samples of children (ADHD) and in clinic-referred samples (ADHD-Clinic) (for reviews, see Barkley, 1991; Kovac, Garabedian, Du Souich, & Palmour, 2001; McInnes et al., 2003). However, at advanced grades, general language disorders were no longer present (McGee, Partridge, Williams, & Silva, 1991), and only specific problems in receptive and expressive language have been documented (McInnes et al., 2003). It is these specific skill deficits found in school-based populations that are summarized next.

FIGURE 7.3

Prevalence of Language and Speech Disorders

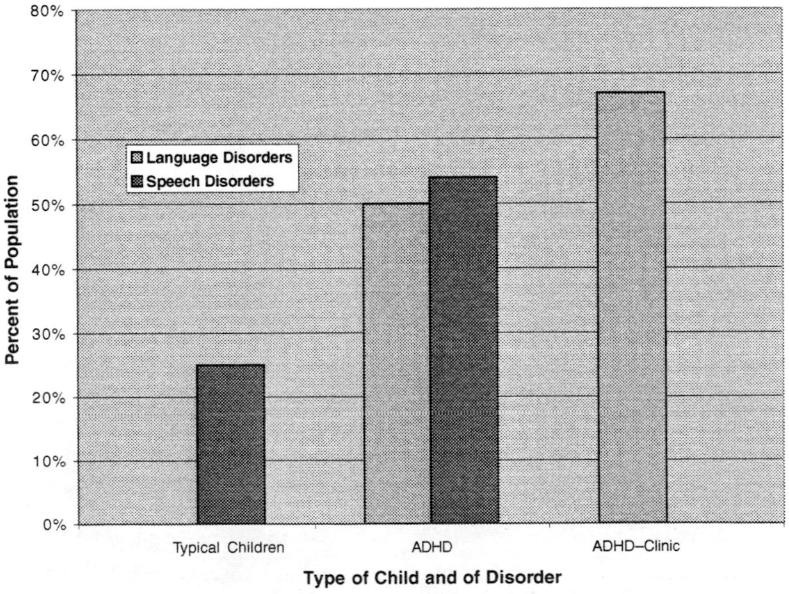

Listening

The literature suggests that children with ADHD are capable of getting the major points when listening to oral directions, discourse, and stories as long as the listening task is not too long, interrupted, or descriptive. The evidence basis follows, with information about how students with ADHD differ from children with verbal learning disabilities:

EVIDENCE-BASED PRACTICES
LISTENING SKILLS

Simple tests of word knowledge or of concepts and listening to oral directions were not more difficult for students with ADHD than for their peers (McInnes et al., 2003; Oram, Fine, Okamoto, & Tannock, 1999; Purvis & Tannock, 1997).

More complex comprehension is often assessed by children's ability to recall sentences and retell stories. With retelling tasks, children with ADHD were able to produce as many major and minor points; in contrast, children with learning and reading disabilities were less able to recall important information (for a review and data, see Oram et al., 1999; Purvis & Tannock, 1997; Zentall, 1988). These studies used school-based samples or controlled for possible IQ differences between groups.

Selective Listening

However, specific difficulties with understanding inferences and specific problems in selective attention were observed. Listening can require attending to a message while ignoring competing (overlapping) information. Thus, listening can be a selective attention task. For example, comprehension questions were answered with less accuracy when children with ADHD listened to a 10-minute story with adjectives added, presented at 200 words per minute (but not in a 10-minute story without adjectives presented slower at 100 words per minute) (Shroyer & Zentall, 1986). Students with ADHD also identified fewer causal links (A leads to B) than matched peers when interruptions occurred in the sequence of a story even though they identified as many cues and concepts (Milch-Reich, Campbell, Pelham, Connelly, & Geva, 1999).

Sustaining Attention and Listening

With longer sequences of language, listening requires the ability to sustain attention. Story retelling is a typical measure of listening comprehension (Harris & Sipay, 1985), but listening to longer stories also assesses sustained attention and memory (Higginbotham & Bartling, 1993). Under these conditions, fewer main points were recalled when retelling two folktales (Lorch et al., 1999; Tannock, Purvis, & Schachar, 1993) but not one story (O'Neill & Douglas, 1991; Purvis & Tannock, 1997; Zentall, 1988; Zentall, Javorsky, & Cassady, 2001). Aaron, Joshi, Palmer, Smith, and Kirby (2002) pointed out that children with attention problems scored worse on those tests of listening comprehension than on tests that were more tolerant of inattention, such as reading comprehension.

Can They Identify Causes and Logical Errors?

Purpose. To determine the receptive language difficulties of students with ADHD in comparison to average peers and students with language learning disabilities.

Participants. Seventy-seven 9- to 12-year-old boys (clinic referred and public school)—39 with ADHD and of those 18 with language learning disabilities. Pure ADHD and typical student groups were significantly higher in IQ scores than were the language learning disability groups.

(Continued)

EVIDENCE-BASED PRACTICES *(Continued)*

Tasks.

1. Four audiotaped passages with questions of factual comprehension and inferences
2. Eight passages with factual and nonlogical errors (e.g., of order)

Findings.

1. Equivalent performance between students with pure ADHD and their peers on factual comprehension.
2. Poorer performance of students with pure ADHD than their peers when
   a. making inferences based on those facts and
   b. detecting errors of information (sequences).

Implications. Lack of compliance with instructions that is often seen in children with ADHD may reflect poorer comprehension of complex instructions, especially when children must find logical errors in sequence or make inferences (McInnes et al., 2003).

Overall, the specific difficulties listening and understanding language were related to attentional problems and not to low IQ, poor motivation, or teacher ratings of hyperactivity/impulsivity (McInnes et al., 2003). Although the difficulties are specific, they may cause considerable problems for students with ADHD in their classrooms because 70% to 80% of elementary and secondary educators rated listening as more important than student compliance—second only and perhaps related to following classroom rules (Kauffman, Lloyd, & McGee, 1989).

Talking

In addition to specific problems in understanding the meaning of language, general problems seem to exist in the amount and the quality of language used to express meaning and in voice tonality. For example, children with ADHD talk excessively and interrupt (turn-taking errors), make sequencing and cohesion errors, make more off-task comments and questions, and fail to plan sufficiently long responses while monitoring their own intended meanings and the listener's perspective. The language of students with ADHD also had fewer connections across ideas and more referents to the immediate external environment than matched comparisons (partially explained by poorer memory [Caplan, Guthrie, Tang, Nuechterlein, & Asarnow, 2001]). These types of expressive language problems are termed errors in pragmatics, or deficits in the social/practical aspects of language. Recent evidence also indicates that boys with ADHD had a higher and less uniform voice pitch than boys with dyslexia and typical boys. In fact, the maximum intensity of voice correctly discriminated between all of the boys with and without ADHD (Breznitz, 2003).

These types of problems were different from those of students with reading disabilities or ADHD plus reading disabilities who have difficulty with the meanings (semantics), grammar, and sound–symbol relationships with spoken and written language (Purvis & Tannock, 1997). Children with both ADHD and RD have the receptive and expressive language problems of both disabilities (Pisecco, Baker, Silva, & Brooke, 2001).

EVIDENCE-BASED PRACTICES
TALKING SKILLS

Spontaneous Talking

The spontaneous talking of students with ADHD is peppered with impulsive statements (e.g., exclamations, commands, interruptions, topic changes) and is more dysfluent (starters, revisions, repetitions) and off task (e.g., more comments about their surroundings and nontask questions) (Redmond, 2004; Stormont-Spurgin & Zentall, 1996; Zentall, 1988; Zentall, Gohs, & Culatta, 1983). Part of the reason for the dysfluency may be that children with ADHD initiate more conversations with adults and peers and use more words and sentences than their peers even when playing alone or during a task (Breznitz, 2003; Zentall, 1988; Zentall et al., 1983).

Requested Talk

However, when asked to tell or retell stories (i.e., without pictures), students with ADHD talked less than their peers (Zentall, 1988). This crossover of effects is infrequently found in the literature (i.e., with students with ADHD showing more behavior in one context and less than peers in another). Some researchers have labeled this a production deficiency or negativism. However, in this case, children with ADHD produced less language in specific conditions (i.e., in the absence of visual cues in two of the story conditions). Visual cues may help these children maintain attention to events from the past and to plan and organize events into the future. Visual cues may be unnecessary for self-initiated conversations, which typically involve commentary about current tasks, objects, conversations, or contexts. For example, boys with ADHD used longer vocalizations than IQ matched comparisons when asked to "speak freely" about their favorite television programs, foods, friends, etc. (Breznitz, 2003, p.432).

Organization and the Social Pragmatics of Language

Organizational problems are reported in the language of students with ADHD (e.g., with and without reading disabilities [Purvis & Tannock, 1997]) in the ordering of words and the formulation and assembly of sentences (Oram et al., 1999). When retelling complex stories (many characters and events), the language of students with ADHD was further characterized by ambiguous references and more sequencing and cohesion errors than their peers (Tannock, Schachar, & Logan, 1993).They also demonstrated more frequent and longer pauses in their conversations than did comparison students with reading disabilities (Breznitz, 2003). These types of errors could indicate a failure to hold information in mind while planning and organizing its expression as well as a failure to self-monitor language and its intended meaning.

A failure to respond to roles in conversational exchanges was also observed. That is, elementary and middle school boys with ADHD were less likely than comparisons to change their communication style when changing roles (from speaking to listening and from interviewee to interviewer ([Landau & Milich, 1988; Whalen, Henker, Collins, McAuliffe, & Vaux, 1979]). For example, they asked more questions as an interviewee and fewer questions as an interviewer.

These role-reversal differences could be attributed to the nature of the roles. That is, asking questions is based on external information and may be easier than creating new questions from "in mind," and talking is more active than listening. In support of the importance of activity in these roles is evidence that students with ADHD had difficulty with a task only when they were assigned the less active helper role and not the more active worker role (Grenell, Glass, & Katz, 1987). They also differ from their peers more when listening than when attempting to send information to others (for a review, see Zentall & Gohs, 1984).

WRITTEN LANGUAGE

Composition

A learning disability in written composition was the most frequently observed academic disability for children with ADHD and was twice more common than reading, math, or spelling learning disabilities (Mayes et al., 2000). It should be noted that composition is the highest-level academic skill, requiring the use of all other skills (e.g., reading, spelling, handwriting). However, even when readability levels were equivalent between students with and without ADHD, differences in written language were still found, as indicated in the following study:

EVIDENCE-BASED PRACTICES

WRITING SAMPLES WITH TOPICS: "HANDS," A PICTURE OF A CAT, AND THE DANGERS OF FIRE.

Purpose. To determine the written language problems of students with ADHD-I and ADHD-H as they differ from normal comparisons.

Participants. Thirty-two 8- to 14-year-old clinic-referred boys with ADHD not taking medication.

Tasks. Wechsler Intelligence Scale for Children—Revised, Bender Visual-Motor Gestalt test, Written Language Assessment test.

Findings. Students with ADHD-H had lower visual-motor scores than either the ADHD-I or comparison groups. Both ADHD groups scored lower than average peers on General Writing Ability, Word Complexity, and Written Language Quotient. On productivity, the ADHD-H group produced less than the typical comparisons.

Implications. Children with ADHD should not be punished for inadequate written language performance or given homework that heavily relies on writing (Resta & Eliot, 1994).

Reading

Reading is a basic component of language that influences many other areas of academic functioning. Children who have difficulties in reading as early as kindergarten remain poor readers (Rabiner & Coie, 2000), and more than 70% of students in the third grade who have reading disabilities still have the same problems in 12th grade (Lerner, 2003). Severe underachievement in reading is found at equivalent and high rates for boys and girls (boys 6.8%; girls 7.7%) (Share & Silva, 2003; Shaywitz, Shaywitz, Fletcher, & Escobar, 1990; but see Barry et al., 2002, for evidence of higher rates in girls). For girls with ADHD, subtypes differ in rates of co-occuring reading disabilities, with the inattentive and combined subtypes displaying higher percentages (15%, 11% respectively) than the average girls (5%) (Hinshaw, 2002).

Although reading disabilities and ADHD are two of the most common disorders of childhood (Willcutt et al., 2001), about 15% of children with ADHD achieve better in reading than predicted (i.e., reading scores more than one standard deviation above age or IQ expectancy, selected from 241 children with ADHD with average IQ or above [Halperin, Gittelman, Klein, & Rudel, 1984]; see Figure 7.4). Note in the figure that the largest, "Other ADHD" group failed to qualify for these predefined groups.

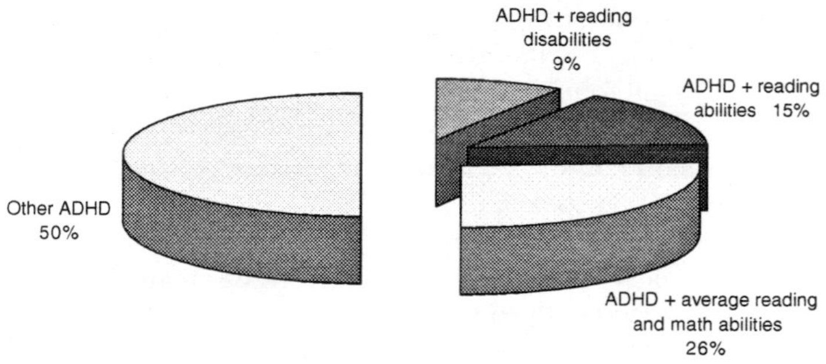

FIGURE 7.4
ADHD and Reading Abilities/Disabilities

To identify students with reading disabilities, a diagnostician could administer a word attack/decoding test (e.g., the Word Attack subtest of the Woodcock Johnson—Revised (WJ-R) [Woodcock & Johnson, 1989]) and a listening comprehension or vocabulary test (e.g., the WJ-R Listening Comprehension subtest). Below-average performance on the word attack test, combined with average to above-average listening comprehension performance, would indicate the presence of a learning disability in reading (Lyon, 1992; Stanovich, 1993).

EVIDENCE-BASED PRACTICES
READING RECOGNITION

Decoding or reading recognition is defined as a mental process that transforms printed symbols into words. Although reading recognition involves the use of both auditory and visual symbols, auditory phonological processes appear to be a marker for poor reading. That is, Foorman and Liberman (1989) compared good and poor readers on visual and phonological processes and reported that above-average readers were better at phonological processing, while poor readers relied more on visual processing. Similarly, Aaron et al. (2002) reviewed data suggesting correlations of reading with (a) rapid naming (auditory memory) at .38, (b) vocabulary (IQ) at .36, and (c) phonological awareness at .46. Verbal IQ appears to contribute to growth in word recognition (Stage, Abbott, Jenkins, & Berninger, 2003). Jimenez, Siegel, & Lopez (2003) pointed out that it is the orthographic structure of the English language that determines the relationship of IQ to reading. That is, no evidence of a relationship exists between IQ and reading disabilities in languages with consistent sound–symbol associations, such as in Spanish.

ADHD and reading disabilities are different disabilities. Phonological disabilities are not typically associated with ADHD (Shaywitz, Fletcher, & Shaywitz, 1994) but do characterize reading disabilities (Stanovich, 1988). Compared to students with pure ADHD, reading disability was associated with lower phonological sensitivity (more errors in sensitivity to rhyme and alliteration) (Ackerman, Anhalt, Dykman, & Holcomb, 1986; Ackerman, Dykman, & Gardner, 1990), difficulties with sound–symbol association, and deficits in short- and long-term memory on verbal tasks (Kaplan et al., 1999; Korkman & Pesonen, 1994).

Reading comprehension Children who are working hard to decode words will have difficulty remembering and comprehending what they read (Kail & Hall, 1999). However, some children learn to read quickly and still have difficulty understanding what they read. They may sound like expert readers when reading aloud but be unable to tell you what happened in a story. For example, students with ADHD were still found to have more problems with reading comprehension than matched comparisons, even when groups were equated in reading recognition (word identification and word attack and speed) and background knowledge and vocabulary (i.e., IQ) (Brock & Knapp, 1996).

Difficulties for students with ADIID in reading comprehension appear to be due to requirements for working memory and sustained attention. Students with ADHD fall behind in comprehension (but not in reading vocabulary), especially when passage lengths were increased (Cherkes-Julkowski & Stolzenberg, 1991; Nussbaum, Grant, Roman, Poole, & Bigler, 1990). In addition, students with ADHD recalled fewer story events than comparisons only when there were more connections in the stories but not when there were only a few casual connections (Lorch, O'Neil, Berthiaume, Milich, Eastham, & Brooks, 2004).

In the following case, Michael clearly has good listening comprehension, and his "boredom" with reading indicates either fatigue from trying to decode material too advanced for a child with a reading disability or the low level of content/interest of the reading material for a bright child with ADHD.

TEACHING STRATEGIES
A READING DISABILITY?

Michael can comprehend what he reads, if he can get through it before he gets bored. However, he loves me to read to him—even junior high school level material. He fails to bring home homework; hides it in the bushes and trash can (unpublished data from Zentall, Moon et al., 2001).

Table 7.1 provides a summary of reading differences between reading disabilities and ADHD.

Spelling

To spell, children must recall both the sequence of sounds (phonological analysis skills) and their corresponding visual symbols (i.e., recalling the order and visual form of letters in words [Mather, 2003]). Children with reading disabilities often have difficulties with spelling because phonological skills underlie both academic areas (Kroese, Hynd, Knight, Hiemenz, & Hall, 2000). Because recognizing visual symbols and translating them to sounds or words (reading/decoding) is easier than recalling sound sequences and then translating those sounds into corresponding visual symbols (spelling), some children who read well may still have difficulties remembering how to spell. Children with ADHD are significantly below grade level or have lower spelling scores than their classmates using both recall and recognition spelling tasks (McGee, Williams, & Silva, 1984; Zentall, 1989a).

TABLE 7.1 Differences between Students with Reading Disabilities and ADHD in Reading

Reading Disabilities	ADHD
A language-based disability (Pisecco, Baker, Silva, & Brooke, 2001) The reading disability group had more auditory-based deficits than visual (Weiler, Bernstein, Bellinger, & Waber, 2002)	Not a language-based disability (Pennington & Ozonoff, 1996) Students with ADHD-I had more deficits in visual search tasks but not on auditory processing tasks (Weiler et al., 2002)
Reading recognition problems associated with poor word attack scores (e.g., decoding nonsense words) (Lyon, 1992; Stanovich, 1993)	Reading comprehension problems (Brock & Knapp, 1996), especially with long and uninteresting passages—associated with sustained inattention (Cherkes-Julkowski & Stolzenberg, 1991; Nussbaum, Grant, Roman, Poole, & Bigler, 1990) More problems in sustained attention than children with reading disabilities (Brown & Wynne, 1984)
Poorer reading comprehension than listening comprehension	Poorer listening comprehension than reading comprehension (for a review, see Aaron, Joshi, Palmer, Smith, & Kirby, 2002)
Phonological skill deficits (Foorman & Liberman, 1989; Stanovich, 1988)	No phonological deficits (Shaywitz, 1992) Slower and less accurate in naming letters and even in naming colors than their peers, even when controlling for phonological skills and vocabulary (Tannock, Martinussen, & Frijters, 2000)
	Early hyperactivity ratings were *not* associated with later reading difficulties (Velting & Whitehurst, 1997)
	Attention ratings and IQ scores had the strongest associations with reading (Rabiner & Coie, 2000)

NONVERBAL SKILLS

Do these children have problems in mathematics? Arithmetic achievement also decreases over time from 8 to 16 years for youth with ADHD (for a review, see Ackerman, Anhalt, Dykman, et al., 1986). More specifically, about a quarter of students with math disabilities (or dyscalculia) also have ADHD, and these rates of math disabilities are higher in students with ADHD-I than in students with only ADHD (Lindsay, et al., 1999). The inattention that characterizes the combined subtype, the inattentive subtype, and students with learning disabilities appears to be predictive of math calculation difficulties (Marshall, Schafer, O'Donnell, Elliott, & Handwerk, 1999, Marshall et al., 1997).

Computations

Performing computations requires initial learning about quantities of objects and their correspondence with number symbols. It then requires sustaining attention in order to memorize facts and sequences of steps while monitoring or going back over answers. Because students with ADHD fail to maintain attention (i.e., practice), they may fail to overlearn basic skills, and they are more likely to make careless errors than their peers (Zentall, 1990).

Math computational performance is an area in which students with ADHD show significant problems (Zentall, 1990; Zentall & Ferkis, 1993; Zentall & Smith, 1993; Zentall, Smith, Lee, & Wieczorek, 1994). Fewer correct facts were calculated and fewer problems attempted by youth with ADHD (with and without aggression) than their peers, even when they were provided with self-paced problems and computer feedback (accuracy and time) and their performance scores were adjusted for IQ and their slower typing speed (Zentall, 1990; Zentall & Smith, 1992).

The speed of math performance may be the best indicator of the severity of attentional problems, especially at older ages when accuracy no longer separates groups (e.g., Cherkes-Julkowski & Stolzenberg, 1991). The slow speed of math computations has been observed for children with ADHD from second grade through middle school and characterized students with ADHD plus aggression even more than students with pure ADHD (MacLeod & Prior, 1996; Zentall & Ferkis, 1993; Zentall et al., 1994). Ackerman, Anhalt, Dykman et al. (1986) further reported that only computational speed (but not naming or writing speed) had *not* become automatized for children with reading disabilities and attention-deficit disorder (with and without hyperactivity) relative to controls matched on age and with IQ controlled. Overall, a continuum of difficulty seems to exist, with the learning disability and ADHD plus aggression groups demonstrating the most severe problems specifically with timed addition facts, followed by pure ADHD groups and then normal comparisons. (For subtraction and multiplication retrieval times, learning disability and ADHD groups performed equivalently.)

Problem solving

Children's word-problem performance is related to accuracy and speed in computing number facts, reading, and the ability to retrieve math strategies. We have found that middle school children who compute answers faster and have better reading skills can solve math problems better than their peers (Zentall, 1990). Memory skills appeared to be the least predictive of problem solving (Kail & Hall, 1999). However, working memory may be a contributing factor. That is, even when reading comprehension and IQ were controlled, students with ADHD still had more difficulty than their peers with word problems requiring mixed actions, mixed operations, and a mixed order of operations (Zentall, 1990), probably because of the greater attentional requirements of reordering information (working memory). An example of mixed operations is as follows: "Julie sold six pencils in the morning. Ann sold two in the afternoon. How many more must they sell before they've sold 10 altogether?" Mixed-problem actions with an action (verb) and a comparison of quantities (e.g., "Carol had eight apples. She gave two apples to Sally. How many more apples did Carol have than Sally?"). Similarly, for students with learning disabilities plus math problems, performance of multistep problems was the single strongest predictor of math achievement (Bryant, Bryant, & Hammill, 2000).

In summary, from the statistical and design controls used, we have concluded that differences in cognitive ability (including working memory) and reading contribute to difficulties with (a) sorting out extraneous information, (b) multiple steps or operations, and (c) a mixed order of verbal information within problems (Zentall & Ferkis, 1993). Thus, when mixed order was no longer a factor (in single-action problems with a single operation), only nonverbal problems with specific mathematical concepts were documented.

EVIDENCE-BASED PRACTICES
ORDER OF INFORMATION AND MATH

Study Purpose. It was hypothesized that children with attention disorders would have greater difficulty than comparisons with the unknown variable in the beginning or middle of the problem because it would require holding the question in working memory while processing the problem data.

Participants. Seventh- through eighth-grade ADHD versus comparison youth.

Word Problems. Using computer control of problem text and structure, it was possible to create three types of problems for each operation that differed only in the placement of the unknown within the problem. That is, we used problems with the unknown in the first position ($? + a = b$), the second position ($a + ? = b$), and the familiar third position ($a + b = ?$). This altered the order of information, with no change in the information or basic vocabulary.

Findings. Problems that required holding the question in working memory and reorganizing the relational sentence produced group differences. However, when reading vocabulary (IQ and reading comprehension) was statistically controlled, most group differences were eliminated. Thus, group differences on problems that involved transforming the order of verbal information were associated with memory requirements of holding information in mind while reordering that information.

Remaining "true" group differences were found in word problems that did not require changing the order of information and specifically in multiplication word problems. This was not attributed to the difficulty of the calculation because children with ADHD performed worse than did comparisons on an assessment of calculation speed and accuracy for all three operations. Because the concepts of distance, money, and sets (objects per container) were present in the multiplication problems, comprehension problems may be attributed to difficulty with these specific mathematical nonverbal concepts.

Implications. Children with ADHD have memory difficulties holding problem information in mind while they must reorganize problem information. (This was presented in the section "Memory" earlier in this chapter.) When reordering information is not involved, differences between students with ADHD and their peers can be seen in specific nonverbal concepts of distance, money, and sets (Zentall et al., 1994).

Similarly, youth with mental disabilities compared to mental-age controls have specific difficulties with the nonverbal concepts of time and money, and students with math learning disabilities compared to equivalent-IQ peers have difficulties with conservation concepts (for a review, see Zentall, & Ferkis, 1993).

Handwriting

The typically illegible handwriting of students with ADHD appears to be the result visual-motor deficits. Students with both subtypes of ADHD have poorer motor control, as young as preschool (Mariani & Barkley, 1997) and slower visual-motor and fine motor speed than their peers (Barkley, Grodzinsky, & DuPaul, 1992; Plomin & Foch, 1981; Zentall & Smith, 1993). In other words, poor motor ability would explain slower performance on many classroom tasks (Piek et al., 2004). Their movements are also less complex than the movement patterns of comparisons (Teicher, Ito, Glod, & Barber, 1996) and less coordinated or organized when performing motor sequences (Carte, Nigg, & Hinshaw, 1996).

Students with ADHD were also less accurate and slower in simple overlearned movements, such as typing (Zentall & Smith, 1993) and tapping (for a review, see Sergeant & Scholten, 1985; but see Leung & Connolly, 1998, for failure to find differences). When visual-motor differences were statistically removed from these analyses, group differences in handwriting errors were no longer found (Zentall & Kruczek, 1988). In addition to the contribution of visual-motor skills to handwriting difficulties is that of sustained inattention or fatigue. That is, when we matched students with ADHD to their peers on initial handwriting scores, they still made more handwriting errors—but only after adaptation/practice (Zentall & Kruczek, 1988). In terms of how handwriting affects classroom functioning, children with ADHD will be slower, work harder, and tire more easily when asked to complete fine motor tasks, such as handwriting or taking classroom notes (Zentall, Falkenberg, & Smith, 1985). Looking back over his experiences, an adult with ADHD said, "I have a very long handwriting career."

Furthermore, children with ADHD-C performed less well than comparisons on gross and fine motor tests (Tseng, Henderson, Chow, & Yao, 2004). Differences obtained appeared to be dependent on those subtests with sustained attention and impulse control requirements. Comparisons of boys and girls with ADHD indicated that boys had somewhat greater underachievement in handwriting than girls, and children with ADHD-H performed worse than ADHD-I on both large motor and fine coordinated movements, including handwriting (for a review, see Lahey & Carlson, 1991). Young children who have ADHD and are gifted may have even more difficulty with handwriting tasks since their ideas come faster than they can express them in writing (Zentall et al., 2001). However, handwriting difficulties for students with giftedness and ADHD may be less of a problem at older age levels and with higher IQ scores, at least as stated by this parent:

FAMILY PRACTICES
ADHD AND THE HIGHLY GIFTED

My [12-year-old] son fits some of the gifted/ADHD group characteristics (losing interest, failing to edit, disorganization, impulsivity, excessive talking, jumping from topic to topic, not paying attention to verbal instructions, loves the computer and science, is very creative, does *not* respond well when privileges are taken away), but not others; [he has] good handwriting, [is a] fast reader, easily writes excellent outlines, does NOT like to work on academic projects in groups. My question relates to the level of IQ, and how this may impact your results [Zentall, Moon et al., 2001]. He tested at IQ 157 and maxed out on 7 of the subtests, while your research had an average IQ in the gifted group of 135 (personal communication from a parent, 2003).

ACADEMIC SELF-CONCEPT

How do these students evaluate their own abilities?

Believing in one's own abilities indicates a high academic self-concept. Self-acceptance appears to be important as a protection against delinquency. That is, children who evaluate their own academic performance as deficient may engage in antisocial behavior to bolster their self-image (Pisecco et al., 2001).

Given the number of coexisting learning disabilities, as well as the specific academic problems of the majority of students with ADHD (e.g., in math, handwriting, spelling), it seems probable that they would have lowered academic self-concept. In particular, math performance is used as a basis for self-judging intellectual ability (Stipek & MacIver, 1989).

Academic self-concept determines how children explain their failure to themselves and is one of the best predictors of children's performance with new tasks and experiences (Dweck, 1986; Licht & Kistner, 1986). When children see themselves as less intelligent and attribute their failures to unalterable factors, such as "being stupid," they have lower expectations for future success and respond to failure with decreased effort (Licht & Dweck, 1984). Evidence suggests that students with ADHD respond to failure with less effort and persistence (Milich, 1994; Milich & Okazaki, 1991). In this work, students with ADHD solved fewer puzzles, gave up more often, performed faster on the second puzzle, and reported more frustration even when no group differences existed in age or IQ.

These responses to failure can be different from what these children initially describe as their expectations. That is, students with ADHD were more optimistic about future puzzle performance and overestimated the amount that teachers liked them, whereas comparison boys were more accurate in their self-appraisals (Ohan & Johnston, 2002). Some of these initial optimistic responses appeared to avoid the social appearance of incompetence because when students with ADHD received positive feedback about how much teachers liked them, they dropped their initial inflated estimates of their own likablility (Ohan & Johnston, 2002). In other words, when they no longer needed to protect their social image of competence, they drop their inflated sense of self.

In the social realm and when asked to predict social outcomes for a main character (someone else), children with ADHD predicted fewer positive outcomes than their peers about what would happen "next week" in stories with unclear outcomes (Zentall, Javorsky et al., 2001). These biased outcome expectations were probably based on prior social experiences. For example, children with hyperactivity have repeated failure in their social lives and more negative events that they perceived as stable and global across settings (Hoza, Pelham, Milich, Pillow, & McBride, 1993; Vitaro, Tremblay, Gagnon, & Pelletier, 1994; Weiss & Hechtman, 1993). A history of unsuccessful experiences appears to make these children overly sensitive to failure and may increase the intensity of their emotional responses to negative feedback (i.e., they overreact).

When children with ADHD suffer both academic and social impairment, their self-esteem can be particularly low. For example, children with learning disabilities and with ADHD plus learning disabilities had lower academic and general self-concept scores than typically achieving comparisons (Tabassam & Grainger, 2002; for a review, see Bussing, 2000). In addition, students with ADHD plus learning disabilities reported a lower self-concept in peer relations than students with learning disabilities alone and a lower self-concept than their typical peers (Tabassam & Grainger, 2002).

These effects are often compounded for teenagers with ADHD. For example, medicated and nonmedicated teens described themselves by what they were not (e.g., friendly, smart) rather than by what they were (Waddell, 1984). Their self-esteem was lower, they had little self-confidence, and their relationships with peers, siblings, and adults were negative and unsatisfactory, contributing to less willingness to face new interpersonal demands (for a review, see Waddell, 1984).

SUCCESSFUL ADAPTATIONS

These probable outcomes for teens with ADHD highlight the importance of providing accommodations for their learning problems or co-occurring disabilities and of encouraging them to compensate with their strengths. In fact, even expectations of competence help these children. That is, when students with ADHD were asked to imagine that they were clever, these increased expectations allowed them to perform optimally (Hartley, 1986).

Students with pure ADHD do have strengths indicated by their preferences and interests (e.g., for sports, building things) as well as in their creative activities (e.g., drawing, using one's imagination, visual/spatial talent, using computers).

Children with giftedness and ADHD are similar to children with pure ADHD in their engagement with sports and social activities. However, they may be better able to develop compensation strategies because of their preferences for additional cognitive and language stimulation (e.g., telling stories, dramatics or imaginative role playing, playing secret service agents) and creative avenues (e.g., creating games, assembling ideas or objects in novel ways, humor and social intelligence, costume design and visual art talent, drawing, building, carving, making paper sculptures). Flint (2001) described a study of 70 gifted children and reported that almost all the students with co-occurring hyperactivity demonstrated creativity. Differences

FAMILY PRACTICES
A DAYDREAMER WITH A BIG IMAGINATION

I am a mother of four children. My second child, Damon, age 7, has been diagnosed as attention-deficit disorder. He does have a limited memory and is a daydreamer; however, he also reads on a sixth-grade level and has a very big imagination. (unpublished data from Zentall, Moon et al., 2001).

between gifted students with and without ADHD were in their ability to organize and finish their creative products/ideas and projects.

When educators do not recognize the strengths and talents of these children, they may provide insufficient challenge or interest, as summarized by this father:

FAMILY PRACTICES
SECOND GRADE WAS A DISASTER!

Second grade was a disaster! The teacher was not very flexible at all. She decided that if he could not do the work that was very easy, that he would never be able to do the work that was hard. Now that was her philosophy and he got nowhere, so we switched schools after that (cited in Zentall, Moon, 2001, p. 509).

FAMILY PRACTICES
ARE LABELS USEFUL?
A PRESCHOOLER: GIFTED, ADHD, OR NEITHER?

Jason crawled at four months, spoke at ten months, and read at four years . . . . He has shown the signs of hyperactivity associated with ADHD all of his life. He was a kicking squirming infant, a five-month old baby who would crawl laps up and down a hallway as though he were in training for a marathon, and a tireless toddler.

Reaching school age, Jason had difficulty making friends as his disruptive behavior was too much to tolerate. At home, excessive noise levels, dented walls, sibling conflict, and difficulty settling down to sleep, are the results of hyperactivity.

Academically, he has always been at least two years ahead of his peers, yet emotionally he seems very immature. Jason's teachers have not recognized the possibility that he may be gifted. The child that they see on a daily basis does not present himself as particularly gifted or talented. He is defiant, angry, restless, impulsive, aggressive, and often rude.

When Jason is stimulated by a subject, he can focus endless amounts of energy toward it; however, he has trouble focusing on his homework.

Though Jason displayed many of the characteristics of ADHD, his kindergarten teacher told his concerned parents that it was not possible because Jason was too smart. As he continued through the grades, teachers focused on behavioral problems rather than his advanced academic achievement. In fact, on his grade 1 report card, his teacher failed to mention that he was reading at grade 4 level. They never suggested testing for ADHD because they could see that he was able to focus when he so chose.

Jason, at age eight, is a gifted child with attention deficit hyperactivity disorder. Now, even though Jason is an energetic third grader who is bright, funny, creative, and talented, he has lost interest in school due to the frustration of unchallenging activities and peer rejection. His self-esteem is low and he is performing at grade level, though group achievement tests have placed him significantly above average. Now Jason's teachers see no reason to consider giftedness or ADHD; they just look at him as a difficult child with an attitude problem.

Jason not only became disruptive, he became oppositional, when frustrated by the tasks that he perceived as dull and restrictive. He simply refused to do these tasks and instead found it more challenging to disrupt those who were attempting the task and engage in a power struggle with his teacher (Leroux & Levitt-Perlman, 2000, pp. 171–172).

However, adult expectations can sometimes be too high for children with ADHD and giftedness (i.e., failing to take into account the influence of ADHD as a disability). Because it was clear that these children had abilities (i.e., they were identified as gifted), they were more likely to be seen as willfully choosing not to organize or complete their academic tasks. In other words, many adults are unable to see children as both ADHD and gifted. Co-occurring giftedness and ADHD may not be identified because professionals believe that low IQ and difficulty with "effortful" tasks are important criteria in the identification of ADHD. For students who are gifted, however, fewer tasks require effort. ADHD is not an inability to sustain attention to all tasks; rather, it is the inability to sustain attention to repetitive (nonstimulating), nonmeaningful, and nonactive tasks. The failure to identify these children can have a number of long-term consequences. See "Family Practices" example on page 147.

SUMMARY

In response to the initial question about whether ADHD is a learning disorder, the answer is both yes and no. Beginning with the "no," ADHD is not a learning disability, although high rates of co-occurring learning disabilities exist. In fact, many children, especially those with ADHD-H, have no learning problems and may achieve higher than would be predicted (e.g., in reading). Furthermore, even when learning problems exist, many children with ADHD can compensate; if co-occurring giftedness is present, they may excel with specific interests or in specific academic areas.

The answer is also "yes" in that the majority of students with ADHD do have academic problems, for example, in mathematics, especially for the subtypes ADHD-I and ADHD-C. In addition, problems may exist in handwriting, reading comprehension, spelling, math computations, and nonverbal math concepts (distance, money, and sets) even when assessment has controlled for possible differences in IQ or the academic area assessed is unrelated to IQ (e.g., spelling, math facts, handwriting). Furthermore, an overlap between reading and math disabilities is explained by working-attention or working–memory deficits. For example, both reading and math require phonological awareness and working memory to manipulate and store letters, math steps, and simple math answers (Hecht, Torgesen, Wagner, & Rashotte, 2000). That is, students with ADHD have difficulty holding and manipulating information in mind (working memory) and specifically with memory-updating skills. These types of skills are proficient in children who can solve math problems, recall text information, and perform computations (Passolunghi & Pazzagliab, 2004).

However, the learning problems observed in the early grades are not due to differences in IQ, at least in school-based samples, even though clinic-referred children do appear to be lower functioning. Poorer fine motor skills do contribute to handwriting difficulties, and inattention contributes to language and academic problems. That is, embedded information requiring selective attention and the recall of information interrupted with delay, added information, or added organizational requirements (sustained attention and working memory) contribute to difficulties with (a) listening tasks with greater length, detail, or description;

(b) speaking and written composition when logical, organized, and extended verbal or written responses are required; and (c) word problems requiring mixed actions, mixed operations, and a mixed order of operations.

Finally, their difficulty sustaining attention and holding information in mind leads to difficulty practicing (and thus failure to overlearn math calculations) and to difficulty completing long and uninteresting reading text. (See cartoon above.)

These academic outcomes for students with ADHD are in addition to the problems experienced by children with co-occurring learning disabilities.

DISCUSSION AND APPLICATION QUESTIONS

1. How would you explain to a parent why her child has started five different books but completed none? How would you help this student finish reading some of the books that she started?
2. How would you explain to the mother of the child described in the box "ADHD and the Highly Gifted" why her son differs from many children with ADHD in terms of easily writing outlines, fast reading, not liking group projects, and good handwriting?
3. The following "Family Practices" box is about Andy, a 9-year old who is having difficulty in school.

FAMILY PRACTICES
GRANDMOTHER'S WORRY AND PARENTS' OBSERVATIONS

Andy's Grandmother's Observations

My 9-year-old grandson needs testing by someone who can give us information about his challenges in education and what to do to help him.

He has been in the XYZ School System special education system. This past school year we enrolled him in a private school that worked one on one with him. He does extremely well in math except when he has to read word problems; then he is at a dead end. If someone reads to him he can do the word math problems.

Andy's Parents' Observations

As far as I can tell, he is not organized in any area of his life. His bedroom is a shambles; he cannot remember to brush his teeth unless he is reminded constantly. He brings home his entire backpack, which I have trouble lifting because it is so heavy, so he doesn't forget something at school.

I should give you some background. Andy is an only child.

He is considered a prince in our home. As much as I find his disorganization frustrating, we find him to be a great joy. He is very creative and independent. He doesn't hold a grudge and rebounds quickly. Spending an unstructured day with my son is something I enjoy immensely.

But recently developments at school have led me to believe that I must take a much more active role in helping his teachers understand how best to get good results from my son. The talents my husband and I admire in our son are not being appreciated as much by his teachers. They are very frustrated by his disorganization, lack of focus, and distractibility. He often appears not to be listening and has trouble understanding the instructions his teachers give. He also doesn't want to be the only kid who raises his hand because he doesn't understand. So he leaves the classroom without knowing what he should be doing.

I think they think he isn't trying. He procrastinates and has difficulty finishing projects. His handwriting is very poor. He also has a friend at school with similar problems. When they are in the same vicinity, they do not seem capable of staying focused on any work. I have asked that he be separated from this child. They have tried to accommodate this, but it has not always been possible. The relationship with this child is not beneficial to my son or to the other child, but he is very loyal. Other children do not want to do academic work with him because they see him as a goof-off. They have said that Andy needs remedial help in English. I found out that Andy was doing his World War I warfare project alone. I asked him why, and he said because no one else wanted to work with him. He said one group reluctantly said he could join their group. He told me he wasn't a "pity case" and said he wanted to do it by himself. I helped him, and he was up until 11:30. Andy told me that he thought it went "awesome" and that one of the children who didn't want him in his group said he did a great job. But the teacher didn't say anything. As a manager it seems kind of basic to give positive feedback to someone who rises to the occasion, especially someone who has difficulty doing so and obviously exerted extra effort. I could go on, but I think you get the idea.

Questions about Andy:

a. What are Andy's school-related problems?
b. What learning disabilities may Andy have?
c. Why do his teachers think that he isn't trying?
d. What abilities does Andy appear to have?
e. What kinds of situations does he do well in?
f. What interests does he have and how would you motivate him?
g. What do you think about his mother's wish to keep him apart from his friend at school?

PART *Three*

Methods

CHAPTER 8

Strategies to Reduce Activity/Impulsivity: Change the Setting

OBJECTIVE

- Recognize that changes of instructional methods, tasks, and settings can be used to reduce the disruptive impulsive and hyperactive behavior of students with ADHD-H.

KEY TERMS

ecological model
positive and negative enabling
universal design for learning
do-rules versus don't rules
setting stimulation
honeymoon effect
cooperative groups
reverse-role peer tutoring
peer interdependence
individual accountability
prompt card

This chapter addresses the effectiveness of changes that can be made to the task and environment to *prevent* inappropriate behavior or to redirect it. "Environmental and task modifications, although less well studied, undoubtedly are critical for these youngsters' success" (Abramowitz & O'Leary, 1991, p. 230). These techniques are less well studied than behavioral consequences (see chapter 9) even though educators (a) rank these antecedent interventions higher (Reid, Vasa, Mang, & Wright, 1994) and (b) are more likely to make accommodations with available task and setting resources in their classrooms (Johnson & Pugach, 1990; Safran, 1982; Whinnery, Fuchs, & Fuchs, 1991).

In addition, changes of task and context meet criteria for effective interventions as listed by Whalen and Henker (1991). These criteria have (a) broad *applicability* across academic domains; (b) *adaptability* to specific children and to groups; (c) ease of *teachability* and *acceptability* to educators (and parents), that is, how easy are strategies learned and how closely do these strategies fit with educators' goals, values, and training; (d) *availability* and *controllability* of the strategies within the school context; (e) *durability* within the school environment; and (f) *constrainability, visibility,* and *feasibility,* or the lack of side effects and the decreased likelihood of stigmatizing the child or causing psychological or economic burden. Antecedent strategies pass all but one criterion, which could explain why they are considered "easier" to implement and ultimately more effective than changes in the consequences that follow behavior (Martens & Kelly, 1993).

The one criterion not met is *generalization.* However, antecedent strategies are context dependent. In other words, social or academic improvement is the result of a change in context or task and would not be

FIGURE 8.1

Setting, Instructional Context, and Task Changes

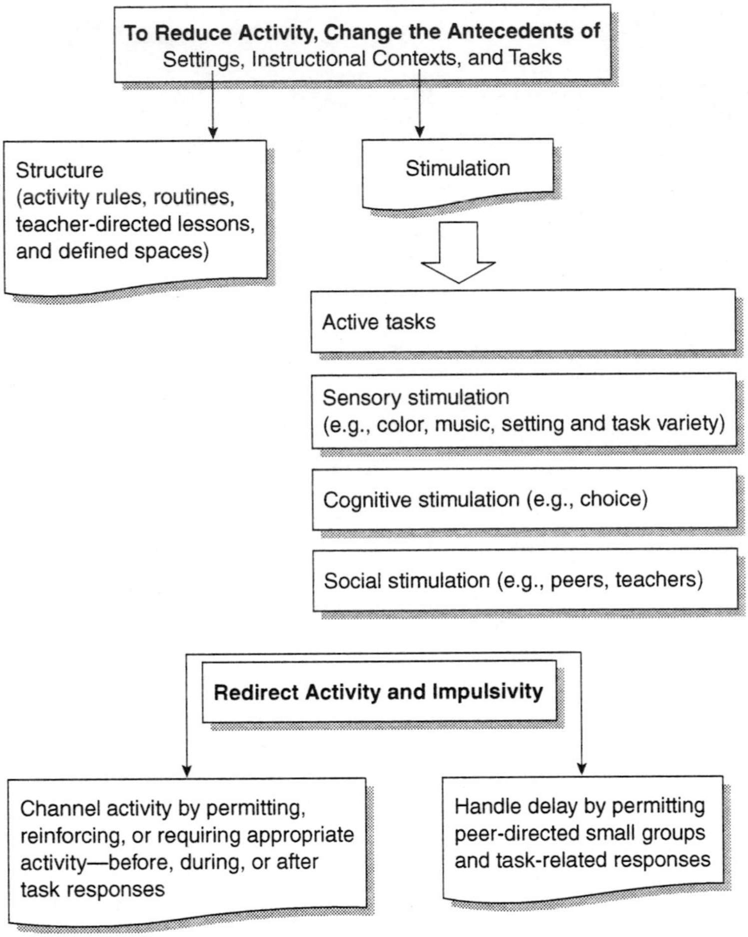

expected to occur in the absence of that change, even though secondary gains could come from successful social interactions or academic improvements.

Even though we can conclude that educators could select these accommodations that are perceived to be within their control and training (see Figure 8.1), we need to consider the controversy over whether they should make changes for children with ADHD.

DO ACCOMMODATIONS BRING OUT ISSUES OF FAIRNESS AND "ENABLE" CHILDREN?

An underlying assumption of the American educational system is "equal education for all." "Equal" is defined not as "the same" but as "opportunities." Educators are more likely to provide equal opportunities when they have accepted the notion of reduced ability, but not if they believe that level of performance is within the child's control. Problems can occur when adults observe that these students are able to perform or behave appropriately under some conditions, which makes nonperformance appear willful, lazy, or lacking in motivation.

No tests can determine how much responsibility a student can be assigned in any setting. The only way teachers can assess whether a child can do something (at least for a short time) is to raise incentives to really make it worthwhile. If the stakes are high enough and the models are appropriate, many children with ADHD will be able to do what they know.

However, even when children recognize what should be done in a particular setting, their ability to apply what they know lags behind. Furthermore, the overemotionality and impulsivity of students with ADHD can interfere with their judgment and behavioral restraint, especially in boring, activity-restricting, peer-conflict, or high-demand academic situations.

We expect a lot from students with ADHD because they can exert great effort for limited periods of time and because they can and do try hard, especially in the beginning of tasks, the day, and the semester (i.e., unless they have a history of failure). However, the costs of this effort may be great. The energy they expend on self-regulation so that they do not look different from their peers may lead to a lack of energy for dealing effectively with their tasks and relationships.

Educators may accept the notion of reduced ability but still resist identifying children because educators feel it could "enable" them. Enabling connotes that we are coddling children and allowing them to make excuses for their behavior. To address this question, it is important to differentiate an excuse from an explanation. We must ask, "Is the student willing to do the task if the conditions were altered?" A difference exists between "I cannot do it" and "I cannot do it under these conditions." Even though children may not understand or know how to tell us optimal conditions for themselves, accommodations are not intended to help them escape from their responsibilities.

The question of responsibility becomes even more acute at the secondary level. At this age, more freedom is available, and students begin to look like adults as they attempt to take on some of the benefits of adulthood. Our society *does* recognize that adolescents have limited capacities because of their age and are granted accommodations. For example, we have created a special justice system for juveniles, and we impose age-related restrictions on alcohol, driving, and voting. Thus, both privileges and consequences are altered for adolescents.

In contrast to the negative connotations of the word "enabling" is its true and positive meaning: "to make able." Accommodations serve an important function in making children able. In addition, accommodations with incentives for small successes provide the bridge that leads to greater independence. Thus, in the true meaning of the word, enabling allows the child to perform at levels equivalent to peers.

Enabling, in the problematic sense, supports negative expectations (i.e., to disable). This occurs only when expectations are lowered (i.e., the destination itself rather than the path to that destination is changed). For example, O'Conner and

Jenkins (1993) reported that when assignments for special education students were the same as those for other group members, more sustained effort and better work quality were observed for these students. Reduced expectations can be a side effect of providing excessive structure or reduced opportunities for independent thinking. Structure may be important initially but it must be faded over time (e.g., from an adult to a peer, or a checklist, or through an electronic device).

Disabling can also occur in the misapplication of information. For example, Barkley (1998b) concluded that students with ADHD were maturationally about 30% behind their peers academically and socially. Such an overall statistic can mislead educators for a number of reasons. First, it cannot apply to most children with ADHD or even to most tasks and situations. For example, statements such as sending an 18-year-old student with ADHD to college is like sending a 12-year-old to college clearly can be misleading. Too many conditions can be used to optimize their performance. Thus, reducing expectations for students across settings based on a 30% statistic is to disable students with ADHD.

ARE ACCOMMODATIONS FAIR TO THE MAJORITY?

Students *without* disabilities need to develop skills and strategies for dealing with differences, conflict, and distractions in their classrooms. They also need to make some changes, for they will encounter conflict and potentially distracting environments throughout their lives (e.g., in study halls, college dorms, the workplace). Focusing only on changing children with disabilities leads to inflexibility on the part of their peers, not to mention the equity issue.

Another concern among educators is the amount of time dedicated to the few at the expense of the many. However, the techniques presented here are also beneficial for average students; it is just that these techniques are essential for children with ADHD.

In the near future, more comprehensive change will be implemented, such as the "Universal Design for Learning" (Hitchcock, Meyer, Rose, & Jackson, 2002), which proposes that the environment be constructed to provide optimal "access," "participation," and "progress" for all children. Principles of this design are built into the architecture and a flexible curriculum to provide optimal learning environments for all children. This is becoming increasingly important because the percentage of children with disabilities who are educated in general education classes increased from about a third in 1988–99 to over a half of these students in 2002 (U.S. Department of Education, 1991; 2002).

When a comprehensive approach to classroom management is designed, it will be unnecessary to patch adaptations for a variety of individual differences into an ongoing curriculum. To design these total management approaches, however, we must first understand variables that are important for optimal functioning of different exceptionalities. These are addressed for students with ADHD in the following section.

CLASSROOM ACCOMMODATIONS

Much can be gained from altering the learning context. This is particularly important because children spend 6 to 7 hours per day for at least 13 years in classrooms. In addition, teachers understand their job as affecting learning through the management of tasks, instruction, and learning contexts.

Modify the classroom environment to reduce the negative impact of this disability
Although youth with ADHD exhibit more activity than classmates in most types of settings, their level of activity does change. Similar to their classmates, students with ADHD can reduce their activity for limited periods of time often until recess or until they arrive home (Madan-Swain & Zentall, 1990). Even though many can comply with setting requirements, it is *difficult* for them to do so, and it may focus their behavior on inhibition rather than on learning.

It is equally difficult for teachers to manage their behavior. In fact, teachers of elementary students with ADHD describe managing the quantity of their students' activity as one of their most difficult tasks (Safran & Safran, 1985). See the cartoon below. Perhaps part of the reason for this difficulty is that teachers expect that they must reduce activity rather than redirect it. Strategies to redirect activity include structuring classroom spaces and children's active responses.

"I had a great time today, Ms. Max; how about you?"

Modify the structure in the classroom without making it restrictive or repetitive

Setting structure Structure can guide physical responding with "what to do" and thereby reduce physical off-task behavior equally for students with and without ADHD (Madan-Swain & Zentall, 1990; Zentall & Leib, 1985). Note that behavioral guidance is more appropriate for children with ADHD-H than for those with ADHD-I because of the former's excessive activity. However, "structure" should not be mistaken for "a very placid classroom, with traditional seating arrangements in neat rows of desks, students' heads bowed quietly over worksheets, one student at a time raising his or her hand to respond to the teacher's questions, and so forth. In fact these types of classrooms and teaching styles are often the worst environments for students with AD/HD" (Rief, 1998, p. 24).

Activity rules Rules can be used to provide guidance for children's active responses. There are "do rules" and "don't rules." "Don't rules" can be helpful in reducing aggression. See "Note" example below.

NOTE
DON'T STEP ON THE CATERPILLARS

Teaching a child *not* to step on a caterpillar is as important for the child as it is for the caterpillar (Richard O'Barry, founder of the "Dolphin Project").

More importantly and more often neglected are "do rules." The following are some best practices for establishing "do rules":

TEACHING STRATEGIES
TAKING RESPONSIBILITY IN SMALL STEPS

1. **Do** stay on topic when talking or entering a group.
2. **Do** set deadlines earlier than the due date to create urgency. Reward yourself with prizes for early drafts.
3. **Do** ask questions when you don't know what to do or when you want to know if you can change something.
4. **Do** plan ahead for wait time (e.g., have other activities on hand).
5. **Do** decide what part of the problem you are willing to accept responsibility for and what part you are not.
6. **Do** stick to the facts—what happened without blame and how am I going to fix it without excuses.

Setting routines A related approach is to teach routines. Routines develop into habits, and habits need few external prompts. However, it is difficult for students with ADHD to maintain routines long enough for them to become habits because routines involve repetition. That is, repetition decreases the amount of stimulation available, resulting in increased activity specifically for students with ADHD (Shroyer & Zentall, 1986). Thus, educators need to incorporate fun, choice, color, or humor into performing routines. In addition, teach motor rather than verbal routines because these are easier for students with ADHD to maintain (Zentall, 1989b).

TEACHING STRATEGIES
Lights and Horns and Other Best Practices for Routines

1. Cue children about upcoming changes in routines. Some students with ADHD also have difficulty responding to changes that others make in routines.
2. Encourage the family to establish routines for the placement of objects and to use time schedules.
3. Cue a routine with novelty because many students with ADHD will resist doing things in the same way, so small changes may need to be introduced, as in the following example:

Place homework in brightly colored boxes with a flashing bicycle light or bicycle horn to facilitate turning in homework each morning. Children could be responsible for changing the box decoration each month. Once the behavior has been cued with novelty, it may or may not need to be rewarded. The teacher may also need to turn the activity into a game or challenge the class to try to achieve a 90% return rate and keep data on the board regarding the percentage of children who turn in 80% of completed homework each day.

Teacher-directed lessons Structure is also provided in the way adults instruct students. Teacher-directed lessons (e.g., brief lectures), in contrast to student-directed lessons, produce less social behavior (prosocial and aggression), out-of-seat behavior, noise, and vocalizations for all children (Huston-Stein, Friedrich-Cofer, & Susman, 1977; Zentall, 1980). Furthermore, students with learning disabilities have been found to be three times more engaged in their lessons during teacher-directed instruction than during seat work (Friedman, Cancelli, & Yoshida, 1988). (This could be explained by a lack of skills or confidence in how to proceed independently for students with learning disabilities.) In sum, teacher direction appears to decrease the amount of social behavior and increase attention to and conformity with adult expectations. These conditions would be important when giving directions or brief periods of high-quality instruction. Thus, teacher direction should be provided at the beginning of a lesson, especially when presenting new information. Student-directed activities, such as cooperative groups, would be more important during later time periods (as discussed later in this chapter).

Defined classroom spaces Students with ADHD learn better when they can move and respond actively during and between tasks (Zentall, 1995). In particular, they need access to teachers, resources, and interesting environments and tasks. Opportunities for appropriate movement are available when the environment is divided into different purposeful spaces, as indicated by the following evidenced-based strategies:

EVIDENCE-BASED PRACTICES
SPACES AND PLACES

1. Provide spaces that are well defined. Wohlwill and Heft (1987) reported that day care centers with more spatial definition and access to those spaces have children who engage in more exploratory activity, interaction, and cooperation than in less well-defined settings. Rosenfield and Black (1985) reported that boundaries around work and study areas reduced off-task talking and looking around. Some teachers use masking tape on the floor. Break up the classroom space with areas dedicated to (a) exploration/new learning, (b) practice, and (c) quiet reflection/reading.
2. Provide learning centers with interesting and educational projects and themes (e.g., pioneers, space travel, computer advancements [Zentall, Moon et al., 2001]). Centers increased on-task behavior as long as resources were not restricted (Zentall, 1995).
3. Travel during brief seat-work activities to provide feedback to students and to monitor their comprehension of the preceding lesson (Stevenson, 1992).
4. Arrange desks in a circle during discussions and presentations to produce more verbal participation than desks in rows (for a review, see Zentall, 1995). Students may need to be provided with things to do with their hands in these contexts.
5. Arrange desks in cluster arrangements to produce more on-task behavior and hand raising than is possible in rows (for a review, see Zentall, 1995).

Additional suggestions are to structure and arrange furniture to make it easy to travel and monitor student progress (for a review, see Zentall, 1995). Some classrooms are too small to provide "traveling" paths, and the space often has permanent fixtures. Under these conditions, teachers can use the wall space to define areas. Students with ADHD need seating that allows them to have (a) proximity or visibility of the teacher, (b) access to other students for peer instruction and collaboration, (c) observation of those children who are potential models, and (d) observation of educational resources (e.g., student artwork interesting photos) and of information (e.g., pets in cages, centers for exploration, bulletin boards). (Visual distraction is not a factor in the distal external environment [see chapter 6].)

LIMITATIONS OF SETTING STRUCTURE

Only during teacher-directed lessons (i.e., setting structure) was more negative behavior for students with behavioral problems observed (including students with ADHD) than for their peers (Beyda, Zentall, & Ferko, 2002). These effects appeared to be due to wait time, which occurred more often during teacher-directed lessons than during student-directed lessons.

Finally, even though it is necessary to provide initial setting support in the form of teacher direction, students with ADHD also need opportunities to experiment with, choose, and create their own learning and study environments (e.g., seating arrangements, bulletin boards). Adding an element of choice can be important, for example, in the placement of desks, as reported here:

STUDENT PRACTICES
TABLE ARRANGEMENT CHOICES

My fifth-grade teacher allowed us to get in a group of four to sit together. She would then allow us to structure our desks any way we wanted to. It was a positive experience, because we were eager to sit at our newly constructed area and learn. We changed seating arrangements every two months. I loved it (Kylee Bassett, personal communication, 2002).

Setting stimulation In schools, stimulation (novelty) is provided by the unfamiliarity of a setting, noise, curriculum content, and access to the teacher, peers, resources, and roles. The behavior of children with ADHD can be similar to their classmates (made more normal) when novelty is present (for a review, see Zentall, 1993, 1995). That is, rather than isolating students away from movement and sound, teachers can *use* sound, movement, and interest as a way to capture and focus students' attention on important events and stimuli. The optimal stimulation theory is assessed through research that compares the behavior of children with and without ADHD in natural or experimentally designed stimulating versus nonstimulating environments and during early versus later time periods in the same environment (i.e., when setting novelty has worn off).

Time in setting Children with ADHD have been described as showing a "doctor's office" or "honeymoon" effect. They look "normal" initially in new settings but soon begin to look different from their peers after adapting (e.g., Schweitzer & Sulzer-Azaroff, 1995; Zentall & Zentall, 1976). That is, once adapted to their setting, they respond with sensation-seeking activity and impulsive responses unless accommodations are in place.

Similarly, a clear morning and afternoon effect exists involving more accurate problem solving and the same level of activity as their peers in the morning in contrast to more behavior problems and activity observed in the afternoon (Dane, Schachar, & Tannock, 2000; Zagar & Bowers, 1983). These effects are due to decreased novelty over time, especially for children with ADHD, and possibly to fatigue (but not to medication wearing off).

Setting and task variety Adding stimulation (e.g., color, movement) to the environment or task improves attention (as reported in chapter 10) but also reduces activity. For example, in classrooms with open spaces with visual stimulation (e.g., colors, animals), children with ADHD showed less behavior over time (Koester & Farley, 1982). Similarly, closed spaces with visual stimulation improved behavior, as derived from the optimal stimulation theory and reported here:

EVIDENCE-BASED PRACTICES
LIGHTS, MICE, AND MUSIC

Purpose. To assess the effects of a broad band of visual and auditory stimulation on the level of activity of children with ADHD.

Participants. Sixteen children with ADHD, 7 to 11 years old.

Tasks. A sitting task and a performance task that required them to cancel out letters in alphabetical order.

Design. Repeated measures crossover (2 condition orders × 2 conditions × 2 sessions).

Treatment Conditions. Low-stimulation room with bare walls versus the same room in a high-stimulation condition filled with pictures, flashing colored lights, mice in cages, and 80-decibel acid-rock music.

Findings. An increase in activity occurred from session 1 to session 2, and the students with ADHD were significantly less active in the stimulating room and performed somewhat better.

Implications. Children with ADHD can use stimulation in their surrounding environments to reduce their need to create stimulation through activity. However, noneducational stimulation fails to significantly improve performance (Zentall & Zentall, 1976).

During simple tasks, added color (Zentall & Dwyer, 1988), color plus movement (Lee, & Zentall, 2002; Zentall & Meyer, 1987; Zentall & Zentall, 1976), and added music (see cartoon, next page) (Schweitzer & Sulzer-Azaroff, 1995) produced more of a decrease in behavior (e.g., fidgeting) for students with ADHD than for their classmates. (The improvements in performance from added stimulation to tasks are described in chapters 10 and 11.)

EVIDENCE-BASED PRACTICES
TO REDUCE ACTIVITY AND IMPULSIVITY

Setting Stimulation

1. Provide stimulating walls and bulletin boards, especially for older children, for whom school settings are overly familiar. Older students with ADHD prefer more novelty than do younger students (Zentall & Smith, 1992). Youth with ADHD may more readily look around, especially during boring or difficult tasks (Steinkamp, 1980), but no performance loss on these tasks was observed (see chapter 6).

(Continued on page 164)

Choice stimulation Critical in the instruction of independence and problem solving is providing opportunities for choice. Choice is a type of cognitive stimulation (i.e., "cognitive-energetic" novelty [Sonuga-Barke, 2002]). We found that students with ADHD talked less and were less noisy when given brief choice than in no-choice conditions. Furthermore, unrelated talking increased over time in the no-choice condition only for students with ADHD (Bennett, Zentall, Giorgetti, & French, 2005).

EVIDENCE-BASED PRACTICES (Continued from page 162)

2. Provide music, exercise, and active learning (e.g., art, fine and gross motor activities), especially during or after routine tasks (Charlebois, Normandeau, Vitaro, & Berneche, 1999; Craft, 1983; Walker, 1980; Zentall & Meyer, 1987). Active tasks can improve the performance of students with ADHD and also appeals to their preferences and need for activity.
3. Use novel classroom settings. Less activity, less talk, and fewer disruptions were observed in the novel classroom settings of tests, films, and free time than in routine lecture settings and seat work (Zentall, 1980).
4. Provide active responses during delays. (See example below.)

Can Preschoolers with ADHD Wait for Cookies?

Three preschool-age children with ADHD were able to delay in order to receive a larger preferred reward (e.g., a cookie) if they were promised an additional activity to do during the delay interval (e.g., naming pictures or repeating self-controlling statements) (Binder, Dixon, & Ghezzi, 2000) but not when math problems were available in the delay intervals (Rapport, Tucker, DuPaul, Merlo, & Stoner, 1986).

Task Stimulation

1. Use novel types of games; this can reduce the activity of children with ADHD to the level of their peers (e.g., computer video games [Farrace-Di Zinno et al., 2001]). However, during a repetitive two-dimensional game, the activity of children with ADHD was greater than their peers (Tannock, 1997). That is, even in games, the degree of novelty (nonrepetitiveness) is important.
2. Add color to repetitive attention tasks; this reduced activity for students with ADHD but not for their peers (Zentall, 1986b).

TEACHING STRATEGIES
Reduce Activity by Redirection

1. Provide several seats to move between or to exchange seats with other students. As stated by one teacher, "Seating options work great!"
2. Allow standing, a stand-up desk, sitting on the floor, or moving during seat work, especially at the end of tasks.
3. Provide opportunities to work on the floor.
4. Make activities, such as indoor and outside recess, field trips, running errands, frequent breaks, and computer time, available to all students and not just to students who complete a certain amount of work.

Choice stimulation is particularly useful for children with oppositionality. For example, Powell and Nelson (1997) found that choice of task content (e.g., spelling, silent reading, grammar) reduced the responses of noncompliance, out-of-seat and off-task behavior, disturbing others, and refusing to work of a young student with ADHD. In addition, children with ADHD plus co-occurring behavioral problems decreased their disruptive and task-avoidant behavior when given task choice, and students with behavioral disorders spent more time on a chosen than on an assigned activity (Dunlap et al., 1993, 1994). Choice may be especially important to accuracy for students with externalizing behavior when presented with difficult tasks (DePaepe, Shores, Jack, & Denny, 1996; Gunter, Shores, Denny, Jack, & DePaepe, 1994) and for students with ADHD when they are given repetitive tasks (Bennett et al., 2005). In conclusion, choice is especially important in the treatment of task-avoidant and noncompliant behavior (Center, Deitz, & Kaufman, 1982; Gunter et al., 1994).

Additional gains from choice could be explained by the interest level or optimal difficulty of the assignments that were chosen. Children will select tasks and activities that challenge their capacities slightly (Danner & Lonky, 1981). For example, students with ADHD who could choose their own pace of learning demonstrated better attention and comprehension than students whose pace of learning was externally controlled (Carrol, Bain, & Houghton, 1994).

These gains are in addition to the gains found for students without disabilities who tolerated more failure and improved social relatedness and task productivity and showed greater creativity, imagination, concentration, and persistence with choice relative to no-choice tasks (Amabile & Gitomer, 1984; Dunlap et al., 1994; Huston-Stein et al., 1977). Even the use of teacher suggestions rather than directives has been found to increase students' persistence (Hamilton & Gordon, 1978).

Choice can also involve (a) learning settings, (b) tasks, (c) responses to tasks, (d) goals, (e) methods of evaluation, (f) materials, (g) types of feedback, (h) ways of demonstrating knowledge, and (i) pacing.

Peer stimulation available in groups Peer attention has been shown to be more powerful in altering behavior than teacher attention for boys with ADHD (Northup et al., 1995). Peer stimulation is available in cooperative groups, which are small groups of students working together toward a common goal.

TEACHING STRATEGIES
Cooperative Learning and Best Practices

Teachers see cooperative groups as a best practice for children with special needs and report gains in self-esteem, feelings of safety, and increases in learning, participation, and the number of products produced (Jenkins, Antil, Wayne, & Vadasy, 2003).

In addition, decreased off-task behavior and increased verbal interactions and helping occur between disabled and nondisabled peers, as does the perception of more cooperative, encouraging, and cohesive classrooms than with individualistic methods (Johnson & Johnson, 1986, 1990). Students who work together will use each other as models and reward each other's behavior and values (Cairns & Cairns, 1994; Dishion, Eddy, Haas, & Spracklen, 1997). Cooperative groups appear to create an appropriate peer climate that promotes positive social interactions among all students. In turn, this climate can increase the social acceptance of children with behavioral disabilities (Chang & Mao, 1999; Kennedy, Shukla, & Fryxell, 1997).

The importance of small groups specifically for students with ADHD may be (a) the greater opportunity for active participation, (b) more frequent and immediate feedback, and (c) greater student control over learning pace (DuPaul & Henningson, 1993). Students with ADHD report that they enjoy participating and learning in small groups (Zentall, Moon et al., 2001; Zentall & Smith, 1992; Zentall & Stormont-Spurgin, 1995). Because children with ADHD are motivated to affiliate and learn with others, it is important to increase their successful contribution in these contexts rather than spending time and energy trying to get them to remain quiet and still.

EVIDENCE-BASED PRACTICES
PEER AND GROUP LEARNING FOR STUDENTS WITH ADHD

1. Brainstorming with a peer prior to writing is more effective in increasing on-task behavior than simply writing without a peer (Ervin, DuPaul, Kern, & Friman, 1998).
2. Peer learning is best suited for guided or independent practice activities (e.g., spelling) that follow and supplement regular instruction (Mathes & Fuchs, 1991) by using colorful, exciting review materials and games (Cartledge & Cochran, 1993).
3. Cooperative games can be designed with altered rules (e.g., each group member must complete one circuit of the game board or reach a certain score, or incorrect responses do not result in elimination [Cartledge & Cochran, 1993]).
4. Classwide peer tutoring decreased activity for one second-grade student with ADHD who was paired with an above-average student in math (as well as twice the amount of attention to task and improved academic performance [DuPaul & Henningson, 1993]). Similar improvements were found in later research in math and spelling for more students (including typical children), specifically in academic engagement and reduced fidgety behavior (DuPaul, Ervin, Hook, & McGoey, 1998).
5. Reverse-role peer tutoring involves a less competent student, perhaps in mathematics or social skills, who tutors a more competent student in his or her area of proficiency, such as reading. After 3 months of reverse-role peer tutoring, the social acceptance of the less competent student and the academic performance of students with externalizing behavior were improved (Kohler, Schwartz, Cross, & Fowler, 1989).

EVIDENCE-BASED PRACTICES *(Continued)*

Teaching Group Skills to All Students

Increase the success of cooperative experiences by the following:

1. Teaching skills to all students before group experiences. Skills included listening, asking and answering questions, sharing ideas and information, taking turns, encouraging others, cooperating, and trust building (responsibility taking), using explanations, modeling, guided practice, role playing, teacher feedback, and student assessment (Gillies, 2003; Ibler, 1997). Specifically, for students with ADHD, 8-week social skill training sessions improved parent ratings on assertiveness and cooperation but not on other social skill areas (Antshel & Remer, 2003).
2. Providing bonus points to group members who help others use social skills more consistently (Johnson & Johnson, 1990). Tangible rewards or stickers might be necessary initially, but over time, emphasis should be placed on social reinforcement (Cartledge & Cochran, 1993; Graves, 1991).
3. Teaching students to perform a number of roles (Ibler, 1997) by initially using role models, such as leader, materials person, record keeper, spokesperson, runner, accuracy coach, facilitator (Mainzer, Mainzer, Slavin, & Lowry, 1993), observer (Anderson, Nelson, Fox, & Gruber, 1988), summarizer, checker, elaboration seeker (Johnson & Johnson, 1986), initiator of positive statements, and demonstrator (Cartlege & Cochran, 1993). Some teachers use laminated "role cards" that contain a description of role responsibilities and appropriate phrasing of verbal statements on the back of the card.
4. Reinforcing peer interdependence rather than relying on adults (O'Conner & Jenkins, 1995). For example, when resistance to working with a student with ADHD arises, require the group to remain together until they have worked out a way to successfully meet the goals. This will increase mutual respect and even friendships (Augustine, Gruber, & Hanson, 1990). Teachers may need to stand near the group initially while reinforcing students' attempts at problem solving.
5. Rewarding students' interest, divergent ideas, and unique approaches to problem solving (Cohen, 1994).
6. Keeping groups together for 4 to 6 weeks at the elementary and secondary grades (Edwards & Stout, 1990; Sapon-Shevin, Ayres, & Duncan, 1994).
7. Using tasks with less emphasis on verbal and written abilities and more emphasis on construction, observation, or artistic skills, such as multimedia, drama, experimental and field study activities (Giangreco, 1996; O'Conner & Jenkins, 1995).
8. Using open-ended tasks with multiple correct solutions, especially later after students have developed some initial group skills, because open tasks encourage interactions among all group members (Pomplun, 1997).
9. Emphasizing individual accountability, which is more difficult to achieve in large than in small groups, by the following:
   a. Awarding points to all group members based on the amount of improvement shown by each and then averaging these scores into a group grade (Rosberg, 1995). Students with lower scores usually show the greatest improvement.
   b. Holding everyone responsible for helping others achieve (Schrag, 1993; Udvari-Solner, 1994).
   c. Requiring individual or peer-pair preparatory work before the cooperative group, which could include
      i. listening to a tape,
      ii. highlighting text to be read (O'Conner & Jenkins, 1993),
      iii. previewing the vocabulary or parts of the material to be covered (Johnson & Johnson, 1986), or
      iv. rehearsing presentations that might assist the group in reaching its goal.
   d. Making each person's individual efforts visible.
   e. Telling children that their contributions are important to the groups.

(Continued)

EVIDENCE-BASED PRACTICES *(Continued)*

f. Making an evaluation by group members before assessment by the teacher so that group members can target areas or skills in which they can help each other before final teacher evaluations.

g. Allowing students to temporarily abandon their roles when they run into problems with group processes in order to facilitate problem solving (Ibler, 1997).

Determining Group Composition

Provide complementary roles or role models for the following:

1. Dominating students. Dishon and O'Leary (1984) recommended that other group members be given more powerful roles.
2. Students with ADHD:
   a. Teach them to use the questioner role as a way to avoid dominating conversations (Zentall, 1995).
   b. Assign assertive peers to work with them (Schultz, 1990).
   c. Identify peer models who are fast, active, loud, and talkative (Copeland & Weissbrod, 1978, 1980; Meyer & Zentall, 1995). Children with ADHD realize they cannot perform like inactive children and may find these children too slow in a small-group context, which would increase their own bossiness, off-task behavior, or interrupting responses. In contrast, students with ADHD but not their classmates copy more active models.
3. Students with behavioral problems. Fowler (1986) found that appointing them to the role of monitoring the behavior of others decreased negative interactions and rule infractions and increased positive behavior in the monitors. Perhaps children with ADHD should monitor only positive behavior, using the checklist in Table 8.1.
4. Students who need attention from peers or who become overly excited in groups. Allow them to first learn the standards for and individually practice the roles of line leader, paper passer, peer tutor, or storyteller.
5. Students initially reluctant to participate. Schultz (1990) indicated that supportive peers would be good models and that a structured role should be assigned to them, such as material gatherer or recorder.

TABLE 8.1 Checklist of Students' Group Skills

Seen on These Dates?	Behavior Observed	Comments
	1. Disagreeing without anger or conflict (Anderson, Nelson, Fox, & Gruber, 1988).	
	2. Making decisions and helping lead the group forward (Johnson & Johnson, 1986).	
	3. Seeking and using help from others and helping others (Johnson & Johnson, 1986).	
	4. Giving positive responses to positive verbalizations from peers (rather than neutral responses as documented for children with behavioral problems) (Pomplun, 1997).	
	5. Reinforcing or paraphrasing others' ideas (Cohen, 1986).	
	6. Initiating ideas and solutions (Udvari-Solner, 1994).	

TABLE 8.1 (*Continued*)

Seen on These Dates?	Behavior Observed	Comments
	7. Making eye contact when speaking to others at least some of the time (Schultz, 1990).	
	8. Listening and questioning (Johnson & Johnson, 1990). Students with ADHD may experience difficulty formulating questions or waiting for a response and might need to be taught (for a review, see Zentall, 1993).	
	9. Describing possible strategies and elaborating on their explanations can be difficult for students with ADHD (Saunders & Chambers, 1996).	
	10. Responding to negative verbalizations from peers (Pomplun, 1997) or ignoring responses from peers by politely repeating requests or input, as if everyone were hearing impaired. O'Conner and Jenkins (1993) reported that students with disabilities were more often ignored when they requested help or attempted to make contributions in cooperative groups.	

TEACHING STRATEGIES
Best Practices for All Students During Group Learning

1. Ask the whole class to exercise or stand for 2 to 3 minutes during lecture after sitting for 15 to 25 minutes (depending on student age).
2. To develop group skills,
   a. begin with easy tasks to promote confidence and so that students can focus on group skill development and not be overwhelmed by the task demands and
   b. begin with more structure, such as studying for spelling or vocabulary tests.
3. To promote group interdependence, use activities such as jigsawing that provide one set of materials with a subset of the total package to each group member (e.g., information about a country, dinosaurs).
4. To promote accountability, these students (and all students) should be asked to do some preparatory group work to gain access to groups; if they stay on task, they could be allowed 5 to 10 minutes of free talking time at the end.

Assembly Line and ADHD Students

"We do several things where we work in pairs or small groups. And he has trouble with that when the structure is not quite as good, then . . . it kind of depends on the partner. . . . The other day we did a social studies activity, an assembly line kind of thing. I was kind of surprised, because he worked so well on that . . . and they just basically assigned the different tasks that this project involved. He had no problem with that at all. . . . He understood exactly what this person wanted him to do. . . and he did it quite well!" (cited in Zentall, Moon et al., 2001, p. 510).

The importance of classroom groups may be based on a growing interest in team skills in business and industry, primarily because teams increase work satisfaction, commitment, and involvement, resulting in higher levels of achievement (Lawler, 1986; Seibert & Gruenfeld, 1992). Small-group learning can help prepare students for success in careers, families, communities, and society (Johnson & Johnson, 1986, 1990).

LIMITATIONS OF STIMULATION

Students with ADHD can become very excited when stimulation is available. This does not mean that stimulation should be removed. That would be like taking children's food away when they expressed excitement over the feast in front of them. It does mean that teachers may need to give students advanced warning about the excitement to come and describe the kinds of responses required (how-to-structure) in order to continue to participate during those times.

Overall, the peer group context can provide a rich learning environment, especially for children with ADHD (Farmer, Pearl, & Van Acker, 1996). That is, students with ADHD habituate or get bored with stimulation faster than their peers and may need dynamic types of stimulation, such as cooperative peer learning. However, not all children prefer groups for completing work. For example, students with pure giftedness preferred to work alone unless it was more efficient to share a project by dividing up the tasks, but children who were moderately gifted with co-occurring ADHD preferred small-group learning experiences (Baska, 1989; Zentall, Moon et al., 2001).

In cooperative groups, a number of potential behavioral problems exist even among typical children:

EVIDENCE-BASED PRACTICES
Problems Typical for Cooperative Learning Activities

1. Passive uninvolvement, or not participating, disengaging, and inattention
2. Active uninvolvement, or off-task verbalization, leaving the group, interfering, or refusing to do one's part
3. Independence of group members, or doing the work alone, ignoring discussion, or being uninvolved, and domination, or doing all the work, refusing help from others, bossing, bullying, and not sharing materials or decisions (Dishon & O'Leary, 1984)

In general, group settings more typically bring out impulsive responses from all students, possibly because attention is directed outward rather than inward to individual self-controlling responses (Carver & Scheier, 1981).

Teachers were very direct about how difficult group situations were for students with ADHD. Even in large groups, teachers reported a greater-than-average need for participation from their students with ADHD:

TEACHING STRATEGIES
THE NEED FOR PARTICIPATION

"I'd say [he works well in] large groups if he's participating, but sometimes if he has his hand up and wants to participate and I'm calling on other children he'll get mad, because I'm not calling on him."

And for a different child: "He wants a lot of attention and he gets it negative or positive. The continuing problem, I think, is the talking out without raising his hand. A lot of times that's just because he's excited about what's going on or really wants to be called on. I think the biggest thing is he's a child in need of attention. He doesn't know what is an appropriate way to get it" (Zentall, Moon et al., 2001, p. 511).

In small groups, students displayed low frustration tolerance, bossiness, over-responsiveness/overexcitement, non–task-oriented behavior, overly social behavior, lack of persistence or carrying their portion of the load, difficulty getting started and in organizing work and time, and an inability to achieve social and participation goals (Grskovic, Zentall, & Stormont-Spurgin, 1995; Moon et al., 2001; Zentall & Smith, 1992; Zentall, Moon et al., 2001). One student with giftedness and ADHD said, "When I am standing around working, I just all of a sudden back out and just go free. They are doing all of my work." Although this behavior gives the appearance of poor effort, King (1993) reported that students who have little confidence in their ability to be contributing group members masked this with low effort.

In small-group contexts, a greater potential for aggression also exists (e.g., from students with ADHD [Nidiffer, Ciulla, Russo, & Cataldo, 1983]). For example, pairs of students, one with ADHD and one without, experienced poorer verbal communication, more aggression, and more withdrawal than when both members were typical children (Saunders & Chambers, 1996). Students with ADHD or other behavioral disorders contributed to aggressive and disruptive behavior in groups, poorer listening, and more verbal interruption than in groups containing all average students (e.g., Dishon, Spracklen, Andrews, & Patterson, 1996; Fergusson & Horwood, 1996; Pomplun, 1997). Under these conditions, these students were more likely to be ignored and excluded by others. These types of potential problems could explain why teachers allocate only 1% of a school day to active student participation, whereas 75% of the day was allocated to teachers instruction (Heward, 1994).

In conclusion, when teachers do not know how to plan ahead for possible problems, they may reduce group learning experiences or exclude children with ADHD. This could reduce valuable learning experiences for all students and specifically the social and academic learning opportunities for students with ADHD. (Specific performance gains from group experiences are addressed in chapter 7.)

EVIDENCE-BASED PRACTICES

Observational Study of Students With and Without ADHD in Problem-Solving Groups: Some Surprises

Groups That Solve Mysteries While Trying Not to Break Eggs

Purpose. To assess the problem-solving performance and behavior of students with ADHD.

Participants. Fourth- through eighth-grade students with and without ADHD-H (66 total children)

Group type: Students were randomly assigned to small groups of three children: group type A—one child with ADHD (Hc) with two comparison children (Ch) or group type B—three comparisons (Cc). This produced six comparison groups, each with three children per group, and 16 Hc + Ch groups of three children.

Tasks.

Verbal: Solve a mystery, such as the following: Laddy, a 5-year-old miniature poodle, has just died. At the dog's memorial service, his owner, Mr. Driscoll, says the following words: "This animal gave his life to protect his humans from a terrible, planned-out crime. We will always be grateful for Laddy's noble sacrifice." How did Laddy die?

Success was defined as three mysteries solved by using the information generated in response to their "yes" or "no" questions

Motor: Build a cushion to catch a plastic egg filled with Skittles (see the cushion example below).

Motor Problem Solving Task: A Cushion to 'Break' the Fall of an Egg

EVIDENCE-BASED PRACTICES *(Continued)*

Success was defined as withstanding a fall of 6 feet.

Design. 2 population group × 2 group type × 2 gender × 2 task × 2 sessions.

Results

Performance During the Verbal and Motor Response Task

Gender Effects:

- Girls demonstrated more positive nonverbal behavior (factor 3: giving, sharing, cooperatively working, and positive rough play) than boys across both tasks.
- Boys demonstrated more passive behavior (factor 4: uncooperative, independently working, and watching others) than did girls.

Task Effects:

The motor response task brought out more

- positive nonverbal behavior than the verbal task and
- negative verbal behavior from all the children than did the verbal task.

The verbal task brought out more positive verbal behavior than the motor task for all children.

Group Effects:

Small groups with one ADHD member had more success than Cc groups.

Behavior During the Verbal and the Motor Task:

- ADHD had less positive nonverbal behavior than comparisons.
- ADHD made more negative verbal and off-task/disruptive noises than comparisons.
- Partners (Ch) of ADHD had less positive nonverbal behavior than Cc.
- Partners (Ch) of ADHD had more negative nonverbal behavior than Cc.

Summary

1. Students with ADHD demonstrated less positive nonverbal behavior in small groups (e.g., cooperatively working) than did comparisons and more negative and off-task verbal behavior in both types of problem-solving tasks.
   - However, the groups in which students with ADHD participated were more successful in solving problems than groups with only comparison children.
2. Groups of girls were more successful problem solvers than boys (which was significant only on the verbal task), and they showed more positive motor behavior (cooperation) and less passive behavior while solving problems than did groups of boys.
3. A problem-solving task requiring the use of motor responses to make a physical product brought out more positive motor behavior from all the children but also more negative verbal behavior than the verbal task.
4. A problem-solving task requiring verbal questioning and responding brought out more positive verbal behavior than the motor task for all children.

Implications

1. In small groups, children with ADHD may sacrifice interpersonal relatedness for achieving competence in a social arena. Supplementary analysis related to goals indicated that students with ADHD less frequently attempted

(Continued)

EVIDENCE-BASED PRACTICES *(Continued)*

to gain positive relatedness than comparison students but only during the motor response task. This could indicate that competence was more important than relatedness, especially during a task with concrete products. Overall, it may be important to cue children with ADHD about the importance of both types of goals.

2. The success rate and cooperative (motor) behavior of girls is what distinguishes them from boys while solving problems. Girls did not sacrifice relatedness for task competence; they achieved both. Perhaps this behavior of girls could serve as a model for boys.
3. Verbal problem solving brought out more positive verbal behavior than when solving motor construction problems. This type of behavior and setting would be an important training setting (i.e., pointing out good verbal models) for boys with ADHD, who typically use less positive verbal behavior than comparisons.
4. Problem solving with visual/concrete objects and physical responses brought out more motor behavior, both positive and negative, than when solving verbal problems. This setting would require more guidance for appropriate nonverbal behavior for all students (Zentall, Kuester, & Craig, 2005).

Change the instructional context to reduce activity

Task structure Structure, as it relates to activity, provides guidance about appropriate behavioral responses. Knowing "what to do" on a task (or the range of acceptable responses) reduces activity and physical off-task behavior for students with and without ADHD (as previously reported for setting structure). Even though both groups respond similarly, children with ADHD may require more task structure when complex tasks, such as those found in sports, social, and task performance, are necessary. Watterson's cartoon dialogue provides a good example:

STUDENT PRACTICES
WE JUST ARGUE OVER THE RULES

Calvin: "I signed up to play baseball every recess, and I don't even like baseball that much. I mean, it's fun playing baseball with just you, because we both get to pitch, bat, run and catch all at once. We get to do everything."

Hobbes: "Mostly we just argue over the rules we make up! That's the part I like!"

Calvin: "But this will be with teams and assigned positions and an umpire! It's boring playing it the real way!"

Hobbes: "Do you even know how to play the real way?"

Calvin: "See, that's another problem! Suppose they make me a halfback. Can I tackle the shortstop or not?" ("Calvin and Hobbes," by Bill Watterson)

Although Calvin's dislike of baseball may be due to the waiting involved in this game (e.g., he may need more active involvement as a pitcher or catcher), it is also clear that he lacks information about the game (see the discussion of selective attention difficulties in chapter 6). In fact, parents reported that the difficulties their children had playing group games was "getting confused with the rules" (for 26% of the boys with ADHD and all the girls) (Berry, Shaywitz, & Shaywitz, 1985).

Parents and teachers of elementary-level students with ADHD (with and without giftedness) and the children themselves (Zentall, Moon et al., 2001) described the following as important to their school success:

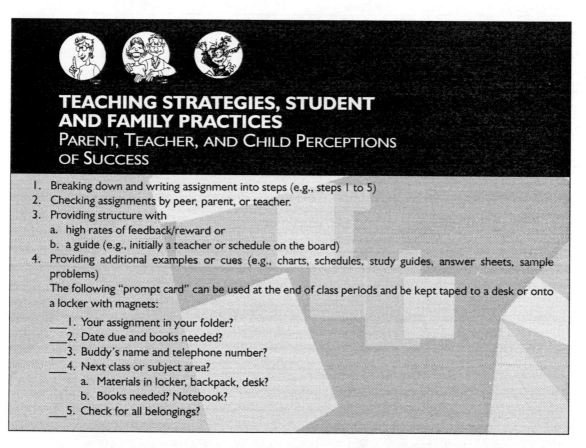

TEACHING STRATEGIES, STUDENT AND FAMILY PRACTICES
PARENT, TEACHER, AND CHILD PERCEPTIONS OF SUCCESS

1. Breaking down and writing assignment into steps (e.g., steps 1 to 5)
2. Checking assignments by peer, parent, or teacher.
3. Providing structure with
   a. high rates of feedback/reward or
   b. a guide (e.g., initially a teacher or schedule on the board)
4. Providing additional examples or cues (e.g., charts, schedules, study guides, answer sheets, sample problems)
   The following "prompt card" can be used at the end of class periods and be kept taped to a desk or onto a locker with magnets:
   ___1. Your assignment in your folder?
   ___2. Date due and books needed?
   ___3. Buddy's name and telephone number?
   ___4. Next class or subject area?
      a. Materials in locker, backpack, desk?
      b. Books needed? Notebook?
   ___5. Check for all belongings?

In addition, a lack of task structure could explain some of the difficulties reported by the parents, teachers, and students with ADHD in their special subject areas of art and physical education (Zentall, Moon et al., 2001). Difficulties in these specialty subjects could also be due to the fact that teachers of music, physical education, or art reported greater reluctance to try new techniques than special or general educators (Zentall & Stormont-Spurgin, 1995). Additional limiting factors common within these specialties are described in Table 8.2.

TABLE 8.2 What Makes "Specials" Difficult for Students with ADHD?

Difficult Setting Variables	**Music**	**Art**	**Physical Education**	**Hall**	**Cafeteria**	**Recess**	**Trips**	**Bus**
*Infrequent feedback (e.g., by grades or charts)	X		X	X	X	X	X	X
Setting associated with fun (expectations)	X	X	X	X	X	X	X	
*Many students waiting their turn	X		X		X		X	X
*Participation mainly for the most skilled students	X		X			X		
*Lessons focus on materials more than students	X	X	X				X	
Time scheduling fixed	X	X	X	X	X	X	X	X
Limited materials	X	X	X			X		
*No defined roles and jobs for students	X	X	X	X	X	X	X	X
*Undefined or uninteresting starting or ending routines	X	X	X				X	X
*Undefined and unpredictable schedule of activities	X	X	X			X	X	
*Not supervised				X	X	X		X
*Spaces without boundaries	X	X	X			X		
*Require sitting for extended periods of time	X							X
*Only the teacher selects goals	X	X	X					
*Only the teacher charts progress	X	X	X					

Note: Variables with an asterisk can be altered.

When structuring the "what to do" of a social task, teachers may need to describe what an appropriate response should "look like." Such a response can be taught with role play or cuing responses right before they are to occur. For example, students with ADHD plus aggression see neutral behavior (e.g., bumping into someone) as hostile (more than boys with pure ADHD) (Madan-Swain & Zentall, 1990; Whalen & Henker, 1985). For this reason, it may be important to help them see the differences between neutral and hostile behavior, perhaps through previous classroom discussion, and to reinterpret events later. Added structure of "what to do" is unnecessary when behavior is clearly hostile or friendly because children with ADHD and aggression are accurate interpreters when the intent of behavior is clear.

Most past research has examined "what to do" rather than "how to do." Some research has been done involving social skill and problem-solving training with students with ADHD (Hoza, Mrug, Pelham, Greiner, & Gragy, 2003). However, this work used only students with ADHD (no comparisons), and the how-to involved multiple sessions of intensive clinical training. The following study examined the effects of teaching students "how" in a single brief session:

EVIDENCE-BASED PRACTICES
Problem Solving with How-To Social Rules

Purpose. To assess the verbal problem-solving performance and behavior of students with ADHD as it may be improved by increased structure of how to respond.

Participants.

- Fourth through eighth grade
- Thirty-four ADHD (16 males, 18 females)
- Ninety-two controls (44 males, 48 females)

Group Type: Students were randomly assigned to small groups of three children: group type A—one child with ADHD (Hc) with two comparison children (Ch) or group type B—three comparisons (Cc). This produced eight comparison groups, each with three children per group, and 34 Hc + Ch groups of three children.

Tasks. Two *verbal* solve-a-survival scenerio tasks.

Similarities Between Tasks:

Difficulty, task time, game-type problem-solving task about survival, physical appearance, choice options, amount of movement, and verbal responses required

Differences Between Task Conditions:

1. Low structure with the unusual survival task
   - Fifteen situations
   - Solution options varied
2. High structure with the daily-living survival task
   - Thirty situations
   - Seven solution options

   Combined social, problem-solving, and cooperative learning skills:
   - Turn taking (social)
   - Justification of possible solutions
   - Required feedback among group members
   - Required group consensus

Design. 2 population group × 2 group type × 2 gender × 2 task condition.

Results. Group Effects:

High active children had more negative verbal behavior (commands, nontask talk, and disruptive noises) than comparison groups and less motor interactive behavior (passive or working alone or watching) than comparisons

Task Condition Effects:

High structure had more success than low structure.

High-structure task condition had:

- Fewer negative verbal, off-task, disruptive behavior and noises
- More positive motor cooperative behavior
- More motor negative behavior (noninteractive, passive) than low structure

High-structure (with rules) task condition:

- Boys had more success than girls.

Group Effects in Each Task Condition:

- ADHD made fewer negative verbal and off-task noises in high than in low structure.
- ADHD had more negative motor (or more passive, noncooperative behavior) in high than in low structure.

(No differences between task conditions for comparisons)

(Continued)

EVIDENCE-BASED PRACTICES *(Continued)*

Summary

In high structure (defined as "how to": take turns, justify answers, give feedback, and arrive at a group consensus),

1. all children had
   - more success in solving problems,
   - more negative motor behavior (or passive, not sharing, working alone, or passively watching),
   - less negative verbal (commands, questions, or non–task-related talk) and off-task disruptive behavior and noises;
2. children with ADHD in high structure more than low structure
   - made fewer negative verbal and disruptive noises and
   - had more negative motor or passive behavior; and
3. boys more than girls had
   - more success.

Implications

The rules of task engagment (e.g., how-to turn taking) appeared to

1. decrease the motor activity of all participants (i.e., increased their passive watching, waiting, and working-alone responses),
2. decrease the negative verbal activity (statements) and off-task disruptive behavior and noises, and
3. allow for greater success in arriving at one answer for all children, possibly by changing a task from divergent thinking to convergent thinking.

This greater success was attributed to

- children with ADHD, who showed more motor passive noninteractive behavior in high than in low structure, and
- boys who showed greater success than girls in the high-structure condition in contrast to the prior study (Zentall et al., 2005), where girls were more successful than boys on the verbal task (i.e., in the absence of rules of task engagement).

LIMITATIONS OF TASK STRUCTURE

Even though increased setting and task information can improve behavioral and task responding initially, the long-term goal for all children is to manage life's challenges with a minimum of adult support. It is important to allow students to make decisions about what is "correct" as they age because there are multiple correct responses (e.g., creative expression, self-management, social behavior, problem solving) and especially in preparation for the increased number of choices and temptations out of school. It is therefore important to decrease structure slowly after the child has demonstrated appropriate responses under "what to do" and "how to do" support conditions (see Table 8.3).

TABLE 8.3 Moving Children from High to Low Structure

Child Dependent on Adults for Initial Success **High-Structure Adult Directed**	**Child Moving Toward Independence and Long-Term Success** **Low-Structure Child Directed**
• High external feedback/reward • Limited choices • Teacher directives	• Less external feedback/reward • More choices • Teacher suggestions • Child goal setting • Peer directed or small groups • Self-directed (self-monitoring with checklists, PDAs, computers, tape players, or mirrors)

BEHAVIORAL REDIRECTION

Move the child in a direction consistent with that child's needs

Redirecting behavior so that it is appropriate to the setting may involve teaching the child "replacement" or alternate behavior that serves the same purpose or function as the original behavior (see chapter 4). Clearly, children with ADHD need alternate ways to be active. Furthermore, children with ADHD are aware of their active learning style, self-report a greater need for working with others and for moving about the classroom, and are, in fact, more active and talkative (see chapter 5). Attempting to stop the flow of activity is difficult, frustrating, and time consuming for both teachers and students.

TEACHING STRATEGIES
BEST PRACTICES FOR CHANNELING ACTIVITY

1. Allow a certain number of student-directed movements in the classroom that are not disruptive (e.g., sharpening pencils standing during seat work). Students might be told how many of these self-initiated activities they are allowed per period or be given "passes" to spend.
2. Give students experience creating and managing their learning environments (e.g., constructing their own bulletin boards, designing poster presentations). This is helpful because it teaches students organization and how to select and present important information.
3. Give students experiences making decisions. Let them discuss and determine "what is fair," for example, with respect to resources. This will be useful for those children with aggression and a low tolerance for frustration. Using some students' ideas about "what is fair," write these rules for sharing on this resource (e.g., on a computer or in a game).

(Continued)

TEACHING STRATEGIES *(Continued)*

4. Encourage diary writing, painting, and drawing as different types of cognitive and sensory stimulation.
5. Allow working at the board or on dry-erase boards during independent work. Some teachers ask students to work initial problems on the surface of dry-erase desks.
6. Allow two seats or the option to move among learning centers.
7. Encourage sports activities outside the classroom, such as bicycling, skating, bowling, karate, swimming.

Swimming Helps

I have a student who is now swimming and his behavior is a lot better. I hope it continues (Laura Dearing, personal communication, 2002).

8. Allow unusual (see the cartoon below) positions or places to work (stand, kneel, straddle chair, or on the floor). Teachers and students may need to evaluate listening comprehension and performance in these different positions.

It is more difficult to redirect impulsivity because the child must first stop a well-practiced response (e.g., blurting out a thought). Success depends on (a) the child's ability to tolerate delay or to control the delay (e.g., during self-paced tasks [Carrol & Bain, 1994; Douglas & Peters, 1979]), (b) the educator's willingness to allow

replacement activities to use during delays (e.g., doodling), and (c) the educator's willingness and skills in reducing instructional delay.

At times, however, we cannot allow the child to control the length of the delay. For example, during listening tasks, children need to either tolerate delay or learn how to use questioning techniques to increase their participation. Difficulties with delays could explain why social skill training that involved listening 88% of the time and practice 12% of the time produced less compliance and more activity (especially over time) than self-regulation training, which involved listening only 30% of the time and individual work 70% (Charlebois et al., 1999). When the length of the delay cannot be shortened, children need control over what to do during the delay.

Complex responses also occur during delay time (e.g., planning and organization) and are addressed in chapter 10 on attentional strategies.

EMPIRICALLY-BASED PRACTICES
TO REDUCE IMPULSIVITY

To Change the Task or Setting

1. Provide self-paced tasks where students proceed at their own speed so they do not have to wait for directions between tasks.
2. Provide more rapid pacing for easy practice tasks. This reduces student wait time and also reduces activity even though it will not necessarily improve performance (Dalby, Kinsbourne, & Swanson, 1991; Schroyer & Zentall, 1986).
3. Cue children with visual reminders (e.g., cue cards) to increase their hand raising (Posavac, Sheridan, & Posavac, 1999).

To Reduce Impulsivity

1. Teach the child to cross out the incorrect answers on multiple-choice assignments or tests rather than circling the correct answer (for a review, see Zentall, 1993). As stated by one teacher, "My students love this."
2. Teach the child to underline or highlight (with magic markers) important information in directions (Zentall & Dwyer, 1988; Zentall & Kruczek, 1988). This can be done by the students.
3. Teach the child to use motor responses during delays. The style of these children is motoric. That is, 90% of boys with ADHD used physical behavior (e.g., pencil tapping) during delay in comparison to only 45% of average boys (Gordon, 1979). Some teachers have used foam on the end of children's pencils or a mouse pad to accommodate this behavior.
4. Teach the child to listen and avoid interrupting peers and teachers by giving additional visual things to look at during listening tasks, such as exposure to windows, artwork, photos, pets, pictures (Zentall & Meyer, 1987; Zentall & Zentall, 1976). Teachers may need to assess the listening comprehension of their children to convince themselves that this approach works for most students with ADHD.

TEACHING STRATEGIES
BEST PRACTICES

1. Use word processors to reorganize written materials.
2. Prepare for wait time by encouraging children to take objects with them (in their pockets or purses) to "play" with (paper clips, colored pipe cleaners, pieces of play-dough, sponges, coated wire, foam, or "stress" balls) and include rules for use during listening activities and classroom delays.
3. Provide practice in identifying conversational lags (as a better time to interrupt) to help them during social interactions whose slow pace brings out their impatience or bossiness.
4. Tell them that as soon as you finish helping child A, you will help them rather than saying you will be there in a minute.
5. Provide attractive, colorful planners that match the color of the texts and teach them how to plan for the day, for after school, and for the weekend. Provide time in groups for this activity.
6. Provide templates for written tasks or fold plain paper into six parts and ask the child to draw a picture for each part of the story to be written to improve organization.
7. Give instructions that are brief and that have visual cues.
8. Provide a worksheet with items labeled easy, moderate, difficult so that students know that if they have answered hard items, they have demonstrated competency. However, they may need to do some easy items first to get started quickly and feel successful.
9. Praise their efforts and abilities to wait and reward successively longer durations of waiting.
10. Provide models of how to take brief notes (even just cue words) or use a computer to take notes. With these notes, they can raise their questions or comments later.
11. Give all students at least 5 minutes before the bell to plan (e.g., prepare for upcoming tasks in their planners or to start homework).
12. Give students a certain number of tickets to talk during specific activities. When you ask the whole class who had a turn to talk, the talkative child sees that some students did not have a turn, and turn taking becomes a clearer notion.
13. Use a "talking stick" (e.g., a popsicle stick) in group activities that gets passed from student to student to indicate who "has the floor."
14. Use individual rather than whole-class transitions to reduce transition time. Individualizing changes of activity can be set up on a schedule or by task completion.
15. Cue children about upcoming difficult times or tasks where extra control or delay activities will be needed.
16. Allow constructive (or at least nondestructive) activities during delays, such as free reading, doodling, crossword puzzles, or weaving.

FAMILY PRACTICES
LAP POTLATCHES AND SEA KAYAKS

A mother of two sons with unidentified ADHD said that her sons adapted well to their classrooms because she had provided them with materials to make pot holders in a small weaving frame (potlatch) to use during listening tasks or delay times. The boys were instructed to keep the materials out of sight as much as possible in their laps, with teacher permission. During nonschool hours, the boys were as active as their mother and father, who at that time were making a living by taking individuals out into the ocean and through caves in sea kayaks.

SUMMARY

The ecological model is emphasized in this chapter because the context (tasks, settings, peers, expectations, and school) contributes to "deviance" and to optimal functioning. The recommended changes involve altering the physical and instructional learning contexts and redirecting activity rather than attempting to reduce activity directly. Activity can be channeled, for example, by teaching activity rules (i.e., "do rules"), using activity routines, and giving children some control of what to do during delay time.

"Enabling" in the negative sense happens only when we fail to teach children independence skills or when we lower our expectations for them across their multiple areas of functioning. Recognizing children's constructive qualities (e.g., energy, spontaneity, enthusiasm, hobbies, humor) is important to adaptive functioning. Teachers can also provide a number of defined spaces with access to educational opportunities and resources, including classroom roles, peers, environmental stimulation, and movement possibilities. Each of these modifications could help students with ADHD who tire (or physiologically habituate) more rapidly than their classmates to familiar tasks and contexts.

Educators can also consider modifying their classroom instructional groupings. When using teacher-directed lessons for students with ADHD, it is important to use brief periods of instruction and to avoid student wait time in order to prevent the inevitable outcome of negative behavior. Structure needs to be balanced with choice or decision making, which also reduces problem behavior in students with ADHD and promotes independence and willingness to tolerate difficult tasks. Choice can also increase creativity and productivity in all students.

Small-group learning experiences provide additional benefits, including decreased off-task behavior and increased cooperative behavior and acceptance between disabled and nondisabled peers. In addition, the importance of small groups for students with ADHD includes active participation, more frequent and immediate peer feedback, control over pace, and self-reported enjoyment of learning in groups. Instructions to students about the importance of both the task (competence) and social goals (relatedness) are important. This can be accomplished by instructing all members to take turns and explain their own choices and decisions to other group members, especially for boys and students with ADHD.

To improve the social status of students with ADHD, we may need to also change the peer context. All children need to make some changes to prevent problems found in group settings, especially in those groups of students with ADHD (e.g., poorer verbal communication, more aggression, more withdrawal behavior, poorer listening, more verbal interruption, low frustration tolerance, bossiness, verresponsiveness/ overexcitedness, difficulty getting started). Because children with ADHD are motivated to be with and learn from others, it should be easier to increase their successful contributions and can improve the problem-solving performance of small groups. This approach is far more useful in the long run than excluding these children from the educational and social opportunities available in group experiences.

DISCUSSION AND APPLICATION QUESTIONS

1. Where and by whom would you seat the child with ADHD in large class discussions, during seat work, or in small groups and why?
2. Provide a well-reasoned and empathetic answer to this question: "What price must the rest of the class pay if there is a classroom with three or four students with attention-deficit disorder?"
3. Under what conditions (e.g., for amount of work, time on task, visual motor skill, task interest) would you assign computer work?
4. Restate your understanding of "disabling" and "enabling."
5. What preventive strategies would you recommend to a teacher who wishes to set up student-directed small groups in a social studies curriculum?
6. You want to put one of your students with ADHD into small-group activities, but the other students complain about him. They say that the group does not get work done, he does not carry his load, and he is disruptive and rude. What can you do?
7. You have just finished instruction on a topic and formed small groups to work. When you monitor the groups' progress, you find the student with ADHD socializing and not doing the assignment. What do you do?
8. Students with ADHD do not like routines because they involve repetition. However, routines are necessary for organization and completing assignments. Select several classroom routines and incorporate change into them to make them more "fun."
9. Here is a story to provide you with an example of a teacher's understanding of the effects of windows:

TEACHING STRATEGIES
WINDOWS OR MATH PERFORMANCE?

"We have a student who sits where he can look out the window, but he just sits and stares and doesn't get his work done. It is only a problem at math time."

10. How will eliminating windows solve this child's problems? What is this child's problem?
11. The perspective of students with ADHD is that we are always asking them to change. How can we make this fair in a group setting?
12. When we alter the environment for the child with ADHD, can you argue that these changes will also benefit other children without ADHD?
13. Design a lesson assigning two or three students to one computer, each student with a different job. (Inservice teachers can do this activity by noting these items in their own classroom.)
14. Observe a classroom and note the items in Table 8.4 to discuss in class (higher-education students who are currently teaching can record their own classroom).

TABLE 8.4 Evaluation of Classroom Resources and Rules

How and where do students access materials?

—— Textbooks

—— Worksheet and workbooks

—— Games and manipulatives

—— Audiovisual equipment

—— Computers and calculators

—— Self-correction materials

—— Writing tools and paper

Other:______________________________

How is the class organized for instruction and practice?

—— Large-group activity area

—— Small-group activity area/centers

—— Individual work areas

—— Bulletin boards designed by teacher or students

—— Boundaries for easy supervision

(Continued)

TABLE 8.4 *(Continued)*

—— Clear path for movement by the teacher and students

—— Learning centers:

Other Areas:______________________________________

How are these variables handled?

—— Conversational noise

—— Student choice of activities

—— Student movement

—— Student interaction

How is feedback provided?

—— Frequency (daily, weekly, hourly):_______________________

—— Type (verbal, written, stickers):________________________

How do students know when and how to make transitions?

	Begin Instruction	**Between Activities in Class**	**To Restroom**	**Between Classes**	**Dismissal**
Type of signal and procedure					
No signal but a procedure					
No procedure					

How do the students know the rules and their jobs?

What jobs and privileges are available?

—— Peer tutor

—— Paper collector/passer

—— Grader of papers

—— Collector of money

—— Assignment monitor

—— Message deliverer

—— Chalkboard eraser

—— Assignment recorder

—— Bulletin captain

—— Class filer

—— Equipment monitor

Other:

TABLE 8.4 (*Continued*)

Basis for jobs/roles:	
—— Good achievement	—— Good behavior
—— Achievement improvement	—— Behavioral improvement
—— Take turns	—— Completed work
—— Student request	—— Good skills
—— Need leadership practice	—— Needs social practice
—— Need activity	—— Needs skills

CHAPTER 9

Strategies to Reduce Activity/Impulsivity: Change the Child

OBJECTIVES

- Recognize that behavioral techniques are available to immediately produce short-term changes in behavior.
- Summarize differences in the way these consequences work for students with ADHD.
- Recognize that psychostimulant medication is also a short-term treatment, which does not solve the major educational or vocational problems of ADHD.

KEY TERMS

'public' teacher reprimands
intrinsically motivated
negative reinforcement
DRA
DRO
DRI
DRL
peer-mediated rewards
'the dessert principle'
inclusionary time-out
cognitive behavioral techniques
self-monitoring

This chapter describes procedures to change behavior. Behavioral consequences, cognitive behavioral techniques, and psychostimulant medication fall into this category of direct interventions. These techniques are very useful, especially as an initial approach to managing behavior. In support, Witzel and Mercer (2003) reviewed evidence indicating that rewards and incentives were used more frequently by beginning teachers than any other technique (see Figure 9.1).

HOW TO MANAGE THE IMMEDIATE BEHAVIOR OF THESE CHILDREN

Behavioral techniques are positive or negative "consequences" that teachers deliver in response to children's behavior (Abramowitz & O'Leary, 1991). Pelham, Wheeler, and Chronis (1998) reported that 23 studies in classroom settings demonstrated the efficacy of behavioral interventions for students with ADHD. Intensive interventions are typically implemented by paraprofessionals, consultants, or master teachers, and special educators spend about 16% of their time in behavioral management (Baker & Zigmond, 1990).

Although these techniques are effective for students with ADHD, a distinction must be made between students with ADHD and students with behavioral disorders. Behavioral consequences, as they are often applied to children with social and behavioral disabilities, are based on assumptions that the child has learned inappropriate behavior and therefore can relearn new behavior. For children with ADHD, this can be correct for many types of behavior. For example, aggression is learned, and the ways that children seek attention or attempt to feel competent or in control may be learned. Therefore, expressions of these social needs can be relearned.

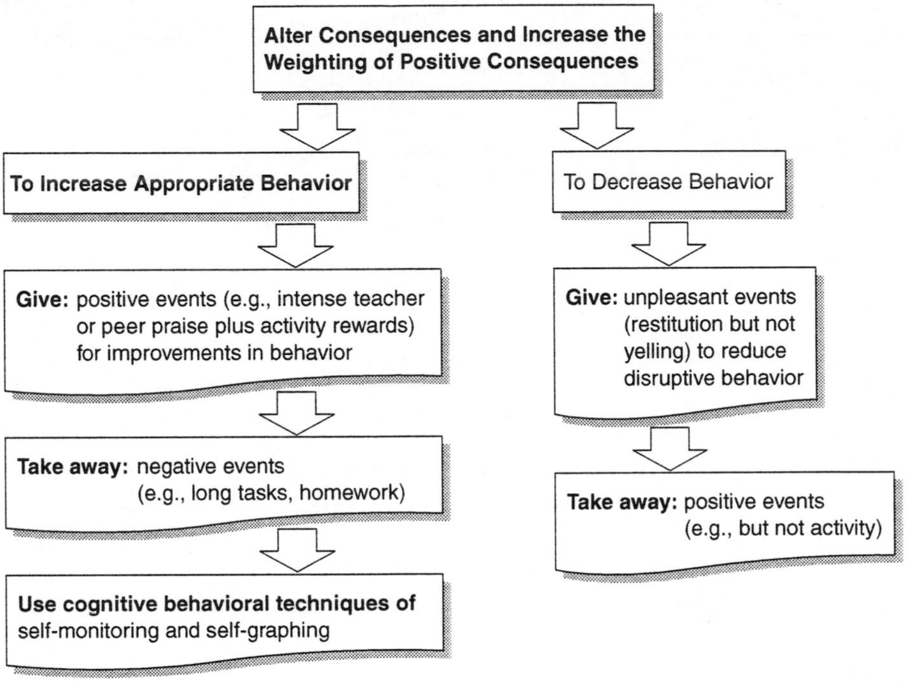

FIGURE 9.1 Behavioral Consequences

However, the need for stimulation (e.g., achieved through increased activity, inattention) and perhaps the need for relatedness are biogenetically determined. Thus, while activity can be redirected or channeled, the quantity of activity is less modifiable. In other words, educators can reduce activity in a setting for short periods of time or even delay or redirect it, but the child still needs active expressions. In addition, children with ADHD have not *learned* to be impulsive. They have a need for active responding or greater difficulty waiting to respond, which leads to responding too early. What is also critical in the differentiation between children with ADHD and those without it is that consequences can serve as stimulation for them, and, depending on the child's relative state of need, any intense positive or negative stimulation can be reinforcing. Thus, optimal stimulation theory and learning theory make joint predictions for students with ADHD (i.e., the behavior of students with ADHD can be increased to the degree that consequences are intense, frequent, and immediate and do not compete in attractiveness with the task at hand). Because students with ADHD respond positively to behavioral interventions does not indicate that ADHD as a complex set of symptoms, is learned; it indicates only that the students are alive and that their behavior (like all organisms) is modifiable by changing consequences.

Use positive consequences

Positive reinforcement Rewards are events, statements, or tangibles (consequences) that are typically positive, follow specific behavior in time, and increase the future occurrence of that behavior. Reinforcement is defined by its outcome rather than by its intended outcome. Although many children will respond similarly to positive consequences, individual differences in the way they respond can be diagnostic. Two children are cleaning chalk erasers, and one child says to the other, "Hey, wait a minute! *You're* cleaning erasers as a punishment? I'm cleaning erasers as a reward!" The child with ADHD would find most types of activity rewarding.

Reid and Maag (1998) have suggested that behavioral techniques of contingency contracting, response cost, token economies, and so on work in the same way for students with and without ADHD. The evidence, however, does not support this. Students with ADHD respond differently from their peers to consequences and to the timing of those consequences.

To understand the basis of these differences, it is important to see that consequences can provide three positive effects for all children: (a) feedback about correct/incorrect, (b) positive/negative social attention, and (c) stimulation. For children with ADHD, stimulation alone can be reinforcing (Brand & Van Der Vlugt, 1989; Lee & Zentall, 2002). Perhaps when positive consequences are not powerful

enough, they fail to "work" as well as negative consequences (Firestone & Douglas, 1975; Pelham et al., 1998). When reward is as intense as punishment, it works as well in reducing impulsive responses for students with ADHD (Oosterlaan & Sergeant, 1998). For example, earning tokens for on-task behavior to be exchanged for an extra minute of recess (or a sticker) was as successful as response cost (losing stickers or recess) for off-task behavior (Sullivan & O'Leary, 1990).

Although reward can be as effective as response cost, studies rarely make a comparison and report only the positive effects of response cost. For example, Bender and Mathes (1995) used a response-cost procedure of reducing Cathy's recess time for each "blurting out." Even though this technique could have decreased blurting-out behavior by increasing her awareness, it is more appropriate for her to earn recess minutes for raising her hand. This more positive technique could produce better long-term self-management while (a) not denying Cathy her needed activity or (b) putting her inappropriate behavior on the chalkboard for her peers to see.

In sum, *intense* praise is as effective as response cost, a mild form of social punishment. In contrast, intense negative social responses can actually increase behavior for students with ADHD. Strong negative social attention can be a reward because children with ADHD prefer strong, social stimulation. Therefore, when aggressive behavior produces an intense emotional response (cry, whine, or yell) from the "victim," this stimulating response can increase their aggressive behavior. For example, students with ADHD (but not typical children) increased their own negative play behavior after witnessing a peer react loudly and intensely to the aggressive behavior of another child (Meyer & Zentall, 1995). Thus, yelling at children with ADHD or even at their peers may quiet them initially but in the long run can actually reinforce or increase subsequent negative behavior.

Research in general education classrooms similarly found that loud "public" teacher reprimands for off-task and aggressive behavior increased rates of that behavior in eight students with ADHD (Rosen, O'Leary, Joyce, Conway, & Pfiffner, 1984) and in first-grade students with hyperactivity (O'Leary, Kaufmann, Kass, & Drabman, 1970). In contrast, "soft reprimands" reduced off-task and increased appropriate behavior.

Evidence also exists that students with ADHD need immediate rewards (Neef, Bicard, & Endo, 2001; Rapport, Tucker, DuPaul, Merlo, & Stoner, 1986). For example, when given a choice of immediate or delayed toys (after 2 days), they chose to complete fewer problems (zero to five) for a smaller reward of one or two toys given immediately compared to their classmates, who chose to complete 15 to 25 problems for a larger delayed reward of three or four toys. It was clear from the Rapport et al. study that immediacy was the important factor because when all rewards were given immediately, the children with ADHD worked more problems for the larger rewards just like their peers.

Given the evidence of the need for immediate rewards, it is also understandable that they would become abnormally frustrated when expected rewards fail to appear and be unusually sensitive to the possible stimulating (and distracting) effects of rewards (Douglas, 1985; Douglas & Parry, 1994). For example, children with ADHD are more likely to get overly excited by appealing rewards, such as toys, but show less physiological sensitivity to rewards (habituate faster [for a review, see Sergeant, Geurts, Huijbregts, Scheres, & Oosterlaan, 2003]) and are more likely than their peers to get bored with the same nonvariable rewards (Houlihan & Van Houten, 1989).

Additional differences were observed within the ADHD population in their response to reinforcement. Children with ADHD who have natural interests in a topic (intrinsically motivated) showed longer task persistence under conditions of self-reward. In contrast, those students who were reliant on others (i.e., perhaps because of skill deficits, lack of background knowledge, or interest) showed greater persistence under external reinforcement (extrinsic reward conditions [Bugental, Whalen, & Henker, 1977]).

Negative reinforcement or taking away unpleasant events The term "negative reinforcement" is often confusing. By definition, reinforcement must increase behavior. Negative reinforcement achieves this effect by removing something unpleasant (a task, sight, sound, person, or bad feeling, such as anxiety). A checklist is a common example; we feel reinforced when we check off an item on our list. Negative reinforcement is not punishment. Both positive and negative reinforcement are at work when a mother gives her crying child a candy bar to stop his crying. In this example, the mother's behavior (giving the candy) was negatively reinforced because the child stopped crying (an unpleasant event was removed) and the child's behavior (crying) was positively reinforced because the child received the candy. Because negative reinforcement involves the removal of unpleasant events or feelings (e.g., anxiety fear), it may be a more potent reward for individuals with co-occurring anxiety or high avoidance behavior (see chapter 4).

EVIDENCE-BASED PRACTICES
To Increase Appropriate Behavior

Social Rewards

1. Use intense or emotional teacher praise to follow specific behavior. Decreased negative behavior and greater use of "friendly" toys were demonstrated by students with ADHD when prosocial behavior was "rewarded" or responded to with loud and emotional social reactions (Meyer & Zentall, 1995).
   a. Use intense praise that gives specific feedback about what students with ADHD are currently doing that is correct or well intentioned.

(Continued)

EVIDENCE-BASED PRACTICES *(Continued)*

b. Use intense praise for *effort* and behavioral improvement rather than waiting for "correct" behavior (i.e., catch the child in the act of improvement). Alternatively, when you see inappropriate behavior, find another child who is showing the opposite behavior and give him or her intense recognition (as a model for the student with ADHD).

c. Use differential reinforcement (DR) of (a) alternative behavior (A), (b) other behavior (O), or (c) behavior incompatible with inappropriate behavior (I)—DRA, DRO, or DRI. These behavioral techniques require identifying a desired alternative or incompatible behavior within the child's ongoing behavior. For example, asking questions is incompatible with off-task talking; both are verbal, but only the former is appropriate. Once the behavior has been identified, the teacher would praise the child for his or her questions.

d. Use differential reinforcement of low-intensity or low-rate behavior (DRL) when the child spontaneously is less intense (e.g., quieter talking) or displays behavior less often (e.g., less monopolizing of conversations). Note that DRL techniques may not work as well with children who are impulsive (Parry & Douglas, 1983).

2. Use immediate rewards because children with ADHD are more responsive to immediate rewards than they are to past experiences with reward or to future delayed rewards (Binder, Dixon, & Ghezzi, 2000; Neef et al., 2001; Tripp & Alsop, 1999). For example, put tallies on the board where all classmates can see for compliance with rules, not for infractions of rules.
3. Use more frequent rewards, which have the effect of helping students with ADHD behave more like their classmates (Sagvolden, Metzger, & Sagvolden, 1993).
4. Use Social Rewards.

a. In individual settings, use peer prompting (e.g., "Let's get moving!") plus peer social praise for math performance (e.g., "Wow, we are going fast, now!"), which reduced off-task behavior and increased the number of math problems for two of the three children with ADHD, while the third child also needed an additional incentive of a preferred task (Flood, Wilder, Flood, & Masuda, 2002).

b. In group settings, Abramowitz and O'Leary (1991) reviewed three types of peer rewards: (a) the behavior of the entire group determined everyone's rewards, (b) each child's own behavior determined his or her rewards, or (c) the behavior of one child determined the rewards for each group member. When using peer-mediated rewards, the peer group needs to have specific information about how to support each child's appropriate behavior; otherwise, they may target the child with ridicule. (These effects have not been studied with students with ADHD.)

Social Rewards plus Small Tangibles

Use praise paired with a variety of small stickers given immediately. Do not use toys or "distracting" objects (Douglas, 1985). The use of tangible rewards was negatively associated with attention to task even for average learners (Newby, 1991).

Social Rewards plus Physical Activities

Provide opportunities for gross motor activities after tasks, such as additional recess, gym time, stretches, or even laps around the gym. This gross motor activity has been shown to decrease absences, out-of-seat behavior, talking out, and teacher ratings of hyperactivity and aggression (Bass, 1985; Berger, 1981; Elsom, 1980; Evans, Evans, Schmid, & Pennypacker, 1985; McGimsey & Favell, 1988; Walker, 1980).

TEACHING STRATEGIES
SOCIAL REWARD BEST PRACTICES

1. Use contingent activity rewards. Activity rewards are very powerful rewards for active children. By using activity, we are using what might be termed "the dessert principle" or technically the Premack Principle. That is, we ask children to work hard in order to "get" a preferred activity. "If you get this less preferred activity done, you can do this more preferred activity."
2. Provide "out-of-seat" rewards using out-of-seat tokens, which allow travel to specific areas (e.g., running errands inside the classroom and then outside the classroom).
3. Provide opportunities for task-related talking as a reward, especially in small groups and in large-group discussions.
4. Provide opportunities for small motor movements as rewards (and incentives) between or during tasks, such as
   a. participating in active games or drills,
   b. using calculators,
   c. organizing or filing materials, or
   d. cleaning the chalkboard.

In order to use preferred activities, educators must know what these are. What does the child do or ask to do? If a child is frequently out of seat, this child will most likely work to sharpen pencils, go on errands, or collect papers—something that has to do with standing and moving out of his seat. One might need to observe what the child does when out of seat. If it is talking to another child, then perhaps the child will work for brief periods of time to talk to or work with another child or teacher. The cartoon below contains cues to this child's preferred activities.

When you assess individual preferences, do not judge the behavior. If a child daydreams a lot, then we might assume this is a preferred activity. And without judging the social acceptability of the behavior, we could have the child work for time to daydream. Otherwise, children will daydream less constructively during lessons. They can learn to daydream contingently (i.e., after appropriate behavior, such as a period of work). This technique was applied below.

TEACHING STRATEGIES
LET THEM EAT PASTE

Glenn, an 8-year-old, socially withdrawn child, ate paste during the art class period and didn't do his art projects. One day I decided to change my approach. I simply said, "Glenn, you work on your art activity for this amount of time and you can eat this amount of paste." I placed a small paper cup full of paste on his desk. Glenn looked at me in disbelief, said nothing, but for the first time he did his art project and then ate his paste. We gradually reduced the paste (but not altogether) and increased the amount of art.

Use negative consequences

Presenting negative events When you chase a behavior with unpleasant consequences (e.g., a reprimand), that behavior "should" decrease. Most often the reprimand does make the child feel badly. However, the question is, Do children with ADHD reduce inappropriate behavior in response to negative consequences differently from their classmates?

To reduce disruptive behavior, it appears that combinations of lost plus gained points may be needed for students with ADHD. For example, points lost for disruptiveness were not effective until points were added for quiet behavior with middle school students (McLaughlin & Malaby, 1972).

Taking away positive events A negative consequence can also be defined as taking away positive things (e.g., fines, response cost, time-out from an activity). Fines are often applied to students with ADHD. Unfortunately, teachers typically take away recess and outdoor activities, such as field trips, because it is clear that these are preferred activities for these children.

The effectiveness of taking things away from children with ADHD may depend on the child's interest in the task and a child's emotional reactivity to loss. For example, taking away and giving produced similar gains during high-interest tasks, but low-interest tasks were performed well only with reinforcement gains for students with ADHD (Carlson & Tamm, 2000). Furthermore, Solanto (1990) reported that getting pennies for accuracy and losing pennies for errors were equally successful in reducing impulsive responding, but a large number of the ADHD group performed worse by responding faster under conditions of response cost.

Time-out also removes the child from a presumably reinforcing social situation and places him or her in a separate nonsocial environment. For successful completion of time-out, a student must stop the offending activity, shift attention to his or her behavior, sit calmly and quietly, and wait (Grskovic et al., 2004). Unfortunately, these requirements are difficult for students with ADHD, who may engage in activity to increase stimulation or use additional avoidance behavior (e.g., talking back), both of which would increase the duration of their time-out (Gunter, Denny, Jack, Shores, & Nelson, 1993). Replacing task-avoidance behavior with something "to do" was the subject of the following study:

EVIDENCE-BASED PRACTICES
TIME-OUT PLUS DELAY ACTIVITIES

Students with emotional and behavioral disorders were taught to use a string of active response beads (ARBs) to move, count, and breathe after the teacher said, "You have a time-out for. . . Get an ARB." Results showed that the ARBs were effective in decreasing the classwide percentage of intervals spent (a) in inclusionary time-out across three academic settings from 20% in baseline to 2% during intervention and (b) in exclusionary time-out from over 30% of the time to 0% to 6% in the three academic settings (Grskovic et al., 2004).

Use combined approaches for whole-classroom programs Level systems and token economies are the combined approaches often used in special education settings where children present more severe problems and teachers can devote more time to management. In these programs, students earn tokens or move up levels (later to be "traded" for additional privileges, activities, or objects). Children also can lose tokens (response cost) or go back down levels. To improve work completion and accuracy, one successful program awarded points, combined with response cost for rule violations, and delayed time-out for harmful or dangerous behavior (Pelham et al., 1993). Daily report cards were sent home, and performance summaries were given at the end of each class. Improvements have also been recorded from intensive and multiple-session programs of cognitive training (Slate et al., 1998).

The limitations of these studies is that they are single-subject designs implemented in controlled settings (e.g., hospitals, university clinics) by trained individuals (Pelham et al., 1998). Their application to most educational settings is thus restricted. "Parents and regular classroom teachers are typically much less willing to implement complex, contingency-management programs" (Pelham et al., 1998, p. 628).

EVIDENCE-BASED PRACTICES
To Decrease Inappropriate Behavior for All Children

Present Negative Consequences

1. Use soft reprimands to decrease disruptive behavior (Abramowitz & O'Leary, 1991)
2. Use soft, private, short reprimands that are delivered calmly (without emotion) and immediately (Abramowitz & O'Leary, 1991)
3. Avoid negative attention to off-task or inappropriate behavior (e.g., do not say "sit down" or "pay attention") and avoid strong social responses (e.g., loud, emotional responses, such as yelling) to negative or aggressive behavior (Meyer & Zentall, 1995)
4. Use firm reprimands, delivered with eye contact and within 1 meter (but not as far away as 3 meters) to quiet behavior, reduce disruptiveness, and increase compliance (Kapalka, 2004; Van Houten, Nau, MacKenzie-Keating, Sameoto, & Colavecchia, 1982)

Withhold Positive Activities

Use inclusionary time-out by asking a child to sit on the periphery of an activity for a specified period of time. During this time, ask the child to observe and/or record predefined appropriate responses by other children (Porterfield, Herbert-Jackson, & Risley, 1976). This may be particularly important for children with ADHD, who are less likely to attend to neutral social information (Zentall, Javorsky, & Cassady, 2001).

TEACHING STRATEGIES
To Decrease Inappropriate Behavior

Present Negative Consequences

1. Use repetitive activities, as these should be experienced as negative because of the loss of desired novelty over time. Thus, techniques such as restitution (whereby the child must repay the "victim" by carrying books or washing their windows) and overcorrection (whereby the child must not only fix the mess he or she created but also do additional cleaning, straightening, repairing, or repaying) should be effective with children with ADHD, although I located no studies to this effect.

Withhold Positive Activities

1. Develop behavioral intervention plans that do not withhold recess, gym, or extracurricular activities, which these children *need* to maintain attention to their tasks.
2. Use a minimum amount of time away from the family, as reported by this parent: "We instituted a period-by-period behavior management system within his school day. He gets evaluated at the end of each period, and then, depending on his total score, he gets an earlier or later bedtime. It has worked well."
3. Use inclusionary time-out with humor. The following is such an example:

TEACHING STRATEGIES *(Continued)*

Chair Timed-Out

After several tippings of his chair over during a classroom activity, the teacher finally walked over to the child with ADHD and said, speaking directly to his chair, "You know chair I am really tired of you falling over all the time and disrupting the class. Now I want you to take yourself outside right now, into the hall, and you may not come back in until after recess!" The child stood there with his mouth open in disbelief. He took the chair outside, came back into the classroom, and just stood where his chair had been, awkwardly, and went out and got his chair after recess.

4. In general, use punishment as if it were a regulated sport—with rules, consequences, and fair play. Remember that children with ADHD do not disregard consequences; they simply do not stop to consider that consequences will follow.

Baseball and Whole-Group Management

A middle school teacher used baseball as a type of whole-class behavior management. When problems were pointed out during the day, he would call a strike. These were usually whole-class noise levels or percentages of the class failing to turn in assignments.

In addition, positive comments, behavior, or performance were called home runs. A run would cancel a strike. If three strikes were accumulated, several outcomes were possible: (a) students would have an in-class test rather than a take-home, (b) students would have a closed-book test rather than an open-book/notes test, and (c) students would have a pop quiz and so on (Zentall & Goldstein, 1999).

LIMITATIONS OF BEHAVIORAL CONSEQUENCES

Many immediate gains can be achieved when using positive behavioral techniques, and typically these are exactly what teachers need in short-term behavioral management. Perhaps teachers are reluctant to use behavioral strategies in a more systematic way or over time because they assume that the curriculum should eventually engage the child through interest and success. Alternatively, they may have observed that improved behavior (a) will revert back when treatment is withdrawn, (b) will not generalize to different situations, (c) is still not normalized to the same level as peers (i.e., it is one standard deviation below), and (d) is not associated with improved academic learning (Fantuzzo & Atkins, 1992; Martens & Kelly, 1993; Pelham et al., 1998). In other words, changing behavior is less likely to result in improved learning, although improved learning can result in improved behavior. In addition, behavior therapy has been demonstrated to be more effective for children than with adolescents (with mean effect sizes of .92 and .58, respectively [Whalen & Henker, 1991]). Finally, girls but not boys with ADHD could inhibit impulsive behavior when punishment was a consequence (Milich, Hartung, Martin, & Haigler, 1994).

Behavioral techniques can also be time consuming. "In all fairness, [behavioral] interventions appropriate for children with moderate-to-severe ADHD can be quite complex and time intensive," and teachers prefer techniques that do not demand a great deal of their time (for a review, see Frank, Sanchez-LaCay, & Fernandez, 2000, p. 99). Other more philosophical criticisms of using some types positive consequences for behavior have been made by the late John Nicholls, a well-known motivational psychologist. When asked what he thought of a program whereby children would get a pizza for every book read, he responded that the consequence would be "a lot of fat kids who don't like to read" (Kohn, 1993). That is, if you must be paid to read, then reading must be an unpleasant task. Kohn similarly stated, "If, like Skinner, you think there is nothing to humans other than what we do, then this criticism will not trouble you. If, on the other hand, you think that our actions reflect and emerge from who we *are* (what we think and feel, expect and will), then you have no reason to expect interventions that merely control actions to work in the long run" (p. 784). This debate, with specific reference to children with ADHD, is represented in an interchange with a colleague of mine in psychology. She said, "I'll get them to sit still, and you get them to learn." I said, "It's going to be a lot harder for me to get them to learn, if they have to sit still."

In sum, positive behavioral techniques are important early steps in behavioral management. Teacher praise will always be important feedback (a) to improve attention and learning, especially for children who have skill deficits (for a review, see Witzel & Mercer, 2003), and (b) to reduce disruptive behavior that may accompany a boring task or a difficult learning task.

More problems may arise when using negative consequences, especially when teachers forget to balance these with similar rates of positives. Furthermore, the rates of negative attention students receive increase over time as they progress in years at school. Baker and Zigmond (1990) documented equal rates of positive and negative statements in elementary math and reading classes. However, negative feedback increased four to five times more often than positive by the intermediate grades, and students spent most of their time on workbooks and other paper-and-pencil tasks. This can be devastating for children who are already receiving more contacts but 50% less praise than their peers (for children with behavioral problems, see Wehby, Symons, & Canale, 1998).

That educators ignore the "normal" behavior of students with externalizing problems may be based on the expression, "Let sleeping dogs lie" or, as translated from Hebrew, "Don't wake the bears." Unfortunately, when the bears do awaken, they are very hungry. In addition, teachers may not realize that the negative attention they deliver to students with ADHD contaminates other students in the classroom. That is, typical children received more negative attention than they would in classrooms without students with hyperactivity (Campbell, Endman, & Bernfeld, 1977).

Furthermore, students with ADHD can respond emotionally to negative feedback. This may explain why problem-solving performance actually deteriorated over time for children with ADHD (Rosenbaum & Baker, 1984). Given the amount of negative feedback these students receive, it is no wonder that they have less emotional tolerance for corrective feedback and less ability to accept responsibility. Even students with conduct disorder were better at accepting responsibility for being emotionally upset and more willing to change than were students with ADHD (Morris, 1993).

Even more hidden costs exist when taking things away from these children, especially activity. Active children need more, not fewer, opportunities for activity. When a student is placed outside the classroom for time-out, he or she also loses opportunities for learning. Perhaps it is for this reason that in some states and for children with individualized education plans, documentation must be placed in the student's eligibility file when he or she is placed in the hallway (Couvillon, 2003).

In practice, teachers and parents begin to observe that keeping students after school or out of recess was ineffective and often made the situation more negative.

TEACHING PRACTICES

Sometimes he has a hard time staying on task and getting his school work done. So the teacher . . . kept him in at recess. And that didn't seem to really do any [good]; it didn't help him to do it (mother of a child with ADHD).

Like one day I asked him to clean his room—this beautiful sunny day—and he didn't. So he stayed in that room until he finished. He never did. He missed the sunny day, and the room was twice as messy as when he started (father of a child with ADHD, cited in Zentall, Moon et al., 2001, p. 512).

OBSERVATIONS OF WORST PRACTICES: HE MISSED THE SUNNY DAY

He generally makes up excuses for why he hasn't done this. And it's an endless battle between the two of us. He misses recess. He misses lunch recess (teacher of a student with ADHD and giftedness, cited in Zentall, Moon et al., 2001, p. 512).

The ineffectiveness of withholding activity until the child complies can be explained by the strength of task avoidance. For students with both giftedness and ADHD, tasks such as cleaning a room, homework, and rote tasks can be unpleasant in both their low intellectual challenge and their low novelty. Only by making the task more pleasant or increasing the rewards can we increase the child's approach to a difficult or unpleasant task.

Taking away activities that the child has earned assumes that the child has somehow "chosen" to digress out of oppositionality, laziness, or not caring. These are assumptions that educators can make when students with ADHD fail their "level systems." They progress up levels, because they can summon energy for a period of time, however, unlike other children in behavioral disorders classes, students with

ADHD were more likely to slip back. The answer lies in several areas: one is their impulsivity and another is that the offending behavior may serve an important function for the child, such as relatedness or stimulation seeking. In the absence of active replacement behavior, the child will fall back down the rungs of the ladder. The highest-frequency problem of children with ADHD in the classroom is a need for something to do, more than a lack of understanding of what is expected.

Use cognitive behavioral techniques

The difficulties of behavioral techniques in achieving long-term change led to a more process-oriented approach (cognitive behavioral management). Of these techniques, the most effective procedure for students with ADHD is self-regulation interventions, including self-monitoring, self-reinforcement, and self-evaluation (Reid, Trout, & Schartz, in press). Self-monitoring procedures typically involve a mechanical device that signals a child to self-attend to behavior and then to record the presence or absence of that behavior. An initial step in self-regulation is defining and tallying target behavior. Typically, a cue (e.g., taped tones presented at random intervals by a multialarm watch or a card prompt to "stop, look, and listen") signals the child to attend to (i.e., self-monitor) his or her own behavior or specific emotional reactions (e.g., anger, anxiety). Examples of current-day mechanical devices are electronic diaries, PDAs, and handheld computers.

Self-monitoring is described more fully in chapter 10 because it is frequently applied to increase attention to task and task completion. However, self-monitoring techniques can also be used to reduce impulsivity and hyperactivity ratings and improve compliance with rules, anger management, and cooperative behavior (for reviews, see Daly & Ranalli, 2003; Zentall, 1989b). Adolescent peers, as well as adults (e.g., paraprofessionals), can be used to signal students with ADHD to self-record, monitor the accuracy of their self-recordings, or cue them to use a previously taught social or emotion regulation skill (Whalen, 2001). This adult involvement can be reduced over time.

The potential of this technique can be observed in natural contexts. That is, children spontaneously use self-regulation.

STUDENT PRACTICES
TALK TO THE HAND

An 8-year-old boy with ADHD spontaneously drew a face on his hand. The thumb formed the lower part of the face, and a mouth was drawn on the thumb joint, which could be moved up and down to represent a mouth talking. The circumference of the head was formed by the index finger on which the child had drawn hair.

The "hand" was examining his paper after he completed each problem and looked up at the child, asking him, in a "funny" voice, whether he had checked this answer. He nodded to each question. The hand appeared to be an internalized teacher.

Other self-monitoring applications are the following:

EVIDENCE-BASED PRACTICES

Cartoons for Self-Monitoring

"Countoons" are cartoon representations of students' appropriate and inappropriate behavior that are delivered to the child on a simple tally counting frame. In addition, small stick-figure pictures can be drawn in small boxes by the child depicting behavior and preferred activities to-be-earned (Daly & Ranalli, 2003).

Video Self-Monitoring

When students were provided with a 30-second viewing of a prior social activity with a self-evaluation (yes/no) written response to a question, "Do I get along with my classmates?" a decrease was found in the inappropriate behavior of children with externalizing behavior. Adding tangible rewards did not produce better effects than the self-monitoring and self-evaluation procedure (Falk, Dunlap, & Kern, 1996).

Specifically with students with ADHD, using the child's own positive behavior on an edited videotape showed the following:

1. Viewing 15-minutes of their own behavior on tape reduced the rate of disruptive behavior by almost one half in a later classroom observation (Boggs, Santagrossi, & Zentall, unpublished data).
2. Viewing behavior over a 5-month period reduced activity and increased math productivity (Woltersdorf, 1992).

LIMITATIONS

Cognitive behavioral techniques

Cognitive behavioral techniques typically involve training children to self-verbalize strategies to use with academic or social tasks. Early reviews reported that cognitive methods failed to maintain self-regulation across time and situation (for a review of children with ADHD, see Abikoff, 1985, 1991) and were less effective in reducing behavior than behavioral (e.g., tokens and response cost) or academic interventions (e.g., peer methods) (DuPaul & Eckert, 1997). Lack of effectiveness may have been due the verbally mediated procedures of most cognitive techniques. Self-verbalization training was even less effective with preschoolers and early elementary schoolchildren (i.e., ages wherein behavior is less regulated by verbalizations [Whalen & Henker, 1991]).

However, recent reviews have documented that 86.6% of the studies from school-based samples reported positive effects for self-regulation interventions with the hyperactive/impulsive behavior of children and adolescents (Robinson, Smith, Miller, & Brownell, 1999). A 29th-percentile-rank improvement in behavior for these interventions, as well as maintenance from 1 to 3 months, was greater than that documented for comparison groups. However, some of these studies did not have nontreatment comparison groups. In addition, a recent review (Reid et al., in press) documented that, on average, student improvements could be greater than one standard deviation for the specific self-regulation interventions of self-monitoring, self-reinforcement, and self-evaluation, with self-monitoring producing the strongest and most consistent gains.

Application of behavioral strategies in the management of aggression

The survival of teachers depends on their ability to manage rates of aggression that can be 90% higher for students with ADHD than for their classmates (Prinz, Connor, & Wilson, 1981). Sometimes this behavior is simply an attempt to achieve social goals, and students need alternative ways to relate. For example, one general education teacher described her student with ADHD:

TEACHING STRATEGIES
FRIENDS

He's a loner. He doesn't have a lot of friends in the room. . . . He wants to have friends but he doesn't know how to relate to them. Now I'm just reflecting to a couple of minutes ago right after lunch. Michael had grabbed onto the boy's arms and had the boy's arms locked behind him. He doesn't have any idea how to play with someone or be friends with someone—other than fight or wrestle (Moon et al., 2001 unpublished data.)

EVIDENCE-BASED PRACTICES

Targeting Aggression

1. Have as many adults present as possible. When the amount of teacher attention (social stimulation) was low (7% to 17%), rates of aggression were relatively high (.5% to 14%), but when the percentage of teacher attention was high (92% to 97%), students with ADHD demonstrated 0% aggression (Nidiffer, Ciulla, Russo, & Cataldo, 1983).
2. Increase the number of available resources. Resources can be defined as those materials and supplies needed for a learning assignment or for enrichment. Aggression occurs primarily when resources are scarce and objects or information are needed but out of reach (Knapczyk, 1988). From the students' perspective, resources can give rise to issues of the "haves" and "have-nots," especially when resources and privileges are made available only to children who complete a standard amount of work. Thus, resources and their availability can give rise to conflicts about "fairness."
3. Provide large spaces within which to play and learn. Restricting space results in reduced access to resources and can increase frustration/aggression. In free play with peers when activity was restricted to one table and one toy, youth with ADHD were less cooperative and more aggressive (for a review, see Zentall, 1985a). Social proximity can be especially threatening for children with aggression.

Targeting Aggression and Excessive Activity

1. Teach children to do the following:
   a. Request brief sessions of physical exercise. Activity programs for individual children with ADHD for 5 to 7 days per week for a 6-week treatment period have been shown to reduce behavioral rating scores relative

(Continued)

EVIDENCE-BASED PRACTICES *(Continued)*

to groups without these exercise programs (Wendt, 2000). Only 30% of teachers who instruct children with behavioral problems report using physical exercise (Ruhl, 1985).

b. Use positive words with setting cues (e.g., when someone disagrees, they would say, "You have a different opinion—that's okay."). Children who were trained to use more prosocial words had fewer aggressive responses than children trained with neutral words (Combs & Slaby, 1977).

c. Practice through role playing. Role playing may be important for children who have an active learning style in order for them to later produce self-controlling responses (Hinshaw, Henker, & Whalen, 1984).

2. Alter antecedents or setting events by doing the following:
   a. Providing both positive and negative examples (models) of social responses to produce better attention and comprehension for students with attentional disorders than only positive and neutral examples (Carrol, Bain, & Houghton, 1994).
   b. First obtaining and then sustaining eye contact (20 to 30 seconds after a request) to increase compliance in boys with ADHD who are oppositional (Kapalka, 2004) when compliance with directives is necessary.
   c. Using mirrors in small-group or other social contexts to reduce emotionality. Mirrors increase attention to the self and also appear to bring a child's own behavioral standards to the forefront. The effectiveness of self-attentional techniques may be found only when the student knows what to do or what is appropriate social behavior (i.e., knows the relevant standards).
   d. Teaching children how to recognize their own body cues that signal intense affect so that they can respond appropriately to teasing and accusations. Boys with ADHD were taught to identify their body and cognitive signs of anger as potential cues of threat and their need for self-control. Each child in the treatment group then rehearsed and used a self-selected strategy when presented with peer taunters. Greater self-control was observed in the self-monitoring-plus-strategy group, whereas psychostimulant medication only reduced the intensity of responses (Hinshaw et al., 1984).
   e. Labeling neutral or ambiguous cues in social situations to encourage positive interpretations of social cues and prevent the hostile interpretations that are typically found for boys with aggression (for a review, see Zentall, Javorsky et al., 2001).
   f. Asking children to verbally restate what the prior events of a social interaction were *before responding*, especially when presented with a challenging interaction (Zentall, Javorsky et al., 2001).
   g. Training students to self-monitor their positive social interactions, which can also decrease the aggressive and impulsive behavior of students with ADHD with their peers (e.g., using taped signals and self-reinforcement [Posavac, Sheridan, & Posavac, 1999]).
   h. Training students to monitor and tally their negative behavior and responses during socialization (playtime period) on personal monitoring notepads (small notebooks that students keep in their pockets). After the playtime, students with ADHD reported the result of their self-monitoring to the teacher, who gave them feedback. Findings were improved positive social interactions and reduced negative interactions with peers (Gumpel & David, 2000).
3. Alter behavioral consequences by doing the following:
   a. Providing loud or emotionally intense responses after children's prosocial behavior to increase that prosocial and decrease negative behavior (Meyer & Zentall, 1995).
   b. Teaching peers to respond with disapproval in low tones or with nonverbal, nonemotional reactions (e.g., by walking away) when confronted by the aggressive social behavior of students with ADHD. However, asking

(Continued)

EVIDENCE-BASED PRACTICES *(Continued)*

peers to ignore aggressive behavior is difficult (Ervin, DuPaul, Kern, & Friman, 1998) and seems to communicate to students with ADHD that aggressive behavior is acceptable (Meyer & Zentall, 1995).

c. Providing response options. Students with ADHD and aggression interpret social situations better when possible responses are provided (i.e., multiple choice produces better performance than free response) (Whalen & Henker, 1985).

TEACHING STRATEGIES
TARGETING INTENSE, NEGATIVE AFFECT AND TALK

Teach verbal routines and place these on prompt cards for the following:

1. How to establish a context for their own topics of conversation.
2. How to ask questions to redirect conversations to interesting subject matter.
3. How to be assertive rather than aggressive. Teach them specific verbal statements, such as, "When in doubt, take a break" or "When you have nothing positive to say—zip it." Anger is produced when the individual says to him- or herself, "Things have to go my way." Teach the child to say, "I want things to go my way, but they won't always."
4. How to talk with others:
   a. When entering and leaving situations (hellos, good-byes, and so on), because these contexts are more likely to elicit aggression (Knapczyk, 1988)
   b. When entering a conversation (e.g., "If you don't mind," "excuse me, but . . .")
   c. When interrupting (i.e., using statements such as, "I hope you don't mind if . . ." or "It really helps me if . . .")
   d. When negotiating their own learning (e.g., by saying, "I have a very hard time in all classes listening for longer than 15 minutes. It helps me when I can talk, ask questions, doodle, or change seats.")
   e. When offering personal opinions (i.e., to make suggestions rather than commands: "It is my opinion or preference that . . .")
   f. To deescalate a difficult situation (e.g., with a lower voice volume)
5. How to show differences between assertive and aggressive behavior by role-playing the following:
   a. Justifying disappointment or displeasure
   b. Refusing requests
   c. Using politeness and reasoning to get some of what they want in social situations (i.e., to convince others)
   d. Dealing with someone's anger
   e. Dealing with your own fear
   f. Standing up for your rights or others', such as dealing with group pressure or persuasion (Adults with ADHD have somewhat greater difficulty handling situations requiring assertion ([Hechtman, Weiss, & Perlman, 1980]).
6. How to use a "hassle log" to record aggressive or emotional reactions in the daily lives of adolescents to begin understanding what events trigger anger (Feindler & Ecton, 1986)
7. How to distinguish between what the child is permitted to do and cannot do (State important rules with reasons about safety, comfort, learning, communication, fairness, life, health, and so on. In this way, behavior and its consequences are rule based rather than person based or person biased.)

Monitor medication to reduce activity, impulsivity, and aggression

General descriptions of the types and effects of psychostimulant medication are available elsewhere (Block, 1998; Wilens, Biederman, & Spencer, 2002). Between 1 million and 3 million children are estimated to use Ritalin (40% of elementary schoolchildren for an average duration of 2 years, 32% of middle school students for an average duration of 4 years, and 15% of high school students with ADHD for an average duration of 7 years [Castellanos et al., 2002; Runnheim, Frankenberger, & Hazelkorn, 1996; Whalen & Henker, 1991]).

What contributes to this number of students is the body of evidence that about 70% to 80% of youth with ADHD show improvements in the core behavioral symptoms of ADHD (hyperactivity and impulsivity) for at least 14 months as well as in reduced disruptive and hostile behavior and more compliant and cooperative social behavior (Abikoff & Hechtman, 1996; Whalen & Henker, 1991). Specifically, it can reduce the level of activity by 28% in classroom contexts (Porrino et al., 1983). The improvement rates are less for preschool children—only 50% of whom can be considered good responders (Sonuga-Barke, 2001).

A comparison of the effectiveness of psychostimulant medication versus psychosocial summer programs (parent training and academic and social skill training, with a buddy) has been summarized:

EVIDENCE-BASED PRACTICES CONCLUSIONS TO MULTIMODAL AND STIMULANT MEDICATION TREATMENT STUDIES

1. Combined treatments of medication plus behavioral/psychosocial were equivalent to medication alone but with lower doses of medication.
2. Combined treatments were superior to traditional community care in required, such as social skills, achievement, and parent–child relations.
3. Combined treatments were superior on 12 of 19 measures; medication alone was superior on 4.
4. Parents were more satisfied with a behavioral component than with medication alone. Medication resulted in decreased parent–child interactions.
5. Medication and psychosocial were equally effective with co-occurring ADHD and anxiety disorders, and both were superior to community care.
6. The highly controlled medication group was superior to medical management in the community (summarized by Whalen, 2001).

TEACHER LIMITATIONS: DO WE HAVE A CURRICULUM OF "READ'N, WRITE'N, AND RITALIN"?

"Despite progress in the assessment, diagnosis, and treatment of ADHD, this disorder and its treatment have remained controversial. . . . The major controversy regarding ADHD continues to be the use of psychostimulant medication both for short-term and for long-term treatment" (National Institutes of Health, 2000, p. 182). These questions that are no longer on the forefront: (a) Will students with ADHD be more likely to abuse other substances (only for children with co-occurring conduct disorder [Lynskey & Fergusson, 1995])? and (b) Are we drugging America's children into nonresponsiveness and passivity? and are depicted in the cartoon. Instead, issues related to effectiveness have come forward.

Medication can improve social behavior, but it can also decrease positive affect and behavior (Mrug, Hoza, & Gerdes, 2001). Even when short-term gains in social behavior have been made, negative interactions, the negative social status of children, and long-term social outcomes have not been impacted (Mrug et al., 2001; National Institutes of Health, 2000; Whalen & Henker, 1991). Overall, the majority of children treated with stimulant medication do not demonstrate fully normalized behavior, often remaining as much as one standard deviation below the mean (Pelham et al., 1998).

That is, children with ADHD continue to show academic, social, and emotional problems into adolescence and adulthood (for a review, see Abikoff & Hechtman, 1996; American Academy of Pediatrics, 2001). In addition, "the positive changes

TEACHING STRATEGIES
MEDICATION AND PERFECT BEHAVIOR?

He's not the perfect child when he's on his medication but off the medication he very obviously doesn't have control of his arms and legs and things like that (cited in Zentall, Moon et al., 2001, unpublished data).

associated with treatment are frequently not maintained when medication is discontinued" (Abikoff & Hechtman, 1996, p. 669).

Compliance with treatment can also be low. That is, 88% of children with ADHD had received methylphenidate at some time, but at any one point in time, only about 6% of these children may be receiving medication, and about 25% of medication dosages were missed in a 3-month period of time (Wolraich et al., 1990). Furthermore, 20% of children had discontinued treatment by the fourth month and 44% by the 10th month, and only 22% survived a 2-year follow-up (for a review, see Whalen & Henker, 1991). The "vast majority" of children with ADHD who were prescribed stimulants, received only 1 to 2 months of medication, indicating that the children or their parents may not have liked the effects (Pelham et al., 1998, p. 192). Although social improvements led to an increase in positive interactions from parents and teachers, the evidence also suggests that parents and peers were more likely to ignore children who were taking medication than children with ADHD who were taking a placebo (for a review, see Landau & Moore, 1991).

Educators also need to monitor the side effects of medication on behavior, especially for preschoolers (Wilens et al., 2002). The behavioral side effects are increased preseverative responses and tics; the somatic side effects are a loss of appetite, sleep difficulties, and various physical aches and pains with rare side effects of slowed growth and increased heart rate and blood pressure; and the emotional side effects are increased moodiness/irritability/crying for no apparent reason (Schulz & Edwards, 1997; Tannock, Schachar, & Logan, 1993). Finally, the symptoms of children with other disorders (e.g., Tourette's syndrome, schizophrenia, depression, autism) can be made worse by psychostimulant medication (Committee on Children with Disabilities, 1987).

Given the number of students on medication, the side effects, and some of the questions of long-term effectiveness, new treatment guidelines for ADHD have been proposed by the American Academy of Pediatrics (2001), which devoted 3 years to reviewing the published literature on the treatment of children with ADHD. See guidelines on the following page.

SUMMARY

Some of the behavioral problems of students with ADHD are disruptive and aggressive learned responses. These learned responses must be relearned. The elements of behavioral interventions include (a) a clear set of treatment goals that recognize

EVIDENCE-BASED, EDUCATIONALLY RELEVANT GUIDELINES FOR USE OF MEDICATION

Guideline #1: When initiating medication treatment, be sure that your child is tested on a full range of doses. The optimum stimulant dosage for a child is not weight dependent, and it is not possible to predict in advance what the best dose—or most effective stimulant—will be for an individual child.

Guideline #2: Before medication treatment is implemented, parents should insist that a systematic procedure is in place to monitor the effectiveness of the different doses being tested. In a recent multisite study (the MTA Cooperative Group study, 1999), only 17% of the children with ADHD continued on the same medication and dosage throughout the entire 13-month maintenance period. The remaining children all experienced at least one change in drug or dosage during this period.

Determining the benefits of medication treatment needs to be far more systematic than anecdotal reports from a teacher that the child seems to be "doing better." In addition to ratings of core inattention and hyperactivity-impulsivity, it is important to obtain information on the child's academic functioning, social relations, and ability/willingness to follow rules at home and school. Effective treatment for ADHD should improve children's functioning in these key areas in addition to reducing core symptoms.

Guideline #3: Alternate types of stimulants should be tried before giving up on stimulant medication. As noted in AAP treatment guidelines, children may respond favorably to one stimulant but not another. For this reason, the guidelines recommend that two or three stimulant medications be tested across a full range of doses before nonstimulant medications are considered.

Results from The MTA Cooperative Group study (1999) suggest that using nonstimulant medications or multiple medications will be necessary for only about 2% of children receiving medication. The only medications other than stimulants for which efficacy in treating ADHD in children has been demonstrated are tricyclic antidepressants, bupropion, and clonidine. These should be considered only after a child has not responded to a careful trial of two or three different stimulants. That is, there is not sufficient research supporting the safety and efficacy of combined pharmacotherapy for children with ADHD. Note: The use of Pemoline/Cylert is not recommended because of potential complications with liver functioning.

Guideline #4: The AAP guidelines compared behavioral techniques with stimulant medication. The guidelines indicated that the stimulants were more effective than behavioral techniques on the core symptoms of ADHD.

However, on some measures, children receiving combined behavioral and medication treatments

1. showed greater improvement than children treated with medication alone,
2. required a significantly lower dose of medication over the 14-month study, and
3. resulted in higher ratings of parent and teacher satisfaction with the treatment plan. As with stimulant medication, behavior therapy typically did not bring a child's behavior into the normal range and did not yield positive changes that persisted beyond the time it was being implemented (American Academy of Pediatrics, 2001).

the functional and biogenetic nature of the behavior of students with ADHD, (b) the use of evidence-based stimulant medication with a close monitoring of the effects and side effects, and (c) the use of evidence-based behavior therapy while monitoring the different responses of students with ADHD to behavioral interventions. In this process, a shift in consequences should occur—from negative to intense positives (e.g., with emotional praise, added preferred activities). See Figure 9.2.

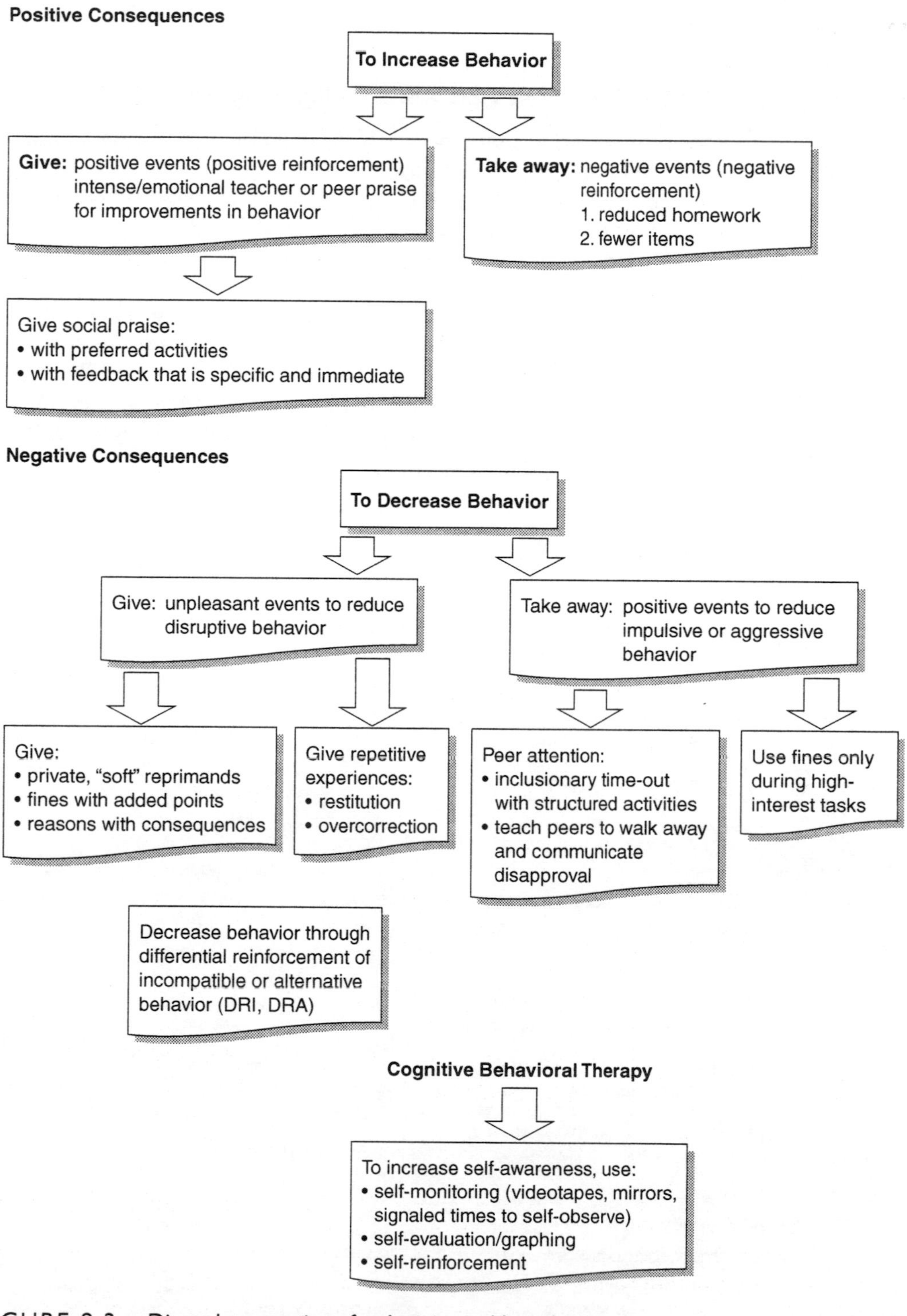

Positive Consequences
To Increase Behavior
Give: positive events (positive reinforcement) intense/emotional teacher or peer praise for improvements in behavior
Take away: negative events (negative reinforcement) 1. reduced homework 2. fewer items
Give social praise: • with preferred activities • with feedback that is specific and immediate
Negative Consequences
To Decrease Behavior
Give: unpleasant events to reduce disruptive behavior
Take away: positive events to reduce impulsive or aggressive behavior
Give: • private, "soft" reprimands • fines with added points • reasons with consequences
Give repetitive experiences: • restitution • overcorrection
Peer attention: • inclusionary time-out with structured activities • teach peers to walk away and communicate disapproval
Use fines only during high-interest tasks
Decrease behavior through differential reinforcement of incompatible or alternative behavior (DRI, DRA)
Cognitive Behavioral Therapy
To increase self-awareness, use: • self-monitoring (videotapes, mirrors, signaled times to self-observe) • self-evaluation/graphing • self-reinforcement

FIGURE 9.2 Direct Interventions for Activity and Impulsivity

DISCUSSION AND APPLICATION QUESTIONS

1. What is the essential difference between children with ADHD and children with behavioral disorders in their response to consequences?
2. How can we make being "good" as much fun, while giving children with ADHD and oppositionality as much control, as being "bad"?
3. Contrast the behavioral treatments of DRL with DRA using what you know about children with ADHD.
4. "My daughter is a fourth grader who had ADHD. Her teacher is asking me for advice about how to manage my daughter's temper outbursts at school. Detention and taking away her recess have not been successful. Any ideas?"
5. "Pete is up and down in his seat. He is disturbing others and getting little work done. The other students are complaining about him. What do I do?"

If you have access to children, select a child for assessment and fill in the information for the plan shown in the following chart.

Behavioral Support Plan—First Steps

Student:		Grade:
Date:		Teacher:
Physician:		
Medication:	Dose:_____	Schedule:_____
Administered by? _____		
Team Meeting:	Date:	
Participants:	Roles:	
#1. Behavioral Concerns:		
a. Setting Events (triggers or antecedents) when Behavior(s) Occur:		
b. How Individuals Usually Respond to the Behavior:		
#2. Select socially desirable replacement behavior:		
__ Friendly verbal and helping behavior (vs. competitive)		
__ Friendly physical and assertive responses (vs. aggression)		
__ Relevant task statements (vs. self-comments)		
__ Requests for participation or to enter group (vs. disruption)		
__ Makes suggestions (vs. being bossy)		
__ Requests structure/help		
__ Requests praise or change of activity		
__ Requests activities during wait time		
__ Responds nonemotionally to failure/frustration		
__ Acceptance of some responsibility (vs. blaming others)		
__ Other		

(continued)

#3. Circle those you have tried:

For disruptive or excessive activity, have you:

a. Assessed the child's knowledge of appropriate behavior?
b. Provided clear rules or routines of activity (how you can be active or when)?
c. Provided substitute responses during the task (turning pages or changing seats) or programmed activity into lessons (e.g., small chalkboards at desks)?
d. Contracted the child—if he or she does what you want for a limited time, he or she can earn a preferred activity (e.g., go on an errand or work with a friend)?
e. Determined the contexts during which this behavior most frequently occurs (specific tasks, with specific adults or children, after lunch, and so on)?
f. Provided the child with alternative ways of obtaining his or her goals of relatedness, mastery, and so on)?
g. Used peer-tutoring activities?
h. Rewarded the whole class for the efforts of that child (e.g., by allowing them to listen to music)?
i. Required the child to make amends by redoing or compensating the victim through his or her efforts?
j. Used baseball strikeouts and home runs for the whole class that are redeemable with open-note tests instead of recall tests?
k. Provided expectations and clear rules (wait until another person has finished and a pause occurs by counting "one elephant, two elephants")?
l. Provided a substitute activity (note taking) or provide small manipulative toys (pipe cleaners, paper clips, journals, books, or tapes) to fill in waiting times?
m. Asked the child to outline, underline, read out loud, rewrite, paraphrase, or talk to a peer about the directions before beginning a task?
n. Helped the child plan thoughts using word processors or picture representations?
o. Taught the child to cross out incorrect responses on multiple-choice tests?

For negativism or noncompliance, have you:

a. Determined the task contexts during which this behavior occurs most frequently (specific tasks)?
b. Given the child choice of goals, methods for completing task/activity, or amount of time?
c. Used clear direct statements, with no further verbalizations or motor prompting while giving the child 5 seconds to comply, and continued visual eye contact to produce better compliance than requests that are vague, interrupted, or with insufficient time to comply (Williams & Forehand, 1984)?
d. Used cooperative learning or peer-tutoring activities?
e. Rewarded the whole class for the compliance and efforts of that child?
f. Given the child some leadership responsibilities?
g. Given the child a prompt list he or she had to read before beginning jobs and check off once they were completed?

For excessive or negative talking, have you:

a. Contracted the child—if he or she responds with positive verbalizations for a limited time, he or she can go on an errand (activity) or work with a friend (social)?
b. Praised the quality of statements and stories (relevance, cohesiveness, assertiveness, and politeness)?
c. Taught the child to ask questions?

CHAPTER 10

Strategies to Improve Attention

OBJECTIVES

- Identify the different types of inattention.
- Select those interventions/accommodations that will work best with each type.

KEY TERMS

practice effects
self-instructional strategies
academic productivity
self-monitoring
normative comparisons
normalized performance
satiate or habituate
metacognition

Failure in school is due primarily to a failure to focus, select/organize, and maintain attention to what is important. Learning to focus on what is relevant rather than on what is bright, moving, or immediately apparent is difficult for students with ADHD. For this reason, it will be easier to use what is bright and moving to capture and focus their attention on what is important. This chapter presents modifications of settings and tasks that have been documented to direct and sustain the attention of students with ADHD.

HOW TO GUIDE THE ATTENTION OF STUDENTS WITH ADHD

Highlight relevant information

Directing attention can be accomplished by structuring the task or providing increased information about appropriate task responses. Structure should not be interpreted as restricted opportunities and inflexibility in the curriculum. When structure is defined as increased information and opportunities, it can have several benefits in guiding the task responses of *all* students, especially when they are given new social or academic tasks. Knowing what to do can also decrease task-avoidance behavior and improve the quality of performance for young children and children with specific learning disabilities (Gunter, Denny, Jack, Shores, & Nelson, 1993).

For students with ADHD, placing attention-getters (bright, intense stimuli) directly onto what is important is useful. (See Evidence-Based Practices box, page 216.) For example, when color was added to letters that were difficult to remember (i.e., irregular nonphonetic letters) in a spelling recognition task, students with ADHD actually outperformed their spelling-matched peers (Zentall, 1989a). Similarly, attention can be focused to the tops of letters (i.e., color added to the top of the letter "O")

EVIDENCE-BASED PRACTICES
PRINCIPLES FOR IMPROVING THE SELECTIVE ATTENTION

1. **Eliminate** irrelevant cues, such as (a) nonrelevant visual novelty that overlaps within complex visual tasks, (b) verbal detail within listening tasks and attractive visual stimuli (toys or cartoons) on the periphery, and (c) conversational noise during complex thinking tasks. If nonrelevant color, movement, or interest is added to complex tasks (e.g., reading, spelling), it should be added only to improve sustained attention and added
   - later after the child has had sufficient practice with that task, as color that is added early to increase task attractiveness is likely to disrupt performance, especially for young students with ADHD more than for their peers, or
   - during the task performance of older children with ADHD because nonrelevant color can reduce activity and slow their responses, relative to comparisons (e.g., Zentall, Falkenberg, Smith, 1985).
2. **Highlight** relevant information with intense visual or verbal cues to guide the attention of students with ADHD to
   - important features of their external social tasks (e.g., to subtle feedback from others)
   - positive outcomes they have experienced or may experience
   - positive behavior and intentions of others
   - important subtleties in their tasks which can reduce errors (Zentall & Dwyer, 1988).
3. Provide additional **practice** in frequently spaced practice sessions.

to improve copying performance of children with ADHD, who typically fail to close up their letters (Zentall & Kruczek, 1988).

Verbal highlighting of important information can be accomplished with alterations in tone, speed, and use of pauses in the teacher's speech. "Children's attention is increased by . . . children's voices, peculiar voices, and animation" (Milich & Lorch, 1994, p. 181). Verbal questions can also guide the attention of children to preceding events in social interactions. Alternatively, provide "the big picture" using analogies or models, especially early in social interactions or when listening to important task instructions (Zentall & Gohs, 1984).

Additionally, provide feedback that is verbal for visual tasks and visual feedback for verbal tasks (Bennett, Zentall, Giorgetti, & French, 2005; Burt & Ryan, 1997). When feedback and the task are the same modality, students with ADHD perform worse than peers. In general, use text, voice, and images in combination to make learning accessible to every child.

To promote social learning, students with ADHD will copy active or talkative peer models who can be used to reduce both aggressive and hyperactive behavior (Goodwin & Mahoney, 1975; for a review, see Meharg & Woltersdorf, 1990). In addition, children with ADHD can perform socially as well as their peers when they are presented with scaffolding cues, such as beginning or ending verbal cues, written choices, or pictured stimuli (for a review, see Zentall, Javorsky et al., 2001). When using verbal scaffolding (self-instructional strategies), teach specific statements for younger students (e.g., "I need to start at the top") and general strategies for older children (e.g., "I should plan out exactly what I need to do") (Copeland, 1981, 1982). These types of scaffolding may direct their attention to a range of alternatives that can be essential for students who typically focus on the bottom line or on latter events in interactions (Milch-Reich; Campbell, Pelham, Cannelly, & Gem, 1999).

Practice

Additional experience with a task will also reduce its selective attention requirements, producing better performance over time (e.g., "practice effects" [French, Zentall, & Bennett, 2003; Malone & Swanson, 1993]. For children identified by teachers for their failure to complete assignments and pay attention in class, repetitive 60-minute selective attention practice sessions were conducted after school in small groups that met twice a week for 18 weeks (Semrud-Clikeman et al., 1999). Visual attention tasks asked students to find a target stimulus embedded among distracters that were initially easy and presented with one target figure among dissimilar figures. Difficult tasks were a number of closely spaced, similar figures. For the auditory tasks presented on a cassette tape, children initially counted a target word and then counted words beginning with specific sounds. Children also reviewed their speed and accuracy scores from prior sessions, discussed and evaluated strategies, and set daily goals (self-evaluation and goal setting). Pre- and posttraining assessments indicated that the ADHD group who received selective attention training scored as well as their non-ADHD classmates and significantly better than the children in the ADHD group who did not receive intervention (Semrud-Clikeman et al., 1999).

Similar studies have been conducted in a game format requiring practice in sorting materials with an increasingly faster pace and with additional nonrelevant stimuli added versus comparison conditions of computer games (Kerns, Eso, & Thomson, 1999). Although children in both sorting and computer game conditions improved with practice, the sorting (selective attention) practice produced greater gains than the control condition on several measures.

EVIDENCE-BASED PRACTICES
KEEPING THE BEAT—ATTENTION PRACTICE

Participants. Boys with ADHD were randomly assigned to one of three conditions, the first two of which involved 15 training sessions, each 1 hour.

Conditions. Interactive metronome (IM) training used a computer-produced beat that the children responded to with various hand and foot exercises. Auditory feedback was provided to indicate whether a response was on time, early, or late. Participants attended for increasing longer periods of time. Video game training involved

(Continued)

EVIDENCE-BASED PRACTICES *(Continued)*

instruction in five nonviolent video games, requiring hand–eye coordination, mental planning, and multiple-task sequencing. In each game, the difficulty increased as boys became more skillful. The control group received no training or additional attention during the 3-week period.

Results. Boys in the no-attention control group had 28 scores improve (pre- to postassessment) and 30 scores decline (consistent with chance findings). Boys in the eye–hand coordination video group gained in 40 of the 58 measures, whereas boys in IM training improved on 53 of the 58 measures, which was greater than the gains for the video game training. Specifically, the IM group showed decreased parent-rated aggression as well as improved reading achievement, motor control, and computerized tests of attention than boys in each of the other conditions (Shaffer et al., 2001).

Reenactment and Retelling Practice

To refocus attention to all events,

1. students with ADHD retold events from a social story, which improved their performance of identifying relevant social solutions to the same level as their peers (Zentall, Javorsky et al., 2001), and
2. students with ADHD and learning disabilities reenacted the events from a puppet show and demonstrated less impulsivity and improved visual attention than a nonreenactment group (Abikoff, 1985).

TEACHING STRATEGIES
TO IMPROVE SELECTIVE ATTENTION

1. Change the visual task:
   a. Before evaluating performance on a task, give students with ADHD early experience with the format and selective attention requirements of the task.
   b. Use formatting for assignments that is clear, with global points, outlines, or steps.
   c. Use films or videos to present an initial global view of a topic area. Show big points, the skeleton structure, and major steps (see the Global Summary, Figure 10.1).
   d. Require children to color math process signs with magic markers to focus their attention to computational changes.
   e. Focus attention to parts of instructions, assignments, and directions with underlining or color emphasis.
   f. Orient students with prompt cards about what to expect during transitions or with unfamiliar tasks.
   g. Provide students with "job cards" or a step-by-step instructional checklist for tasks or jobs.
   h. Provide sample problems with self-correcting flash cards, folders, or answer tapes.
2. Change verbal task instructions:
   a. Use auditory signals (bells or flashing lights) to indicate changes in topic or activities.
   b. Use nonverbal signals to focus attention to listening for brief 4- to 5-minute periods of time.
   c. Eliminate detail and description from directions or lecture material.
   d. Ask children to repeat verbal instructions or the contents of a conversation because they may have heard only the emotional content.

(Continued)

TEACHING STRATEGIES *(Continued)*

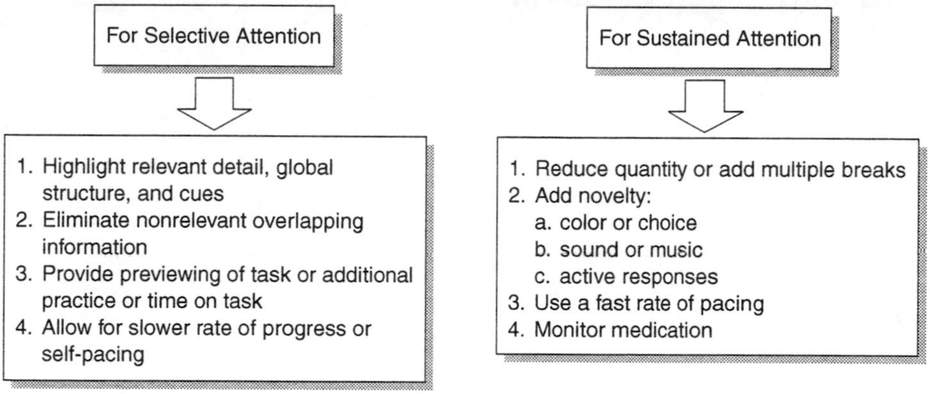
For Selective Attention
1. Highlight relevant detail, global structure, and cues
2. Eliminate nonrelevant overlapping information
3. Provide previewing of task or additional practice or time on task
4. Allow for slower rate of progress or self-pacing
For Sustained Attention
1. Reduce quantity or add multiple breaks
2. Add novelty:
a. color or choice
b. sound or music
c. active responses
3. Use a fast rate of pacing
4. Monitor medication

FIGURE 10.1 Global Summary of Accommodations

e. Use analogies, stories, or pictures from related experiences to make broad points.
f. Use verbal outlines with numbered points (e.g., "There are three things I want you to remember.").
g. Use emotional emphasis during the presentation of important material.
h. Orient students verbally to what to expect during transitions. For example, for individuals with ADHD, it is not uncommon to walk into glass doors. It would be helpful if a taped voice were audible close to the door (as on moving walkways at airports) that said, "Be careful of the glass door. The handle is on the right, and it is brass," or "Don't forget to take your pills, lunch, and homework."
i. Orient students to past positive outcomes they have experienced and to the positive behavior and intentions of others. In other words, they may need direct instruction in interpreting neutral or ambiguous experiences.

3. Change the setting:
   a. Use sound, movement, and interest as a way to capture and focus attention to important events or objects in the environment (e.g., on bulletin boards).
   b. Allow *all* children in the classroom the option of working in areas away from conversations during new or complex tasks—as long as this placement is temporary, self-selected, and provides access to visual stimulation, peers, resources, and opportunities for movement.
4. Teach students with ADHD skills in the following:
   a. Finding important information in outlines, headings, topic sentences, and end-of-chapter questions.
   b. Organizing materials and events by time, topic, date, and so on.
   c. Representing information globally. For example, have them draw a coat of arms to describe their understanding of setting, characters, and main activities of a book.
   d. Asking and answering big questions as they plan. Older, brighter, and more verbal students can learn to examine the whole in reading assignments by asking such questions as "How many pages/problems are there?" or "Are there any instructions on the page?" or "Are there any questions in the chapter?"

HOW TO HELP STUDENTS WITH ADHD MAINTAIN ATTENTION OVER TIME

EVIDENCE-BASED PRACTICES
PRINCIPLES FOR IMPROVING THE SUSTAINED ATTENTION (PRESENTED IN CHAPTER 6)

1. Reduce the quantity of material or reduce the time dedicated to practicing or redoing a task at any one sitting
2. Increase novelty at various intervals during and within the task—but especially toward the end of repetitive or rote tasks
3. Enrich the environment with novelty (visual and auditory) and avoid isolating children in cubicles
4. Use behavioral consequences and academic skill training as it applies specifically to students with ADHD (see chapter 9)
5 Monitor the use of medication (see chapter 9)

Change the child

Most research has been devoted to interventions designed to directly change the child as described in this section (i.e., rather than changing the task or setting, see Chapter 8). These direct interventions are medical and behavioral in nature.

Monitor medication The most effective intervention is psychostimulant medication (Hoagwood, Kelleher, Feil, & Comer, 2000). Medication is particularly effective in improving measures of sustained attention and memory and reducing careless errors related to sustained attention (Miranda, Presentacion, & Soriano, 2002). Performance improvements have been found most often in the amount of work completed (academic productivity), with about half the children showing improved work quality (accuracy); the remainder make no gains or decline in performance (Abikoff & Hechtman, 1996; Rapport, Denney, DuPaul, & Gardner, 1994).

Long-term, positive vocational outcomes or academic achievement outcomes have been disappointing, including failure to find gains in higher-level skills, such as reading comprehension, math problem solving, creative expression (American Academy of Pediatrics, 2001b; Hinshaw, 1994; Mrug, Hoza, & Gerdes, 2001; MTA Cooperative Group, 1999; Richters et al., 1995; Runnheim, Frankenberger, & Hazelkorn, 1996; Swanson, McBurnett, Christian, & Wigal, 1995). In other words, medication cannot teach or promote cognitive reorganization (Miranda et al., 2002). Although medication can improve the length of attention, it cannot tell children what is important to pay attention to (i.e., cannot remediate selective inattention).

In addition to the behavioral and somatic side effects reported in chapter 9, Sprague and Sleator (1977) further cautioned that the dose of medication that was optimal for change in behavior was two thirds stronger than what was needed for optimal learning. Attentional side effects include increased passivity or reduced responsiveness, overfocusing of attention, and an inability to shift strategies or think divergently in problem-solving tasks (Schulz & Edwards, 1997; Tannock, Schachar, & Logan, 1993). These performance effects are as important for educators to communicate to parents as behavioral effects; parents can then report the effects and side effects of medication to their physicians (i.e., unless the educator has obtained permission to communicate directly to the physician).

Behavioral strategies The second most frequently used intervention to improve the attention of students with ADHD involves the application of learning principles. Although the major focus for this is given in chapter 9, specific applications of consequences to improve attention are presented here.

EVIDENCE-BASED PRACTICES
APPLICATIONS OF CONSEQUENCES TO IMPROVE ATTENTION (FROM EVIDENCE PRESENTED IN CHAPTER 9)

1. Identify areas where persistence of attention already exists (e.g., with computers) and use these interests to mediate or reinforce persistence in other content areas.
2. Adapt learning principles for students with ADHD by increasing the intensity (loudness or rate) of reinforcers and decreasing the intensity of negative social consequences, especially as they are applied to off-task attention. Stimulus intensity reinforces or increases the behavior of students with ADHD.
3. Teach students to self-monitor their own immediate behavior and feedback from the self (i.e., behavioral standards, thoughts, strategies, feelings, a history of past experiences and their consequences, and future positive expectations), for example, by questioning students and teaching them to self-question.

Intense consequences Children with ADHD need consequences that are more immediate, frequent, and stimulating or paired with other incentives or preferred activities (see chapter 9). More frequent reinforcement is needed to encourage sufficient practice to overlearn rote skills (Hallahan, Tarver, Kauffman, & Graybeal, 1978).

Self-monitoring Teaching children to self-monitor behavior requires little teacher effort to achieve positive attentional gains in students. Only adult presence was necessary for children to comply with self-monitoring procedures of checking off behavioral events when signaled by a taped tone (Cameron & Robinson, 1980; Varni & Henker, 1979). Children can also be taught to self-attend to internal emotional reactions, such as anger or anxiety, and then to record the presence or absence of a behavior in response to those internal states.

Self-monitoring procedures increase the number of academic problems attempted, number correct, task persistence, and on-task attention of children with mild disabilities (De Haas-Warner, 1991; Harris, Graham, Reid, McElroy, & Hamby, 1994; Maag, Reid, & DiGangi, 1993; Prater, Hogan, & Miller, 1992; Levendoski & Cartledge, 2000). Self-monitoring procedures can even improve on-task behavior for children currently receiving psychostimulant medication (Mathes & Bender, 1997). The latter intervention was implemented in a resource room with three boys with ADHD who were trained to ask whether they were doing what they should have been doing when they heard a random-interval tone. Self-monitoring can also be used (a) with self-graphing (self-evaluation) to double the amount of on-task behavior of children with ADHD and learning disabilities, relative to baseline (Shimabukuro, Prater, Jenkins, & Edelen-Smith, 1999) or (b) with reinforcement that the child self-administers (e.g., stars, stamps). Self-monitoring using a handheld computer increased homework production for three of the four children with ADHD (Currie, Lee, & Scheeler, in press). The failure of these techniques for specific children can be attributed to the difficulty of specific tasks. That is, self-monitoring directs attention to the self, helping children with ADHD persist and monitor responses they *can already make* (e.g., to go slower, to review responses [Zentall, 1989b]). If a skill deficit exists, then increased attention alone is insufficient.

The use of mirrors is another simple self-monitoring technique to increase task persistence, productivity, and accuracy. Mirrors can be placed such that the child can view him or herself while performing a task. With typical children, evidence exists that mirrors can improve performance on a concept-learning task (Ellis, Hawkins, Pryer, & Jones, 1963). For middle school students with ADHD, mirrors (presented in the context of a "homework station" with additional stimulation and access to preferred activities) improved their homework production to levels equivalent to their peers (Hall & Zentall, 2000). For the two students who used the homework station, homework completion and accuracy rates were tripled. A related study examined the effects of just a mirror and found that it was especially beneficial for those children with ADHD who looked at the mirror (i.e., were "distracted") and less beneficial for those who did not look relative to comparison children (Zentall, Hall, & Lee, 1998).

When students also engage in self-graphing or self-evaluation, with *private* feedback from adults, they are more likely to increase effort and improve performance. Motivational researchers suggest that public or normative comparisons (e.g., displaying grades on bulletin boards) emphasize negative aspects of functioning for those children not displayed, particularly when the child compares unfavorably with classmates (Jagacinski & Nicholls, 1987; Zimmerman, 2000).

Change the task

Changes of the task are familiar modifications for educators. One often-cited task change is reducing task length. This can be accomplished by increasing the pace of responding, especially for rote practice tasks (van der Meere, Shalev, Borger, &

Gross-Tsur, 1995). However, fast pacing does not improve creativity, planning, or complex task performance. Students may need to regulate their own instructional pace during these complex selective attention tasks. In addition to reducing the amount of task time, educators can shorten task instructions by using fewer words (concise and global verbal directions [Zentall & Gohs, 1984]).

A few changes in task novelty have actually documented better sustained attention performance for students with ADHD than for matched controls when stimulation was added (a) prior to a visual creativity task (i.e., an exciting car-chase video [Shaw & Brown, 1999]) and (b) at the same time as a simple attentional coding task (i.e., colorful pictures, paper streamers, toys, comic books, balls, a mirror, a Bobo clown, a punching bag, an audio recording, and a candy reward—but not in the nondistracting or in the nonreward-plus-distracting condition [Worland, North-Jones, & Stern, 1973]). To sustain attention on this simple boring task, children with ADHD appeared to need a "high dose" of concurrent stimulation as well as an anticipated candy incentive. It will also be important to decrease the frequency and intensity of negative consequences that follow off-task attention.

For all students, especially those with mild disabilities, quality of instruction(s) may be more important than quantity:

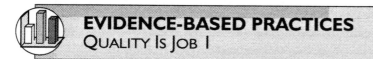

EVIDENCE-BASED PRACTICES
Quality Is Job 1

When the quality of instruction in regular education produced task engagement for the typical student at 75% to 80% or higher, students with learning disabilities were also engaged at high rates (60% to 87%). However, when overall class engagement was generally low (less than 80%), students with learning disabilities were engaged at even lower rates (43% to 62%).

Implications. High-quality instruction reduces attentional differences between students with learning disabilities and their classmates (Friedman, Cancelli, & Yoshida, 1988).

It has often been documented that students with ADHD can sustain attention for relatively long periods of time when the task is engaging (e.g., television [Milich & Lorch, 1994]). Another way to increase instructional quality is to eliminate repetitiveness, which has the effect of decreasing off-task and behavioral problems for children with ADHD (Shroyer and Zentall, 1986).

For less interesting tasks or simple practice tasks (attentional search, sustained attention, handwriting, copying, or matching figures), relevant or nonrelevant color novelty can be added (Zentall, 1985b, 1986b; Zentall & Dwyer, 1988; Zentall et al., 1985). For example, students with ADHD read familiar stories less accurately in the traditional black-and-white print conditions. However, they read as accurately as their classmates when color was added late (Zentall, Grskovic, Javorsky, & Hall, 2000). That is, even nonrelevant color can produce normalized performance for students with ADHD during simple or familiar tasks.

Tasks that have active responses can also improve attention. For example, when children could push a button to see slides during a listening task, their performance was equivalent to the performance of their peers (Zentall & Meyer, 1987), especially during slow-rate listening tasks (Leung, Leung, & Tang, 2000). Whole-class active learning also improved attention and rates of learning for students with and without learning problems (for a review, see Heward, Courson, & Narayan, 1989; Kinder & Carnine, 1991). Whole-class choral responding produced better attention to task because of the increased active responding and the fast presentation rate. That is, in a 30-minute period, rates of active whole-class responding were 21.8 compared to a mean of 1.5 academic responses when teachers called for oral responses by individual students (Heward, 1996).

Change the setting

Settings that decrease off-task attention for students with ADHD are more novel (tests, films, and free time) than routine lecture and seat-work settings (Zentall, 1980). Similar attention gains have been reported by parents who rated their child's responses to after-school or weekend outdoor and "green" activities (e.g., playing in the woods) as significantly better than indoor nongreen activities (e.g., shopping, watching television [Taylor, Kuo, & Sullivan, 2001]). This research was based on the hypothesis that directed attention is fatiguing and needs involuntary attention directed to stimulating events, such as "strange things, moving things, wild animals, bright things, pretty things . . . blood" (James, 1962, as cited by Taylor et al., 2001, p. 57).

Although considerable empirical support indicates that novel settings are important for students with ADHD, the experience of educators tells them that when the child is placed in a cubicle, he or she will have nowhere else to look except at the task. Cruickshank was one of the first to advocate the use of cubicles for students with hyperactivity to reduce distractions (Cruickshank, Bentzen, Ratzeburg, & Tannhauser, 1961).

LIMITATIONS: PRACTICE WITHOUT EVIDENCE—FAILURE TO SUPPORT CUBICLES

Cruickshank's 12-month study and other similar research has failed to support the use of cubicles (e.g., not in reaction time, achievement test scores, or task completion times during perceptual/motor tasks) even in comparison to distracting classrooms with tape-recorded noises, toys, flying paper airplanes or bouncing balls. This body of research has assessed samples of students with brain injury, hyperactivity, distractibility, aggression, and emotional disturbance and compared their performances with IQ-matched controls.

Even though past research has failed to support cubicles and current research no longer assesses the use of cubicles and carrels, many current sources still recommend their use for students who are ADHD (Bussing, Gazy, Leon, & Garvan 2002; Paul & Epanchin, 1991; Reid, 1999). Perhaps educators assume that the environment "causes" children to look away from their tasks, as stated by this educator:

TEACHING STRATEGIES
WATCHING EVERYTHING ELSE

He isn't disturbing other people but it's just watching everything else that's going on. And he's always the last one to get finished because he's just so distracted when this person, clear across the room drops his pencil. He's got to watch and think about other things (cited in Zentall, Moon et al., 2001, unpublished date).

However children are not necessarily looking at an interesting environment, as much as they are looking for any excuse to avoid a task that is too easy, too difficult, or too boring. This is a problem with the task. When the task holds no attraction, the child will find some distraction. Eliminating the external distraction does not improve the task.

NOTE
A CLINICIAN'S OBSERVATION OF A STUDENT WITH ADHD

A teacher had placed a child with ADHD in a cubicle, and for 20 minutes the child was quiet. The teacher was delighted with his apparent concentration.

Dr. Goldstein decided to see what the child was doing and walked back into the cubicle. He found the child observing a worm making its way through a maze that the child had constructed (Sam Goldstein, personal communication, 1996).

Educators may also continue to use cubicles because they observe decreased off-task behavior. However, it is important to make a distinction between looking away from a task and poor performance. Even very young children can understand this distinction:

STUDENT PRACTICES

Mom, if I wasn't paying attention, how come I got all the answers right on the test? (6-year-old, cited in Zentall, Moon et al., 2001, p. 505).

Setting modifications can also involve changing the position of the child in the classroom. Placing the child near the teacher is both a best and empirically based practice. Although teacher presence alone does not eliminate performance errors, it does help children maintain attention (Steinkamp, 1980; van der Meere et al., 1995). In other words, teacher presence can increase social stimulation, but without a change instruction, teacher presence alone was insufficient.

Another easy-to-implement, empirically based practice is to arrange activities between tasks. Additional recess, gym time, or even laps around the gym have been shown to decrease absences, out-of-seat behavior, talking out, and teacher ratings of hyperactivity and aggression (e.g., Bass, 1985; Berger, 1981; Elsom, 1980; Evans, Evans, Schmid, & Pennypacker, 1985; McGimsey & Favell, 1988; Walker, 1980). Unfortunately, many schools nationwide are eliminating recess and gym time, with detrimental effects on students with ADHD as well as their peers. Recess and gym time are important for all students. Stevenson and Stigler (1992) reported, "Attention is more likely to falter after several hours of classes than it is, if opportunities for play and relaxation precede each class, as is the case in Asian schools" (p. 75).

Readin', rhythm, and 'rithmetic Music is easy to implement and improves performance on familiar tasks for students with ADHD (Abikoff, Courtney, Szeibel, & Koplewicz, 1996; Scott, 1970). Even typical students were more likely to do homework and without a loss in performance when there was music than when it was quiet at home (Bryan & Nelson, 1994; Pool, Kodstra, & van der Voort, 2003). However, music tempo must be considered during visual-motor performance because students with ADHD have poorer fine motor skills (see chapter 11). Perhaps for this reason, they make more errors under fast music conditions than their peers when asked to perform a precision motor task or a free drawing task (Klein, 1982).

TEACHING STRATEGIES
Best Practices for Helping Children Maintain Attention

1. Eliminate goals of completing long tasks during one time period:
   a. Use shorter more frequent tasks and tests (e.g., fewer spelling words or math problems).
   b. Break one task into smaller parts to be completed at different times—three short reports instead of one long one.
   c. Use multiple breaks within rote tasks.
   d. Use distributed practice rather than massed practice.
   e. Allow children to switch among tasks on their own, providing that each task is finished in the end.
   f. Have students proofread and edit work when it is "cold" (i.e., after time intervening) or with a buddy, tape-recorded list, in small groups, and so on.

TEACHING STRATEGIES *(Continued)*

2. Increase novelty and use performance standards:
   a. Provide students with certain quality standards as a challenge ("Can you do it this well?") for shorter assignments.
   b. Use technology (e.g., computers, videos, films).
   c. Incorporate student interests about science fiction, Native Americans, science, and pioneers (as self-reported by elementary students [Zentall, Moon et al., 2001]).
   d. Use pictures, anecdotes, collections, art, treasure hunts, games, group projects, and graphs during the performance of familiar tasks.
   e. Provide "real-world" projects or dramatics as application activities rather than relying on memorization. For example, the game "What's My Verb?" requires one team to act out a verb and another team to guess and use the verb in a sentence.
   f. Alternate low- and high-interest tasks so that child can complete less interesting tasks while looking forward to interesting tasks.
   g. Add noise stimulation to increase arousal and narrow the attentional field, which is what is needed during the performance of repetitive practice tasks.
   h. Introduce novel pets to the educational environment. One teacher reported that she brought a parrot to school, with the outcome that the whole class showed attentional improvements even though they looked at the pet.
3. Increase opportunities for motor responding during or after task performance (see also chapter 9):
   a. Allow children to "play with" objects (task- and non-task-related) during longer tasks or while listening to lectures.
   b. Use peer or small-group practice, which can be more stimulating when peers work together with games, flash cards, miniquizzes, timed drills, and so on.
   c. Do not take away recess or other special classes when children fail to attend. As stated by Ben, a 16-year-old student with ADHD-I, "I just learned to dawdle even more because I never got recess anyway." Furthermore, this was a heavy child who needed exercise.
   d. Encourage hobbies and collections.
   e. Provide opportunities for task-related talking (e.g., in small groups, in large-group discussions, and while children are seated in circles or half circles or clustered at tables rather than isolated in rows). This may be particularly important for girls with ADHD (Grskovic & Zentall, 2005).
4. Increase opportunities for self-monitoring:
   a. Use an audience, observer, or camera to help children self-monitor their behavior and attend to their own strategies and standards (Carver, 1979; Carver & Scheier, 1981).
   b. Involve children in fantasy or journal writing to focus attention to the self, as recommended by Meichenbaum (1979).
5. Assign unique topics and assignments.
6. This is an example of one student's unique interests:

Anne said she wanted to become a dermatologist because she wanted to study all the "gross stuff" that grew on people's skin.

1. Provide opportunities for choice.

STUDENT PRACTICES
Choice and Cereal Boxes

Ben, the same student with ADHD-I described previously, recalled his best assignment in school. He described one teacher who gave an assignment to create an advertisement for a cereal. They had to present this advertisement to the class, and they could choose how: they could design their own cereal box by creating a poster, a poem, a short play, or a video. Ben completed all of them.

TEACHING STRATEGIES
Jack: Off and On Medication

When off medication, he did miss assignments. He just wouldn't take it home, or wouldn't think about it, or he'd lose it . . . and his grade suffered because of that. . . . When he's on his medication he's a lot more focused, a lot more on-task, and participates in the discussions appropriately . . . [but when he was on medication] he was almost fastidious about making sure things were done. And then he was very tense and stressed . . . he would burst into tears cause it was all just too much. So that stress level wasn't good (cited in Zentall, Moon et al., 2001, p. 507).

Monitor the Effects and Side Effects of Medication

1. Learn which children have medication to be taken at school and know that a student has a right to privacy about his or her medications.
2. Communicate to the child that the pill can improve attention, but it is the child's effort and not the pill that is responsible for improved skills.
3. Assess attentional performance (e.g., math facts or handwriting quality using self-selected work arranged chronologically in a portfolio) or social behavior (e.g., the appropriateness of verbal statements or acts of kindness using self-recordings on colorful bar graphs).
4. Monitor medication side effects (e.g., irritability, sadness, tics, stress).

APPLICATIONS TO IMPROVE ORGANIZATION AND ASSIGNMENT COMPLETION

Organization can be learned from practice, similar to other selective attention skills, but it is not necessarily learned from living in an organized environment or with an organized person. Children can learn to comply with some of the routines of adults, but they must learn to organize the events, tasks, and time requirements in their own lives. Because students with ADHD were aware that they lacked object placement and retrieval routines, personal neatness, and organization (Zentall et al., 1992), interventions should be easier to implement.

TEACHING STRATEGIES
ORGANIZATION THROUGH SORTING

1. Teach children to put like objects with like objects.
2. Assign organizational roles and responsibilities in the classroom (e.g., for collecting materials).
3. Verbalize the sequence of activities in the day and of lessons.
4. Teach the student to set priorities for assignments (e.g., according to importance, time due, length, outside resources required).
5. Suggest that parents give children responsibility for sorting the laundry, the mail, the silverware drawer, and so on.
6. Teach the child to take notes on lectures or on written materials in three columns (main points, supporting points, and questions).
7. Teach word processing to reorder ideas.

Object-Placement Routines

1. Encourage routines of pocket folders with new work on one side, completed graded work on the other, and class notes organized chronologically in the middle.
2. Encourage parents to establish places for certain things at home (books and a homework outbox).
3. Provide storage space for materials (e.g., desk, locker, closet, container).
4. Have the child organize his or her desk or locker with spatial organizers and labels.
5. Set up the child's environment so that what the child uses is closest at hand.
6. Teach verbal routines of self-questioning—"Do I have everything I need?"—especially before leaving one place for another.
7. Observe the methods that individual children attempt to organize themselves in areas of their interests and use these ways in other areas.

Individual Organizational Systems

A student with ADD was reported by his teacher to have poor organizational skills. When the teacher was asked whether he organized anything well, she said yes; he had a great card file system of organizing ideas and notes for the stories he planned and loved to write. If this system worked in one area, it most likely could be transferred other areas. The teacher was surprised and pleased at how easily this organizational method transferred to other areas, such as classroom notes, homework assignments, and so on.

Time Routines

1. Teach the child routines to put the current date and the date to be completed on each piece of paper.
2. Give the child duplicate sets of materials to use at home and in school, in class A and in class B.
3. Provide the student with a schedule of daily events or teach the student to draw or use pictures so that the student knows exactly what and how much there is to do in a day, a period, and so on.
4. Develop monthly calendars to keep track of long-term events, due dates, assignments.
5. Use assignment organizers (notebooks or folders).
6. Provide the student with checklists (e.g., materials needed and steps to follow). Tape these prompt cards in desks, on books, or on assignment folders.

(Continued)

TEACHING STRATEGIES *(Continued)*

7. Ask students with stronger verbal abilities to verbalize their steps in planning activities as models for the student with ADHD.
8. Teach students to repeat or chant the thing to be remembered. They can turn it into a rap song or a poem.
9. Write homework assignments on the board in red chalk in the same place each time.

Applying Principles of Behavioral Management to Improve Organization

1. Write a contract with the student specifying what behavior is expected (e.g., having necessary materials for specified activities) and what reinforcement will be made available when the terms of the contract have been met.
2. Communicate with parents (e.g., notes home, phone calls, e-mail) in order to share information concerning the student's progress so that they may reinforce the student at home for being organized/prepared for specified activities at school (see chapter 12).
3. Have the student chart the number of times he or she is organized/prepared for specified activities (self-monitoring).

LIMITATIONS

Adding stimulation to important parts of tasks and the environment has several limitations. First, it takes time. Teachers will need to abstract the main points, make global outlines, and emphasize important details in tasks. However, these procedures will help all the students in their classes. To supplement these procedures, students with ADHD and their peers can be taught to highlight important information and how to use self-monitoring.

In addition, several limitations of interventions exist for sustained attention. These children will adapt (satiate or habituate) or get bored more rapidly to novelty than will their peers. This will require greater teacher flexibility and creativity to make periodic changes in the environment, task, and rewards or by allowing children to choose content or direct their own pacing, topics, task order, or peer groupings.

SUMMARY

Most individuals cannot attend to tasks that are too difficult (e.g., astrophysics), too simple (e.g., reading *Dick and Jane*), or not meaningful. Meaningfulness can be enhanced by explaining why a task is relevant to students. This was more effective than tangible rewards for increasing the on-task behavior of typical students (Newby, 1991). Meaningful tasks relate to children's interests and prior experiences.

For children with mild disabilities, tasks are often too difficult, producing earlier fatigue from the amount of effort required. For these children, simplified tasks or requirements will be helpful (e.g., decrease fine motor, perceptual, memory, or conceptual requirements). In the absence of assessment information to make informed decisions, educators can experiment with a range of difficulty levels and alternate response modes (e.g., computer, taped assignments, drama). When the appropriate task level and response requirement for that child have been identified, adapting instruction to improve selective attention would be the next step.

Selective attention. Two approaches can be used to improve the selective attention of students with ADHD: (1) highlight a task's global structure or relevant task details (parts of problems, words, sentences, or instructions) and (2) provide additional task practice. Again, when relevant detail is highlighted, students with ADHD can actually perform significantly better than their matched peers. An alternative to highlighting details is to highlight the structure of a task or situation by using global points, diagrams, analogies, and so on.

In addition, repeated practice can improve selective attention performance. That is, task errors generally occur early in selective attention performance (e.g., when new formatting is used) and decrease with additional practice, experience, or age. Perhaps for this reason, gains in selective attention performance, motor control, and reading were achieved from repeated practice training sessions with

(a) visual and auditory selective attention tasks and (b) hand/foot motor responses timed in response to a metronome.

Selective attention can be disrupted only when nonrelevant "stuff" overlaps with relevant task information. For this reason, visual environmental stimulation that is distant from a task typically will not interfere (unless cartoons are adjacent [see chapter 6]). Similarly, cubicles are not supported by research and produce no academic gains and can further isolate children socially and educationally.

However, conversations in the environment can overlap with listening and thinking that are required for learning new or complex tasks. Complex tasks must be presented where few ongoing conversations can be heard. The disruptive effects of conversations are even worse for young children or children with verbal learning disabilities for whom many verbal tasks are complex. Furthermore, high levels of noise stimulation can disrupt visual complex search or problem-solving tasks that require a wide attentional field or the generation of multiple solutions.

Finally, educational methods using self-monitoring charts and self-evaluation as well as self-focusing mirrors have demonstrated improved self-focused attention and performance. Other self-attentional techniques that have potential as best practices include journal writing, instruction in self-questioning, and fantasy applications of the instructional content.

Sustained attention. To help students maintain attention, common educational accommodations involve decreasing time and/or increasing novelty (e.g., activities, color, movement, noise, music). Most empirical work demonstrates that students with ADHD respond differently from their classmates to novelty added to the environment, to the end of task performance (an academic period or a day), or on tasks that require practice, repetition, and a narrow focus of attention (memory or rote tasks). That is, their performance can be improved to the same level as their peers when color or visual novelty is added, and some novelty interventions have documented sustained attention performance that is better for students with ADHD than for their classmates.

Added stimulation can also come from peer groups. The presence of any other person adds social stimulation, which facilitates already practiced (but not new) responses ("social facilitation effects" [Zajonc, 1965]). In addition, when children externalize their thinking with their peers, it allows them to think about their thinking (metacognition). For this reason, one-on-one interactions with a peer or a small group can be preferable to one teacher and a large group. However, social stimulation can be used only to facilitate responses. It is similar to psychostimulant medication, which "does not, by itself, educate" (Whalen & Henker, 1991, p. 129). Medication, like social stimulation, can improve sustained attention, but it does *not* appear to improve selective attention. That is, psychostimulants *cannot* teach children to look at parts of the curriculum, although peers could be trained to help students with ADHD understand task directions, how to study, and so on.

DISCUSSION AND APPLICATION QUESTIONS

1. Does it take longer for students with ADHD to practice rote tasks, or does it take more practice sessions?
2. Which would students with ADHD prefer for a written assignment: poetry or prose. Why?
3. Students with ADHD often need objects to hold during delays. List some appropriate objects.
4. Students with ADHD do not like routines because they require repetition. But routines are necessary for many classroom activities. How can you incorporate change into routines to make them novel or stimulating? Give three examples.
5. How and what does the teacher monitor when the student is taking medication?
6. Sue is avoiding working on her math-facts assignment and is rummaging through her desk. You tell her that when she has completed each row of her assignment, she can check it with a calculator. In addition, at the end of the total assignment, she could use a bar graph to indicate the number of problems per row that matched on the first try. What are you assuming about Sue, and what approach are you using?
7. You are the teacher of a high school course, and you assign a big research paper that is worth half the semester grade. When checking on progress, you discover that several of your students have not started the paper. Without the paper, they will receive an F for the grading period and will not get credit. What can you do?
8. What conversations might you have with a teacher who has behavioral contracts with her student that requires him to sit still? This teacher's attitude is that if he is on psychostimulant medication, he should be able to perform like everyone else.
9. What are the features within this textbook that apply principles of providing accommodations for students with selective and sustained attention problems?
10. You are the teacher in the following middle school. What do you do?

TEACHING STRATEGIES
USE OF COLOR TO ORGANIZE HOMEWORK PAPERS

Hi, my name is Maria, and I am a social studies teacher in a middle school. Our building effectiveness team has decided with the principal's approval that a "white only" rule will be instituted for using copy paper.

As a classroom teacher, the rule has not been very effective. Students cannot organize their materials and cannot find their assignments because they are looking through every "white" piece of paper they own. I believe the ADHD students are most harmed by this policy. ADHD students benefit from the use of colored paper on their daily assignments.

CHAPTER 11

Strategies to Improve Learning

OBJECTIVES

- Use this chapter as a resource for interventions for the specific learning problems of children with ADHD, ADHD plus learning disabilities, and ADHD plus giftedness.
- Understand what helps this group of children learn so that you can design learning plans.

KEY TERMS

- distributed practice
- global cues
- task-relevant self-talk
- decode
- whole-language approach
- phonological awareness
- peer-assisted learning
- story maps
- classwide peer tutoring
- mastery learning
- relevant task details
- intrinsic motivation
- extrinsic motivation
- cognitive stimulation
- homework coupons

Only about 17% to 30% of students with ADHD receive special education services (e.g., for reading and learning disabilities [Fischer, Barkley, Edelbrock, & Smallish, 1990; Zentall, 1986; Zentall & Smith, 1993]), and only 20% of adolescents with ADHD were receiving some type of intervention besides medication (Topplski et al., 2004). Under IDEA, students with ADHD are entitled to "access," "participation," and "progress" (Hitchcock, Meyer, Rose, & Jackson, 2002). In order to participate and make progress, students with ADHD, who have deficits in attention, need tasks that (a) are presented with their relevant or global features highlighted (e.g., outlines, general topics), (b) have active, well-defined responses possible with little delay time, and (c) maintain the child's interest and active participation with others over time. Strategies appropriate for students with ADHD for their specific learning and academic problems will be presented in the "map" order shown in Figure 11.1.

HOW CAN WE HELP STUDENTS WITH ADHD REMEMBER?

In chapter 7, we concluded that children with ADHD recalled less information only when they were required to hold information throughout a delay period, especially when there were internal or external interferences or additional tasks (e.g., requirements for ordering that information). Thus, they need strategies to help them hold information as they cognitively or behaviorally engage in other activities.

FIGURE 11.1 Academic Development Map

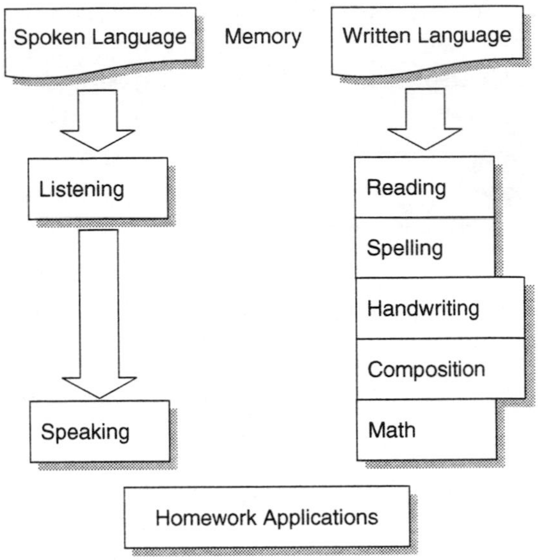

EVIDENCE-BASED MEMORY PRACTICES

1. Present information to be recalled with possible negative outcomes to help students with ADHD attend. Negative outcomes (e.g., unforeseen consequences of accidents) may arouse more intense affect and thus provide optimal conditions to help students with ADHD maintain activation of memory (Milch-Reich, Campbell, Pelham, Connelly, & Geva, 1999).
2. Ask them to sort words they need to remember, which can improve the performance of students with ADHD to the level of their peers (August, 1987). However, these sorting trials need to be short because over time their failure to sustain attention will wash out the initial gains from sorting.
3. Teach chunking or ordering strategies. Material can be presented verbally by time chronology, by topics, or by cause-and-effect relationships. These strategies produce gains for children with and without ADHD (French et al., 2003).
4. Provide practice when many items are to be remembered to improve the memory performance of children with ADHD to the memory performance level of peers (French et al., 2003).
   a. Distributed practice (5 to 10 minutes each day) is better for long-term recall than massed practice (25 to 50 minutes per sitting), especially for children with ADHD. Short practice sessions allow the teacher to reduce the quantity to be learned and emphasize quality (e.g., what is acceptable performance or performance improvement, and how does it look?).
   b. Games are ideal in getting children to practice materials (e.g., by bettering his or her own performance or team competition).
   c. Use self-monitoring procedures (see chapter 9) with taped signals and self-reinforcement to improve academic productivity and accuracy. Gains are typically found with lower-level skills (e.g., number of correct

EVIDENCE-BASED MEMORY PRACTICES *(Continued)*

problems or handwritten words) but not with higher-level skills (e.g., finding the main idea, study skills, or strategy use) (Reid, Trout, & Schartz, in press).

d. Ask children to self-monitor their task-unrelated thoughts as they proceed through a practice task because this can improve their immediate memory scores (French et al., 2003). That is, when students knew they would need to report the number of task-unrelated thoughts (internal interferences), it appeared to act as a form of self-monitoring.

5. Provide a signaling device:

Don't Forget to: Turn in Homework, Take Meds, and Get Your Books Ready!

Purpose. To determine whether an external device could be used to signal children to remember daily tasks.

Participants. One student with ADHD-I.

Treatment. Three-week baseline plus 3-week intervention—a computer program provided games to be used for daily or weekly rewards for remembering daily tasks that were signaled by a vibrating pager with 10 possible prompts per day.

Findings. Improved compliance with taking meds and getting books ready. Putting homework away showed an immediate gain that was not maintained and more global types of behavior, such as attentional ratings and home behavior, were not affected.

Implications. External signaling or paging can remind children with ADHD-I to complete specific events at a particular point in time (Epstein, Willis, Conners, & Johnson, 2001).

CAN WE HELP STUDENTS WITH ADHD LISTEN AND EXPRESS THEIR THOUGHTS MORE CLEARLY?

When teachers constantly call children to attention (e.g., "pay attention!"), children soon learn to attend only when "called." When this happens frequently, children will begin to tire of reminders, as indicated by this story written by a very young child with ADHD: "Once upon a time there lived a cow whose name was mooooo. Moo got tired of all the cows calling his name when they didn't even need him."

Listening

Calvin tries to tell his father what he needs in listening tasks:

STUDENT PRACTICES
CALVIN DESCRIBES EXACTLY WHAT IS IMPORTANT IN STORIES

Calvin: "What's this story you're going to read me, Dad? It doesn't have any romance does it?"

Dad: "Uhhh."

(Continued)

STUDENT PRACTICES *(Continued)*

Calvin: "Edit it out if it does. I hate romance.
Does it have any boring description in it?"

Dad: "Wellllll."

Calvin: "Skip it if you see any. I like my stories fast and gripping. It doesn't have a moral does it? I hate being told how to live my life. Skip the moral too."

Dad: "Does his majesty prefer color pictures or black and white?"

Specific evidence-based applications to improve listening for students with ADHD are as follows:

EVIDENCE-BASED LISTENING STRATEGIES

1. Reduce the length, repetitiveness, and descriptiveness of instructions to improve the listening performance for youth with ADHD (Shroyer & Zentall, 1986).
2. Present instructions with a visual model to increase the time listening to instructions and decrease memory errors (Carter & Shostak, 1980) and to improve performance over verbal instructions (Neef et al., 2004).
3. Add visual cue reminders (e.g., color, small pictures) to normalize the skills of following directions, specifically for students with ADHD, although it appears to be unnecessary for comparison children (Hamlett, Pellegrini, & Conners, 1987; Weingartner et al., 1980).
4. Ask students to write answers to questions on response cards (dry erase or chalk boards) because it is preferred by the majority of students and produces better scores on daily quizzes than volunteering answers orally (Narayan, Heward, Gardner, Courson, & Omness, 1990).
5. Allow active responses during listening tasks. For example, when children could push a button to see pictures during the performance of a listening attention task, their listening performance was equivalent to the performance of their peers (Leung, Leung, & Tang, 2000; Zentall & Meyer, 1987).
6. Provide task-relevant active responses. For example, in a single-subject design, a child with ADHD was asked to take notes during lectures, which produced less off-task behavior (55%) than when he passively listened (98% off task) (DuPaul & Eckert, 1998). See the following study as well:

Guided Notes for Notes

Purpose. To demonstrate that teacher prompts can help students selectively attend to lecture information.
Participants. Sixteen adolescents with ADHD (13 boys).
Tasks. Listening to lecture material.
Condition. A teacher-provided outline of main ideas and details that eventually became just a blank page.

EVIDENCE-BASED LISTENING STRATEGIES *(Continued)*

Findings. Improvements in the quality of notes and recording of details over baseline were found in study 1 and increased on-task behavior and improved daily assignment performance in study 2 (but not quiz grades or disruptive behavior). However, for those students with higher-quality notes, better comprehension and decreased disruptiveness were found.

Implications. Students can improve daily performance and on-task attention with guided notes (Evans, Pelham, & Grundberg, 1995).

7. Give them a global view, such as demonstrated in the following study:

Give Preschoolers "The Big Picture"

Purpose. The present investigation tested the hypothesis that listening problems were specifically in response to detailed types of information. To control for possible differences in ability and motivation to request additional information, the children were given a buzzer to signal the need for additional information.

Participants. Thirteen boys with ADHD and 13 average nursery school to first-grade peers equivalent in age and IQ.

Tasks. Communication tasks were presented with the student in the role of listener and the experimenter providing input. These tasks require children to (a) listen to descriptors of six block forms and (b) place the correct block on a stick. Global cues were "it looks like" versus detailed cues like "it has the following parts." For example, "it looks like a ray gun" or "it has two parts on the side that curve up, with a hole in the middle."

Design. Half the children in each group received a global cue first and then a detailed one, while the other half had the reverse order.

Findings. Students with ADHD experienced listening problems with longer response times and impulsivity only when given detailed information or when detail was available as the next cue. In contrast, they made more requests for global cues, and the availability of global cues reduced performance problems.

Implications. Data suggest overall that the problems children with ADHD have listening are due not to low IQ, poor motivation to get additional information, or overall difficulties listening but rather to the detail that was presented.

Use *global cues, metaphors, analogies, or models* to focus attention onto "the big picture," especially early in performance and during directions, listening, or social tasks when important task information can be embedded (Zentall & Gohs, 1984).

Speaking

Initially, we need to recognize the strengths of students with ADHD. That is, the stories they spontaneously tell are more novel and creative than those told by their peers (Zentall, 1988). This could be due to their attraction to novelty. Students with ADHD do, however, fail to produce extended or organized verbal responses, and their social conversations are marked by interrupting and turn-taking errors. To help them organize their language, the following evidence-based strategies may be useful:

EVIDENCE-BASED PRACTICES
ORGANIZING LANGUAGE IS LIKE JUGGLING ORANGES

1. Provide visual cues or scaffolding (e.g., pictures or beginning or ending verbal cues [Zentall, 1988]). For example, require them to design a framework for their spoken responses (e.g., draw a series of pictures first).
2. Allow self-talking during problem solving because Lawrence et al. (2002) reported that students with ADHD used more task-relevant self-talk. The researchers concluded that thinking aloud helped students with ADHD maintain arousal and focus.
3. Practicing speaker roles appears to help students with ADHD, although observation of a skilled partner was not helpful (Whalen, Henker, Collins, McAuliffe, & Vaux, 1979).

TEACHING STRATEGIES
BEST-PRACTICES TO:

Reduce Interrupting and Turn-Taking Errors

1. Teach the children specific manners to use when they interrupt (e.g., "excuse me" or "I'm sorry for interrupting, but . . .").
2. Allow talkative children a set number of talking times, questions, or comments per period that they can spend like tokens.

Reduce Errors of Sequencing and Cohesion

1. Ask them to tell you what the ongoing topic of conversation was and how what they said was related.
2. Ask them to reexplain what they just said in the exact order that it happened (from beginning to the end) or in the order of greatest importance or interest.
3. Invite them to plan different activities for picnics, parties, overnights, trips, and so on (e.g., what is needed, how to break tasks into parts, or how to make a time schedule, a map, or a budget) and then to present that information to a small group. Make planning fun.
4. Teach them outlining skills. Children can organize their own thoughts with spatial cues (i.e., dividing the paper into three columns for main points, supporting points, and questions) or by using magic markers with a specific color indicating main points and another denoting supporting points.
5. Allow them to contribute at the right time and place using visual placeholders.

Put It in the Parking Lot

When the teacher was conducting a discussion and students offered off-task ideas, one master teacher described a technique she had learned, called "Put It in the Parking Lot" (Heather Nymus, personal communication, 2002). On the board, Heather had drawn a parking lot space, and when children came up with a topic, she didn't dismiss the idea and the child's attempt to participate. Instead, she put the idea in the parking lot for later discussion at a more appropriate time.

Follow-up independence goals would be to teach children to keep their own parking lots (e.g., on sticky notes) for later discussion. Another teacher used the last 5 minutes of class for "chat time" while students went through their transition checklists.

CAN WE HELP STUDENTS WITH ADHD READ WITH BETTER COMPREHENSION?

Comprehension is the primary goal of reading. However, in order to capture the meaning from words, children must first be able to decode those words. A strong positive correlation exists between children's ability to read and reading comprehension (Torgesen, 2000).

Reading recognition

Learning to decode words and sentences requires the integration of many skills. Children must learn to (a) follow print from left to right across the page; (b) recognize that written symbols are equivalent to sounds and that a letter such as "b" represents a different sound from a similar turned-around letter, a "d" (even though a chair is a chair regardless of its orientation); and (c) combine sounds into words and words into sentences. To become a reader, a child must also have good information processing skills (discussed in chapter 7) and appreciate books as a source of pleasure and information. In other words, make reading enjoyable and take away social embarrassment.

Contributors to this learning process include the home and school reading environments, time allocated, and the methods used. Vaughn, Levy, Coleman, and Boss (2002) summarized observational research suggesting that critical instructional variables were time devoted to reading and the intensity of instruction (i.e., one on one). An imbalance in reading instruction occurs when too little time is dedicated to silent reading and reading comprehension and too much to worksheets and seatwork activities. At the youngest ages, when reading instruction is most critical, students appear to spend the least amount of time reading (25% reading time in grades 1 to 3 during the time allocated to reading, 35% in grade 4, and 50% in grade 5) and more time doing independent seat work, with delay time for organizing, consuming 20% of class time in math and reading (Baker & Zigmond, 1990). In addition, students with reading disabilities report that unhelpful aspects of their reading instruction included repetitive instruction, emphasis on sounding out words to the exclusion of other strategies, and unmotivating materials (Kos, 1991).

The instructional setting also appears to be important. Those teachers who emphasized whole-group reading instruction over combinations of small- and large-group instruction had more students with negative interpersonal behavior (e.g., hyperactivity) and more referrals of students exhibiting this negative interpersonal or academic behavior (Drame, 2002). This may be due to the increased wait time in large groups.

Methods and principles of teaching reading are also important. The "sight" method of teaching involves visual attention to and memory for a whole word. The phonetic method is a direct, explicit teaching of the relationships between letters and sounds and how they correspond to reading words in text. Reviews of broad principles for teaching phonological awareness, word analysis, fluency, and comprehension can be found elsewhere (e.g., Levy, Coleman, & Alsman, 2002). Both methods use visual symbols and oral requirements. In an attempt to integrate all parts of language and learning, the whole-language approach was constructed, wherein the rules of language are "discovered."

Debate is ongoing about which method is preferable. Comparison studies indicate that phonological code instruction for kindergarten to first-grade children produced greater gains in follow-up assessments than did context- or literature-enriched programs (for a review, see Torgesen, 2000). In addition, the whole-language approach produced fewer gains for students in special education than for general education students, whereas the basal reading program produced the strongest effects (Drecktrah & Chiang, 1997).

In terms of actual usage, the whole-language approach is used most often by teachers in general education, and this approach increases in frequency of use at higher grade levels as students achieve independence. In contrast, over half the number of special educators use "direct instruction" during small-group reading (Drecktrah & Chiang, 1997). The majority of all teachers, across grade level and type of setting, felt that a combination of whole-language and direct instruction was the most effective. Additional general reading strategies include (a) reading aloud to students, (b) providing time for independent reading with follow-up discussion and writing, (c) instructional emphasis on comprehension, and (d) providing choice of a range of literature and novels related to social studies, art, and so on.

The following are strategies that have been specifically assessed with students with ADHD. The techniques presented relate to learning new reading vocabulary and to practicing those skills. When addressing these reading goals, remember that students with ADHD need less verbal repetition than do children with reading disabilities (Dewey, Kaplan, Crawford, & Fisher, 1998). If children have both disabilities, they will need more repetition spread out over longer periods of time and interspersed with more novelty.

EVIDENCE-BASED READING RECOGNITION PRACTICES FOR CHILDREN WITH ADHD

1. Deliver phonological awareness training (e.g., rhyming, sound blending and segmenting, reading, and spelling) with reinforcement for participation and correct responding, which produced reading gains (e.g., word attack and oral reading fluency) and social gains (e.g., reduced negative social behavior) for most of the seven first-grade children with symptoms of ADHD plus poor reading skills (Lane, 2001).
2. Implement peer-assisted learning to improve reading achievement by using alternating roles with the following:
   a. Higher-functioning readers delivering instruction to lower achievers several times a week, alternating roles between coach and reader (for a review, see Falk & Wehby, 2001). This method was applied to teaching sound blending and segmentation to one child with ADHD, with improvements noted in letter-sound identification and blending but not in segmentation.

EVIDENCE-BASED READING RECOGNITION PRACTICES FOR CHILDREN WITH ADHD *(Continued)*

b. Three boys with ADHD and borderline IQ in self-contained classrooms reading to a partner for 5 minutes while the partner monitored and corrected errors and then reversed roles (Locke & Fuchs, 1995). Behavioral findings relative to baseline were increased on task from 52% to 88% and positive social interaction from 4% to 18%.

3. Encourage parents of children with ADHD and reading difficulties *to* practice reading by asking their children to read and reread small 5-minute segments of text with error corrections and praise for errorless rereading to produce greater fluency at home and improve reading performance at school (Hook & DuPaul, 1999). Some of the additional treatment components for the four families were daily stickers for participation traded for special activities/tangibles and goal setting with video review sessions.
4. Use computer-assisted technology (speaking and highlighting the words from left to right) to reduce off-task behavior and increase sustained reading by 60% and increase the rate of reading (but not comprehension) by 54% for college students with ADHD (Hecker, Burns, Elkind, Elkind, & Katz, 2002).
5. Use colored overlays, especially blue, to improve the recognition of single words for students with ADHD, with and without reading disabilities (Iovino, Fletcher, Breitmeyer, & Foorman, 1998). However, altering the font in color or style (e.g., outline, bold, shadow) does not appear to improve single-word recognition of the three students (ages 10 to 11) with reading disabilities and ADHD (Belfiore, Grskovic, Murphy, & Zentall, 1996). In other words, all three students learned sight words equally well in both the black-on-white and the novelty-added condition, perhaps because the added novelty called attention to irrelevant aspects of the words to be read.
6. Reduce classroom conversational noise during verbal tasks, such as sequencing the alphabet, as the background conversations can produce more errors than low-conversational-noise conditions for young students with ADHD (Zentall & Shaw, 1980). Use headsets with or without music as an application.
7. Place pictures and illustrations at the end of story segments to review or reinforce prior reading experiences (Brody & Legenza, 1980).
8. Use classwide token points (exchanged for 15 minutes of video game play) combined with peer tutoring in special education settings for gains in (a) reading vocabulary and (b) nine times the number of tasks completed for students with ADHD (Robinson, Newby, & Ganzel, 1981).
9. Allow children to make active responses:

And Who Is Holding the Cards?

Purpose. To demonstrate that children with ADHD who were allowed active responding during reading recognition would show less inappropriate activity and perform better.

Participants. Twenty-two 6- to 12-year-old students with ADHD and 25 comparisons matched in reading performance and IQ.

Tasks. Reading single words selected from grade-level texts.

Treatment Conditions. Active stimulation: the children presented words to themselves from a stack of cards and turned over the words completed.

Passive Condition: The examiner presented word cards to the children in response to their cues.

Findings. The two groups of students responded differentially to the active/passive conditions. Children with ADHD were more verbally and physically active in the passive condition than their peers. In fact, a correlation between their hyperactivity scores and their behavioral data was obtained only in the passive conditions of this study.

(Continued)

EVIDENCE-BASED READING RECOGNITION PRACTICES FOR CHILDREN WITH ADHD *(Continued)*

Both groups of children attempted and decoded more words correctly (a) in the active condition and (b) when easy words were presented first and difficult words second.

Implications. Task-appropriate active responses (reading with flash cards) can differentially help students with ADHD reduce inappropriate levels of activity. When tasks have active responses available, all children will attempt more words and provide more correct responses. In addition, all children performed better when words were organized for decoding from easy to hard (Zentall & Meyer, 1987).

Reading comprehension

Reading comprehension strategies can be understood by what college students with ADHD (undiagnosed for reading disabilities) reported: 70% say they missed or skipped important parts of text—from elements of words to whole sentences—and 70% did not recall what they read (Hecker et al., 2002). From these self-observations, it seems likely that helping students stay on track and recall text would be helpful.

These college students also chose a variety of self-help strategies that could be used with children: (a) 75% read in quiet places, (b) 75% used active responses such as underlining and note taking, (c) more than half used a stimulant like coffee, (d) 60% took frequent breaks, and (e) 75% read and reread the material for meaning and memory.

EVIDENCE-BASED PRACTICES
READING COMPREHENSION STRATEGIES FOR CHILDREN WITH ADHD

1. Use red-colored overlays to differentially improve the reading comprehension of groups of students with ADHD, with and without reading disabilities, relative to the effects of no overlays, blue overlays, and the non-ADHD group (Iovino et al., 1998).
2. Use interesting stories, as students had clear preferences for specific stories (Belfiore et al., 1996). Story interest may be more novel than color because color was repeated, while story plot changed across and within each session. In addition, story interest has been found with typical students to produce better learning and recall, especially for younger students who decide importance based on what is interesting (for a review, see Shirey & Reynolds, 1988).
3. Use story maps to increase reading satisfaction, recall, and comprehension (identification of main characters, story setting, problem, events and outcome, but not main idea) fourth- and fifth-grade students with behavioral difficulties—one of whom was ADHD (Babyak, Koorland, & Mathes, 2000).The effectiveness of story maps, especially for students with ADHD, could be in attending to causal links, which they have difficulty identifying and recalling, even when listening to stories (see chapter 7). In addition, it may be a way to teach the global structure.

EVIDENCE-BASED PRACTICES *(Continued)*

4. Teach self-management skills during reading tasks to improve the reading comprehension of three elementary-age students with ADHD. At the sound of a prerecorded tone on a beep tape, students asked themselves whether they were on or off task (Edwards, Salant, Howard, Brougher, & McLaughlin, 1995). Comparisons in accuracy of self-report were made with an adult, and tokens were delivered for 60% correspondence. These techniques improved attention to task and therefore production of correct responses in reading.
5. Encourage talking out loud or subvocalizing when reading, problem solving, or planning. Dubey and O'Leary (1975) reported that two youth with ADHD and delayed reading comprehension performed with significantly fewer errors (e.g., skipping words, phrases, and lines) and with improved reading comprehension when they read the stories privately but out loud in contrast to reading silently. Reading out loud may slow down reading rate.
6. Use magic markers:

Markers *Can* Be Magic

Purpose. To determine whether color added late would increase reading comprehension.

Participants. Three students (ages 10 to 11) were identified as having ADHD and reading disabilities.

Design. A single-subject alternating-treatments design was used, with order of conditions counterbalanced.

Measures. Percent correct on comprehension tests of story facts and concepts using 10 written questions per story.

Tasks. Students were assigned to reading level.

Treatment Conditions. Stories were in a black-on-white condition and in a color condition. Each story was divided into three passages of equivalent line length and highlighted with colored markers. The first third of the story was left in the traditional, black-on-white format. The second third was highlighted with one of seven pastel washable markers. The last third was highlighted with one of seven bright, bold, or fluorescent-colored markers. Students were asked to read two stories per session silently, one in the black-on-white and one in the color-added-late condition. When they had finished, they were given the 10 questions, and the process was repeated with the second story and questions.

Findings: Reading Comprehension. Improvements were observed in reading comprehension, within and across sessions, for all three students under the color condition. (Tim did not perform as well as the other two students initially because he covered the lower portion of the page where the color was overlaid until the top portion was completed, saving the potential early effects of the additional color.)

Implications. Color can improve the reading comprehension performance of students with reading disabilities and ADHD. However, early performance gains decreased after repeated exposure to the color. Thus, practitioners need to plan for loss of novelty over time (Belfiore et al., 1996).

CAN WE HELP STUDENTS WITH ADHD BECOME BETTER SPELLERS?

When attempting to spell, children with ADHD need (a) help selectively attending to the sounds and to the irregular (nonvoiced) visual letters and (b) techniques to help them sustain attention and practice.

Selective attention techniques

Selective attention techniques include teaching students finger spelling with the deaf alphabet (for work done with learning-disabled youth, see Vernon, Coley, Hafer, & Dubois, 1980; for work done with regular classroom children, see McKenzie & Henry, 1979). For children with ADHD, we have proposed that because they are attracted to salient stimuli (e.g., color), it should be possible to direct their attention selectively to relevant cues by color highlighting those cues. To this purpose, we demonstrated that color added late improved spelling performance:

EVIDENCE-BASED PRACTICES
COLOR YOUR SPELLING LETTERS

Purpose. To demonstrate that attention can be directed selectively by color highlighting cues.

Participants. A school-based sample of elementary-age boys with ADHD.

Tasks. Children with ADHD performed worse on spelling tasks than controls when a five-response, multiple-choice format was used but not with a two-choice format (Hoy, Weiss, Minde, & Cohen, 1978). So this study similarly used a word presented verbally with an array of six printed words, one of which was the correctly spelled word. This made the task sufficiently demanding in its selective attentional requirements to allow for improvement, even though ability level was controlled.

Conditions. High stimulation involved coloring specific letters that were irregular, such as **k**ni**gh**t (nonphonetic or nonvoiced letters). Four colors were assigned randomly to the irregular letters in words, with no more than two of the same consecutive colors. In the black condition, all the letters were black.

Design. Pairs of comparison children and children with ADHD were randomly assigned to color order (color in the first half of the experimental session and black in the second half or the reverse order).

Findings. All the students made more errors on their first trial than on their second, suggesting that the task was difficult, and performance improved with practice. Findings relevant to the color conditions indicated that the children with ADHD who practiced the task with all black letters first and color added later outperformed their peers.

Implications. Color can be added late to direct attention to hard parts of spelling words and improve the performance of children with ADHD above the performance level observed for their peers (Zentall, 1989a).

Even nonrelevant color and shapes can improve performance of a spelling task as long as this stimulation is added during later trials (Zentall, Zentall, & Booth, 1978).This finding also indicates that techniques leading to success in spelling are to some degree problems of sustaining attention.

Sustained attention techniques

Once children can selectively attend to the sounds and the corresponding letter sequences, they will need help practicing. Simply allowing children a choice of spelling activities was demonstrated with one student with ADHD to result in increased engagement in spelling and reduced disruptive behavior (Dunlap et al., 1994). In addition, studying in peer groupings can improve math, spelling, and reading basic skills from 22% during baseline to 82% during peer interventions (DuPaul & Eckert, 1998). An additional peer intervention study follows:

EVIDENCE-BASED PRACTICES
PEER TUTORING INCREASES ON-TASK BEHAVIOR AND SPELLING

Purpose. To demonstrate that peer tutoring can help children with ADHD sustain attention sufficiently to master lower-level skills of spelling.

Participants. Nineteen students (16 boys, 3 girls) with ADHD grades 1 to 5, 10 peer comparisons, and 18 general education teachers

Treatment. Teachers paired students with ADHD with a student with appropriate behavior and on-grade-level performance. Teachers modeled peer-tutoring practices, and the tutors were given a script and awarded points for the correct answers (or corrected) by their tutee during 10-minute lessons, and then roles and procedures were reversed for a 20-minute session three or four times per week. Classes were divided into two overall teams with winning teams applauded.

Task and Procedures. Teachers dictated 10 to 20 spelling words, and students wrote answers. Pretests were on Monday and posttests on Friday.

Findings. The on-task behavior of students with ADHD was improved over baseline and was equivalent to their peers during treatment conditions. Fidgeting decreased for the majority of students with ADHD. Overall treatment success was found for half the students with ADHD and one third of the comparisons. The majority of teachers and students were satisfied with this treatment and would recommend it.

Implications. Peer tutoring is an effective method for about half of students with ADHD who only need help practicing, but the selective attention problems in the spelling performance of the other half of the students may need to be addressed initially (DuPaul, Ervin, Hook, & McGoey, 1998).

CAN WE HELP STUDENTS WITH ADHD BECOME MORE PROFICIENT IN MATH?

Strategies are reviewed elsewhere for students with learning disabilities (Miller & Mercer, 1997; Xin, 1999). However, some of these strategies are related to evidence presented earlier for improving the attention of students with ADHD, for example, to (a) make "big ideas" clearly evident (e.g., the big idea of subtraction is finding differences), (b) directly (but briefly) instruct students in explicit strategies, (c) integrate different concepts within one lesson, and (d) ensure that prerequisite skills have been mastered. In addition to these applications from evidence in the field of learning disabilities differences in the learning of mathematics exist for students with ADHD.

Math calculation

As presented in chapter 7, students with ADHD are slower in their calculations even into middle school. This slower computation requires attention that detracts from attention to the problem-solving process. If educators could improve students' speed or provide assistive technology aids, it might improve students' problem-solving performance. For example, one child could perform math as long as he had a calculator in his hands.An active response helped him even when his teacher was working at the board. But because this was not a "typical" way of taking notes, this child was prohibited from using his calculator. So, he failed each math class assignment and test that did not allow a calculator even though he could perform his independent work. Thus, some children may need calculators on a continuous basis, and if the purpose of math is problem solving and understanding, then this is an important accommodation. However, when improving speed in calculations is an objective, educators could allow the use of hand calculators to check work or as an incentive and reward after students had achieved mastery (e.g., 80% completed or 80% correct on a prior lesson).

EVIDENCE-BASED PRACTICES FOR MATH

1. Use games, especially competitive games with peers, more than competitive games with the computer (Ford, Poe, & Cox, 1993). These procedures were used over a 4-week period of time and also resulted in more attending behavior with animated computer games than with just computer drill and practice.
2. Use active responses (talking and computers) to practice math facts because this is prefered by children with and without ADHD (Zentall & Smith, 1992).
3. Have students verbalize the problem and then write the answers to math problems, which can produce greater accuracy than just writing the answers (Lovitt & Curtiss, 1968).
4. Use classwide peer tutoring to improve the on-task behavior and math performance of students with ADHD. In addition to the spelling gains cited previously (DuPaul et al., 1998), math problems (addition, subtraction, multiplication, or division) were also included in those findings. As well, for a single 7-year-old child with ADHD, math gains were found primarily during later trials (i.e., when sustained attention would be a factor) as well as decreased fidgeting and increased on-task behavior (DuPaul & Henningson, 1993).
5. Assess the use of psychostimulant medication on math calculations because it can increase the number of math facts attempted, number correct, number correct per minute, and number of self-corrected errors (relative to placebo) (Douglas, Barr, O'Neill, & Britton, 1986).
6. Add color to math practice materials to increase production and decrease the off-task behavior of students with co-occurring learning disabilities and ADHD/ADHD-I in classroom settings (Lee & Asplen, in press).
7. Use music during the performance of rote math tasks. Students with ADHD performed more math problems and were more accurate in the presence of music than in the presence of silence (or with speech) in the background. These positive effects were not found for their elementary-level peers (Abikoff, Courtney, Szeibel, & Koplewicz, 1996; Scott, 1970). The beneficial effects of music on the number of math problems and decreased

(Continued)

EVIDENCE-BASED PRACTICES FOR MATH *(Continued)*

rule-breaking behavior have also been reported for children with behavioral problems, especially for those with high levels of "stimulus-seeking and over-activity, closely resembling the 'hyperactivity syndrome,' " according to Hallam and Price (1998, p. 90). Music that was provided contingent on number correctly solved per minute was also useful for middle school typical students (McLaughlin & Helm, 1995).

8. Use color and animation stimulation within math tasks:

Novel Math Tasks and Improved Performance

Purpose. To demonstrate differential gains from within-task novelty for students with ADHD.
Participants. Seventeen children, ages 8 to 14, with ADHD.
Tasks. A series of single-digit addition problems presented on the computer monitor for 20 minutes.
Study 1

Treatment conditions. Task stimulation (colored numbers and movement) was presented and contrasted with low stimulation (black numbers on a gray computer screen) across two sessions in different orders.

Findings. Students with ADHD completed more problems with greater accuracy and were less active in the high task stimulation condition.

Implications. Novelty within rote calculations tasks improves the performance and behavior of students with ADHD when it is first introduced, although these effects may decrease over time on a rote mathematics task.

Study 2

Purpose. To demonstrate that children with ADHD would persist less on math calculations when there was competing stimulation (i.e., when cartoon animations were available).

Treatment Conditions. Competing cartoons versus low levels of competing stimulation (a gray computer screen) were presented to the same students during the same within-task stimulation condition in the first study that earlier resulted in better performance.

Findings. Students with ADHD completed fewer problems in the competing stimulation condition than in the low. In the competing stimulation condition, the student could gain stimulation by (a) viewing the cartoons, (b) working on the task, or (c) self-generating stimulation. Of these choices, viewing cartoons required the least amount of effort and the greatest novelty.

Implications. Within-task stimulation can be used to increase the on-task behavior of students with ADHD but is effective only to the extent that it can compete with highly attractive stimulation available in the environment.

It is not a matter of reducing competing stimulation but rather one of increasing task stimulation so that children spend most of their time gaining stimulation through assigned tasks. Because movement and color increased the number of problems attempted and the number correct, stimulation appears to serve as a reward for academic behavior (Lee & Zentall, 2002).

Problem solving

For students with learning disabilities, effective strategies for teaching computations and problem solving were the use of self-monitoring and self-evaluation, step-by-step procedures and manipulative devices with drawings (for a review, see

Miller, Butler, & Lee, 1998). Direct instruction and computer-assisted instruction were also found to be promising. Although self-monitoring has demonstrated effectiveness for students with learning disabilities and for many types of attentional tasks for students with ADHD, it has not been assessed with students with ADHD for higher-level skills, such as problem solving (for a review, see Reid et al., in press).

For students with ADHD and learning disabilities, additional effective instructional factors are the following:

Instructional Practices for Math Problem Solving for Students with ADHD and Learning Disabilities

1. Mastery learning, which builds on prerequisite skills.
2. Verbal teacher interactions with the child to assess and stimulate problem strategies and the active construction of meanings rather than teachers who teach strategies and monitor students' written products. That is, teachers' knowledge of math strategies did not predict their students' achievement scores. Instead, the best predictor of math achievement was teachers' knowledge of individual students' problem-solving skills based on questioning them about methods they used to solve problems and listening to their explanations of solutions (Peterson, Carpenter, & Fennema, 1989).
3. Strategies that first address the memory and reading comprehension problems of children with reading disabilities, and especially for multiple-step problems (for a review, see Zentall & Ferkis, 1993).

Students with pure ADHD preferred to work with other children and with their teachers in the general education classroom (i.e., increased social exchange) and to stand and move more (active engagement) during math problem solving than their peers reported (Zentall & Smith, 1992). Active problem solving experiences are particularly important to use because psychostimulant medication does not improve higher level skills (reading comprehension, math problem solving, or language comprehension). Furthermore, students with ADHD appear to have success with problem solving. That is, when students with ADHD participated in problem-solving tasks with two average comparison children, their small groups arrived at a higher percentage of correct solutions than small groups of three comparison children (Zentall, Kuester, & Craig, 2005).

CAN WE HELP STUDENTS WITH ADHD WRITE SO THAT WE CAN READ IT?

Handwriting is often an overlooked skill, even though a deficit in this area can contribute to significant impairment in written assignments. Educators often complain about the messy, irregular handwriting of students with ADHD and may interpret these errors as a sign of immaturity, low motivation, or noncompliance (Zentall,

Falkenberg, & Smith, 1985). Children with learning disabilities are more likely to have difficulty remembering the form of letters. However, youth with ADHD "see" that their work is of poor quality but still have difficulty with the fine motor or visual motor requirements of handwriting. The "seeing" but inability "to do" can be assessed, for example, by the number of erasures. Because of these problems and the negative feedback these students receive, they are more likely than their peers to avoid, become frustrated with, or rush through tasks that require handwriting (Zentall, 1993; Zentall, Grskovic, Javorsky, & Hall, 2000). Keyboarding could reduce this frustration.

Attending to letter details (selective attention) and maintaining attention to repeated practice can also contribute to the handwriting difficulties for these children. Unfortunately, educators ask students to redo work or continue working on materials with the expectation that performance will meet quality or quantity standards. Asking children with ADHD to redo or continue working on material typically results in work that gets progressively worse instead of better (see Figure 11.2, provided by Jayme Miller, 2003). That is, even when matched in handwriting to their peers, their writing deteriorates more rapidly over time (Zentall & Kruczek, 1988).

FIGURE 11.2
Handwriting Gets Worse with Practice

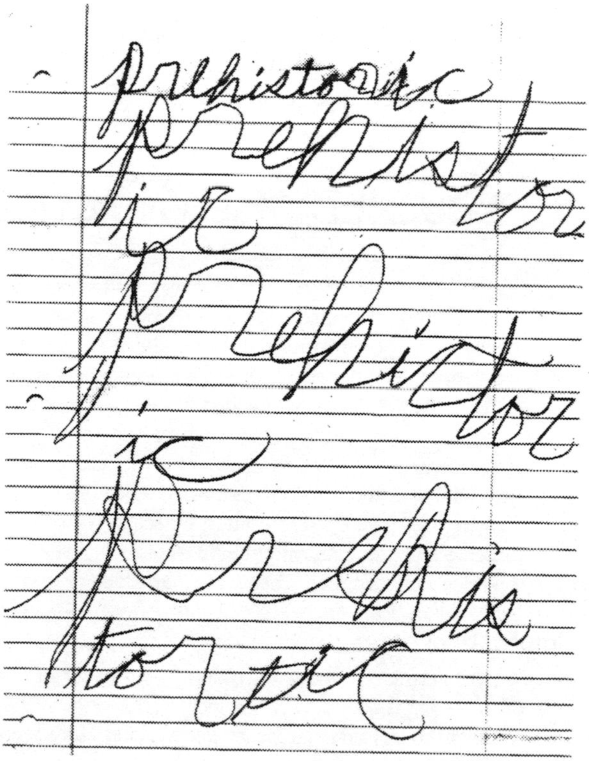

Thus, editing could be done at a later time or with a partner. Rather than redoing work, it would be useful to reduce the quantity of written work required or accept typed or taped assignments. Different methods of response or motivating writing tasks should be more successful. Alternatively, educators could lower the standards of acceptable work for some assignments and keep particularly good samples of the child's work in a portfolio to demonstrate specific quality standards for other assignments or final drafts.

Problems in sustained attention can be improved by simply using colored paper. That is, Imhof (2004) administered either white or a choice of colors of ruled paper during the spelling practice periods. Findings were that children with ADHD performed better with the colored paper than they did with the white paper and showed worse performance than their matched peers only in the white-paper condition (note this study manipulated choice as well as color).

We have proposed that if children with ADHD are attracted to color, it should be possible to direct their attention selectively to difficult-to-form letters in copying tasks. In research assessing copying (handwriting), color added to relevant parts of letters reduced handwriting errors of adolescent boys with attention problems but had negligible effects on the performance of matched adolescents (Zentall et al., 1985).Thus, color stimulation can be added to increase the scanning of relevant task details (crossing t's, dotting i's, and opening or closing letters).

As a follow-up to this study, we examined the hypothesis that because color can captivate the attention of these children, it should be placed on relevant and not irrelevant details in a task.

EVIDENCE-BASED PRACTICES
COPYING IN COLOR

Purpose. To demonstrate that color can produce positive or negative effects specifically for students with ADHD, depending on whether color is placed on relevant or irrelevant details.

Students. Seventeen attention-problem and 17 elementary-age comparison boys.

Treatment Conditions. Color was added to the closure points of certain letters that are difficult to form (i.e., the letters found in the acronym "kity-fog-pads") and contrasted with randomly placed color.

Design. Students were exposed to either high stimulation first or low stimulation first conditions.

Findings. Both groups of children performed worse over time, indicating the sustained attention requirements of the copying task. Failure to close letters, which is a common handwriting error, accounted for the majority of errors observed for students with ADHD. Attention-problem children performed better with color emphasis placed on relevant details than when color was added randomly.

Implications

1. Color can guide attention of children with ADHD and should be used to focus attention onto relevant stimuli.
2. When color is added to simply increase the attractiveness of a task, it may disrupt performance for attention-problem children more than for peers (Zentall & Kruczek, 1988).

Improvements in handwriting can also be achieved through self-monitoring and self-evaluation. Students with ADHD and learning disabilities charted or graphed the amount of work and its accuracy in math, reading, and written expression; corrected their work in groups; and graphed results. These procedures increased their productivity and, to a lesser degree, their accuracy (Shimabukuro, Prater, & Jenkins, Edelen-Smith, 1999; Shimabukuro & Serena, 1999). Mirrors can also be used to self-monitor performance. Research using mirrors to improve copying performance has not been assessed with students with ADHD. However, mirrors have been used with a letter-to-word tracking task, which is similar to self-monitoring one's own handwriting performance:

EVIDENCE-BASED PRACTICES
MIRROR, MIRROR ON THE WALL

Purpose. To determine if a mirror could increase self-monitoring.
Participants. Seventh- and eighth-grade students, 16 ADHD (8 boys, 8 girls) and 27 comparisons (15 boys, 12 girls).
Task. Partially solvable word puzzles within which the child located words (e.g., diagonally, vertically). Students were told that not all the words on their list of words to be found were actually there.
Treatment Conditions. A mirror or picture on the wall was across from a child's desk.
Findings. The mirror increased the letter/word search accuracy performance of students with ADHD to levels equivalent to their peers. The effects of the mirror were especially beneficial for those children with ADHD, who looked at the mirror (i.e., were "distracted") and detrimental for those who did not relative to comparison children.
Implications. We proposed that an external focus of attention, which characterizes students with ADHD, would prevent self-focusing of attention. Methods to help children monitor what they are producing include the use of mirrors, cameras, and journals. These techniques can be used to improve the quality or rate of production of skills already obtained, such as handwriting, reading, and social behavior (Zentall, Hall, & Lee, 1998).

It has also been documented that handwriting is one of the academically related skills, in addition to math calculations, that can be improved by psychostimulant medication (for a review, see Zentall et al., 1985).

CAN WE HELP STUDENTS WITH ADHD EXPRESS THEMSELVES IN WRITING?

Written composition is the highest academic skill because it requires the combined skills of reading, spelling, and handwriting. Principles that have been shown to be effective in teaching written expression to students with learning disabilities include (a) a basic outline of written language components—planning, writing, and revising; (b) "explicitly" teaching these different components and (c) providing "feedback"

(Harris & Graham, 1999). In addition, the use of word processing on computers has been shown to improve the composition skills of all children (Lewis, 1998).

For students with ADHD, work that has been done in this area suggests the use of compensatory techniques. In a functional assessment of a child with ADHD, paper and pencil tasks produced off-task rates of behavior at about 32% of the time. When computers were provided for written assignments and the child was allowed to brainstorm with a peer, off-task behavior fell to about 5% (Ervin, DuPaul, Kern, Friman, 1998).

CAN WE SPARK SELF-ACCEPTANCE AND MOTIVATION?

What we know about the motivation of average learners could be important in the instruction of children with ADHD. Pintrich and Schunk (1996) reviewed strategies for improving academic motivation as (a) focusing on meaningful aspects of learning activities; (b) designing tasks for novelty, variety, diversity, and interest; (c) designing tasks that are challenging but reasonable; (d) providing opportunities for students to have some choice and control over activities in the classroom; (e) focusing on individual improvements; (f) making evaluation private, *not* public; (g) recognizing student effort; and (h) helping students see mistakes as opportunities for learning.

Each of these principles focuses on pleasure that can exist within the activity itself and is called intrinsic motivation. In contrast, extrinsic motivation uses external rewards (e.g., grades and other signs of recognition) as outcomes of performance. Intrinsic motivation is considered important in the long term because it is independent of outside conditions and has been found to increase students' task involvement and the use of more effective study strategies (i.e., than students who were extrinsically motivated or assigned to extrinsic conditions [Schunk, 1996]).

However, motivational researchers also agree that extrinsic rewards are necessary for boring or repetitive practice tasks. For example, all students who attempt more difficult tasks or tasks on which they have a history of failure would need extrinsic incentives. Even average students reported that getting positive feedback or grades reinforced their efforts (studying), increased pride in learning, and reduced worries about failing, which freed them to learn more (Covington, 2000). Finally, certain types of extrinsic reward can lead to intrinsic motivation. A recent review of research reported that teacher praise (but not tangibles) led to increased intrinsic motivation and attention similar to the gains from teacher explanations of the relevance of content (for a review, see Witzel & Mercer, 2003). Verbal praise has an especially positive effect when it is informational (feedback) rather than controlling.

Many students with learning difficulties also have low self-acceptance. Students with this kind of profile often spend considerable energy avoiding feelings of failure and bolstering self-concept. For example, blaming others avoids possible punishment. Similarly, dependency and a need for perfection avoid possible failure. More constructive ways to get mastery require learning how to ask for help or how to ask for permission to join in a group or activity. The following are evidence-based practices to improve academic self-acceptance:

EVIDENCE-BASED PRACTICES
Emphasize Strengths and Successes and Help Children Avoid Failure

1. Prepare the student for new situations, tasks, and transitions. Teach students how to ask for permission to enter groups. It may protect them from acting aggressively when they attempt to get what they need or enter groups (Knapczyk, 1988).
2. Communicate a personal interest in students with ADHD. As reported by these students, the most helpful motivational strategies were teachers who gave individual attention and took personal interest (Zentall, Moon et al., 2001; for similar reports by students with behavioral problems, see Morse, 1994). From these caring individuals, children learn to lead with their strengths and to be patient with their own weaknesses.
3. Involve students in cooperative learning groups because they
   a. provide a supportive environment that contributes to children valuing themselves and feeling valued by others more than in traditional classes (Augustine, Gruber, & Hanson, 1990; Slavin, 1987);
   b. increase motivation and self-esteem for students with behavioral disorders (Rife & Karr-Kidwell, 1995);
   c. improve social behavior, friendships, and acceptance within general education classrooms (Schrag, 1993; Slavin, 1991); and
   d. can generalize to other classroom and school situations (Johnson, Johnson, Warring, & Maruyama, 1986).
4. Provide opportunities for students with ADHD to tutor younger students to improve their social and affective skills. Outcomes for students with behavioral disorders included improvement in social interactions and communication skills, kindness and empathy, a sense of responsibility toward others, and awareness of the needs of others (Fitzsimmons-Lovett, 1998).
5. Comment on the contributions of students with disabilities to enhance their status within groups (O'Conner & Jenkins, 1993).

TEACHING STRATEGIES
Best Practices to Increase Academic Motivation

Help Children Avoid Failure

1. If the child has strength in math but not reading, ask the child to chart progress in reading with a bar chart or use interesting math word problems for him or her to read.
2. Instruct students how to continue on easier parts of tasks (or do a substitute task) while waiting for teacher help.
3. Give the student a small stand-up flag to indicate that the child needs help or small amounts of play-dough to form a question mark to leave on a corner of his or her desk.
4. Take away blame from the student who fears failure. Find a small area within a task that the child can choose to be independent or responsible.

(Continued)

TEACHING STRATEGIES *(Continued)*

5. Help students who make small assignments into huge projects and then are chronically late by having them
   a. define the basic assignment,
   b. make a wish list of additional elements in priority, and
   c. make a time schedule with enough time to at least complete one element of the wish list.
6. Provide 5 minutes before starting an in-class assignment so that pairs of students can get together to compare their understanding of assignments.
7. Ask a group of students "what is fair" for a student who needs to move more or has difficulty sharing, writing, remembering directions, bringing materials, taking notes, or finishing his or her tasks and is left out of many opportunities.

Help Children Deal with Making Mistakes

1. Discuss with all students how they have learned to respond to experiences of failure, embarrassment, or being left out.
2. Reinforce students' handling of mistakes, not knowing things, and asking questions, especially for those students who spend too much time on perfect papers and keep erasing their written work.

Help Children Be Successful

1. Provide high-status jobs with higher levels of responsibility and leadership (e.g., team captain, organizer and distributor of equipment, scorekeeper, peer tutor, line leader, paper passer, storyteller). Ask students to describe, for example, what a captain does. Then appoint those children who can describe this role the position of captain with badges or armbands to serve as initial role models for others on the playground, in the cafeteria, or in groups. Other children could then learn these roles from this modeling.
2. Call attention to areas of children's strengths by allowing for a time each day or week during which children can review talents or accomplishments (e.g., in a portfolio). Cohen (1986) suggests increasing the status of low-achieving students by selecting tasks in which they might be able to demonstrate particular knowledge or expertise.

   Remember the positive qualities—(a) that excessive activity can also mean increased energy and productivity, (b) that bossiness can also be leadership potential, and (c) that impulsiveness can lead to spontaneity and humor. Even though bossiness appears aggressive, that is not necessarily the intent.
3. Call attention to the social skills of taking turns, team cooperation, and small improvements in sports.

HOW CAN WE HELP STUDENTS WITH HOMEWORK?

One of the first questions to answer in analyzing homework problems and before implementing intervention is, Does the child (a) know what to do, (b) know how to do it, or (c) simply dislike the task? To delineate homework problems for specific children, see "Inventory of Homework Skills" (Zentall & Goldstein, 1999, pp. 26–27). Knowing what to do is typically a selective attention problem (although it could also reflect problems with reading or understanding language), and knowing how to do is typically a skill deficit, which was addressed more fully in chapter 7. Disliking tasks could be resistance to a rote nonmeaningful task, which would be a sustained attention problem. Those students who know what and how to do their homework can begin their assignments but soon move off task. This indicates that the child was having difficulty sustaining interest or effort (arousal). Students differ in how long they can work on a task before getting bored or restless.

Assuming that the child can do the work, reducing the time children spend in a holding pattern (difficulty getting started or procrastination) can be done in several ways. The more interesting a task, the materials, and the setting or the more attractive a payoff, the more likely is the child with ADHD to engage in homework. Thus, teachers can make homework interesting, make payoffs valuable, and assign homework that focuses on process (e.g., problem solving, observing, and recording) rather than repetitive practice (e.g., 50 math problems) (Zentall & Goldstein, 1999). It is important to understand that homework is not like medicine. It does *not* have to taste bad to be good for the student, as indicated by the following:

EVIDENCE-BASED PRACTICES
MAKING AND COLLECTING ASSIGNMENTS

1. Communicate why an assignment is important. Fewer homework problems are experienced when children see how schoolwork relates to their skills or experiences (Nicholls et al., 1994).
2. Communicate the next day's assignment early in the lesson rather than at the end of the period, which may penalize young students and students with ADHD.
3. Establish a routine place for assigning, collecting, and returning homework. Students with ADHD report that they do their homework but fail to turn it in (Zentall, Harper, & Stormont-Spurgin, 1993). Parents confirm these reports when they help clean out a desk or locker at school and find assignments that were not turned in.
   a. Assign a homework buddy to help students with assignment placement and retrieval tasks. If assignments must be given at the end of a period or day, the student with ADHD and a buddy can spend a few moments together making certain that they agree on what has been assigned and what must be done that evening. If disagreement occurs, they can seek clarification from the teacher.
   b. Alternatively, ask some students to repeat the assignment in their own words or do a sample problem.
4. Use colored folders for different subject areas that match the texts used.
5. Use colorful plastic bins placed next to student desks. These bins are easier to organize and to see into than a desk.
6. Notify parents at the first signs of incomplete or missing homework. It may be necessary to suggest ways for parents to monitor their own children (see examples in Zentall & Goldstein, 1999).

Design Study Spaces and Schedules

1. Make the environment or place of study pleasant and approachable.

A Homework Station

Purpose. To see if a homework station could help organize homework tasks, maintain interest, and improve self-management.

(*Continued*)

EVIDENCE-BASED PRACTICES *(Continued)*

Participants. A single-subject design with three students with ADHD.

Intervention. The homework station was a freestanding, three-sided panel that was portable, decorated by the student in bright colors, and placed on a desk in any room of the house or in a classroom with the following:

1. Each of the three panels had places to organize and hold supplies and related materials. Work to be completed was placed in a folder in the left panel and moved to a folder in the right panel when completed.
2. A grab bag of reinforcement activities was available (five to seven, 5-minute activity breaks or preferred activities) that the children preidentified and wrote down as possible:
   [Alan chose to draw, shoot baskets, eat, stretch, play with his dog, and clean his room. Anita chose to eat a snack, chat with Mom, play with her cat, clean her room, run around the block, get clothes out for the next day, and draw. Shane chose to watch television, eat a snack, chat with his Mom, run, and work on a model. Note that for two children, cleaning their room or parts of their room was seen as a more rewarding activity than homework.]
3. A mirror was placed in the center panel so that the child could self-monitor. Other self-monitoring charts, task goal and accomplishment checklists, and strategy prompt cards could be available.
4. Music was available to listen to while the child was working or while checking work. Experiment with types of music to see which works best.

Components. Organization (pockets), external stimulation (color, music options, and breaks for activities), cognitive stimulation (choice of activity breaks and task order), mirrors for self-monitoring, and positive consequences (preferred activities during breaks).

Findings. The homework stations produced an increase in math homework completion and accuracy that was three times what it had been (Hall & Zentall, 2000; Zentall & Goldstein, 1999).

2. Create an agreed-on schedule and routine for homework with parent and child.
3. Provide choice in setting, task order, and times to work.
4. Make an order of the assignments checklist (e.g., from easy to hard).
5. Make sure the child knows how to use the organizational tools that he or she has. Dr. Bill Jensen tells the story of a middle school student whose locker was taken away from him because he wasn't using it. The child was carrying around all his books, gym clothes, assignments, and so on and losing things. When asked why he was carrying everything, the child said he didn't know how to use the lock on his locker.

Assignments: Their Requirements and Consequences

1. Direct attention:
   a. Use highlighters or ask students to underline the important parts. If there are multi-part directions, use different colors.
   b. Give feedback to students. Assignments with teacher feedback produced gains in achievement over those assignments with no feedback (for a review, see Rosenberg, 1989).
   c. See also practices in chapter 10 for selective attention.
2. Increase sustained attention:
   a. Increase urgency by using a timer or by setting goals to accomplish so much work in so much time in order to have access to this preferred activity.

(Continued)

EVIDENCE-BASED PRACTICES *(Continued)*

b. Decrease assignment length, which also reduces teachers' grading time (e.g., completing five math problems to demonstrate mastery rather than 20 or several smaller assignments or chapters rather than one long assignment or report). Remember that for students with ADHD, less is more.
c. Offer more choices of ways to practice materials (e.g., computer games).
d. Get feedback from students on how much time the assignment took to complete (e.g., put start and end time at top of page) and quality ratings on interest (e.g., faces to be circled).
e. Emphasize demonstration of concepts and problem solving (e.g., finding, describing, and recording the habitat of 200 different birds for high school biology) rather than memorizing assignments.
f. Use the behavioral management and self-monitoring principles, which extend information in chapter 9:
   i. Use incentives of activity breaks and do not use homework as punishment (Salend & Schliff, 1989).
   ii. Allow students with ADHD (especially if they are older or without learning problems) to work assignments, organize tasks, edit, or plan during television in the background. Students with ADHD can multitask with some homework tasks, perhaps because they attend to TV half the amount of time that typical children do (Milich & Lorch, 1994). Note that difficult language-based task performance of typical eighth graders was made worse by soap operas in the background but not by music (Pool, van der Voort, Beentjes, & Koolstra, 2000; Pool, Koolstra, & van der Voort, 2003).
   iii. Ask students to keep a log of their excuses.

A Big Fat Lizard Ate It

Susan Davis attempted to correct her students' failure to turn in homework using punishment (detentions first and then counting homework as a part of the final grade). Those solutions produced more detentions and failing grades. When it was clear that punishment was not the answer, she gave students an excuse sheet to explain why the homework was not done. At the bottom of the excuse sheet were clear consequences, requiring them to still complete the work. After using the sheet for one term, over 60% of the 140 students raised their grades. It was especially helpful for students whose homework grades were below 50%. Perhaps over time students looked at the pattern in their excuses (self-monitoring and self-evaluation) and eventually took responsibility (Davis, 1990).

   iv. Teach students to graph the percentage of homework completed per day using colorful bar graphs to improve homework completion (Bryan & Sullivan-Burstein, 1997).
   v. Use reduced homework and reduced class time as an incentive.

Homework Coupons

Middle and secondary students completed their week's assignments and improved their organization and grades when they could earn "free homework" coupons for reduced homework. Middle school students with behavioral problems will also work to improve their behavior if they can get reduced homework (Cooper & Nye, 1994, p. 476; McLaughlin, Swain, Brown, & Fielding, 1986).

Early Exit Passes

Similarly, gains were found for elementary-level students who got to leave school 15 minutes early if they completed their homework at an 80% accuracy level (for a review, see Miller & Kelley, 1994).

SUMMARY

Educators have often approached the learning problems of students with ADHD using the perspective of the field of learning disabilities. Although many strategies from this field are useful, especially for those children with co-occurring learning disabilities, this approach does not target the specific problems or strengths of children with ADHD. The field of learning disabilities, with its emphasis on task analysis and prerequisite skills, assumes that effective instruction is tightly controlled, step by step and repetitive and that the learner is passive (Poplin, 1988). These assumptions do not match the more fluid and nonlinear learning style of children with ADHD. It also does not relate to their active response style, which is intolerant of delays and thrives on problem solving and active participation with others.

For children with ADHD, it is also important to accommodate differences in their attentional style, which is improved by highlighting global features and relevant task detail. It is especially important to establish academic priorities with a primary emphasis on engaged and productive time and on performance quality (accuracy and creativity), with less emphasis on surface behavior (e.g., looking at a task) or on the appearance of good performance (neatness, organization, and length). These "appearance" indicators of organization and so on would be secondary goals.

Table 11.1 provides a brief summary of practices based on the above evidence for students with ADHD.

TABLE 11.1 Academic Accommodations and Interventions Summary

Academic Areas	Accommodations and Interventions
Listening comprehension	1. Reduce the length, descriptiveness, repetitiveness 2. Use visual models 3. Provide visual response cards or dry-erase boards 4. Allow active responses such as holding objects or doodling 5. Provide the big picture, metaphors, and models before the details 6. Require whole-class or choral responding
Speaking	1. Teach verbal manners, turn taking, and specific times to talk 2. Allow self-talking during problem solving 3. Ask for reexplanations 4. Ask students to draw pictures to provide a framework for talking (or writing) in a logical sequence 5. Use creative verbal assignments
Reading	1. Phonological awareness training (ADHD + reading disabilities) 2. Peer-assisted groups 3. Stack of word cards (self-administered) 4. Blue overlays 5. Pictures at the end of stories

TABLE 11.1 (*Continued*)

Academic Areas	Accommodations and Interventions
Reading comprehension	1. Frequent breaks 2. Red overlays or colored highlighting at the end of passages 3. Interesting stories that relate to student interests 4. Story maps that include characters, setting, conflicts, major events, and outcomes 5. Self-monitoring of attention 6. Encourage self-talking and other active responses 7. Silent reading of self-selected books
Spelling	1. Coloring specific parts of spelling words that are irregular (nonvoiced) after initial exposure to regular print 2. Use the "deaf alphabet" (finger spelling), magnetic letters, and so on 3. Choice of order of spelling activities 4. Peer practice sessions with reversible roles (tutor/tutee)
Math calculations	1. Highlight changes of operation 2. Require active responses (speak answer before writing, hand calculators, or computer practice) 3. Use peer tutoring or games 4. Add color or movement within math calculation practice sessions 5. Provide music during practice
Math problem solving	1. Emphasize big ideas 2. Verbally engage and question the child about his or her use of strategies and reasoning 3. Allow working in pairs or small groups 4. Allow standing while working out problems
Handwriting	1. Reduce the quantity of written work 2. Allow printing, as it is faster and easier 3. Lower standards of acceptable work for some assignments and keep samples of quality work in a portfolio (as models) 4. Add color stimulation to those parts of letters that children fail to close ("kity fog pads") and provide specific practice with difficult letters 5. Require self-monitoring and self-evaluation and the use of mirrors 6. Teach children as early as preschool how to keyboard or use a shorthand note system when computers are unavailable
Composition	1. Use computers instead of handwriting 2. Have children write stories from a series of self-generated pictures rather than from group discussion 3. Ask for poetry or work done in segments rather than one long report
Self-acceptance and avoidance of failure	1. Teach nonverbal methods to ask for help (e.g., a help magnet) 2. Teach verbal methods to ask for permission and the use of apologies 3. Provide high-status jobs, responsibilities, and cooperative learning experiences

DISCUSSION AND APPLICATION QUESTIONS

1. What seems particularly important from this site in teaching students with ADHD? **http://www.sp.uconn.edu/%7Edjleu/third.html**
2. "I'm a special education collaboration teacher for grades 6 to 8. I'm trying to locate teaching strategies for ADHD students, specifically in writing and reading. Why do ADHD students have such an aversion to writing? How can I help them besides scribing for them? I want them to become independent members of society, and it seems to me that scribing for them is defeating that goal."
3. You have arranged for Jack to have access to (a) several seats to move between and (b) the computer for practicing math facts and written assignments. Now several other students are complaining. What do you say or do?
4. "My third-grade son was diagnosed with ADHD-I 2 years ago. Although medication has been useful to his work in other areas, he is struggling in math." Where might this child be struggling in math, and why?
5. List the important components for students with ADHD (preschool, elementary, and/or secondary) of
   a. a reading program,
   b. a spelling program, and
   c. a math program.
6. For the case study of Travis presented in chapter 4, how would you address his probable verbal learning difficulties and handwriting difficulties?
7. "My daughter currently is taking Adderall. She has a 504 plan at school. She did pass her annual achievement test, however, she is failing 7th grade. I believe most of her problems are social and organizational. What homework she does turn in is in the A to B range. However, the homework that does not get done results in failing the class. The teachers have their expectations, but if the work doesn't make it home, then I can't help her. She does not qualify enough for special education assistance, but she is not a successful 7th grader. They say she is immature and needs retention.
8. The following questions relate to the following vignette about David: (See "Student Pratices" example, next page.)
   a. What are the areas of learning difficulty for David?
   b. What is the teacher's instructional approach? Is that working, and, if not, how would you change it?
   c. What does David prefer to do? What is your evidence, and how would you use that to help him with his learning?
   d. Why is David now having difficulties in science, and how would you help his science teacher?
   e. What are his high-frequency get payoffs and avoid payoffs (see chapter 4)? How will knowing about this information help you design lessons for him?
   f. In what ways is David a "hard case," and in what ways does he show us that progress is possible?

STUDENT PRACTICES

David

David is a 12-year old boy in the seventh grade at B. Middle School. He has been identified as having a learning disability and ADHD and receives services in the resource room for 60% of his day (i.e., he takes science and industrial arts with his general education peers but is now showing behavioral difficulties in science as well). He is very smart but has a number of behavioral problems. About one third of his behavior is avoidance based. Of this, 54% avoids instruction, 15% avoids failure, 15% avoids punishment, and 16% avoids loss of self-determination control. The majority (68%) of his behavior functions to get payoffs—peer or adult relatedness (25%); social/emotional stimulation through behavior such as calling people names (29%); kinesthetic stimulation, primarily activity (29%); self-determination/control (14%); and novelty sitmulation (3%).

From his log are the following incidents, which will provide some indication of his learning difficulties:

David is in a "direct instruction" reading class with a group of six other students that meets for 45 minutes daily in the morning.

September 10

9:50 David opened his book to the correct lesson.
9:53 Working in workbook rather than doing oral practice.
10:10 This time David could not find his place when he was called on to read. He then decided to close his book and not participate at all.

September 24

10:02 David was called on to read but refused.
10:12 David did his work in his workbook without problems.

October 2

10:15 David is working on homework.
10:22 Talking without permission.
10:24 David got up and walked around during teacher reading time.

October 9

9:49 Still not participating in oral practices.
10:00 David is throwing pieces of erasers at others and refused to read when called on. Playing with his pencil.

October 14

9:45 Not repeating words during vocabulary review.
10:00 David gets up and walks around and is very argumentative during reading time.
10:10 Puts his things away and begins drawing. He is quiet, so the teacher does not say anything to him.

CHAPTER 12

Collaborating to Support Students with ADHD

OBJECTIVES

- Understand the commonalities and different perspectives of children, families, teachers, and administrators.
- Identify parent and educator practices and how they influence children with ADHD.
- List ways to improve communication among teachers and between teachers and parents.
- List the important contributions of administrative personnel.

KEY TERMS

disengagement
IFSP
protective practices
family-centered
"insular" mothers
ecological model
teachers' professional style
negative teacher practices
monitoring comprehension
problem-based communication
school-to-home notes
introductory letter
testimonials
administrative centralization
in-service education
severe school problems
mild school problems

Knowledge about how to collaborate within and outside the school system is the overall focus of this chapter. Collaboration traditionally involves general educators with their invaluable skills of observation and knowledge of subject matter, parents with their rich knowledge and experiences, and the expertise of special educators and related professionals.

Bringing these perspectives together to advance the educational program of children is the art of school administrators. This is an art based on mutual respect. Thus, productive collaboration asks professionals to evaluate their own biases and inaccurate assumptions about students with ADHD and about their families (Mathur and Smith, 2003; Smith, Salend, & Ryan, 2001).

To these purposes, this chapter will examine the perspectives and needs of families, educators, and school personnel. Interestingly, commonality exists among the diverse experiences, perspectives, and practices of educators and parents (see Figure 12.1).

PERSPECTIVES OF THE FAMILY

What are some of the challenges of families with preschoolers?

One of the major tasks of families of preschool children is the establishment of a climate within which children can express emotions and negotiate conflict. Angry and distressed families are less likely to support feelings (Dunn & Brown, 1994). Regulating emotions and negotiating conflict are difficult in a negative family climate, especially for preschool

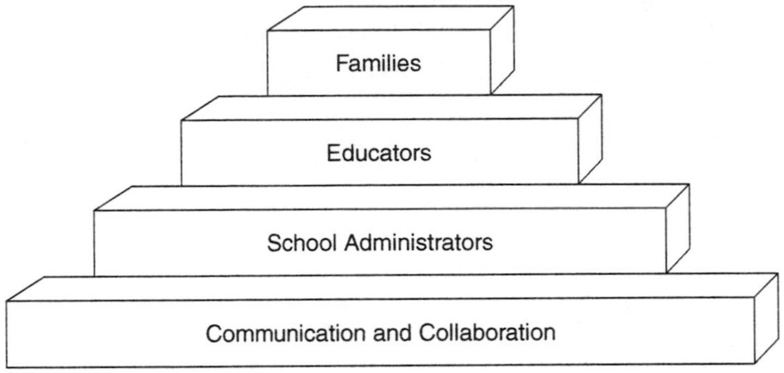

FIGURE 12.1
Perspectives and Needs of Families, Educators, and Administrators Share Common Elements

FAMILY PRACTICES
Perspectives of the Family

"Having a disability in the family is, as Emily Perl Kingsley writes, like taking a plane trip for an Italian vacation, and hearing the stewardess announce, 'Welcome to Holland.'" In response to this unforeseen trip, parents can respond with overinvolvement with the child to the neglect of other family and personal interests or respond with intolerance—interpreting the child's behavior as purposefully against the parent. Either can negatively affect marital and sibling relationships (Ferguson, 2002). Even when neither pattern characterizes a family, family challenges can still become magnified at different developmental stages and in transition to these stages.

children who appear to be particularly vulnerable to the effects of adverse parenting (Keown & Woodward, 2002). At this early developmental stage, the child's nature interacts with family practices to facilitate or discourage the learning of oppositionality (oppositional defiant disorder) (Johnston & Mash, 2001).

Parental conflict and a retaliatory style of management were more characteristic of families with preschoolers with hyperactivity plus aggression than for families of preschoolers with pure hyperactivity (Stormont-Spurgin & Zentall, 1995). Mothers in these families reported giving more physical aggression to their partners (threatening, attempting, or actually hitting, pushing, shoving, grabbing, or throwing something at her partner or throwing things or smashing objects) and receiving more verbal aggression (arguing, yelling, insulting, or sulking) from partners during conflict than mothers of preschoolers with only ADHD (Stormont-Spurgin & Zentall, 1995). In fact, in longitudinal studies, family fights were most frequently cited as a contributing factor to child difficulties (for a review, see Cunningham, Benness, & Siegel, 1988).

Fathers of children with ADHD plus aggression differed from fathers of children with only ADHD in their greater restrictiveness with preschoolers and greater indulgence and permissiveness with their older children (Stormont-Spurgin & Zentall, 1995,

1996). It is possible that fathers' early control strategies failed to produce intended results, so they disengaged from the disciplinary process. Although disengagement avoids feelings of failure, it can also have long-term negative consequences, including failure to monitor children, which appears to protect them from learning aggression (Johnston & Mash, 2001). Disengagement has also been reported for parents in other disability groups (for a review, see Stormont-Spurgin & Zentall, 1996).

Mothers used more lax parenting with their preschoolers (Keown & Woodward, 2002) but more punishment (time-outs or taking away privileges) with their elementary-age children than did comparison mothers (Stormont-Spurgin & Zentall, 1996). Disengagement for mothers was seen in decreased interactions during play, especially when mothers were experiencing stress (Mash, 1983). The statements of mothers of children with ADHD can indicate their reactions to some parenting tasks. For example, when asked what were the rules in their family, one mother replied, "Keep their rooms clean, which they don't; do the dishes, which they don't; take care of these pets, which they don't." In contrast, when mothers were confident in their parenting skills and knowledge, they were more likely to be active in their task interactions with their children (Mash, 1983).

Parents and support personnel have little control over many family factors that predict later aggression (i.e., initial child manageability, maternal depression, and low income [Stormont-Spurgin & Zentall, 1995, 1996]). However, parents' feelings of not being supported or helped by others (Cunningham et al., 1988; Woodward, Taylor, & Dowdney, 1998) is modifiable and becomes increasingly important over time. That is, parents of older children with ADHD reported lower parenting self-esteem and parenting satisfaction than did parents of younger children with ADHD (Mash & Johnson, 1983). In addition, lower self-esteem, more guilt, and a greater sense of isolation are often reported by mothers and fathers of children with ADHD (Cunningham et al., 1988).

Because of the importance of supporting families at this young age, Congress decided to increase families' abilities to meet the special needs of infants and toddlers with handicaps. To help the whole family, an individualized family service plan (IFSP) was developed to guide early intervention services. Parents and professionals work together as partners in writing the IFSP, which typically includes both family and child goals. The emphasis in the IFSP is on enabling the family to support the child. This can be seen in the following listing of some of the important ingredients of the IFSP:

NOTE

COMPONENTS OF AN IFSP

1. The child's present level of functioning or development in vision, hearing, and health status, cognition, language/speech, psychosocial, and self-help skills
2. The family's strengths and needs that can be used to enhance the child

(Continued)

NOTE *(Continued)*

3. The outcomes expected for the child and family
4. The criteria, procedures, and method of assessing progress and of determining changes
5. The specific early intervention services needed to meet the needs of the child and family, including the methods, frequency/intensity of services, and payment arrangements, where necessary
6. The projected dates for starting and completing services
7. The name of the case manager
8. The procedures to support transition to another program

What are the challenges of families with elementary-age children?

Even though early family dysfunction is infrequently found in school-based samples of children, parental coping may become crystallized into a clear discipline style by the elementary school years (Woodward et al., 1998). That is, the child's core symptoms of hyperactivity, impulsivity, and inattention, as well as frequent instances of children's noncompliance, can contribute to negative expectations for these children and a parenting style that is control oriented.

Parents of elementary-level children with ADHD used more negative, reactive, and directive or controlling practices and less praise and fewer positive practices than did parents of children who were not ADHD (for reviews, see Hinshaw & McHale, 1991; Johnston & Mash, 2001; Johnston, Murray, Hinshaw, Pelham, & Hoza, 2002; Madan-Swain & Zentall, 1990). Aggressive discipline, parental feelings of anger and hostility, and poor parental coping were associated with hyperactivity even after controlling for conduct disorders and parents' mental health (Woodward et al., 1998). Noncompliance is typically dealt with by adults who assert power, thereby intensifing parent–child conflict (Woodward et al., 1998).

At this age, conflicts around schoolwork and homework appear to be a major challenge for families (Bursuck et al., 1999). Difficulties with daily school and homework assignments and classroom conduct may lead parents to underestimate their children's actual capabilities (Hartsough & Lambert, 1982). For example, parents of school-age children with hyperactivity had lower academic aspirations and less of a desire to participate in the learning activities of their children (Hartsough & Lambert, 1982).

Schoolwork and homework difficulties are made worse by difficulties with organization (see chapter 6). For example, mothers and fathers of children with ADHD reported that their children organized their time and toys and planned important events more poorly than was reported by parents of typical children (Zentall, Harper, & Stormont-Spurgin, 1993).

In response to these organizational problems, fathers of students with ADHD (but not mothers) reported that they were more likely than comparison fathers to suggest that their child make lists for multiple jobs or tasks. In contrast, mothers of children with ADHD were (a) less likely to teach their child routines for placing objects, (b) more likely to get upset when their child was late for a planned meeting or activity, and (c) rated themselves as significantly less able than mothers of typical children to mentally organize tasks (Zentall et al., 1993). Similarly, in their interactions with their sons with ADHD, mothers used less effective scaffolding (instructional support appropriate to their child's needs) (for a review, see Johnston, Murray, Hinshaw, Pelham, & Hoza, 2002).

Even parents of children with ADHD and giftedness found that enforcing rules was difficult, especially those rules related to morning and eating routines (Moon et al., 2001). One parent described eating as not very structured and that it *wasn't* "uncommon to find food all over the house."

What are the challenges of families with teenagers?

As children develop into adolescents and demonstrate failing grades, noncompliance with family rules, and forgetfulness, it can be interpreted as irresponsibility and bring out additional conflicts with parents, especially when the teen has ADHD (Barkley, Edwards, Laneri, Fletcher, & Metevia, 2001). Parents report more conflicts with teens with ADHD, negative interactions, and intense anger during these conflicts than parents of comparison adolescents (Barkley et al., 1992). To indicate the specific contribution of ADHD symptomology to these family interactions, boys with ADHD (more than their brothers) had antisocial behavior and more self-reported illegal acts, specifically more crimes against persons (Loney, Whaley-Klahn, Kosier & Conboy, 1983). Conflicts are also at school, especially with secondary educators, who expect increased student independence (Bursuck et al., 1999). At the secondary level, students were quite aware of the social consequences, as indicated in the following study:

EVIDENCE-BASED PRACTICES

HOW DO ADOLESCENTS WITH ADHD SEE THEMSELVES?

Purpose. To assess the perceptions of adolescents with ADHD about their overall quality of life and specifically their family and peer relationships.

Participants. Eleven- to 18-year-old clinic-referred and medicated boys with ADHD versus comparison samples of students with and without chronic health conditions

(Continued)

EVIDENCE-BASED PRACTICES *(Continued)*

Tasks. The adolescents completed a depression scale and a Youth Quality of Life Instrument. The environment domain included the quality of school, their engagement in interesting activities, their sense of personal safety, and their view of their future. The quality-of-life scale asked about overall satisfaction with their lives, including theamount of enjoyment adolescents experienced on a day-to-day basis and their feelings about life being worthwhile.

Findings. Adolescents with ADHD reported lower quality-of-life ratings than both comparison groups of adolescents in each domain (e.g., physical health, mental health, belief in themselves). They indicated that they more frequently needed help with emotional/mental health problems, were in a good mood less often, and their problems were more likely to create problems in their families.

Implications. The quality-of-life ratings provided by adolescents with ADHD were comparable to those provided by adolescents with significant mobility impairments even though self-reported depressive symptoms were controlled and the students were all taking medication.

Quality of life can be enhanced when children and teens maintain good relationships with parents and peers, experience success in school, and participate in activities that are enjoyable and in which they are successful (Topplski et al., 2004). Educators need to address these positive qualities earlier and collaborate with parents to achieve success.

Given these developmental challenges, what do parents need from the educational system?

The closest literature relevant to this question is from parents of children identified with emotional and behavioral problems (Petr & Allen, 1997). The primary perception of these parents was that the services they had received were not family centered. They wanted to be involved in decision making and specifically to have access to information about their child and about their rights as parents. Their top five concerns were the following:

1. Failure of providers to get them assistance from other agencies
2. Lack of help in tapping their own family strengths and resources
3. Failure to provide adequate information to the family
4. Failure to inform them of their rights
5. Lack of respect for parents' decision-making responsibilities

The second concern can be addressed perhaps not by understanding an individual family's strengths but by knowing the protective practices of parents of students with ADHD in general:

EVIDENCE-BASED PRACTICES
FAMILY PROTECTIVE PRACTICES

Dysfunction is not typical of the families of young students with pure ADHD (Cunningham & Boyle, 2002). In addition, family strengths may exist.

Mothers who overprotected their children from getting hurt, from strangers, or from people with different values were less likely:

1. to have children with ADHD plus aggression (Stormont-Spurgin & Zentall, 1995, 1996) and
2. to have children with poor social outcomes in young adulthood (i.e., job changes, unemployment, and vagrancy [Loney et al., 1981]).

Parents of children with hyperactivity who rated themselves as strict and demanding in their child-rearing practices were

1. more likely to have children with higher self-esteem (Whaley-Klahn & Loney, 1977) and
2. less likely to use punitive and physical punishment or withdrawal of love.

Mothers who have many contacts outside the family were less likely to have children with serious behavioral problems than "insular" mothers (Wahler, 1975). Parental involvement can be an indicator of parental monitoring that supports the long-term positive outcomes of children with ADHD (Johnston & Mash, 2001). Families who share out-of-school activities and sports with their children provide one positive way to stay engaged with their children (Moon et al., 2001).

An additional family variable of warmth and caring may also be necessary for the development of positive self-esteem in children with ADHD (Hartsough & Lambert, 1982).

In sum, better child outcomes are found for children whose parents provide overprotective strategies with strict expectations, who are engaged with and monitor their children within a supportive context, and who are engaged in other relationships and community activities..

The fourth concern in the previous list can be easily addressed by a handout of rights:

NOTE
SAMPLE NOTICE OF RIGHTS TO PARENTS/STUDENTS

As granted by Section 504 of the Rehabilitation Act of 1973, you as a guardian/parent have the right to the following:

1. Have the school district advise you of your rights under federal law.
2. Receive notice with respect to identification, evaluation, and placement of your child.
3. Have evaluation, educational, and placement decisions based on a variety of informational sources and by persons who know the student and are knowledgeable about the evaluation data and placement options.
4. Examine all relevant records relating to decisions regarding your child's identification, evaluation, and placement.

(Continued)

NOTE *(Continued)*

5. Have your child participate and receive benefits from public education programs without discrimination because of his or her disabling condition(s).
6. Have your child receive a free and appropriate public education.
7. Have your child receive an equal opportunity to participate in nonacademic and extracurricular activities offered by the district.
8. Have your child receive services and be educated in facilities that are comparable to those provided to nondisabled students.
9. Have your child transported to and from an alternative placement setting (if the setting is a program not operated by the district) at no greater cost to you than if the student were placed in a program operated by the district.
10. Have a mediator or impartial due process hearing related to your child's identification, evaluation, educational program, or placement. You may file a local grievance, take part in the hearing, and be represented by counsel. Requests for hearings must be made to your local superintendent.

To improve involvement in decision making (the fifth concern), parents need to understand that their involvement is critically important in the areas of eligibility, educational planning, and the individualized education plan (IEP) meetings (see chapter 2). Although parents have always had input at the assessment stage and a large role in developing the IEP, the reauthorization of IDEA in 1997 increased expectations of parental involvement in prereferral and eligibility meetings (Bos, Nahmias, & Urban, 1999). The contributions that parents can make to the IEP meeting are the following:

NOTE
IEP Meetings

1. Prior to the meeting, review the notebook prepared and described in chapter 1.
2. During an initial IEP meeting,
   a. get an explanation of all terms and results (tape-record or take notes at these meetings),
   b. present your summary of the child's strengths and weaknesses (including those listed from the notebook) and your academic and vocational goals for your child,
   c. discuss the type and amount of related and special education services that the child requires, and
   d. discuss the modifications to the child's general education classes that may be necessary.
3. At the end of the IEP meeting,
   a. make sure all the services, modifications, and the amount of time in general education appear on the IEP and
   b. make sure you agree with the content of the IEP.
4. During a follow-up to the IEP meeting, find out what progress has been made toward the goals and objectives previously proposed (Fowler, 1994).

Additional contributions that parents can make are based on information that only parents have about how the child is handling homework (Zentall & Goldstein, 1999), and only parents can communicate to physicians about the effects and side effects of medication (see chapter 9) (i.e., parent permission is required for educators to communicate with physicians [Bos et al., 1999]).

PERSPECTIVES OF EDUCATORS

The complexity of being a "good" teacher is described in the following:

TEACHING STRATEGIES
A Secondary Educator's Job Perspective

I started teaching at [Jane Doe] High School in the fall of 1998. As you know, for any teacher [who] starts a new job, there are many changes that take place. You have to become familiar with the mission of that particular school, the curriculum they are using, and the personalities of the people you work with. If you are lucky enough to be involved in inclusion, you spend a lot of time developing lesson plans that encompass the experiences and expertise of the teachers involved. Along with that you spend the first semester getting to know and striving to understand the complex yet intriguing nature of the students (Debbie Yocum, personal communication, 2000).

Teachers' personal style

The personal style of teachers contributes significantly to outcomes. Teachers' acceptance and support appear to be especially important for student achievement (Bos et al., 1999). For example, teachers who were warm, accepting, and responsive to students were also more likely to believe that it was possible to produce desired learning outcomes. In turn, their students demonstrated more enthusiasm, higher levels of initiation with their teachers, and higher achievement (for a review, see Beyda, Zentall, & Ferko, 2002). Similarly, students with ADHD said they were motivated when teachers gave them individual attention and took a personal interest in them (Zentall, Grskovic, Javorsky, & Hall, 2000); this has also been reported for children with behavioral problems (Morse, 1994).

Unfortunately, children with hyperactivity perceived that teachers responded to them with greater demandingness and with less acceptance than children without hyperactivity (Peter, Allan, & Horvath, 1983). These perceptions of children were supported (a) by observational research finding more teacher disapproval directed to students with ADHD (for a review, see Peter et al., 1983) and (b) by elementary teachers who reported that their lowest confidence was in their ability to manage the stress "caused" by instructing students with ADHD (Bussing, Gary, Leon, & Garvan, 2002).

Teachers' professional style and practices

Qualities of professional style include the settings and the practices that teachers select. Teacher practices are modifiable and appear to have a direct influence on student behavior.

One management practice that is highly valued among educators is control (Kauffman, Lloyd, & McGee, 1989). Control, however, must be shared. Morrison (1979) assessed student participation in high- versus low-control and high- versus low-activity classrooms. Teacher control increased students' work involvement, whereas low-control classrooms were higher in social involvement of both intimacy and disruption (not aggression). Morrison's review concluded that even though teacher control does reduce pupil talk, it has no effect on deviant behavior and does not foster the learning of social skills, self-direction, or creativity (Morrison, 1979).

When low teacher control was defined as opportunities for student choice, behavioral outcomes were positive for students with ADHD. Flynn and Rapoport (1976) compared the behavior of youth with ADHD in child-directed classrooms with formal classrooms (low choice and movement restricted). In this study, ratings of hyperactivity *decreased* over time in choice and movement classrooms but not in the formal classrooms. In low-choice/low-movement classes, students with ADHD may inhibit activity initially, but it increased significantly over time. This activity increase did not occur in classes where active participation was expected.

One nonadaptive way of meeting a teacher's need for control is through a punitive classroom management style. Negative teacher practices (verbal reprimands or physical restraint) have been linked to increased disruptive, off-task, and negative behavior in average elementary students and in students with emotional and behavioral disorders (Thomas, Becker, & Armstrong, 1968; Van Acker, Grant, & Henry, 1996). Negative student behavior may bring out negative teacher practices (and vice versa) or some combination of the two. The cyclical nature of teacher practices and similar responding by students is suggested in the evidence that practices, such as response cost and suspension, serve as cues suggesting to students that their teachers have hostile intentions that in turn bring out students' reactive aggression (Hartman & Stage, 2000).

The study on page 275 examines the practices that teachers select in specific settings in general education and how these practices influenced the behavior of students with ADHD or with externalizing behavior.

Sometimes it is certain types of student behavior that elicit negative responses from teachers. In particular, the perception of a violation of authority (but not of rules) and the subsequent interpretation ("lack of respect") can lead to serious disciplinary consequences (Beyda & Zentall, 1998). Noncompliance is usually construed as willful disobedience, especially if it is paired with talking back or arguing.

Finally, educators' practices may be in response to written or unwritten policy. Educators will avoid possible disapproval from their administrators when school rules prohibit the use of specific evidence-based practices (Johnson & Pugach, 1990) or require punitive nonevidence-based practices (e.g., writing sentences as a

EVIDENCE-BASED PRACTICES
TEACHERS' PRACTICES AFFECT STUDENTS' BEHAVIOR

Purpose. To assess predictions that negative behavior would be greater (a) in teacher-directed setting for students with externalizing behavior more than for their classmates and (b) in classrooms where teachers exhibited higher rates of negative practices.

Participants. Most of the students met criteria for impulsivity/hyperactivity from teacher ratings on the *DSM–IV*, and all met the criteria either for interpersonal difficulties or inappropriate behavior on the Behavior Evaluation Scale-2. The rates of negative behavior were five times higher for these students than for students with average behavior. However, most students had not been identified as having emotional and behavioral disorders, and this could be attributed to the fact that they were achieving within the normal range.

Settings.

1. Student-directed settings
2. Teacher-directed settings
3. Independent seat-work settings
4. Transitions

Behavior.

1. Task-appropriate behavior (task-related statements or questions and compliance with teacher instructions)
2. Academic—not appropriate, negative/physical; social—not appropriate

Findings Related to Practices.

1. Positive/social teacher practices were related to task-appropriate and positive social behavior of their students.
2. Cooperative practices (e.g., use of divergent tasks and solutions, different concurrent activities, and student-directed learning) were associated with more task-appropriate behavior, specifically for students with ADHD, and other externalizing behavior
3. Teacher directives (reminders and redirects) were associated with task-appropriate behavior for all the students, but it was significant only for students with average behavior. Only in student-directed settings were teacher directives associated with positive task-appropriate behavior for students with ADHD or externalizing behavior. That is, in small-group settings (but not in large-group settings), students with externalizing behavior may derive benefits when teachers are explicit about task requirements.
4. High levels of teachers' negative practices were found in association with high levels of negative student behavior for students with ADHD or externalizing behavior in three of the four settings (teacher directed, independent seat work, and transitions).
5. High rates of coaching/feedback were associated with high rates of task-appropriate behavior that was significant only for students with ADHD or externalizing behavior during independent seat work (i.e., a setting with individual pacing and no waiting).

Findings Related to Settings.

1. The rate of task-appropriate behavior was higher in small-group, student-directed settings than in teacher-directed or in independent seat-work settings. However, the self-pacing of independent settings was more beneficial for students with ADHD and externalizing behavior than for their classmates.
2. The rate of negative behavior for students with ADHD and externalizing behavior was greater in the teacher-directed setting than for their classmates. Teacher-directed settings were also associated with higher rates of teachers' coaching/feedback, which may have increased wait time and set the occasion for negative behavior specifically for these students.

(Continued)

EVIDENCE-BASED PRACTICES *(Continued)*

Implications. Small-group and self-directed settings appeared to normalize the negative behavior of students with externalizing behavior. Small-group activities afforded greater access to information, feedback, social stimulation, choice, interest, and pacing. In these less-structured settings, experienced teachers shaped student behavior with increased use of positive statements and directives.

Teachers could alter their large-group instruction by reducing its length and wait time that often is a by-product of providing individual coaching and feedback during large-group instruction (Beyda et al., 2002).

punishment for swearing). Teachers will also avoid practices that depart from their past experience or educational training. For example, general educators reported feeling less successful implementing individualized accommodations (e.g., use of private signals, use of fewer words in explaining tasks) and were less willing than special educators to try new individualized methods (e.g., highlighting, coloring, circling parts of assignments/directions, or alternating high- and low-interest tasks) or to "change standards" (e.g., altering task length or time) (Zentall & Stormont-Spurgin, 1995). They generally did not and would not implement accommodations for students with ADHD that diverged from group instruction (e.g., allowing alternative response modes, determining places for certain items, and taping prompt cards in desks, on books, or on assignment folders). This indicates that special educators may need to provide support for these modifications or that children may need to be taught how to alter their own materials.

Under some conditions, educators are more willing to attain new competencies and make changes. For example, middle school and secondary-level educators reported that they had tried and succeeded more in altering groupings or seating arrangements during classroom performance (Zentall & Stormont-Spurgin, 1995). Secondary educators appeared to experiment with independent and small group activities more than elementary educators, who, in turn, felt more comfortable altering instructional methods. Across grade levels, other conditions facilitated change. See "Evidence-Based Practices" example on page 277.

Monitoring behavior and performance

Monitoring children with ADHD is just as important a task for educators as it was reported for parents. In examples on page 277, both a mother and an educator indicated an understanding of the importance of monitoring comprehension of directions.

Parent–teacher communication is also an important way to monitor children (Bursuck et al., 1999). Teachers who immediately initiated communication with parents about potential problems had better outcomes with students with ADHD than teachers who delayed this communication (Beyda & Zentall, 1998; Zentall, Moon

EVIDENCE-BASED PRACTICES
General Educators Are Willing to Make Changes When:

1. The problems they observe are modifiable by changing students' tasks or settings (see chapter 8), whereas special educators are more successful or skilled with making changes in the consequences of behavior (see chapter 9) (Zentall & Stormont-Spurgin, 1995).
2. The accommodation can be implemented with available resources and with little time (Johnson & Pugach, 1990). No obstacles were reported by educators who needed specialized equipment or materials to teach students with ADHD (Reid, Vasa, Maag, & Wright, 1994), although it was documented in chapter 11 that children with ADHD do need computers to accommodate for visual-motor skill deficiencies and can profit from electronic equipment that improves organization, such as PDAs (see chapter 10).
3. The accommodation is viewed as a positive technique (praise or a setting/task modification) that does not have side effects for the target child or others.
4. The problem falls within the normal distribution of problems they typically address (Safran, 1982; Whinnery, Fuchs, & Fuchs, 1991; Witt, Elliott, & Martens, 1984). For example, the teachers' perceived ability to manage behavior was related to the quantity of that active behavior (Safran & Safran, 1985). Educators may be put off by descriptions of students with extreme symptomology (Kallas, Reeve, Welch, & Wright, 1997) that are based on clinical samples of children and do not include students' strengths.
5. The accommodations are appropriate for the whole group and not just one individual (Greene, 1996).
6. The accommodation is about directions and assignments more than changes of content, instructional method, or individualized instruction (Munson, 1986).
7. The accommodations are supported by reduced class size and by training the teacher (Bussing et al., 2002).

TEACHING STRATEGIES
Monitoring Comprehension of Directions

After I've given directions, then often times I'll walk to him [and say], "now, you explain to me, what do you think you should do here" (cited in Zentall, Moon et al., 2001, p. 511).

FAMILY PRACTICES

He can be in the same room, and you can be teaching him something, and he can be doing something else . . . but he will know exactly what you're saying, because you can question him on it and he'll be able to give you the answers (cited in Zentall, Moon et al., 2001, p. 511).

et al., 2001). To solve immediate problems and to monitor projects and assignments, teachers rated direct contact methods with parents (e.g., school-to-home notes) as most helpful (Zentall & Goldstein, 1999). School-to-home notes can also fulfill one requirement of IEPs that parents must be regularly informed.

When communicating potential problems to parents, language that describes behavior, interactions, settings, or performance was more successful than statements that evaluated or judged. Evaluative statements move parents into a defensive position where they focus on how they appear, might be seen more favorably, could avoid future attacks, or could control the situation. Defensive exchanges do not lead to effective collaboration. In contrast, when the educator has no prejudgment and simply describes behavior, it allows the parent to think proactively and set goals and make decisions (Gibb, 1961).

School-to-home notes plus a behavioral contract (rewarded by an activity or snack) were evaluated by the parents and the teachers of five children with either inattentiveness or ADHD (Kelley & McCain, 1995). The school-to-home notes plus behavioral contracts were effective in improving classroom behavior and academic productivity for all the children with ADHD, with improved accuracy for four of the five children. Similar school-to-home note programs can decrease disruptiveness and activity for 5-year-old children (McCain & Kelley, 1993). However, it is important to keep these notes descriptive and positive, as reported by the mother of a first-grade child with both giftedness and ADHD:

FAMILY PRACTICES
School-to-Home Notes Must Be Positive, Especially for Preschoolers to First Graders

When he was in first grade he was in trouble a lot. Oh gosh, he was always standing on line. . . . That's their discipline. They don't get to play at recess. They stand on a line. He was bringing notes home on a daily basis that he was not listening; he was not paying attention . . . and he had to carry those [notes] home daily. It was terrible for his self-esteem (cited in Zentall, Moon et al., 2001, p. 505).

When only bad news is communicated, parents feel that they are to blame and must take some action. Parents are partners on the team and not disciplinarians for school events they have not witnessed (Davern, 2004).

In addition to the importance of this type of problem-based communication, daily feedback to parents can be accomplished through (a) telephone hotlines and access tapes, (b) Web addresses, (c) a checklist of performance or behavior that is tabulated and compared over time, and (d) school-to-home (and back-to-school) notebooks or assignment books that communicate progress, strategies that worked well, and daily school events or special events to increase participation from home (Davern, 2004). Table 12.1 provides an example that is descriptive.

Communication in the reverse order from parents to teachers has been anecdotally reported to be successful when an introductory letter was sent to the teacher in the beginning of the school year that described such child characteristics as intentions, variability, possible difficulties, interests/strengths, hobbies, and home strategies

TABLE 12.1 School-to-Home Note Template

School-to-Home Note Teacher's Name ______________ Student Name ______________ Date ______________	
Teacher's observations in subject area, time period, etc.	Parents' home observations and comments:
A. Changes noted: 1. In school effort: 2. In behavior: 3. In school work: 4. In peer relations:	A. Changes noted: 1. In family events: 2. In homework: 3. In relations with brothers and sisters: 4. In relations with parents: 5. In mood or eating/sleeping: 6. Other______________
B. Homework: completed or incomplete Specific difficulties: Progress observed:	Time spent: Difficulties: Interest in assignments: Homework habits:
C. Progress on project: ______________ Expected Progress: Current progress:	
D. Behavioral Contract Behavior: ______________ Points earned: Suggested activities earned or lost: • TV time: ______________ • Earlier/later bedtime • Snacks • Points toward purchase of object Other ______________________	Child's responses to earned/lost privileges:
Teacher's comments and observations (see back):	Parent comments (see back) and signature:

that work and past teachers' strategies, references on ADHD, plans for meetings, requests for feedback, and so on.

Keeping up with fads and new "cures"

"Magic pills" arrive in a variety of forms, including megavitamin, motor training, auditory and visual or perceptual training, dietary restrictions, and biofeedback. "Convention, convenience, dogma, folklore, fashion, and fad—more so than the results of scientific research—have influenced theory and practice in education over the years" (for a review, see Heward, 2003, p. 194). Educators and other professional groups must be ready to evaluate and help parents evaluate these therapies. Miracles are brightly packaged with exaggerated claims (e.g., "an amazing discovery") and advertised with glowing individual testimonials. They also typically require an investment of time, hope, and money and produce minimal short-lived outcomes, similar to those produced by a placebo (a nonactive medication or sugar pill that produces effects because an expectation of gain is present).

PERSPECTIVES OF SCHOOL PERSONNEL

The climate of a classroom that supports children's learning is determined not only by the professional and personal style of the teacher but also by the expectations and support from the school administration (Culbertson & Silovsky, 1996). The culture of some schools may need a few small repairs to create such an environment. Those schools most in need of reframing are those with administrative centralization and high student-to-teacher ratios as well as high rates of suspensions. These, in turn, are associated with lower-quality instruction and more time relegated to discipline (for a review, see Peterson, 2003). In schools such as these, suspension allows for children to escape an unpleasant environment (i.e., it functions as a negative reinforcer for some children [Peterson, 2003]). Repairs that are easily made by administrators to address these problems are listed in the following sections.

Selection and assignment of teachers

Administrators can support students with ADHD by selectively hiring and retaining teachers. Teacher–student compatibility has been identified as a very important when placing students with ADHD (Greene, 1995). If teachers believe that students are irresponsible and undisciplined, they are more likely to use controlled settings with punitive responses for misbehavior. For example, the higher the percentage of teachers who agree that pupils are generally incapable of solving their own problems, the more likely the students are to have antisocial attitudes or behavior and to be suspended from that school (Wu, Pink, Crain, & Moles, 1982). Negative teacher attitudes have also been linked to higher suspension and absentee rates, more negative reactions from students, lower student satisfaction with school, and lower commitment to class work (see Beyda & Zentall, 1998).

Encourage teacher and parent participation

Teachers, like parents and children, are more effective when they are actively participating. When teachers have more adult-to-adult interactions, they are more open to experimentation, ongoing professional development and change, collaborative problem solving, and strong personal relationships with students (Beyda & Zentall, 1998). Participation can be encouraged by asking for input from teachers and by supporting teacher participation with others in problem-solving teams and in common planning times. For example, common planning times can increase teachers' access to the knowledge of other professionals. In addition, bimonthly teams of general educators, master teachers, school counselors, special educators, parent representatives, the school corporation's Section 504 coordinator, and other personnel or community volunteers can be used to represent a wider set of perspectives. These perspectives can address disciplinary decisions, especially for repeat offenders (Freiberg, Stein, & Parker, 1995) and the failure of punitive methods to address these repeat offenders. Such teams could review behavioral records, teachers' disciplinary referrals, and a functional analysis of student behavior (see chapter 4) in order to make recommendations regarding discipline or accommodations to the administrator.

Participation is equally important in increasing parents' perceptions of being supported. Participation can be facilitated through schoolwide committees, newsletters with parent involvement, incentives for parents to attend meetings (e.g., food, babysitting services), and information available to parents about local services to families. In addition, special educators have recommended that (a) students receive after-school sessions and peer tutoring, (b) parents receive frequent communication from teachers to include evening conferences, and (c) special educators receive release time to meet with parents (survey data by Bursuck et al., 1999).

Support innovative practices and provide in-service education

In a sample of 353 schools, encouragement for innovative practices, as measured by two teacher survey items ("In this school, I am encouraged to experiment with my teaching" and "The principal is interested in innovation and new ideas"), were found to relate to teacher's perception that teaching was personally satisfying and worth the effort (Newmann, Rutter, & Smith, 1989).

Administrators can encourage innovation through periodic feedback/monitoring and through in-service education. General educators report that few opportunities for in-service education contributed to their resistance to implementing accommodations (Galis & Tanner, 1995). Those general educators with more experience with students with ADHD or education about them were more willing to make instructional changes (Reid et al., 1994). This opinion was also expressed by an anonymous secondary-level general educator. (See "Teaching Strategies" page 282.)

Addressing the knowledge that teachers need to reduce their own frustration has been defined as a phase I intervention (Marchant & Siperstein, 1997) and can be found in chapters 5 through 7. Immediate, short-term strategies that reduce student frustration are phase II interventions and are described in chapters 8 through 11. These are environmental and task changes, which include the use of intense teacher praise to improve attention, academic performance, and activity. Phase III interventions, according to Marchant and Siperstein, focus on improving the climate of the

TEACHING STRATEGIES
Frustration and Willingness to Accommodate

Personally, it is much easier to invest time and energy working with a student who has an identifiable "problem" that is interfering with his or her classroom performance than it is to work with one who just has a lack of interest or motivation. I think just knowing more about problems that interfere with students learning can help with my own frustration levels, but knowing some specific things I can do to help students to lower their frustration levels and raise their achievement levels in my class (and frequently decrease their behavior problems) is even better.

classroom. These changes require more teacher time and training and include interventions, such as classwide peer tutoring, more systematic use of behavioral strategies, coaching/modeling, and the use of functional assessment, which are presented in chapters 4, 8, and 9. It may be important for consultants to gradually increase the strength of interventions through such a phase approach. The following study examined such an incremental approach to in-service education:

EVIDENCE-BASED PRACTICES
Phases in a Field Study of In-Service Education

Purpose. To assess the implementation of in-service education to promote knowledge, empathy, and effective practices for teachers of students with ADHD.

Participants. Forty-nine teachers were scheduled to attend in-service education from a large intermediate school district supporting 85,000 students and their families.

Conditions. Three levels of training: (1) knowledge, implemented during 1 day by the local educational agency drawing on a number of local professionals; (2) knowledge plus empathy, similarly implemented in 1 day; and (3) knowledge plus empathy plus practice (i.e., 1 additional day of practice), implemented by the author and a doctoral student. Knowledge training was designed to facilitate cognitive understanding of major concepts, characteristics, outcomes, and strategies for students with ADHD. Empathy training was designed to facilitate understanding and empathy with these students so that teachers were motivated to make modifications in instruction. The preceding two elements plus an emphasis on functional assessment (see chapter 4) were the elements of the third training component.

Findings Across Conditions

1. Across conditions, participants were more willing to learn about ADHD and were more confident in teaching these students at post–in-service than at pre–in-service.
2. Across conditions, self-rating on the Classroom Environment Scale, a measure of a teacher's flexibility and willingness to accommodate for individual differences, also increased.
3. Both conditions reported a reduction in the level of hyperactivity, oppositionality, and inattention as well as an improvement in social skills (e.g., peer interactions) in their classrooms 3 months after attending an in-service education program on ADHD.

(Continued)

EVIDENCE-BASED PRACTICES *(Continued)*

Findings Indicating Differences Between Knowledge (Condition 1) and Knowledge plus Empathy (Condition 2).

1. Significant differences were found in ratings on the reported use of two categories of classroom behavior (classroom removals to outside the class plus detentions) and classroom discipline (inside the classroom time-outs plus loss of privileges). The Condition 1 group (school in-service), knowledge only, used significantly more disciplinary practices than the Condition 2 (university knowledge plus empathy) group. Data representing actual classroom incidents showed that the Condition #1 group doubled their use of classroom removals over their pre–in-service mean, and used twice as many negative consequences for misbehavior and "don't rules" in their classroom than the Condition #2 group.
2. In the analysis of the actual classroom data, we found that type of in-service also had a significant influence on the average number of times per week students received an outside-the-classroom time-out or a detention. Prior to the in-service program, both groups employed time-out at similar rates per week. Three months after in-service education, participants in Condition #1 were more likely to use practices associated with the local school agency in-service program (e.g., time-out, posting of consequences), and Condition #2 participants were more likely to use practices associated with the university curriculum (e.g., colorful/interesting bulletin boards, short transition times, and choral responding).

Findings of Differences Between Knowledge plus Empathy (Condition 2) and Knowledge plus Empathy plus Functional Assessment Practice (Condition 3).

1. Condition #3 teachers rated students one half a standard deviation improvement on the Hyperactivity Scale from pre– to post–in-service, which was not found for Condition #2.
2. Condition #3 teachers rated a significant decrease in oppositionality ratings of approximately one third a standard deviation, which was not found for Condition #2. This group may have been more skilled in reducing or redirecting these behaviors by analyzing the function of behavior.
3. The additional day of in-service education led to an average of only two classroom discipline (time-out plus loss of privileges) practices per week specifically during weeks 4, 5, and 6 of the study, whereas the Condition #2 group used an average of 6.1. This finding suggests that the Condition 3 group was applying different approaches to address disruptive behavior even though they received general information on positive practices.

Implications. These changes in teaching practices were consistent with the materials that the participants were exposed to during their sessions. In other words, in-service recommendations are learned by participants. Unfortunately, sometimes the practices taught are not positive practices. That is, one disadvantage of local educational agencies is their reliance on local professionals who may be less knowledgeable about empirically supported positive practices. Functional assessment is an important component of in-service education because it can result in decreased child oppositionality and decreased disciplinary actions by educators (Zentall & Javorsky, 2005).

Other models of in-service education that appear to have merit include using teachers as peer coaches and identifying a "trainer of trainers" model in which an in-service program is used to update an individual from each school district who consults with a building member and acts as a liaison to a team (Bradley-Klug, Shapiro, & DuPaul, 1997; Worthington et al., 1997).

Provide formalized procedures and policies

Administrators can use rules, policies, and procedural guidelines to protect educators and students. At a procedural level, administrators can alter the schedules of students with ADHD so that more novel and active classes (e.g., physical education, music, arts) are interspersed regularly throughout the day. They can also distribute students with behavioral challenges over a number of classes. This practice will *decrease* educators' primary focus on classroom control (Eccles et al., 1993).

Administrator may also need to provide individualized support to teachers who use restrictive approaches, such as reprimand, withdrawal of privileges, removal. These teachers can be recognized by the frequency of their referrals.

Support will also be necessary for specific students who are repeatedly referred for misconduct and for conflict. For recurrent problems, administrators can design alternatives to exclusionary and punitive discipline. The magnitude of any conflict is usually reflected in the distance between a student's expectation and that of an adult (Algozzine, Audette, Ellis, Marr, & White, 2000). That is, preventive practices include making expectations clear on both parts, which can depersonalize conflict.

In addition, school personnel need to see infractions in relation to their severity. Severe school problems are those that represent a threat to the safety of persons, whereas mild school problems are those that threaten the order and flow of activities and the immediate comfort of individuals (Algozzine et al., 2000) (see Table 12.2).

Other types of policies that are useful are those that specify homework modifications for students with ADHD. Unfortunately, only about 35% of school districts had a homework policy, and of those, 64% included modifications for students with disabilities (Roderique, Polloway, Cumblad, Epstein, & Bursuck, 1994). Homework policies could include guidelines for the amount of time students would be ex-

TABLE 12.2 Mild Problems of School Order or Severe Problems of Safety

	Aggression		**Activity/Impulsivity**
Severity of Misconduct	Severe	Moderate	Mild
Examples of Misconduct	1. Chronic fighting 2. Bullying 3. Malicious teasing, racism, and sexism	1. Destroying school property 2. Truancy	1. Running in hallways 2. Class disruptiveness 3. Talking back or arguing 4. Missing assignments
Examples of Intervention	Involvement of other consultants (e.g., counselors and psychologists)	1. Have the child repair it 2. Other consultants 3. Establish a peer mediation review board 4. Use functional assessment	1. Assign role responsibilities during difficult activities 2. Time-out within the class from an in-class activity 3. Behavioral contracts 4. Use functional assessment (chapter 4)

pected to work on homework (15 to 45 minutes at the elementary level, 1 to 2 hours in junior high, and up to 2.5 hours in high school [Cooper & Nye, 1994]) and consequences for failure to complete homework assignments (e.g., turn it in the following day, during an after-school study period, or by Friday with a loss of a percentage of points or with an excuse sheet [see chapter 11]). For children who need more time than suggested for their age-group, reductions in the amount of work and adaptations for handwriting would be part of the policy. Administrative policies could also formalize procedures for voice-mail assignments, homework buddies, homework hotlines, or an after-school homework program for small groups of students with recurrent failure to complete homework assignments.

Schoolwide grading policies can also be beneficial for students with ADHD. When neither the task nor the content is changed (i.e., only the amount of material, amount of time, task input, or task response is changed), grading should not be altered. Examples are for following directions that are highlighted, completing assignments given an opportunity to discuss the assignment with a buddy after teachers' instructions, or completing assignments with the aid of a computer or hand calculator. However, when a task change is made, with different information, curriculum content, and performance goals, then the objective of the lesson has *not* been met, and the learning is not comparable to other students in class. When these types of content changes are made, a student's recommended maximum grade might be a B, not an A. However, even for students for whom a task change has been made and who put forth reasonable effort, a minimum grade would be a D.

Finally, administrators can design templates to meet the legal requirements of meetings as sampled in the following:

NOTE
Developing the IEP and Transition Requirements: A Checklist

1. Did the public agency (school) invite the student to the case conference (IEP) meeting?
2. Did the student attend the case conference (IEP) meeting?
3. Did the public agency take steps to ensure that the student's preferences and interests were considered in developing the IEP? [When Zach was given the opportunity to add goals during his case-conference, his response was, "bug hunting."]

4a. Did the public agency (school) invite a representative from any other public agency that is likely to be responsible for providing or paying for transition services?

4b. If a representative from any agency did not attend, did the public agency take other steps to obtain their participation in the planning of transition services? (Reauthorization H.R. 1350 [2004] modifies transition activities to begin no later than the first IEP and to be in effect when the child is 16 years old with measurable postsecondary goals related to training, education, employment, and, where appropriate, independent living skills.)

(Continued)

NOTE (Continued)

5. Was the parent provided with notice?
6. Does the parents' notice:
   a. indicate that one of the purposes of the meeting will be the development of a statement of needed transition services?
   b. indicate that the public agency will invite the student?
   c. identify (by agency, position, and title) any other agency that will be invited to send a representative?
   d. indicate the date, time, and location of the meeting and who will attend?
   e. inform the parents that they may invite other individuals who have knowledge or special expertise regarding their child, including related services personnel, as appropriate?
7. Does the IEP contain a statement of:
   a. current performance related to transition services?
   b. transition service needs that specifies the student's courses of study that will be meaningful to the student's future and motivate the student to complete his or her education?
   c. needed transition services?
   d. that at least 1 year before the student reaches the age of majority under state law, the student has been informed of the rights under Part B of IDEA 97 that will transfer to him or her on reaching the age of majority?
8. Does the statement of needed transition services consider the following?
   - Related services
   - Instruction
   - Community experiences
   - Development of employment and other postschool adult living objectives
   - Daily living skills
   - Functional vocational evaluation
9. Are the activities in the statement of needed transition services presented as a coordinated set of activities that:
   a. promote movement from school to the student's desired postschool goals? or the interagency responsibilities or any needed linkages if appropriate?
   b. reviewed at least annually?
10. Did any participating agency from outside the school system fail to provide agreed-on transition services contained in the IEP?
    a. Did the public agency responsible for the student's education initiate a meeting to identify alternative strategies to meet the transition objectives and, if necessary, revise the student's IEP? (adapted from Indiana Department of Education, 2002).

SUMMARY

School is socially and academically stressful for children with ADHD and stressful as well for their parents and teachers. All parties—parents, teachers, and students—need support and a sense of control and competence (empowerment). Families can provide a rich source of support for the child and, indirectly, for the teacher to the extent that parents can master their own challenging tasks at each stage of development.

At the preschool level, the primary challenge is interacting with a difficult and often noncompliant child who many fathers attempt to manage with a strong hand. These restrictive practices apparently fail to achieve desired effects, often contributing to fathers' disengagement. Fathers may be viewing their role as that of disciplinarian (control orientation) and may need to refocus to other strengths in the male role, including an emphasis on directing activity and playing and a focus on mastery. In contrast, many mothers begin with a lax parenting style with their preschoolers (perhaps as a counterweight to their husbands), setting the stage for aggressive child outcomes, especially when used in a family that resolves conflicts through vindictiveness and negative interactions. However, a number of family strengths can be supported (e.g., parental protectiveness, strict rules, caregiving, child monitoring, verbal management practices, and active participation of both parents in the educational process).

At the elementary level, struggles between the child and parent were often expressed over homework and other routines. Family strengths were observed in nonroutine activities, such as family outings and shared activities (Moon et al., 2001). For students with ADHD, the primary challenges were in organization and completion of homework. Homework is particularly punishing for these children because it typically is a repetition of tasks the student failed to complete during the day. Fathers can offer considerable support here in teaching organizational skills, and educators may need to draw fathers into the educational process.

At the secondary level, the challenges of the previous stages are present in addition to significant peer and adult relationship problems. At this age, these problems increase in number and severity. To improve relationships, parents and educators may need to help secondary students with ADHD recognize their own assets, interests, and specific liabilities (Whalen, 2001). If these students also have oppositional defiant disorder or conduct disorder, anger management training may be needed.

Educators are similar to parents in their struggle to get "appropriate" behavior from these children (get control) and to feel competent in their roles. Teachers reported feeling overwhelmed by the quantity of activity and their inability to manage stress that resulted from attempting to handle this activity. Reciprocally, children with ADHD, more than typical children, perceived their teachers to be more demanding and less accepting.

Protective personality factors were teachers' warmth and an expressed personal interest in individual children. The professional practices that teachers select can also support students with ADHD. To reduce negative behavior, self-directed settings (not teacher controlled) are important, and small-group activities increased task-appropriate behavior. These less control-oriented settings provided movement opportunities for students with ADHD, but they were guided by experienced teachers' use of positive statements and directives.

Finally, the contributions of school administrators were valuable assets in the support of students with ADHD. Administrators provide support through (a) selective hiring and retaining of teachers; (b) encouragment of communication and participation among teachers and between parents and teachers, (c) support of innovation in the classroom, in-service education, and individual support and redirection for teachers who make frequent referrals; and (d) establishing and maintaining rules, policies, and

Student + Principal + Parents = Student's Success

procedural guidelines for nonpunitive discipline, homework accommodations, and templates for grading students and for meeting legal requirements.

In this chapter, the ecological model has been emphasized because it focuses on teachers, parents, and administrators as members of the same team. This is the appropriate model for educational collaboration (Marchant & Siperstein, 1997). When using this model, we need to recognize that our common ground is supporting students with ADHD. Positive practices that support these children were used (a) by parents, that is, warmth plus strict expectations and involvement/monitoring of their child; (b) by teachers, that is, personal interest and positive statements as well as high expectations (not demandingness) and the use of student-directed learning opportunities; and (c) by administrators, that is, positive rules and policies as well as support for innovation and in-service education.

The most difficult task is assumed by educators and parents, who provide direct services on a daily basis. It is, therefore, not surprising that educators and parents also expressed their own need for support—requesting more participation and communication, involvement in the decision-making process, and access to information or in-service education.

DISCUSSION AND APPLICATION QUESTIONS

1. How can you help parents using this web site? **http://www.ldonline.org/finding_help/online_help/online-help.html**
2. If you go to the "Technology" link, what are some of the interesting resources?
3. You talked to the parents of your student with ADHD and discovered that they are punishing him for not completing his homework. He never gets to go out to play, must stay in his room every evening, rarely watches TV or plays with

friends, and now has been restricted from going on the family vacation. The student is depressed and anxious about the situation. You feel bad about it, but the homework is mostly his class work that he failed to complete during the day, and your rule is that if it doesn't get done, it becomes homework. What can you do?

4. Referring to Discussion Question 7 in chapter 10, how can you involve the family?
5. List ways you might enlist children and parents into participating with the goals listed in the left column of the following chart.

Collaborative Responsibilities

Goals to increase:	 Teacher	 Student	 Parents
Channeled Motor Activity	Reduce wait time Allow activity fillers (doodling) Active response curriculum (e.g., whole-class voting, choral responding) Provide jobs and responsibilities Allow short activity breaks between assignments; do not take away recess	Join a club or a sport Set specific times for activities Take things with you to be prepared for delays Keep a small notebook to write ideas or tasks	Encourage daily time for physical activity and do not take away sports Provide constructive activities during delay time (e.g., church) Require jobs and reasonable responsibilities around the house/yard
Channeled Verbal Activity	Seating arrangements in clusters Use peer tutoring as both tutor and tutee	Keep conversations on the topic of the current subject Plan out conversations using small pictures	Bring a child friend over for supervised structured fun activities and reinforce appropriate behavior Bring student back to focus of conversation (on track)
Self-Esteem	Focus on student's strengths (avoid disability areas) (e.g., grade content and originality, separately from handwriting or spelling) Provide access to privileges	List those things about yourself you like List those things in others you like Ask questions when you don't understand	Focus on the child's strengths Set goals that can be easily reached

(Continued)

Goal to increase:	 Teacher	 Student	 Parents
	Suggest parent readings	Ask for praise when you feel you have done something well Ask for feedback in areas you feel you get criticism	
Appropriate Reactions to Frustration	Do not take away physical education or recess Give choice whenever possible Suggest parental/family counseling Suggest parent support groups (e.g., Children and Adults with Attention Deficit Disorders)	Keep a picture diary or log of feelings with events Identify settings or events that trigger emotional overreactions Decide what to say and do for these difficult moments Remove self from group when upset (self time-out)	Spend fun time together as a family; tell stories at dinner Reward efforts at attempts to control Provide active ways to release energy or require time intervening to "cool down" Accept the child's feelings even though the behavior may not be acceptable
Increase Compliance	Allow choices Set limits on what the child *cannot* choose or a few important rules with reasons about safety, comfort, learning, and communication (i.e., rule directed and not personal). Identify alternatives to physical punishment or taking away sports and club activities Assign peer or group projects Set up communication with parents	Establish several routines, with reasons why to do them Follow the routines you have established by making them fun Follow directions by making them your own (e.g., rewriting, restating, or rephrasing)	Give choice of which assignment to work on first Reward for completed work with a desired activity/privilege Allow choice of the order of tasks

References

Aaron, P. G., Joshi, R. M., Palmer, H., Smith, N., & Kirby, E. (2002). Separating genuine cases of reading disability from reading deficits caused by predominantly inattentive ADHD behavior. *Journal of Learning Disabilities, 35*, 425–437.

Abikoff, H. (1985). Efficacy of cognitive training interventions in hyperactive children: A critical review. *Clinical Psychology Review, 5*, 479–512.

Abikoff, H. (1991). Cognitive training in ADHD children: Less to it than meets the eye. *Journal of Learning Disabilities, 24*, 205–209.

Abikoff, H., Courtney, M. E., Szeibel, P. J., & Koplewicz, H. S. (1996). The effects of auditory stimulation on the arithmetic performance of children with ADHD and nondisabled children. *Journal of Learning Disabilities, 29*, 238–246.

Abikoff, H. B., & Hechtman, L. (1996). Multimodal therapy and stimulants in the treatment of children with attention deficit disorder. In E. D. Hibbs & P. Jensen (Eds.), *Psychosocial treatment for child and adolescent disorders: Empirically based strategies for clinical practice* (pp. 668–696). Washington, DC: American Psychological Association.

Abikoff, H. B., Jensen, P. S., Arnold, L. L. E., Hoza, B., Hechtman, L., Pollack, S., et al. (2002). Observed classroom behavior of children with ADHD: Relationship to gender and comorbidity. *Journal of Abnormal Child Psychology, 30*, 349–359.

Abramowitz, A. J., & O'Leary, S. G. (1991). Behavioral interventions for the classroom: Implications for students with ADHD. *School Psychology Review, 20*, 220–234.

Ackerman, P. T., Anhalt, J. M., Dykman, R. A., & Holcomb, P. J. (1986). Effortful processing deficits in children with reading and/or attention disorders. *Brain and Cognition, 5*, 22–40.

Ackerman, P. T., Anhalt, J. M., Holcomb, P. J., & Dykman, R. (1986). Presumably innate and acquired automatic processes in children with attention and/or reading disorders. *Journal of Child Psychology and Psychiatry, 27*, 513–529.

Ackerman, P. T., Dykman, R. A., & Gardner, M. Y. (1990). ADD students with and without dyslexia differ in sensitivity to rhyme and alliteration. *Journal of Learning Disabilities, 23*, 279–283.

Adelman, H. S., & Taylor, L. (1990). Intrinsic motivation and school misbehavior: Some intervention implications. *Journal of Learning Disabilities, 23*, 541–550.

Aleman, S. R. (1991). Special education for children with attention deficit disorder: Current issues. Washington, DC: Congressional Research Service.

Allessandri, S. M. (1992). Attention, play, and social behavior in ADHD preschoolers. *Journal of Abnormal Child Psychology, 20*, 289–302.

Algozzine, B., Audette, B., Ellis, E., Marr, M. B., & White, R. (2000). Supporting teachers, principals—and students—through unified discipline. *Teaching Exceptional Children, 33*, 42–54.

Allen, T. W. (1986). Styles of exploration in control, attention deficit disorder with hyperactive and learning disabled children. *Journal of Learning Disabilities, 19*, 351–353.

Amabile, T. M., & Gitomer, J. (1984). Children's artistic creativity: Effects of choice in task materials. *Personality and Social Psychology Bulletin, 10,* 209–215.

American Academy of Pediatrics. (1994). *Understanding the child with ADHD: Information for parents about attention deficit hyperactivity disorder.* Elk Grove, IL: Author.

American Academy of Pediatrics. (2001a). Clinical practice guideline: Diagnosis and evaluation of the child with attention-deficit/hyperactivity disorder (AC0002). *Pediatrics, 105,* 1158–1170.

American Academy of Pediatrics. (2001b). Clinical practice guideline: Treatment of the school-aged child with attention-deficit/hyperactivity disorder. *Pediatrics, 108,* 1033–1044.

American Psychiatric Association. (2000). *Diagnostic and statistical manual of mental disorders* (4th ed., revised). Washington, DC: Author.

Ames, C., & Ames, R. (1984). Systems of student and teacher motivation—Toward a qualitative definition. *Journal of Educational Psychology, 76,* 535–556.

Anderson, M., Nelson, L. R., Fox, R. G., & Gruber, S. E. (1988). Integrating cooperative learning and structured learning: Effective approaches to teaching social skills. *Focus on Exceptional Children, 20,* 1–8.

Antshel, K. M., & Remer, R. (2003). Social skills training in children with attention deficit hyperactivity disorder: A randomized-controlled clinical trial. *Journal of Clinical Child and Adolescent Psychology, 32,* 153–165.

Armstrong, T. (1995a). *The myth of the A.D.D. child: 50 ways to improve your child's behavior and attention span without drugs, labels, or coercion,* New York: Dutton Press.

Armstrong, T. (1995, October 18). ADD as a social intervention. *Education Week, 33, 40.*

Armstrong, T. (1996). ADD: Does it really exist? *Phi Delta Kappan, 1,* 424–428.

Arndorfer, R. E., Miltenberger, R. G., Woster, S. H., Rortvedt, A. K., & Gaffaney, T. (1994). Home-based descriptive and experimental analysis of problem behaviors in children. *Topics in Early Childhood Special Education, 14,* 64–87.

Atkins, M. S., Pelham, W. E., & Licht, M. H. (1989). The differential validity of teacher ratings of inattention/overactivity and aggression. *Journal of Abnormal Child Psychology, 17,* 423–435.

August, G. J. (1987). Production deficiencies in free recall: A comparison of hyperactive, learning-disabled, and normal children. *Journal of Abnormal Child Psychology, 15,* 429–440.

August, G. J., Realmuto, G. M., Joyce, T., & Hektner, J. M. (1999). Persistence and desistance of oppositional defiant disorder in a community sample of children with ADHD. *Journal of the American Academy of Child and Adolescent Psychiatry, 38,* 1262–1270.

August, G. J., Realmuto, G. M., MacDonald, A. W., III, Nugent, S. M., & Crosby, R. (1996). Prevalence of ADHD and comorbid disorders among elementary school children screened for disruptive behavior. *Journal of Abnormal Child Psychology, 24,* 571–595.

Augustine, D. K., Gruber, K. D., & Hanson, L. R. (1990). Cooperation works! *Educational Leadership, 47,* 4–7.

Aylward, G. P., Gordon, M., & Verhulst, S. J. (1997). Relationships between continuous performance task scores and other cognitive measures: Causality or commonality? *Assessment, 4,* 325–336.

Babyak, A. E., Koorland, M., & Mathes, P. G. (2000). The effects of story mapping instruction on the reading comprehension of students with behavioral disorders. *Behavioral Disorders, 25,* 239–258.

Baker, J. M., & Zigmond, N. (1990). Are regular classes equipped to accommodate students with learning disabilities?. *Exceptional Children, 56,* 515–526.

Banaschewski, T., Brandeis, D., Heinrich, H., Albrecht, B., Brunner, E., & Rothenberger, A. (2003). Association of ADHD and conduct disorder—Brain electrical evidence for the existence of a distinct subtype. *Journal of Child Psychology and Psychiatry, 44,* 356–376.

Bandura, A. (1969). *Principles of behavior modification.* New York: Holt, Rinehart and Winston.

Barkley, R. A. (1985). Do as we say, not as we do. In J. Swanson & H. Bloomingdale (Eds.), *Emerging trends in research on attention deficit disorders.* New York: LEA Publications.

Barkley, R. A. (1991). Attention deficit hyperactivity disorder. *Psychiatric Annals, 21,* 725–733.

Barkley, R. A. (1995). *Taking charge of ADHD.* New York: Guilford Press.

Barkley, R. A. (1997a). *ADHD and the nature of self-control.* New York: Guilford Press.

Barkley, R. A. (1997b). Behavioral inhibition, sustained attention, and executive functions: Constructing a unifying theory of ADHD. *Psychological Bulletin, 121,* 65–94.

Barkley, R. A. (1998a). Attention-deficit hyperactivity disorder. *Scientific American, 279,* 66–71.

Barkley, R. A. (1998b). *Attention-deficit hyperactivity disorder: A handbook for diagnosis and treatment* (2nd ed.). New York: Guilford Press.

Barkley, R. A., & Biederman, J. (1997). Toward a broader definition of the age-of-onset criterion for attention-deficit hyperactivity disorder. *Journal of the American Academy of Child and Adolescent Psychiatry, 36,* 1204–1210.

Barkley, R. A., DuPaul, G. J., & McMurray, M. B. (1990). Comprehensive evaluation of attention deficit disorder with and without hyperactivity as defined by research criteria. *Journal of Consulting and Clinical Psychology, 58,* 775–789.

Barkley, R. A., Edwards, G., Laneri, M., Fletcher, K., & Metevia, L. (2001). Executive functioning, temporal discounting, and sense of time in adolescents with attention deficit hyperactivity disorder (ADHD) and oppositional defiant disorder (ODD). *Journal of Abnormal Child Psychology, 29,* 513–528.

Barkley, R. A., Fischer, M., Edelbrock, C. S., & Smallish, L. (1990). The adolescent outcome of hyperactive children diagnosed by research criteria: I. An 8-year prospective follow-up study. *Journal of the American Academy of Child and Adolescent Psychiatry, 29,* 546–557.

Barkley, R. A., Grodzinsky, G., & DuPaul, G. J. (1992). Frontal lobe functions in attention deficit disorder with and without hyperactivity: A review and research report. *Journal of Abnormal Child Psychology, 20,* 163–188.

Barkley, R. A., Guevremont, D. C., Anastopoulos, A. D., DuPaul, G. J., & Shelton, T. L. (1993). Driving-related risks and outcomes of attention deficit hyperactivity disorder in adolescents and young adults: A 3- to 5-year follow-up survey. *Pediatrics, 92,* 212–218.

Barkley, R. A., Koplowitz, S., Anderson, T., & McMurray, M. B. (1997a). Sense of time in children with ADHD: Effects of duration, distraction, and stimulant medication. *Journal of International Neuropsychological Society, 3,* 359–369.

Barry, T. D., Lyman, R. D., & Klinger, L. G. (2002). Academic underachievement and attention-deficit/hyperactivity disorder: The negative impact of symptom severity on school performance. *Journal of School Psychology, 40,* 259–283.

Baska, L. (1989). Characteristics and needs of the gifted. In J. Feldhusen, J. Van Tassel-Baska, & K. Seeley, (Eds.), *Excellence in educating the gifted* (pp. 15–28) Denver: Love.

Bass, C. K. (1985). Running can modify classroom behavior. *Journal of Learning Disabilities, 18,* 160–161.

Battle, E. S., & Lacey, B. (1972). A context for hyperactivity in children, over time. *Child Development, 43,* 757–773.

Begley, S. (1995, March). Gray matters. *Newsweek,* p. 53.

Belfiore, P. J., Grskovic, J., Murphy, A. M., & Zentall, S. S. (1996). The effects of antecedent color on reading for students with learning disabilities and co-occuring attention deficit hyperactivity disorders. *Journal of Learning Disabilities, 29,* 432–438.

Bender, W. N., & Mathes, M. Y. (1995). Students with ADHD in the inclusive classroom: A hierarchial approach to strategy selection. *Intervention in School and Clinic, 30,* 226–233.

Benezra, E., & Douglas, V. I. (1988). Short-term serial recall in ADDH, normal, and reading-disabled boys. *Journal of Abnormal Child Psychology, 16,* 511–525.

Bennett, D. E., Zentall, S. S., Giorgetti, K., & French, B. F. (estimated 2006). *Computer-administered choice and modality of math instruction for students with and without attention deficit hyperactivity disorder.* Manuscript submitted for publication.

Berger, M. (1981). Remediating hyperkinetic behavior with impulse control procedures. *School Psychology Review, 10,* 405–407.

Berry, C. A., Shaywitz, S. E., & Shaywitz, B. A. (1985). Girls with attention deficit disorder: A silent minority? A report on behavioral and cognitive characteristics. *Pediatrics, 76,* 801–809.

Beyda, S. D., & Zentall, S. S. (1998). Adminstrative responses to AD/HD. *Reaching Today's Youth, 2,* 21–36.

Beyda, S. D., Zentall, S. S., & Ferko, D. J. K. (2002). The relationship between teacher practices and the task-appropriate and social behavior of students with behavioral difficulties. *Behavioral Disorders, 27,* 236–255.

Biederman, J., Faraone, S., Keenan, K., Knee, D., & Tsuang, M. (1991). Family-genetic and psychosocial risk factors in DSM-III attention deficit disorder. *Journal of the American Academy of Child and Adolescent Psychiatry, 29,* 526–533.

Binder, L. M., Dixon, M. R., & Ghezzi, P. M. (2000). A procedure to teach self-control to children with attention deficit hyperactivity disorder. *Journal of Applied Behavior Analysis, 33,* 233–237.

Blachman, D. R., & Hinshaw, S. (2002). Patterns of friendship among girls with and without attention deficit/hyperactivity disorder. *Journal of Abnormal Child Psychology, 30,* 625–640.

Block, S. L. (1998). Attention-deficit disorder: A paradigm for psychotropic medication intervention in pediatrics. *Child and Adolescent Psychopharmacology, 45,* 704–734.

Bloomingdale, L., Swanson, J. M., Barkley, R. A., & Satterfield, J. (1991). *Response to the notice of inquiry by the professional group for ADD and related disorders.* (Available from the Professional Group for Attention and Related Disorders, Student Development Center, University of California, 19262 Jamboree, Irvine, CA.)

Boggs, J., Santagrossi, D., & Zentall, S. S. *Videotaped self-observation: A method for reducing disruptive behaviors in the classroom.* Unpublished manuscript.

Bonafina, M. A., Newcorn, J. H., McKay, K. E., Koda, V. H., & Halperin, J. M. (2000). ADHD and reading disabilities: A cluster analytic approach for distinguishing subgroups. *Journal of Learning Disabilities, 33,* 297–307.

Borger, N., van der Meere, J., Ronner, A., Alberts, A., Geuze, R., & Bogte, H. (1999). Heart rate variability and sustained attention in ADHD children. *Journal of Abnormal Child Psychology, 27,* 26–33.

Bos, C. S., Nahmias, M. L., & Urban, M. A. (1999). Targeting home-school collaboration for students with ADHD. *Teaching Exceptional Children, 31,* 4–11.

Bradley-Klug, K. L., Shapiro, E. S., & DuPaul, G. J. (1997). Attention deficit disorder and kids in the middle: A field test of a school-based consultation model. *Teacher Education and Special Education, 20,* 179–188.

Brand, E., & van der Vlugt, H. (1989). Activation: Base-level and responsivity—A search for subtypes of ADDH children by means of electrocardiac, dermal and respiratory measures. In T. Sagrolden & T. Archer (Eds.), *Attention Deficit Disorder: Clinical and Basic Research* (pp. 137–150). Hillsdale, NJ: Lawrence Erlbaum Associates.

Brandeis, D., Banaschewski, T., Baving, L., Georgiewa, P., Blanz, B., Schmidt, M. H., et al. (2002). Multicenter P300 brain mapping of impaired attention to cues in hyperkinetic children. *Journal of the American Academy of Child and Adolescent Psychiatry, 41,* 990–998.

Bremer, D. A., & Stern, J. A. (1976). Attention and distractibility during reading in hyperactive boys. *Journal of Abnormal Child Psychology, 4,* 381–387.

Breznitz, Z. (2003). The speech and vocalization patterns of boys with ADHD compared to boys with dyslexia and boys without learning disabilities. The *Journal of Genetic Psychology, 164,* 425–452.

Brock, S. E., & Knapp, P. K. (1996). Reading comprehension abilities of children with attention-deficit hyperactivity disorder. *Journal of Attention Disorders, 1,* 173–185.

Brody, P. J., & Legenza, A. (1980). Can picturial attributes serve mathemagenic functions? *Education, Communication, and Technology, 28,* 55–59.

Broussard, C. D., & Northup, J. N. (1995). An approach to functional assessment and analysis of disruptive behavior in regular education classrooms. *School Psychology Quarterly, 10,* 151–164.

Brown, R. T., & Wynne, M. E. (1984). Attentional characteristics and teachers ratings in hyperactive, reading disabled, and normal boys. *Journal of Clinical Child Psychology, 13,* 38–43.

Bryan, T., & Nelson, C. (1994). Doing homework: Perspectives of elementary and junior high school students. *Journal of Learning Disabilities, 27,* 488–499.

Bryan, T., & Sullivan-Burstein, K. (1997). Homework how-to's. *Teaching Exceptional Children, 29,* 32–37.

Bryant, D. P., Bryant, B. R., & Hammill, D. D. (2000). Characteristic behaviors of students with LD who have teacher-identified math weaknesses. *Journal of Learning Disabilities, 33,* 168–177.

Bugental, D. B., Whalen, C. K., & Henker, B. (1977). Causal attributions of hyperactive children and motivational assumptions of two behavior-change approaches: Evidence for an interactionist position. *Child Development, 48,* 874–884.

Burns, G. L., & Walsh, J. A. (2002). The influence of ADHD-hyperactivity/impulsivity symptoms on the development of oppositional defiant disorder symptoms in a 2-year longitudinal study. *Journal of Abnormal Child Psychology, 30,* 245–256.

Bursuck, W. D., Harniss, M. K., Epstein, M. H., Polloway, E. A., Jayanthi, M., & Wissinger, L. A. (1999). Solving commnunication problems about homework: Recommendations of special education teachers. *Learning Disabilities Research and Practice, 14,* 149–158.

Burt, K. L., & Ryan, C. L. (1997). An investigation of the effects of medication and the use of computerized feedback in task performance of AD/HD children. *Issues in Special Education and Rehabilitation, 12,* 56–70.

Bussing, R. (2000). Self-esteem in children in special education with ADHD: Relationship disorder characteristics and medication use. *Journal of the American Academy of Child and Adolescent Psychiatry, 39,* 1260–1269.

Bussing, R., Gary, F. A., Leon, C. E., & Garvan, C. W. (2002). General classroom teachers' information and perceptions of attention defict hyperactivity disorder. *Behavioral Disorders, 27,* 327–339.

Bussing, R., Zima, B. T., Perwien, A. R., Belin, T. R., & Widawski, M. (1998). Children in special education: Attention deficit hyperactivity disorder, use of services, an unmet need. *American Journal of Public Health, 88,* 1–7.

Cadesky, E. B. (2000). Beyond words: How do children with ADHD and/or conduct problems process nonverbal information about affect? *Journal of the American Academy of Child and Adolescent Psychiatry, 39,* 1160–1167.

Cairns, R. B., & Cairns, B. D. (1994). *Lifelines and risks: Pathways of youth in our time.* Cambridge: Cambridge University Press.

Calabi, P. (1997). *Ecology: A systems approach.* Dubuque, IA: Kendall/Hunt.

Callaway, E., Halliday, R., & Naylor, H. (1983). Hyperactive children's event-related potentials fail to support underarousal and maturational-lag theories. *Archives of General Psychiatry, 40,* 1243–1248.

Cameron, M. I., & Robinson, V. M. J. (1980). Effects of cognitive training on academic and on-task behavior of hyperactive children. *Journal of Abnormal Child Psychology, 8,* 405–420.

Campbell, S. B. (1990). *Behavior problems in preschool children.* New York: Guilford Press.

Campbell, S. B., Endman, M. W., & Bernfeld, G. (1977). A three-year follow-up of hyperactive preschoolers into elementary school. *Journal of Child Psychology and Psychiatry, 18,* 239–249.

Cantwell, D. P., & Baker, L. (1991). Association between attention deficit-hyperactivity disorder and learning disorders. *Journal of Learning Disabilities, 24,* 88–95.

Caplan, R., Guthrie, D., Tang, B., Nuechterlein, K. H., & Asarnow, R. F. (2001). Thought disorder in attention-deficit hyperactivity disorder. *Journal of the American Academy of Child and Adolescent Psychiatry, 40,* 965–972.

Carlson, C. I., & Tamm, L. (2000). Responsiveness of children with attention deficit-hyperactivity disorder to reward and response cost: Differential impact on performance and motivation. *Journal of Consulting and Clinical Psychology, 68,* 73–83.

Carlson, C. L., Booth, J. E., Shin, M., & Canu, W. H. (2002). Parent-, teacher-, and self-rated motivational styles and ADHD subtypes. *Journal of Learning Disabilities, 35,* 104–113.

Carlson, E. A., Jacobvitz, D., & Sroufe, L. A. (1995). A developmental investigation of inattentiveness and hyperactivity. *Child Development, 66,* 37–54.

Carrol, A., Bain, A., & Houghton, S. (1994). The effects of interactive versus linear video on the levels of attention and comprehension of social behavior by children with attention disorders. *School Psychology Review, 23,* 29–43.

Carte, E. T., Nigg, J. T., & Hinshaw, S. P. (1996). Neuropsychological functioning, motor speed, and language processing in boys with and without ADHD. *Journal of Abnormal Child Psychology, 24,* 481–498.

Carter, E. N., & Shostak, D. A. (1980). Imitation in the treatment of the hyperkinetic behavior syndrome. *Journal of Clinical Child Psychology, 9,* 63–66.

Carter, J. D., & Swanson, H. L. (1995). The relationship between intelligence and vigilance in children at risk. *Journal of Abnormal Child Psychology, 23,* 201–220.

Cartledge, G., & Cochran, L. (1993). Developing cooperative learning behaviors in students with behavior disorders. *Preventing School Failure, 37,* 5–10.

Carver, C. S. (1979). A cybernetic model of self-attention processes. *Journal of Personality and Social Psychology, 37,* 1251–1281.

Carver, C. S., & Scheier, M. F. (1981). *Attention and self-regulation: A control therapy approach to human behavior.* New York: Springer.

Caseau, D. L., Luckasson, R., & Kroth, R. L. (1994). Special education services for girls with serious emotional disturbance: A case of gender bias? *Behavioral Disorders, 20,* 51–60.

Castellanos, F. X., Lee, P. P., Sharp, W., Jeffries, N. O., Greenstein, D. K., Clusen, L. S., et al. (2002). Developmental trajectories of brain volume abnormalities in children and adolescents with attention-deficit/hyperactivity disorder. *Journal of the American Medical Association, 288*(14), 1740–1748.

Center, D. B., Deitz, S. M., & Kaufman, M. E. (1982). Student ability, task difficulty, and inappropriate classroom behavior. *Behavior Modification, 6,* 355–374.

Chaang, H. T., Klorman, R., Shaywitz, S. E., Fletcher, J. M., Marchione, K. E., Holahan, J. M., et al. (1999). Paired-associate learning in attention-deficit/hyperactivity disorder as a function of hyperactivity-impulsivity and oppositional defiant disorder. *Journal of Abnormal Child Psychology, 27,* 237–245.

Chang, C. Y., & Mao, S. L. (1999). The effects on students' cognitive achievement when using the cooperative learning method in earth science classrooms. *School Science and Mathematics, 99,* 374–379.

Charlebois, P., Normandeau, S., Vitaro, F., & Berneche, F. (1999). Skills training for inattentive, overactive, aggressive boys: Differential effects of content and delivery method. *Behavioral Disorders, 24,* 137–150.

Cherkes-Julkowski, M. (1998). Learning disability, attention deficit disorder, and language impairment as outcomes of prematurity: A longitudinal descriptive study. *Journal of Learning Disabilities, 31,* 294–306.

Cherkes-Julkowski, M., & Stolzenberg, J. (1991). The learning disability of attention deficit disorder. *Learning Disabilities: A Multidisciplinary Journal, 2,* 8–15.

Chhabildas, N. A., Pennington, B. F., & Willcutt, E. G. (2001). A comparison of the neuropsychological profiles of the DSM-IV subtypes of ADHD. *Journal of Abnormal Child Psychology, 29,* 529–540.

Cohen, E. (1994). Restructuring the classroom: Conditions for productive small groups. *Review of Educational Research, 64,* 1–35.

Cohen, E. G. (1986). *Designing groupwork: Strategies for the heterogeneous classroom.* New York: Teachers College Press.

Cohen, M. J., Riccio, C. A., & Gonzalez, J. J. (1994). Methodological differences in the diagnosis of attention-deficit hyperactivity disorder: Impact on prevalence. *Journal of Emotional and Behavioral Disorders, 2,* 31–38.

Cohen, N. J., Weiss, G., & Minde, K. (1972). Cognitive styles in adolescents previously diagnosed as hyperactive. *Journal of Child Psychology and Psychiatry, 13,* 203–209.

Combs, M. L., & Slaby, D. A. (1977). Social skills training with children. *Advances in Clinical Child Psychology, 1,* 161–201.

Committee on Children with Disabilities, Committee on Drugs (1987). Medication for children with an attention deficit disorder. *Pediatrics, 80,* 758–760.

Cooley, E. L., & Morris, R. D. (1990). Attention in children: A neuropsychologically based model of assessment. *Developmental Neuropsychology, 6*, 239–274.

Cooper, H., & Nye, B., (1994). Homework for students with learning disabilities: The implications of research for policy and practice. *Journal of Learning Disabilities, 27*, 470–479.

Copeland, A. P. (1981). The relevance of subject variables in cognitive self-instructional programs for impulsive children. *Behavior Therapy, 12*, 520–529.

Copeland, A. P. (1982). *Individual difference factors in children's self-management: Toward individualized treatment.* New York: Pergamon Press.

Copeland, A. P., & Weissbrod, C. S. (1978). Behavioral correlates of the hyperactivity factor of the Conners teacher questionnaire. *Journal of Abnormal Child Psychology, 6*, 339–343.

Copeland, A. P., & Weissbrod, C. S. (1980). Effects of modeling on behavior related to hyperactivity. *Journal of Educational Psychology, 72*, 875–883.

Copeland, A. P., & Weissbrod, C. S. (1983). Cognitive strategies used by learning disabled children: Does hyperactivity always make things worse? *Journal of Learning Disabilities, 16*, 473–477.

Copeland, A. P., & Wisniewski, N. M. (1981). Learning disability and hyperactivity: Deficits in selective attention. *Journal of Experimental Child Psychology, 32*, 88–101.

Cotugno, A. J. (1987). Cognitive control functioning in hyperactive and nonhyperactive learning disabled children. *Journal of Learning Disabilities, 20*, 563–567.

Couvillon, M. A. (2003). Understanding restraint and time-out in schools: Positive steps for Texas. *Beyond Behavior, 12*, 10–11.

Covington, M. V. (2000). Intrinsic versus extrinsic motivation in schools: A reconciliation. *Current Directions in Psychological Science, 9*, 22–25.

Craft, D. H. (1983). Effect of prior exercise on a cognitive performance task by hyperactive and normal boys. *Perceptual and Motor Skills, 56*, 979–982.

California Research Institute. (1992). Educational practices in integrated settings associated with positive student outcomes. *Strategies on the Inclusion and the Integration of Students with Severe Disabilities, 3*(3), 7, 10.

Cruickshank, W. M., Bentzen, F. A., Ratzeburg, F. H., & Tannhauser, M. T. (1961). *A teaching method for brain-injured and hyperactive children.* Syracuse, NY: Syracuse University Press.

Culbertson, J. L. & Silovsky, J. F. (1996). Learning disorders and attention deficit hyperactivity disorder: Their impact on children's significant others. In F. W. Kaslow (Ed.), *Handbook of relational diagnosis and dysfunctional family patterns.* (186–209) New York: Wiley.

Cunningham, C. E., Benness, B. B., & Siegel, L. S. (1988). Family functioning, time allocation, and parental depression in the families of normal and ADDH children. *Journal of Clinical Child Psychology, 17*, 169–177.

Cunningham C. E., & Boyle M. H. (2002). Preschoolers at risk for attention-deficit hyperactivity disorder and oppositional defiant disorder: Family, parenting, and behavioral correlates. *Journal of Abnormal Child Psychology, 30*, 555–569.

Cunningham, C. E., Siegel, L. S., & Offord, D. R. (1985). A developmental dose-response analysis of the effects of methylphenidate on the peer interactions of attention deficit disordered boys. *Journal of Child Psychology and Psychiatry, 26*, 955–971.

Currie, D., Lee, D. L., & Scheeler, M. C. (in press). Using a personal data assistant to increase homework production. *Journal of Evidence-Based Practices for Schools.*

Cutting, L. E., Koth, C. W., Mahone, E. M., & Denckla, M. B. (2003). Evidence for unexpected weaknesses in learning in children with attention-deficit disorder without reading disabilities. *Journal of Learning Disabilities, 36*, 259–269.

Dalby, J. T., Kinsbourne, M., & Swanson, J. M. (1989). Self-paced learning in children with attention deficit disorder with hyperactivity. *Journal of Abnormal Child Psychology, 17*, 269–275.

Daly, P. M., & Ranalli, P. (2003). Using countoons to teach self-monitoring skills. *Teaching Exceptional Children, 35*, 30–33.

Dane, A., Schachar, R., & Tannock, R. (2000). Does actigraphy differentiate ADHD subtypes in a clinical research setting? *Journal of the American Academy of Child and Adolescent Psychiatry, 39,* 752–760.

Danner, F. W., & Lonky, E. (1981). A cognitive-developmental approach to the effects of rewards on intrinsic motivation. *Child Development, 52,* 1043–1052.

Davern, L. (2004). School-to-home notebooks: What parents have to say. *Teaching Exceptional Students, 36,* 22–27.

Davila, R. R., Williams, M. L., & MacDonald, J. T. (1991). *Memorandum to chief state school officers re: Clarification of policy to address the needs of children with attention deficit disorders within general and/or special education.* Washington, DC: U.S. Department of Education.

Davis, S. J. (1990). The dog ate my homework: A middle school dilemma and a solution. *Middle School Journal, 21,* 43.

Deci, E. L., & Ryan, R. M. (1985). *Intrinsic motivation and self-determination in human behavior.* New York: Plenum Press.

De Haas-Warner, S. J. (1991). Effects of self-monitoring on preschoolers' on-task behavior: A pilot study. *Topics in Early Childhood Special Education, 11,* 59–73.

de Haas, P. A., & Young, R. D. (1984). Attention styles of hyperactive and normal girls. *Journal of Abnormal Child Psychology, 12,* 531–546.

DePaepe, P. A., Shores, R. E., Jack, S. L., & Denny, R. K. (1996). Effects of task difficulty on the disruptive and on-task behavior of students with severe behavior disorders. *Behavioral Disorders, 21,* 216–225.

Dewey, D., Kaplan, B. J., Crawford, S. G., & Fisher, G. C. (1998). Predictive accuracy of the wide range assessment of memory and learning in children with attention deficit hyperactivity disorder and reading difficulties. *Developmental Neuropsychology, 19,* 173–189.

Dienske, H., de Jonge, G., & Sanders-Woudstra, J. A. R. (1985). Quantitative criteria for attention and activity in child psychiatric patients. *Journal of Child Psychology and Psychiatry, 26,* 895–916.

Dishion, T. J., Eddy, J. M., Haas, E., & Spracklen, K. M. (1997). Friendships and violent behavior during adolescence. *Social Development, 6,* 207–223.

Dishion T. J., Spracklen K. M., Andrews D. W., & Patterson, G. R. (1996). Deviancy training in male adolescent friendships. *Behavior Therapy, 27,* 373–390.

Dishon, D., & O'Leary, P. W. (1984). *A guidebook for cooperative learning.* Holmes Beach, FL: Learning Publications.

Dodge, K. A., Price, J. M., Bachorowski, J., & Newman, J. P. (1990). Hostile attributional biases in severely aggressive boys are exacerbated under conditions of threats to the self. *Child Development, 58,* 213–224.

Douglas, V. I. (1972). Stop, look, and listen: The problem of sustained attention and impulse control. *Canadian Journal of Behavioral Science, 4,* 259–282.

Douglas, V. I. (1985). The response of ADD children to reinforcement: Theoretical and clinical implications. In L. M. Bloomindale (Ed.), *Attention deficit disorder: Identification, course and rationale* (pp. 49–66). New York: Spectrum Publications.

Douglas, V. I., Barr, R. G., O'Neill, M. E., & Britton, B. G. (1986). Short term effects of methylphenidate on the cognitive learning and academic performance of children with attention deficit disorder in the laboratory and the classroom. *Journal of Child Psychology and Psychiatry, 27,* 191–212.

Douglas, V. I., & Parry, P. A. (1994). Effects of reward and non-reward on frustration and attention in attention deficit disorder. *Journal of Abnormal Child Psychology, 22,* 281–302.

Douglas, V. I., & Peters, K. G. (1979). *Toward a clearer definition of the attentional deficit of hyperactive children.* New York: Plenum Press.

Drame, E. R. (2002). Sociocultural context effects on teachers' readiness to refer for learning disabilities. *Exceptional Children, 69,* 41–53.

Drecktrah, M. E., & Chiang, B. (1997). Instructional strategies used by general educators and teachers of students with learning disabilities: A survey. *Remedial and Special Education, 18,* 174–181.

Dubey, D. R., & O'Leary, S. G. (1975). Increasing reading comprehension of two hyperactive children: Preliminary investigation. *Perceptual and Motor Skills, 41,* 691–694.

Dumas, M. C. (1998). The risk of social interaction problems among adolescents with ADHD.

Education and Treatment of Children, 21, 447–460.

Dunlap, G., dePerczel, M., Clarke, S., Wilson, D., Wright, S., White, R., et al. (1994). Choice making to promote adaptive behavior for students with emotional and behavioral challenges. *Journal of Applied Behavior Analysis, 27,* 505–518.

Dunlap, G., Kern, L., dePerczel, M., Clarke, S., Wilson, D., Childs, K. E., et al. (1993). Functional analysis of classroom variables for students with emotional and behavioral disorders. *Behavioral Disorders, 18,* 275–291.

Dunn, J., & Brown, J. (1994). Affect expression in the family, children's understanding of emotions, and their interactions with others. *Merrill-Palmer Quarterly, 40,* 120–137.

DuPaul, G. J. (1991). Parent and educator ratings and ADHD symptoms: Psychometric properties in a community-based sample. *Journal of Clinical Child Psychology, 20,* 245–253.

DuPaul, G. J., & Eckert, T. J. (1997). Interventions for students with attention-deficit/hyperactivity disorder: One size does not fit all. *School Psychology Review, 26,* 369–382.

DuPaul, G. J., & Eckert, T. J. (1998). Academic interventions for students with attention-deficit/hyperactivity disorder: A review of the literature. *Reading and Writing Quarterly, 14,* 59–82.

DuPaul, G. J., & Ervin, R. A. (1996). Functional assessment of behavior related to attention-deficit/ hyperactivity disorder: Linking assessment to intervention design. *Behavior Therapy, 27,* 601–622.

DuPaul, G. J., & Ervin, R. A., Hook, C. L., & McGoey, K. E. (1998). Peer tutoring for children with attention deficit hyperactivity disorder: Effects on classroom behavior and academic performance. *Journal of Applied Behavior Analysis, 31,* 579–592.

DuPaul, G. J., & Henningson, P. N. (1993). Peer tutoring effects on the classroom performance of children with attention deficit hyperactivity disorder. *School Psychology Review, 22,* 134–143.

DuPaul, G. J., & Stoner, G. (1994). *ADHD in schools: Assessment and intervention strategies.* New York: Guilford Press.

DuPaul, G. J., Volpe, R. J., Jitendra, A. K., Lutz, G., Lorah, K. S., & Gruber, R. (2004). Elementary school students with AD/HD: predictors of academic achievement. *Journal of School Psychology, 42,* 285–301.

Dweck, C. S. (1986). Motivational processes affecting learning. *American Psychologist, 41,* 1040–1048.

Dykman, R. A., Ackerman, P. T., & Oglesby, D. M. (1979). Selective and sustained attention in hyperactive, learning disabled, and normal boys. *Journal of Nervous and Mental Disease, 167,* 288–297.

Eccles, J. S., Wigfield, A., Midgley, C., Reuman, D., MacIver, D., & Feldlaufer, H. (1993). Negative effects of traditional middle schools on students' motivation. *Elementary School Journal, 93,* 553–574.

Edelbrock, C., Costello, A. J., & Kessler, M. D. (1984). Empirical corroboration of attention deficit disorder. *Journal of the American Academy of Child Psychiatry, 23,* 285–290.

Edmonds, E. M., & Smith, L. R. (1985). Students' performance as a function of sex, noise, and intelligence. *Psychological Reports, 56,* 727–730.

Edwards, L., Salant, V., Howard, V. F., Brougher, J., & McLaughlin, T. F. (1995). Effectiveness of self-management on attentional behavior and reading comprehension for children with attention deficit disorder. *Child and Family Behavior Therapy, 17,* 1–17.

Edwards, C., & Stout, J. (1990). Cooperative learning: The first year. *Educational Leadership, 47,* 38–41.

Eisenberg, N., Gutherie, I. K., Fabes, R. A., Reiser, M., Murphy, B. C., Holgren, R., et al. (1997). The relations of regulation and emotionality to resiliency and competent social functioning in elementary school children. *Child Development, 68,* 295–311.

Ellis, N. R., Hawkins, W. F., Pryer, M. W., & Jones, R. W. (1963). Distraction effects in oddity learning by normal and mentally defective humans. *American Journal of Mental Deficiency, 68,* 576–583.

Elsom, S. (1980). Self-management of hyperactivity: Children's use of jogging. *Dissertation Abstracts International, 41*(08), 3176B. (UMI No. 8104639)

Epstein, J. N., Willis, M. G., Conners, C. K., & Johnson, D. E. (2001). Use of a technology prompting device to aid a student with attention deficit hyperactivity disorder to initiate and complete daily tasks: An exploratory study. *Journal of Special Education Technology, 16*, 19–28.

Ervin, R. A., DuPaul, G.J., Kern, L., & Friman, P. C. (1998). Classroom-based functional and adjunctive assessments: Proactive approaches to intervention and selection for adolescents with attention deficit hyperactivity disorder. *Journal of Applied Behavior Analysis, 31*, 65–78.

Ervin, R. A., Radford, P. M., Bertsch, K., Piper, A. L., Ehrhardt, K. E., & Poling, A. (2001). A descriptive analysis and critique of the empirical literature on school-based functional assessment. *School Psychology Review, 30*, 193–210.

Evans, S. E. (1995). Reflections on "The efficacy of notetaking to improve behavior and comprehension of adolescents with attention deficit hyperactivity disorder." *Exceptionality, 5*, 45–48.

Evans, S. W., Pelham, W. E., & Grundberg, M. V. (1995). The efficacy of notetaking to improve behavior and comprehension of adolescents with attention deficit hyperactivity disorder. *Exceptionality, 5*, 1–17.

Evans, W. H., Evans, S. S., Schmid, R. E., & Pennypacker, H. S. (1985). The effects of exercise on selected classroom behaviors of behaviorally disordered adolescents. *Behavioral Disorders, 1*, 42–51.

Executive Summary of the President's Commission on Excellence in Special Education. (2002, October 2). A new era: Revitalizing special education for children and their families. *ISEAS Cable, 23*(10), 1–2.

Executive Summary. (1995). *ISEAS Cable, 16*(3), 5.

Falk, G. D., Dunlap, G., & Kern, L. (1996). An analysis of self-evaluation and videotape feedback for improving the peer interactions of students with externalizing and internalizing behavioral problems. *Behavioral Disorders, 21*, 261–276.

Falk, K. B., & Wehby, J. H. (2001). The effects of peer-assisted learning strategies on the beginning reading skills of young children with emotional or behavioral disorders. *Behavioral Disorders, 26*, 344–359.

Fantuzzo J., & Atkins, M. (1992). Applied behavior analysis for educators—Teacher centered and classroom based. *Journal of Applied Behavior Analysis, 25*, 37–42.

Faraone, S. V., Biederman, J., Krifcher, B., Keenan, K., Moore, C., Ugaglia, K., et al. (1992). Evidence for the independent transmission in families for attention deficit hyperactivity disorder and learning disability: Results from a family genetic study of ADHD. *American Journal of Psychiatry, 150*, 891–895.

Farmer, T. W., Pearl, R., & Van Acker, R. M. (1996). Expanding the social skills deficit framework: A developmental synthesis perspective, classroom social networks, and implications for the social growth of students with disabilities. *Journal of Special Education, 30*, 232–256.

Farrace-Di Zinno, A. M., Douglas, G., Houghton, S., Lawrence, V., West, J., & Whiting, K. (2001). Body movements of boys with attention deficit hyperactivity disorder (ADHD) during computer video game play. *British Journal of Educational Technololgy, 32*, 607–618.

Feindler, E. L., & Ecton, R. B. (1986). *Adolescent anger control: Cognitive-behavioral techniques.* New York: Pergamon Press.

Felton, R. H., Wood, F. B., Brown, I. S., & Campbell, S. K. (1987). Separate verbal memory and naming deficits in attention deficit disorder and reading disability. *Brain and Language, 31*, 171–184.

Ferguson, P. M. (2002). A place in the family: An historical interpretation of research on parental reactions to having a child with a disability. *Journal of Special Education, 36*, 124–147.

Ferguson, P. M., & Horwood, L. J. (1996). Attention deficit and reading achievement. *Journal of Child Psychology and Psychiatry and Applied Disciplines, 33*, 375–385.

Fischer, M., Barkley, R. A., Edelbrock, C. S., & Smallish, L. (1990). The adolescent outcome of hyperactive children diagnosed by research criteria: II. Academic, attentional, and neuropsychological status. *Journal of Consulting and Clinical Psychology, 58*, 580–588.

Fitzsimmons-Lovett, A. (1998). *Enhancing self-respect: A challenge for teachers of students with emotional-behavioral disorders.* Reston, VA: Council for Children with Behavioral Disorders. (ERIC Document Reproduction Service No. ED412676)

Firestone, P. & Douglas, V. I. (1975). The effects of reward and punishment on reaction times and autonomic activity in hyperactive and normal children. *Journal of Abnormal Child Psychology, 3*, 201–215.

Flint, L. J. (2001). Challenges in identifying and serving gifted children with ADHD. *Teaching Exceptional Children, 33*, 62–69.

Flood, W. A., Wilder, D. A., Flood, A. L., & Masuda, A. (2002). Peer-mediated reinforcement plus prompting as treatment for off-task behavior in children with attention deficit hyperactivity disorder. *Journal of Applied Behavior Analysis, 35*, 199–204.

Flynn, N. M., & Rapoport, J. L. (1976). Hyperactivity in open and traditional classroom environments. *Journal of Special Education, 10*, 285– 290.

Foorman, B.R., & Liberman, D. (1989). Visual and phonological processing of words: A comparison of good and poor readers. *Journal of Learning Disabilities, 22*, 349–355.

Ford, M. J., Poe, V., & Cox, J. (1993). Attending behaviors of ADHD children in math and reading using various types of software. *Journal of Computing in Childhood Education, 4*, 183–196.

Fowler, M. (1994). *Maybe you know my kid: A parents' guide to identifying, understanding, and helping your child with attention deficit hyperactivity disorder.* Secaucus, NJ: Carol Publishing Group.

Fowler, S. A. (1986). Peer-monitoring and self-monitoring: Alternatives to traditional teacher management. *Exceptional Children, 52*, 573–581.

Frank, E. A. R., Sanchez-LaCay, A., & Fernandez, M. C. (2000). Teacher understanding of ADHD as reflected in attributions and classroom strategies. *Journal of Attention Disorders, 4*, 91–101.

Freiberg, H. J., Stein, T. A., & Parker, G. (1995). Discipline referrals in an urban middle school. *Education and Urban Society, 27*, 421–440.

French, B. F., Zentall, S. S., & Bennett, D. (2003). Short-term memory of children with and without characteristics of attention deficit hyperactivity disorder. *Learning and Individual Differences, 13*, 205–225.

Friedman, D. L., Cancelli, A. A., & Yoshida, R. K. (1988). Academic engagement of elementary school children with learning disabilities. *Journal of School Psychology, 26*, 327–340.

Galis, S. A., & Tanner, C. K. (1995, October). Inclusion in elementary schools: A survey and policy analysis [Online]. *Education Policy Analysis Archives, 3*(15).

Gathercole, S. E., & Pickering, S. J. (2000). Working memory deficits in children with low achievements in the national curriculum at 7 years of age. *British Journal of Educational Psychology, 70*, 177–194.

Gaub, M., & Carlson, C. I. (1997). Gender differences in ADHD: A meta-analysis and critical review. *Journal of the American Academy of Child and Adolescent Psychiatry, 36*, 1036–1045.

Geary, D. C. (1993). Mathematical disabilities: Cognitive, neuropsychological, and genetic components. *Psychological Bulletin, 114*, 345–362.

Giangreco, M. F. (1996). What do I do now? A teacher's guide to including students with disabilities. *Educational Leadership, 53*, 56–59.

Gibb, J. R. (1961). Defensive communication. *Journal of Communication, 11*, 141–148.

Gillies, R. M. (2003). The behaviors, interactions, and perceptions of junior high school students during small group learning. *Journal of Educational Psychology, 95*, 137–147.

Gillis, J. J., Gilger, J. W., Pennington, B. F., & DeFries, J. C. (1992). Attention deficit disorder in reading-disabled twins: Evidence for a genetic etiology. *Journal of Abnormal Child Psychology, 20*, 303–315.

Goldman-Rakic, P. S. (1992). Dopamine mediated mechanisms of prefrontal cortex. *Seminar in the Neurosciences, 4*, 149–159.

Goodman, G., & Poillion, M. J. (1992). ADD: Acronym for any dysfunction or difficulty. *Journal of Special Education, 26*, 37–56.

Goodman, R., & Stevenson, J. (1989). A twin study of hyperactivity—II. The aetiological role of genes, family relationships and perinatal adversity. *Journal of Child Psychology and Psychiatry, 30*, 691–709.

Goodwin, S. E., & Mahoney, M. J. (1975). Modification of aggression through modeling: An experimental probe. *Journal of Behavior Therapy and Experimental Psychiatry, 6*, 200–202.

Gordon, M. (1979). The assessment of impulsivity and mediating behaviors in hyperactive and nonhyperactive boys. *Journal of Abnormal Child Psychology, 7,* 317–326.

Graves, T. (1991). The controversy over group rewards in cooperative classrooms. *Educational Leadership, 48,* 77–79.

Greenblatt, A. P. (1994). Gender and ethnicity bias in the assessment of attention deficit disorder. *Social Work in Education, 16,* 89–95.

Greene, R. W. (1995). Students with ADHD in school classrooms: Teacher factors related to compatibility, assessment, and intervention. *School Psychology Review, 24,* 81–93.

Greene, R. W. (1996). Students with attention deficit hyperactivity disorder and their teachers: Implications of a goodness-of-fit perspective. *Advances in Clinical Child Psychology, 18,* 205–230.

Greene, R. W., Biederman, J., Faraone, S. V., Quellette, C. A., Penn, C., & Griffin, S. M. (1996). Toward a new psychometric definition of social disability in children with attention-deficit disorder. *Journal of The American Academy of Child and Adolescent Psychiatry, 35,* 571–578.

Grenell, M. M., Glass, C. R., & Katz, K. S. (1987). Hyperactive children and peer interaction: Knowledge and performance of social skills. *Journal of Abnormal Child Psychology, 15,* 1–13.

Grskovic, J. A., Hall, A. M., Montgomery, D. J., Vargas, A. U., Zentall, S. S., & Belfiore, P. J. (2004). Reducing time-out assignments for students with emotional/behavioral disorders in a self-contained classroom: Class-wide implications. *Journal of Behavioral Education, 13,* 25–36.

Grskovic, J., & Zentall, S. S. (2006). *The behavioral, social, and emotional characteristics and self-concepts of a school-based sample of girls with symptoms of ADHD.* Manuscript submitted for publication.

Grskovic, J. A., Zentall, S. S., & Stormont-Spurgin, M. (1995). Time estimation and planning abilities: students with and without mild disabilities. *Behavioral Disorders, 20,* 197–203.

Gumpel, T. P., & David, S. (2000). Exploring the efficacy of self–regulatory training as a possible alternative to social skills training. *Behavioral Disorders, 25,* 131–141.

Gunter, P. L., Denny, R. K., Jack, S. L., Shores, R. E., & Nelson, C. M. (1993). Aversive stimuli in academic interactions between students with serious emotional disturbance and their teachers. *Behavioral Disorders, 18,* 265–274.

Hall, A. M., & Zentall, S. S. (2000). The effects of a learning station on the completion and accuracy of math homework for middle school students. *Journal of Behavioral Education, 10,* 123–137.

Hallahan, D. P., Tarver, S. G., Kauffman, J. M., & Graybeal, N. L. (1978). A comparison of the effects of reinforcement and response cost on the selective attention of learning disabled children. *Journal of Learning Disabilities, 11,* 430–438.

Hallam, S. & Price, J. (1998). Can the use of background music improve the behavior and academic performance of children with emotional and behavioral difficulties? *British Journal of Special Education, 25,* 88–91.

Hallowell, E., & Ratey, J. (1995). *Driven to distraction.* New York: Simon & Schuster.

Halperin, J. M., Gittelman, R., Klein, D. F., & Rudel, R. G. (1984). Reading disabled hyperactive children: A distinct subgroup of attention deficit disorder with hyperactivity? *Journal of Abnormal Child Psychology, 12,* 1–14.

Hamilton, V. J., & Gordon, D. A. (1978). Teacher-child interactions in preschool and task persistence. *American Educational Research Journal, 15,* 459–466.

Hamlett, K. W., Pellegrini, D. S., & Conners, C. K. (1987). An investigation of executive processing in problem solving of attention deficit disorder hyperactive children. *Journal of Pediatric Psychology, 12,* 227–240.

Harris, A. J., & Sipay, E. R. (1985). *How to increase reading ability: A guide to developmental and remedial methods.* New York: Longman.

Harris, K., & Graham, S. (1999). Programmatic intervention research: Illustrations from the evolution of self-regulated strategy development. *Learning Disability Quarterly, 22,* 251–262.

Harris, K. R., Graham, S., Reid, R., McElroy, K., & Hamby, R. S. (1994). Self-monitoring of attention versus self-monitoring of performance: Replication and cross-task comparison studies. *Learning Disability Quarterly, 17,* 121–139.

Harris M. J., Milich R., Johnston E. M., & Hoover, D. W. (1990). Effects of expectancies on childrens' social interactions. *Journal of Experimental Social Psychology, 26,* 1–12.

Hart, E. L., Lahey, B. B., Loeber, R., Applegate, B., & Frick, P. J. (1995). Developmental change in attention-deficit hyperactivity disorder in boys: A four-year longitudinal study. *Journal of Abnormal Child Psychology, 23,* 729–749.

Hartley, R. (1986). "Imagine you're clever." *Journal of Child Psychology and Psychiatry, 27,* 383–398.

Hartman, R., & Stage, S. A. (2000).The relationship between social information processing and in-school suspension for students with behavioral disorders. *Behavioral Disorders, 25,* 183–195.

Hartmann, T. (1998). What's good about AD/HD: A different perception. *Reaching Today's Youth: The Community Circle of Caring Journal, 2,* 19–23.

Hartsough, C. S., & Lambert, N. M. (1982). Some environmental and familial correlates of antecedents of hyperactivity. *American Journal of Orthopsychiatry, 52,* 272–287.

Harvey, P. D., Weintraub, S., & Neale, J. M. (1984). Distractability in learning-disabled children: The role of measurement artifact. *Journal of Learning Disabilities, 17,* 234–236.

Hebb, D. O. (1955). Drives and the CNS (conceptual nervous system). *Psychological Review, 62,* 234–254.

Hecht, S. A., Torgesen, J. K., Wagner, R. K., & Rashotte, C. A. (2000). The relations between phonological processing abilities and emerging individual differences in mathematical computation skills: A longitudinal study from second to fifth grades. *Journal of Experimental Child Psychology, 79,* 191–227.

Hechtman, L., Weiss, G., & Perlman, T. (1980). Hyperactives as young adults. *Canadian Journal of Psychiatry, 25,* 478–483.

Hecker, L., Burns, L., Elkind, J., Elkind, K., & Katz, L. (2002). Benefits of assistive reading software for students with attention disorders. *Annals of Dyslexia, 52,* 243–273.

Henker, B., & Whalen, C. K. (1989). Hyperactivity and attention deficits. *American Psychologist, 44,* 216–223.

Heward, W. L. (1994). Three "low-tech" strategies for increasing the frequency of active student response during group instruction. In R. Gardner III, D. M. Sainato, J. O. Cooper, T. E. Heron, W. L. Heward, J. Eshleman, & T. A. Grossi (Eds.), *Behavior analysis in education: Focus on measurably superior instruction* (pp. 283–320). Monterey, CA: Brooks/Cole.

Heward, W. L. (1996). *Exceptional children: An introduction to special education* (5th ed.). Englewood Cliffs, NJ: Prentice Hall/Merrill.

Heward, W. L. (2003). Ten faulty notions about teaching and learning that could hinder the effectiveness of special education. *Journal of Special Education, 36,* 186–205.

Heward, W. L., Courson, F. H., & Narayan, J. S. (1989). Using choral responding to increase active student response. *Teaching Exceptional Children, 21,* 72–75.

Higginbotham, P., & Bartling, C. (1993). The effects of sensory distractions on short-term recall of children with attention deficit-hyperactivity disorder versus normally achieving children. *Bulletin of Psychonomic Society, 31,* 507–510.

Hinshaw, S. P. (1994). *Attention deficits and hyperactivity in children* (Vol. 29). Thousand Oaks, CA: Sage.

Hinshaw, S. P. (2002). Pre-adolescent girls with attention-deficit/hyperactivity disorder: I. Background characterisitics, comorbidity, cognitive and social functioning, and parenting practices. *Journal of Consulting and Clinical Psychology, 70,* 1086–1098.

Hinshaw, S. P., Henker, B., & Whalen, C. K. (1984). Self-control in hyperactive boys in anger-inducing situations: Effects of cognitive-behavioral training and of methylphenidate. *Journal of Abnormal Child Psychology, 12,* 55–77.

Hinshaw, S. P., & McHale, J. P. (1991). Stimulant medication and the social interactions of hyperactive children: Effects and implications. In D. G. Gilbert & J. J. Connolly (Eds.), *Personality, social skills, and psychopathology: An individual differences approach* (pp. 229–253). New York: Plenum Press.

Hitchcock, C., Meyer, A., Rose, D., & Jackson, R. (2002). Providing access to the general curriculum. *Teaching Exceptional Children, 35,* 8–17.

Hoagwood, K., Kelleher, K. J., Feil, M., & Comer, D. M. (2000). Treatment services for children with ADHD: A national perspective. *Journal of the American Academy of Child and Adolescent Psychiatry, 39*, 198–206.

Holzwarth, C. L. (2001, May). A different story: Brain surgeon eases trauma for kids. *Journal of American Association of Retired Persons Bulletin*, p. 26.

Hook, C. L., & DuPaul, G. J. (1999). Parent tutoring for students with attention-deficit/hyperactivity disorder: Effects on reading performance at home and school. *School Psychology Review, 28*, 60–75.

Houlihan, M. & Van Houten, R. (1989). Behavioral treatment of hyperactivity: A review and overview. *Education and Treatment of Children, 12*, 265–275.

Hoy, E., Weiss, G., Minde, K., & Cohen, N. (1978). The hyperactive child at adolescence: Cognitive, emotional, and social functioning. *Journal of Abnormal Child Psychology, 6*, 311–324.

Hoza, B., Mrug, W., Pelham, W. E., Greiner, A. R., & Gnagy, E. M. (2003). A friendship intervention for children with attention-deficit/hyperactivity disorder: Preliminary findings. *Journal of Attention Disorders, 6*, 87–98.

Hoza, B., Pelham, W. E., Milich, R., Pillow, D., & McBride, K. (1993). The self-perceptions and attributions of attention deficit hyperactivity disordered and nonreferred boys. *Journal of Abnormal Child Psychology, 21*, 271–286.

Huessy, H. R., & Howell, D. C. (1988). The behaviors associated with ADD followed from age seven to twenty-one: Differences between males and females. In L. M. Bloomingdale (Ed.), *Attention deficit disorder: (Vol. 3). New research in attention, treatment, and psychopharmacology* (pp. 20–28). Sausalito, CA: High Point Symposium in ADD.

Huston-Stein, A., Friedrich-Cofer, L., & Susman, E. J. (1977). The relation of classroom structure to social behavior, imaginative play, and self-regulation of economically disadvantaged children. *Child Development, 48*, 908–916.

Ibler, L. S. (1997). *Improving higher order thinking in special education students through cooperative learning and social skills development.* Master's thesis, Saint Xavier University, Chicago IL. (ERIC Document Reproduction Service No. ED410732)

Imhof, M. (2004). Effects of color stimulation on handwriting performance of children with ADHD without and with learning disabilities. *European Child and Adolescent Psychiatry, 13*, 191–198.

Indiana Department of Education. (2002). *ISEAS Cable, 23*(10), 15–16.

Iovino, I., Fletcher, J. M., Breitmeyer, B. G., & Foorman, B. R. (1998). Colored overlays for visual perceptual deficits in children with reading disability and attention deficit/hyperactivity disorder: Are they differentially effective? *Journal of Clinical and Experimental Neuropsychology, 20*, 791–806.

Jagacinski, C. M., & Nicholls, J. G. (1987). Competence and affect in task involvement and ego involvement: The impact of social comparison information. *Journal of Educational Psychology, 79*, 107–114.

James, W. (1962). Psychology: The briefer course. New York: Collier Books. (Original work published in 1892.)

Jenkins, J. R., Antil, L. R., Wayne, S. K., & Vadasy, P. F. (2003). How cooperative learning works for special education and remedial students. *Exceptional Children, 69*, 279–292.

Jensen, P. S. (2001). AD/HD: What's up, what's next? *Attention! 7*, 24–27.

Jimenez, J. E., Siegel, L. S., & Lopez, M. R. (2003). The relationship between IQ and reading disabilities in English-speaking Canadian and Spanish children. *Journal of Learning Disabilities, 36*, 15–23.

Johnson, D. W., & Johnson, R. T. (1986). Mainstreaming and cooperative learning strategies. *Exceptional Children, 52*, 553–561.

Johnson, D. W., & Johnson, R. T. (1990). Social skills for successful group work. *Educational Leadership, 47*, 29–33.

Johnson, D. W., Johnson, R. T., Warring, D., & Maruyama, G. (1986). Different cooperative learning procedures and cross-handicap relationships. *Exceptional Children, 53*, 247–252.

Johnson, L. J., & Pugach, M. C. (1990). Classroom teachers' views of intervention strategies for learning and behavior problems: Which are reasonable and how frequently are they used? *Journal of Special Education, 24*, 479–491.

Johnston, C., & Mash, E. J. (2001). Families of children with attention-deficit/hyperactivity disorder: Review and recommendations for future research. *Clincial Child and Family Psychology Review, 4,* 183–208.

Johnston, C., Murray, C., Hinshaw, S. P., Pelham, W. E., & Hoza, B. (2002). Responsiveness in interactions of mothers and sons with ADHD: Relations to maternal and child characteristics. *Journal of Abnormal Child Psychology, 30,* 77–88.

Jones, E., & Nisbett, R. (1971). The actor and the observer: Divergent perceptions of the causes of behavior. In E. E. Jones, D. E. Kanouse, H. H. Kelley, R. E. Nisbett, S. Valins, & B. Weiner (Eds.), *Attribution: Perceiving the causes of behavior* (pp. 79–94). Morristown, NJ: General Learning Press.

Jones, N. M., Loney, J., Weissenburger, F. E., & Fleischmann, D. J. (1975). The hyperkinetic child: What do teachers know? *Psychology in the Schools, 12,* 388–392.

Jonsdottir, S., Bouma, A., Sergeant, J. A., & Scherder, E. J. A. (2005). The impact of specific language impairment on working memory in children with ADHD combined subtype. *Archives of Clinical Neuropsychology, 20,* 443–456.

Kaidar, I., Wiener, J., & Tannock, R. (2003). The attributions of children with Attention-Deficit/Hyperactivity Disorder for their problem behaviors. *Journal of Attention Disorders, 6,* 99–109.

Kail, R., & Hall, L. K. (1999). Sources of developmental change in children's word problem performance. *Journal of Educational Psychology, 91,* 660–668.

Kalff, A. C., Hendriksen, J. G. M., Kroes, M., Vles, J. S. H., Steyaert, J., Feron, F. J. M., et al. (2002). Neurocognitive performance of 5- and 6-year-old children who met criteria for attention deficit/hyperactivity disorder at 18 months follow-up: Results from a prospective population study. *Journal of Abnormal Child Psychology, 30,* 589–598.

Kallas, A., Reeve, R. E., Welch, A. B., & Wright, J. V. (1997). A continuing education program on attention deficit/hyperactivity disorder. *Teacher Education and Special Education, 20,* 114–122.

Kapalka, G. M. (2004). Longer eye contact improves ADHD children's compliance with parental commands. *Journal of Attention Disorders, 8,* 17–23.

Kaplan, B. J., Crawford, S. G., Dewey, D. M., & Fisher, G. C. (2000). The IQs of children with ADHD are normally distributed. *Journal of Learning Disabilities, 33,* 425–432.

Kaplan, B. J., Dewey, D., Crawford, S. G., & Fisher, G. C. (1999). Deficits in long-term memory are not characteristic of ADHD. *Journal of Clinical and Experimental Neuropsychology, 20,* 518–528.

Kaplan, B. J., Dewey, D. M., Crawford, S. G., & Wilson, B. N. (2001). The term comorbidity is of questionable value in reference to developmental disorders: Data and theory. *Journal of Learning Disabilities, 34,* 555–565.

Karatekin, C., & Asarnow, R. F. (1999). Exploratory eye movements to pictures in childhood-onset schizophrenic and attention-deficit/hyperactivity disorder (ADHD). *Journal of Abnormal Child Psychology, 27,* 35–49.

Kataria, S., Hall, W. C., Wong, M. M., & Keys, F. G. (1992). Learning styles of LD and NLD ADHD children. *Journal of Clinical Psychology, 48,* 371–378.

Kauffman, J. M., Lloyd, J. W., & McGee, K. A. (1989). Adaptive and maladaptive behavior: Teachers' attitudes and their technical assistance needs. *Journal of Special Education, 23,* 185–200.

Kauffman, J. M., Wong, K. L. H., Lloyd, J. W., Hung, L., & Pullen, P. L. (1991). What puts pupils at risk? An analysis of classroom teachers' judgments of pupils' behavior. *Remedial and Special Education, 12,* 7–16.

Kavale K. A., & Forness, S. R. (1996). Social skill deficits and learning disabilities: A meta-analysis. *Journal of Learning Disabilities, 29,* 226–237.

Kelley, M. L., & McCain, A. P. (1995). Promoting academic performance in inattentive children: The relative efficacy of school-home notes with and without response cost. *Behavior Modification, 19,* 357–375.

Kennedy, C. H., Shukla, S., & Fryxell, D. (1997). Comparing the effects of educational placement on the social relationships of intermediate school students with severe disabilities. *Exceptional Children, 64,* 31–47.

Keown, L. J., & Woodward, L. J. (2002). Early parent-child relations and family functioning of preschool boys with pervasive hyperactivity. *Journal of Abnormal Child Psychology, 30*, 541–553.

Kerns, K. A., Eso, K., & Thomson, J. (1999). Investigation of a direct intervention for improving attention in young children with ADHD. *Developmental Neuropsychology, 16*, 273–295.

Kimberg, D. Y., D'Esposito, M., & Farah, M. J. (1997). Cognitive functions in the prefrontal cortex working memory and executive control. *Current Directions in Psychological Science, 6*, 185–192.

Kinder, D., & Carnine, D. (1991). Direct instruction: What it is and what it is becoming. *Journal of Behavioral Education, 1*, 193–213.

King, L. H. (1993). High and low achievers' perceptions and cooperative learning in two small groups. *Elementary School Journal, 93*, 399–416.

Klein, P. S. (1982). Responses of hyperactive and normal children to variations in tempo of background music. *Israel Journal of Psychiatry and Related Science, 18*, 157–166.

Klingberg, T., Fernell, E., Olesen, P. J., Johnson, M., Gustafsson, P., Dahlstrom, K., et al. (2005). Computerized training of working memory in children with ADHD–A randomized, controlled trial. *Journal of the American Academy of Child and Adolescent Psychiatry, 44*, 177–186.

Knapczyk, D. (1988). Reducing aggressive behaviors in special and regular class settings by training alternative social responses. *Behavioral Disorders, 14*, 27–39.

Koester, L. S., & Farley, F. H. (1982). Psychophysiological characteristics and school performance of children in open and traditional classrooms. *Journal of Educational Psychology, 74*, 254–263.

Kohler, F. W., Schwartz, I., Cross, J., & Fowler, S. A. (1989). The effects of two alternating intervention roles on independent work skills. *Education and Treatment of Children, 12*, 205–218.

Kohn, A. (1993). Rewards versus learning: A response to Paul Chance. *Phi Delta Kappan, 74*, 783–786.

Korkman, M., & Pesonen, A.E. (1994). A comparison of neuropsychological test profiles of children with attention deficit-hyperactivity disorder and/or learning disorder. *Journal of Learning Disabilities, 27*, 383–392.

Kos, R. (1991). Persistence of reading disabilities: The voices of four middle school students. *American Educational Research Journal, 28*, 875–895.

Kovac, I., Garabedian, B., Du Souich, C., & Palmour, R. M. (2001). Attention deficit/hyperactivity in SLI children increases risk of speech/language disorders in first-degree relatives: A preliminary report. *Journal of Communication Disorders, 34*, 339–354.

Kroese, J. M., Hynd, G. W., Knight, D. F., Hiemenz, J. R., & Hall, J. (2000). Clinical appraisal of spelling ability and its relationship to phonemic awareness (blending, segmenting, elision, and reversal), phonological memory, and reading in reading disabled, ADHD, and normal children. *Reading and Writing: An Interdisciplinary Journal, 13*, 105–131.

Krupski, A. (1980). Attention processes: Research, theory, and implications for special education. In B. K. Keogh (Ed.), *Advances in special education* (Vol. 1, pp. 101–140). Greenwich, CT: JAI Press.

Kuester, D.A. & Zentall, S. S. (2006). *Effects of social problem-solving rules on the behavior of students with ADHD during group interactions.* Manuscript in preparation.

Kuhne, M., Schachar, R., & Tannock, R. (1997). Impact of comorbid oppositional or conduct problems on attention-deficit hyperactivity disorder. *Journal of the American Academy of Child and Adolescent Psychiatry, 36*, 1715–1725.

Kupietz, S. S., & Richardson, E. (1978). Children's vigilance performance and inattentiveness in the classroom. *Journal of Child Psychology and Psychiatry, 19*, 145–154.

Ladd, G. W. (1999). Peer relationships and social competence during early and middle childhood. *Annual Review of Psychology, 50*, 333–359.

Ladd, G. W., Price, J. M., & Hart, C. H. (1988) Predicting preschoolers' peer status from their playground behaviors. *Child Development, 59*, 986–992.

Lahey, B., Applegate, B., & McBurnett, K. E. (1994). DSM-IV field trials for attention deficit hyperactivity disorder in children and adolescents. *American Journal of Psychiatry, 151*, 1673–1685.

Lahey, B. B., & Carlson, C. L. (1991). Validity of the diagnostic category of attention deficit disorder without hyperactivity: A review of the literature. *Journal of Learning Disabilities, 24*, 110–120.

LaHoste, G. J., Swanson, J. M., Wigal, S. B., Glabe, C., Wigal, T., King, N., et al. (1996). Dopamine D4 receptor gene polymorphism is associated with attention deficit hyperactivity disorder. *Molecular Psychiatry, 1*, 121–124.

Lambert, N. M., & Sandoval, J. (1980). The prevalence of learning disabilities in a sample of children considered hyperactive. *Journal of Abnormal Child Psychology, 8*, 33–50.

Landau, S., & Milich, R. (1988). Social communication patterns of attention-deficit-disordered boys. *Journal of Abnormal Child Psychology, 16*, 69–81.

Landau, S., & Milich, R., & Diener, M. B. (1998). Peer relations of children with attention-deficit hyperactivity disorder. *Reading and Writing Quarterly: Overcoming Learning Difficulties, 14*, 83–105.

Landau, S., & Moore, L. A. (1991). Social skill deficits in children with attention-deficit hyperactivity disorder. *School Psychology Review, 20*, 235–252.

Lane, K. L. (2001). The efficacy of phonological awareness training with first grade students who have behavior problems and reading difficulties. *Journal of Emotional and Behavioral Disorders, 9*, 219–231.

Laursen, B., & Hartup, W. W. (1989). The dynamics of preschool children's conflicts. *Merrill-Palmer Quarterly, 35*, 281–297.

Lawler, E. E., III. (1986). *High-involvement management.* San Francisco: Jossey-Bass.

Lawrence, V., Houghton, S., Tannock, R., Douglas, G., Durkin, K., & Whiting, K. (2002). ADHD outside the laboratory: Boys' executive function performance on tasks in videogame play and on a visit to the zoo. *Journal of Abnormal Child Psychology, 30*, 447–462.

Lerner, J. (2003). *Learning Disabilities: Theories, diagnosis, and teaching strategies.* (9th ed.). Boston: Houghton Mifflin Company.

Lee, D. L., & Asplen, J. (in press). The effects of added color on the math performance of children with co-occurring learning disabilities and attention deficits. *Journal of Learning Disabilities.*

Lee, D. L., & Zentall, S. S. (2002). The effects of visual stimulation on the mathematics performance of children with attention deficit/hyperactivity disorder. *Behavioral Disorders, 27*, 272–288.

Leibowitz, G. (1991). Organic and biophysical theories of behavior. *Journal of Developmental and Physical Disabilities, 3*, 201–243.

Leroux, J. A., & Levitt-Perlman, M. (2000). The gifted child with attention deficit disorder: An identification and intervention challenge. *Roeper Review, 22*, 171–177.

Leuba, C. (1955). Toward some integration of learning theories: The concept of optimal stimulation. *Psychological Reports, 1*, 27–33.

Leung, J. P., Leung, P. W. L., & Tang, C. S. K. (2000). A vigilance study of ADHD and control children: Event rate and extra-task stimulation. *Journal of Developmental and Physical Disabilities, 12*, 187–201.

Leung, P. W. L., & Connolly, K. J. (1996). Distractibility in hyperactive and conduct-disordered children. *Journal of Child Psychology and Psychiatry, 37*, 305–312.

Leung, P. W. L., & Connolly, K. J. (1998). Do hyperactive children have motor organization and/or execution deficits? *Developmental Medicine and Child Neurology, 40*, 600–607.

Leung, P. W. L., Ho, T. P., Luk, S. L., Taylor, E., Bacon-Shone, J., & Mak, F. L. (1996). Separation and comorbidity of hyperactivity and conduct disturbance in Chinese schoolboys. *Journal of Child Psychology and Psychiatry, 37*, 841–853.

Levendoski, L. S. & Cartledge, G. (2000). Self-monitoring for elementary school children with serious emotional disturbances: Classroom applications for increased academic responding. *Behavioral Disorders, 25*, 211–224.

Levy, S., Coleman, M., & Alsman, B. (2002). Reading instruction for elementary students with emotional/behavioral disorders: What's a teacher to do? *Beyond Behavior, 11*, 3–10.

Lewis, R. B. (1998). Assistive technology and learning disabilities: Today's realities and tomorrow's promises. *Journal of Learning Disabilities, 31,* 16–26.

Lewis, T. J., & Sugai, G. (1996a). Descriptive and experimental analysis of teacher and peer attention and the use of assessment based intervention to improve the pro-social behavior of a student in a general education setting. *Journal of Behavioral Education, 6,* 7–24.

Lewis, T. J., & Sugai, G. (1996b). Functional assessment of problem behavior: A pilot investigation of the comparative and interactive effects of teacher and peer social attention on students in general education settings. *School Psychology Quarterly, 11,* 119.

Licht, B., & Kistner, J. A. (1986). Motivational problems of learning-disabled children: Individual differences and their implications for treatment. In J. K. Torgesen & B. Y. L. Wong (Eds.), *Psychological and educational perspectives on learning disabilities* (pp. 225–255). San Diego: Academic Press.

Licht, B. G., & Dweck, C. S. (1984). Determinant of academic-achievement—The interaction of children's achievement orientations with skill area. *Developmental Psychology, 20,* 628–636.

Light, J. G., & DeFries, J. C. (1995). Comorbidity of reading and mathematics disabilities: Genetic and environmental etiologies. *Journal of Learning Disabilities, 28,* 96–117.

Lindsay, R. L., Tomazic, T., Levine, M. D., & Accardo, P. J. (1999). Impact of attentional dysfunction in dyscalculia. *Developmental Medicine and Child Neurology, 41,* 639–642.

Locke, W. R., & Fuchs, L. S. (1995). Effects of peer-mediated reading-instruction on the on-task behavior and social-interaction of children with behavior disorders. *Journal of Emotional and Behavioral Disorders, 3,* 92–99.

Loeber, R., Burke, J. D., Lahey, B. B., Winters, A., & Zera, M. (2000). Oppositional defiant disorder and conduct disorder: A review of the past 10 years, part I. *Journal of the American Academy of Child and Adolescent Psychiatry, 39,* 1468–1484.

Loeber, R., Green, S. M., Keenan, K. & Lahey, B. B. (1995). Which boys will fare worse? Early predictors of the onset of conduct disorder in a six-year longitudinal study. *Journal of the American Academy of Child and Adolescent Psychiatry, 34,* 499–509.

Loney, J. (1974). The intellectual functioning of hyperactive elementary school boys: A cross-sectional investigation. *American Journal of Orthopsychiatry, 44,* 754–762.

Loney, J. (1987). Hyperactivity and aggression in the diagnosis of attention deficit disorder. *Advances in Clinical Child Psychology, 10,* 99–135.

Loney, J., Kramer, J., & Milich, R. S. (1981). The hyperactive child grows up: Predictors of symptoms, delinquency and achievement at follow-up. In K. D. Gadow & J. Loney (Eds.), *Psychosocial aspects of drug treatment for hyperactivity* (pp. 381–416). Boulder, CO: Westview Press.

Loney, J., Whaley-Klahn, M. A., Kosier, T., & Conboy, J. (1983). Hyperactive boys and their brothers at 21: Predictors of aggressive and antisocial outcomes. In K. T. V. Dusen & S. A. Mednick (Eds.), *Prospective studies of crime and delinquency* (pp. 181–206). Boston: Kluwer Nijhof.

Lorch, E. P., Diener, M. B., & Sanchez, R. P., Milich, R., Welsh, R., & van den Broek, P. (1999). The effects of story structure on the recall of stories in children with attention deficit hyperactivity disorder. *Journal of Educational Psychology, 91,* 273–283.

Lorch, E. P., O'Neil, K., Berthiaume, K. S., Milich, R., Eastman, D., & Brooks, T. (2004). Story of comprehension and the impact of studying on recall in children with attention deficit hyperactivity disorder. *Journal of Clinical Child and Adolescent Psychology, 33,* 506–515.

Lou, H. C., Henricksen, L., Bruhn, P. Borner, H., & Nielsen, J. B. (1989). Striatal dysfunction in attention deficit hyperkinetic disorder. *Archives of Neurology, 46,* 49–52.

Lou, H. C., Henricksen, L., & Bruhn, P., (1984). Focal cerebral hypoperfusion in children with dysphasia and/or attention deficit disorder. *Archives of Neurology, 41,* 825–829.

Lovitt, T. C., & Curtis, K. A. (1968). Effects of manipulating an antecedent event on mathematics response rate. *Journal of Applied Behavior Analysis, 1,* 329–333.

Lynskey, M. T., & Fergusson, D. M. (1995). Childhood conduct problems, attention deficit behaviors, and adolescent alcohol, tobacco, and illicit drug use. *Journal of Abnormal Child Psychology, 23*, 281–302.

Lyon, G. R. (1992). *Research in learning disabilities.* Washington, DC: U.S. Department of Health and Human Services.

Maag, J. W., & Reid, R. (1996). Treatment of attention deficit hyperactivity disorder: A multimodal model for schools. *Seminars in Speech and Language, 17*, 37–57.

Maag, J. W., Reid, R., & DiGangi, S. A. (1993). Differential effects of self-monitoring attention, accuracy, and productivity. *Journal of Applied Behavior Analysis, 26*, 329–344.

MacDonald, K., & Parke, R. D. (1984). Bridging the gap: Parent-child play interaction and peer interactive competence. *Child Development, 55*, 1265–1277.

MacLeod, D., & Prior, M. (1996). Attention deficits in adolescents with ADHD and other clinical groups. *Child Neuropsychology, 2*, 1–10.

Madan-Swain, A., & Zentall, S. S. (1990). Behavioral comparisons of liked and disliked hyperactive children in play contexts and the behavioral accommodations by their classmates. *Journal of Consulting and Clinical Psychology, 58*, 197–209.

Maedgen, J. W., & Carlson, C. I. (2000). Social functioning and emotional regulation in the attention deficit hyperactivity disorder subtypes. *Journal of Clinical Child Psychology, 29*, 30–42.

Mainzer, R. W. J., Mainzer, K. W., Slavin, R. E., & Lowry, E. (1993). What special education teachers should know about cooperative learning. *Teacher Education and Special Education, 16*, 42–50.

Malone, M. A., & Swanson, J. M. (1993). Effects of methylphenidate on impulsive responding in children with attention-deficit hyperactivity disorder. *Journal of Child Neurology, 8*, 157–163.

Marchant, C., & Siperstein, G. N. (1997). Meeting the social needs of students with AD/HD by addressing the professional development needs of their teachers. *Teacher Education and Special Education, 20*, 92–102.

Margalit, M., & Almougy, K. (1991). Classroom behavior and family climate in students with learning disabilities and hyperactive behavior. *Journal of Learning Disabilities, 24*, 406–412.

Mariani, M. A., & Barkley, R. A. (1997). Neuropsychological and academic functioning in preschool boys with attention deficit hyperactivity disorder. *Developmental Neuropsychology, 13*, 111–119.

Marshall, R. M., Hynd, G. W., Handwerk, M. J., & Hall, J. (1997). Academic underachievement in ADHD subtypes. *Journal of Learning Disabilities, 30*, 635–642.

Marshall, R. M., Schafer, V. A., O'Donnell, L., Elliott, J., & Handwerk, M. J. (1999). Arithmetic disabilities and ADD subtypes: Implications for DSM-IV. *Journal of Learning Disabilities, 32*, 239–247.

Martens, B. K., & Kelly, S. Q. (1993). A behavioral analysis of effective teaching. *School Psychology Quarterly, 8*, 10–26.

Mash, E. J. (1983). The prediction of mothers' behavior with their hyperactive children during play and task situations. *Child and Family Behavior Therapy, 5*, 1–13.

Mash, E. J., & Johnston, C. (1983). Parental perceptions of child behavior problems, parenting self-esteem, and mothers' reported stress in younger and older hyperactive and normal children. *Journal of Consulting and Clinical Psychology, 51*, 86–99.

Mather, D. (2003). Dyslexia and dysgraphia: More than written language difficulties in common. *Journal of Learning Disabilities, 36*, 307–317.

Mathes, M. Y., & Bender, W. N. (1997). The effects of self-monitoring on children with attention-deficit/hyperactivity disorder who are receiving pharmacological interventions. *Remedial and Special Education, 18*, 121–128.

Mathes, P. G., & Fuchs, L. S. (1994). The efficacy of peer tutoring in reading for students with mild disabilities: A best-evidence synthesis. *School Psychology Review, 12*, 59–80.

Mathur, S., & Smith, R. (2003). Collaborate with families of children with ADD. *Intervention in School and Clinic, 38*, 311–315.

Mayes, S. W., Calhoun, S. L., & Crowell, E. W. (2000). Learning disabilities and ADHD: Overlapping spectrum disorders. *Journal of Learning Disabilities, 33*, 417–424.

McBurnett, K. (1995). The new subtype of ADHD: Predominantly hyperactive-impulsive. *Attention, 1*(3), 10–15.

McBurnett, K., Lahey, B. J., & Pfiffner, L. J. (1993). Diagnosis of attention deficit disorders in DSM-IV: Scientific basis and implications for education. *Exceptional Children, 60,* 108–117.

McCain, A. P., & Kelley, M. L. (1993). Managing the behavior of an ADHD preschooler: The efficacy of school-home note intervention. *Child and Family Behavior Therapy, 15,* 33–44.

McGee, R., Partridge, F., Williams, S., & Silva, P. A. (1991). A twelve-year follow-up of preschool hyperactive children. *Journal of the American Academy of Child and Adolescent Psychiatry, 30,* 224–232.

McGee, R., & Share, D. L. (1988). Attention deficit disorder-hyperactivity and academic failure: Which comes first and what should be treated? *Journal of the American Academy of Child and Adolescent Psychiatry, 27,* 318–325.

McGee, R., Williams, S., Moffitt, T., & Anderson, J. (1989). A comparison of 13-year-old boys with attention deficit and/or reading disorder on neuropsychological measures. *Journal of Abnormal Child Psychology, 17,* 37–53.

McGee, R., Williams, S., & Silva, P. A. (1984). Behavioral and developmental characteristics of aggressive hyperactive and aggressive-hyperactive boys. *Journal of the American Academy of Child Psychiatry, 23,* 270–279.

McGimsey, J. F., & Favell, J. E. (1988). The effects of increased physical exercise on disruptive behavior in retarded persons. *Journal of Autism and Developmental Disorders, 18,* 167–179.

McInnes, A., Humphries, T., Hogg-Johnson, S., & Tannock, R. (2003). Listening comprehension and working memory are impaired in children with ADHD irrespective of language development. *Journal of Abnormal Child Psychology, 31,* 427–433.

McKenzie, G. R., & Henry, M. (1979). Effects of test-like events on on-task behavior, test anxiety, and achievement in a classroom rule-relearning task. *Journal of Educational Psychology, 71,* 370–374.

McKinney, J. D., Montague, M., & Hocutt, A. M. (1993). Educational assessment of students with attention deficit disorder. *Exceptional Children, 60,* 125–131.

McLaughlin, T. F., & Helm, J. L. (1995). Use of contingent music to increase academic performance of middle school students. *Psychological Reports, 72,* 658.

McLaughlin, T., & Malaby, J. (1972). Reducing and measuring inappropriate verbalizations in a token classroom. *Journal of Applied Behavior Analysis, 3,* 329–333.

McLaughlin, T. F., Swain, J. C., Brown, M., & Fielding, L. (1986). The effects of academic consequences on the inappropriate social behavior of special education middle school students. *Techniques: A Journal for Remedial Education and Counseling, 2,* 310–316.

Meharg, S. S., & Woltersdorf, M. A. (1990). Therapeutic use of videotape self-modeling—A review. *Advances in Behaviour Research and Therapy, 12,* 85–99.

Meichenbaum, D. (1979). Teaching children self-control. *Advances in Clinical Child Psychology, 2,* 1–27.

Melnick, S. M., & Hinshaw, S. P. (1996). What they want and what they get: The social goals of boys with ADHD and comparison boys. *Journal of Abnormal Child Psychology, 24,* 169–185.

Meyer, M. J., & Zentall, S. S. (1995). Influence of loud behavioral consequences on attention deficit hyperactivity disorder. *Behavior Therapy, 26,* 351–370.

Milberger, S., Biederman, J., Faraone, S. V., Chen, L., & Jones, J. (1996). Maternal smoking during pregnancy a risk factor for attention deficit hyperactivity disorder in children? *American Journal of Psychiatry, 153,* 1138–1142.

Milch-Reich, S., Campbell, S. B., Pelham, W. E., Connelly, L. M., & Geva, K. (1999). Developmental and individual differences in children's on-line representations of dynamic social events. *Child Development, 70,* 413–431.

Milich, R. (1994). The response of children with ADHD to failure: If at first you don't succeed, do you try, try again? *School Psychology Review, 23,* 11–28.

Milich, R., Hartung, C. M., Martin, C. A., & Haigler, E. D. (1994). Behavioral disinhibition and underlying processes in adolescents with disruptive behavior disorders. In D. K. Routh (Ed.), *Disruptive behavior disorders in childhood.* (pp. 109–138) New York: Plenum Press.

Milich, R., & Lorch, E. P. (1994). Television viewing methodology to understanding cognitive processing of ADHD children. *Advances in Clinical Child Psychology, 16*, 177–201.

Milich, R., & Okazaki, M. (1991). An examination of learned helplessness among attention-deficit hyperactivity disordered boys. *Journal of Abnormal Child Psychology, 19*, 607–623.

Miller, C. D., & Mercer, C. D. (1997). Educational aspects of mathematics disabilities. *Journal of Learning Disabilities, 30*, 47–56.

Miller, S. P., Butler, F. M., & Lee, K-h. (1998). Validated practices for teaching mathematics for students with learning disabilities: A review of literature. *Focus on Exceptional Children, 31*, 1–24.

Miller, D. L., & Kelley, M. L. (1994). The use of goal setting and contingency contracting for improving children's homework performance. *Journal of Applied Behavior Analysis, 27*, 73–84.

Miranda, A., Presentacion, M. J., & Soriano, M. (2002). Effectiveness of a school-based multicomponent program for the treatment of children with ADHD. *Journal of Learning Disabilities, 35*, 546–562.

Monastra, V. J., Lubar, J. F., Linden, M., Van Deusen, P., Green, G., Wing, W., Phillips, A., Fenger, T. N. (1999). Assessing ADHD via quantitative electroencephalography. *Neuropsychology, 13*, 424–433.

Moon, S., Zentall, S. S., Grskovic, J., Hall, A. M., & Stormont, M. (2001). Social and family characteristics of boys with giftedness and/or attention deficit/hyperactivity disorder. *Journal for the Education of the Gifted, 24*, 207–247.

Moore, L. A., Hughes, J. M., & Robinson, M. (1992). A comparison of the social information-processing abilities of rejected and accepted hyperactive children. *Journal of Clinical Child Psychology, 21*, 123–131.

Morgan, A., Hynd, G., Riccio, C., & Hall, J. (1996). Validity of DSM-IV ADHD predominantly inattentive and combined types: Relationship to previous DSM diagnoses/subtype differences. *Journal of the American Academy of Child and Adolescent Psychiatry, 35*, 325–333.

Morris, G. B. (1993). A rational-emotive treatment program with conduct disorder and attention-deficit hyperactivity disorder adolescents. *Journal of Rational-Emotive and Cognitive- Behavioral Therapy, 11*, 123–134.

Morrison, J. R. (1979). Diagnosis of adult psychiatric patients with childhood hyperactivity. *American Journal of Psychiatry, 136*, 955–958.

Morse, W. C. (1994). The role of caring in teaching children with behavior problems. *Contemporary Education, 65*, 132–136.

Munson, S. M. (1986). Regular education teacher modifications for mainstreamed mildly handicapped students. *Journal of Special Education, 20*, 489–502.

Mrug, S., Hoza, B., & Gerdes, A. C. (2001). Children with attention-deficit/hyperactivity disorder: Peer relationships and peer-oriented environments. *New Directions for Child and Adolescent Development, 91*, 51–76.

MTA Cooperative Group. (1999). A 14-month randomized clinical trial of treatment strategies for attention deficit/hyperactivity dis-order. *Archives of General Psychiatry, 56*, 1073–1086.

Narayan, J. S., Heward, W. L., Gardner, R., III, Courson, F. H., & Omness, C. (1990). Using response cards to increase student participation in an elementary classroom. *Journal of Applied Behavior Analysis, 23*, 483–490.

National Institutes of Health. (2000). Consensus Development Conference Statement: Diagnosis and treatment of attention-deficit/hyperactivity disorder (ADHD). *Journal of the American Academy of Child and Adolescent Psychiatry, 39*, 182–193.

Neef, N. A., Bicard, D. F., & Endo, S. (2001). Assessment of impulsivity and the development of self-control in students with attention deficit hyperactivity disorder. *Journal of Applied Behavior Analysis, 34*, 397–408.

Neef, N. A., Marckel, J., Fereri, S., Jung, S., Nist, L., & Armstrong, N. (2004). Effects of modeling versus instructions on sensitivity to reinforcement schedules. *Journal of Applied Behavior Analysis, 37*, 267–281.

Neuringer, A. (2002). Operant variability: Evidence, functions, and theory. *Psychonomic Bulletin and Review, 9*, 672–705.

Newby, T. J. (1991). Classroom motivation: Strategies of first-year teachers. *Journal of Educational Psychology, 83*, 195–200.

Newmann, F. M., Rutter, R. A., & Smith, M. S. (1989). Organizational factors that affect school sense of efficacy, community, and expectations. *Sociology of Education, 62*, 221–238.

Nicholls, J., McKenzie, M., & Shufro, J. (1994). Schoolwork, homework, life's work: The experience of students with and without learning disabilities. *Journal of Learning Disabilities, 27*, 562–569.

Nidiffer, F. D., Ciulla, R. P., Russo, D. C., & Cataldo, M. F. (1983). Behavioral variability as a function of noncontingent adult attention, peer availability, and situational demands in three hyperactive boys. *Journal of Experimental Psychology, 36*, 109–123.

Nigg, J. T. (2001). Is ADHD a disinhibitory disorder? *Psychological Bulletin, 127*, 571–598.

Northup, J., Broussard, C., Jones, K., George, T., Vollmer, T. R., & Gering, M. (1995). The differential effects of teacher and peer attention on the disruptive classroom behavior of three children with a diagnosis of attention deficit hyperactivity disorder. *Journal of Applied Behavior Analysis, 28*, 227–228.

Nussbaum, N. L., Grant, M. L., Roman, M. J., Poole, J. H., & Bigler, E. (1990). Attention deficit hyperactivity disorder and the mediating effect of age on academic and behavioral variables. *Developmental Behavioral Pediatrics, 11*, 22–26.

O'Conner, R. E., & Jenkins, J. R. (1993, April). *Cooperative learning as an inclusion strategy: The experience of children with disabilities.* Paper presented at the annual meeting of the American Educational Research Association, Atlanta, GA. (ERIC Document Reproduction Service No. ED360778)

O'Conner, R. E., & Jenkins, J. R. (1995, April). *Cooperative learning for students with learning disabilities: Teacher and child contributions to successful participation.* Paper presented at the annual conference of the American Educational Research Association, San Francisco. (ERIC Document Reproduction Service No. ED390189)

Ohan, J. L., & Johnston, C. (2002). Are the performance overestimates given by boys with ADHD self-protective? *Journal of Clinical Child Psychology, 31*, 230–241.

O'Leary, K. D., Kaufmann, K. F., Kass, R. E., & Drabman, R. S. (1970). The effects of loud and soft reprimands on the behavior of disruptive students. *Exceptional Children, 37*, 145–155.

O'Neill, M. E., & Douglas, V. I. (1991). Study strategies and story recall in attention deficit disorder and reading disability. *Journal of Abnormal Child Psychology, 19*, 671–692.

O'Neill, M. E., & Douglas, V. I. (1996). Rehearsal strategies and recall performance in boys with and without attention deficit hyperactivity disorder. *Journal of Pediatric Psychology, 21*, 73–88.

Oosterlaan, J., Sergeant, J. A. (1998). Effects of reward and response cost on response inhibition in AD/HD, disruptive, anxious, and normal children. *Journal of Abnormal Child Psychology, 26*, 161–174.

Oram, J., Fine, J., Okamoto, C., & Tannock, R. (1999). Assessing the language of children with attention deficit hyperactivity disorder. *American Journal of Speech-Language Pathology, 8*, 72–80.

Parry, P. A., & Douglas, V. I. (1983). Effects of reinforcement on concept identification in hyperactive children. *Journal of Abnormal Child Psychology, 11*, 327–340.

Passolunghi, M. C., & Pazzagliab, F. (2004). Individual differences in memory updating in relation to arithmetic problem solving. *Learning and Individual Differences, 14*, 219–230.

Passolunghi, M. C., & Siegel, L. S. (2004). Working memory and access to numerical information in children with disability in mathematics. *Journal of Experimental Child Psychology, 88*, 348–367.

Paul, J. L., & Epanchin, B. C. (1991). *Educating emotionally disturbed children and youth: Theories and practices for teachers.* New York: Macmillan.

Pelham, W. E., Carlson, C., Sams, S. E., Vallano, G., Dixon, M. J., & Hoza, B. (1993). Separate and combined effects of methylphenidate and behavior modification on boys with attention deficit-hyperactivity disorder in the classroom. *Journal of Consulting and Clinical Psychology, 61*, 506–515.

Pelham, W. E., Wheeler, T., & Chronis, A. (1998). Empirically supported psychosocial treatments for attention deficit hyperactivity disorder. *Journal of Clinical Child Psychology, 27*, 190–205.

Pennington, B. F. (1991). *Diagnostic learning disorders: A neuropsychological framework*. New York: Guilford Press.

Pennington, B. F., & Ozonoff, S. (1996). Executive functions and developmental psychopathology. *Journal of Child Psychology and Psychiatry, 37*, 51–87.

Peter, D., Allan, J., & Horvath, A. (1983). Hyperactive children's perceptions of teachers' classroom behavior. *Psychology in the Schools, 20*, 234–240.

Peterson, P. L., Carpenter, T., & Fennema, E. (1989). Teachers' knowledge of students' knowledge in mathematics problem solving: Correlational and case analyses. *Journal of Educational Psychology, 81*, 558–569.

Peterson, R. (2003). Teaching the social curriculum: School discipline as instruction. *Preventing School Failure, 47*, 66–73.

Petr, C., & Allen, R. (1997). Family-centered professional behavior: Frequency and importance to parents. *Journal of Emotional and Behavioral Disorders, 5*, 196–204.

Piek, J. P., Dyck, M. J., Nieman, A., Anderson, M., Hay, D., Smith, L. M., et al. (2004). The relationship between motor coordination, executive functioning and attention in school aged children. *Archives of Clinical Neuropsychology, 19*, 1063–1076.

Pintrich, P., & Schunk, D. (1996). *Motivation in education: Theory, research and applications.* Englewood Cliffs, NJ: Prentice Hall.

Pisecco, S., Baker, D. B., Silva, P. A., & Brooke, M. (2001). Boys with reading disabilities and/or ADHD: Distinctions in early childhood. *Journal of Learning Disabilities, 34*, 98–106.

Pisecco, S., Wristers, K., Swank, P., Silva, P. A., & Baker, D. B. (2001). The effect of academic self-concept on ADHD and antisocial behaviors in early adolescence. *Journal of Learning Disabilities, 34*, 450–461.

Pliszka, S. R. (1989). Effect of anxiety on cognition, behavior, and stimulant response in ADHD. *Journal of the Academy of Child and Adolescent Psychiatry, 28*, 882–887.

Pliszka, S. R., McCracken, J. T., & Maas, J. W. (1996). Catecholamines in attention-deficit hyperactivity disorder: Current perspectives. *Journal of the Academy of Child and Adolescent Psychiatry, 35*, 264–272.

Plomin, R., & Foch, T. T. (1981). Hyperactivity and pediatrician diagnoses, parental ratings, specific cognitive abilities, and laboratory measures. *Journal of Abnormal Child Psychology, 9*, 55–64.

Pomplun, M. (1997). When students with disabilities participate in cooperative groups. *Exceptional Children, 64*, 49–58.

Pool, M. M., Koolstra, C. M., & van der Voort, T. H. A. (2003). The impact of background radio and television on high school students' homework performance. *Journal of Communications, 53*, 74–87.

Pool, M. M., van der Voort, T. H. A., & Koolstra, C. M. (2000). Background television as an inhibitor of performance on easy and difficult homework assignments. *Communication Research, 27*, 293–326.

Poplin, M. S. (1988). The reductionistic fallacy in learning disabilities: Replicating the past by reducing the present. *Journal of Learning Disabilities, 21*, 389–396.

Porrino, L. J., Rapoport, J. L., Behar, D., Sceery, W., Ismond, D. R., & Bunney, W. E. (1983). A naturalistic assessment of the motor activity of hyperactive boys. *Archives of General Psychiatry, 40*, 681–687.

Posavac, H. D., Sheridan, S. M., & Posavac, S. S. (1999). A cueing procedure to control impulsivity in children with attention deficit hyperactivity disorder. *Behavior Modification, 23*, 234–253.

Powell, S., & Nelson, B. (1997). Effects of choosing academic assignments on a student with attention deficit hyperactivity disorder. *Journal of Applied Behavior Analysis, 30*, 181–183.

Prater, M. A., Hogan, S., & Miller, S. R. (1992). Using self-monitoring to improve on-task behavior and academic skills of an adolescent with mild handicaps across special and regular education settings. *Education and Treatment of Children, 15*, 43–55.

Prinz, R. J., Connor, P. A., & Wilson, C. C. (1981). Hyperactive and aggressive behaviors in childhood: Intertwined dimensions. *Journal of Abnormal Child Psychology, 9*, 191–202.

Purvis, K. L., & Tannock, R. (1997). Language abilities in children with attention deficit hyperactivity disorder, reading disabilities, and normal controls. *Journal of Abnormal Child Psychology, 25,* 133–145.

Rabiner, D., & Coie, J. D. (2000). Early attention problems and children's reading achievement: A longitudinal investigation. *Journal of the American Academy of Child and Adolescent Psychiatry, 39,* 859–867.

Radosh, A., & Gittelman, R. (1981). The effect of appealing distractors on the performance of hyperactive children. *Journal of Abnormal Child Psychology, 9,* 179–189.

Rapoport, J. L., & Benoit, M. (1975). The relation of direct home observations to the clinic evaluation of hyperactive school age boys. *Journal of Child Psychology and Psychiatry, 16,* 141–147.

Rapport, M. (2001). Bridging theory and practice: Conceptual understanding of treatments for children with attention deficit hyperactivity disorder (ADHD), obsessive-compulsive disorder (OCD), autism, and depression. *Journal of Clinical Child Psychology, 30,* 3–7.

Rapport, M. D., Denney, C., DuPaul, G. J., & Gardner, M. J. (1994). Attention deficit disorder and methylphenidate: Normalization rates, clinical effectiveness and response prediction in 76 children. *Journal of the American Academy of Child and Adolescent Psychiatry, 33,* 882–893.

Rapport, M. D., Tucker, S. B., DuPaul, G. J., Merlo, M., & Stoner, G. (1986). Hyperactivity and frustration: The influence of control over and size of rewards in delaying gratification. *Journal of Abnormal Child Psychology, 14,* 191–204.

Redmond, S. M. (2004). Conversational profiles of children with ADHD, SLI and typical development. *Clinical Linguistics and Phonetics, 18,* 107–125.

Reeve, R., Schrag, J., & Walker, R. (1994). *Policy and administrative issues: Module IV.* Continuing Education Program on Attention Deficit Disorder. Reston, VA: The Council for Exceptional Children.

Reid, R. (1999). Attention-deficit hyperactivity disorder: Effective methods for the classroom. *Focus on Exceptional Children, 32,* 1–20.

Reid, R., & Maag, J. W. (1998). Functional assessment: A method for developing classroom-based accommodations and interventions for children with ADHD. *Reading and Writing Quarterly, 14,* 9–34.

Reid, R., Trout, A. L., & Schartz, M. (in press). Self-regulation interventions for children with attention deficit hyperactivity disorder. *Exceptional Children.*

Reid, R., Vasa, S. F., Maag, J. W., & Wright, G. (1994). An analysis of teachers' perceptions of attention deficit-hyperactivity disorder. *Journal of Research and Development in Education, 17,* 195–202.

Reilly, R. (2004, August). Water boy. *Sports Illustrated 101*(8), 110.

Rief, S. F. (1998). Redefining "structure" for students with AD/HD. *Reaching Today's Youth, 2,* 24–27.

Resta, S. P., & Eliot, J. (1994). Written expression in boys with attention deficit disorder. *Perceptual and Motor Skills, 79,* 1131–1138.

Riccio, C. A., Hynd, G. W., Cohen, M. J., & Gonzalez, J. J. (1993). Neurological basis of attention deficit hyperactivity disorder. *Exceptional Children, 60,* 118–124.

Richardson, A., & Puri, B. K. (2002). A randomized double-blind, placebo-controlled study of the effects of supplementation with highly unsaturated fatty acids on ADHD-related symptoms in children with specific learning disabilities. *Progress in Neuro-Psychopharmacology and Biological Psychiatry, 26,* 233–239.

Richters, J. E., Arnold, L. E., Jensen, P. S., Abikoff, H., Conners, C. K., Greenhill, L. L. (1995). NIMH Collaborative Multisite Multimodal Treatment Study of Children with ADHD. I: Background and rationale. *Journal of the American Academy of Child and Adolescent Psychiatry, 34,* 987–1000.

Rife, R. M., & Karr-Kidwell, P. J. (1995). *Administrative and teacher efforts for elementary emotionally disturbed and behaviorally-disordered students: A literary review and recommendations for an inclusion program.* Denton, Texas: Texas Woman's University (ERIC Document Reproduction Service No. ED 396497).

Robinson, P. W., Newby, T. J., & Ganzell, S. L. (1981). A token system for a class of under-achieving hyperactive children. *Journal of Applied Behavior Analysis, 14,* 307–315.

Robinson, T. R., Smith, S. W., Miller, M. D., & Brownell, M. T. (1999). Cognitive behavior modification of hyperactivity/impulsivity and aggression: A meta-analysis of school-based studies. *Journal of Educational Psychology, 91,* 195–203.

Roderique, T. W., Polloway, E. A., Cumblad, C., Epstein, M. H., & Bursuck, W. D. (1994). Homework: A survey of policies in the United States. *Journal of Learning Disabilities, 27,* 481–487.

Roodenrys, S., Koloski, N., & Grainger, J. (2001). Working memory function of attention deficit hyperactivity disordered and reading disabled children. *British Journal of Developmental Psychology, 19,* 325–337.

Rosberg, M. (1995, May). *Responsible inclusion of students with disabilities.* Paper presented at the Study Conference on Cued Speech in Malay, Perpustakaan Negara, Malaysia. (ERIC Document Reproduction Service No. ED387973)

Rosen, L. A., O'Leary, S. G., Joyce, S. A., Conway, G., & Pfiffner, L. J. (1984). The importance of prudent negative consequences for maintaining the appropriate behavior of hyperactive children. *Journal of Abnormal Child Psychology, 12,* 581–604.

Rosenbaum, M., & Baker, E. (1984). Self-control behavior in hyperactive and nonhyperactive children. *Journal of Abnormal Child Psychology, 12,* 303–318.

Rosenberg, M. S., Wilson, R. J., & Legenhausen, E. (1989). *The assessment of hyperactivity in preschool populations: A multidisciplinary perspective, 9,* 90–105.

Rosenfield, P., Lambert, N. M., & Black, A. (1985). Desk arrangement effects on pupil classroom behavior. *Journal of Educational Psychology, 77,* 101–108.

Rosenthal, J. H. (1973). Neurophysiology of minimal cerebral dysfunctions. *Academic Therapy, 8,* 291–294.

Rosenthal, R. H., & Allen, T. W. (1978). An examination of attention, arousal, and learning dysfunctions of hyperkinetic children. *Psychological Bulletin, 85,* 689–715.

Rosenthal, R. H., & Allen, T. W. (1980). Intratask distractibility in hyperkinetic and nonhyperkinetic children. *Journal of Abnormal Child Psychology, 8,* 175–187.

Rucklidge, J. J., & Tannock, R. (2001). Psychiatric, psychosocial, and cognitive functioning of female adolescents with ADHD. *Journal of the American Academy of Child and Adolescent Psychiatry, 40,* 530–540.

Rueda, R., Gallego, M. A., & Moll, L. C. (2000). The least restrictive environment: A place or a context? *Remedial and Special Education, 21,* 70–78.

Ruhl, K. L. (1985). Handling aggression: Fourteen methods teachers use. *The Pointer, 29,* 30–33.

Runnheim, V. A., Frankenberger, W. R., & Hazelkorn, M. N. (1996). Medicating students with emotional and behavioral disorders and ADHD: A state survey. *Behavioral Disorders, 21,* 306–314.

Safran, S. P. (1982). Resource consultant communication and teacher expectations of behaviorally disordered children. *Behavioral Disorders, 8,* 25–31.

Safran, S. P., & Safran, J. S. (1985). Classroom context and teachers' perceptions of problem behaviors. *Journal of Educational Psychology, 77,* 20–28.

Sagvolden, T., Metzger, M. A., & Sagvolden, G. (1993). Frequent reward eliminates differences in activity between hyperkinetic rats and controls. *Behavioral and Neural Biology, 59,* 225–229.

Salend, S. J., & Schliff, J. (1989). An examination of homework practices of students with learning disabilities. *Journal of Learning Disabilities, 22,* 621–623.

Salisbury, C. L. (1993, November). *Effects of inclusive schooling practices: Costs to kids and organizations.* Paper presented at the 1993 Conference of the Association for Persons with Severe Handicaps, Chicago.

Sapon-Shevin, M., Ayres, B. J., & Duncan, J. (1994). Cooperative learning and inclusion. In J. S. Thousand, R. A. Villa, & A. I. Nevin (Eds.), *Creativity and collaborative learning: A practical guide to empowering students and teachers* (pp. 45–58). Baltimore: Paul H. Brookes.

Satterfield, J. H., Schell, A. M., Nicholas, T. W., Satterfield, B. T., & Freese, T. E. (1990). Ontogeny of selective attention effects on event-related potentials in attention-deficit hyperactivity disorder and normal boys. *Biological Psychiatry, 28,* 879–903.

Saunders, B., & Champbers, S. M. (1996). A review of the literature on attention-deficit hyperactivity disorder children: Peer interactions and collaborative learning. *Psychology in the Schools, 33*, 333–340.

Schab, D. W., & Trinh, N-H. T. (2004). Do artificial food colors promote hyperactivity in children with hyperactive syndromes? A meta-analysis of double-blind placebo controlled trials. *Development and Behavioral Pediatrics, 25*, 423–434.

Schaefer, E. S., & Bayley, A. (1963). Maternal behavior, child behavior and their intercorrelations from infancy through adolescence. *Monographs of the Society for Research in Child Development, 28*, 1–127.

Scheres, A., Oosterlaan, J., Geurts, H., Morein-Zamir, S., Meiran, N., Schut, H., et al. (2004). Executive functioning in boys with ADHD: Primarily an inhibition deficit? *Archives of Clinical Neuropsychology, 19*, 569–594.

Schrag, J. A. (1993). *Organizational, instructional, and curricular strategies to support the implementation of unified, coordinated, and inclusive schools.* Reston, VA: Council for Exceptional Children.

Schultz, J. L. (1990). Cooperative learning: Refining the process. *Educational Leadership, 47*, 43–45.

Schulz, E. G., & Edwards, M. C. (1997). Stimulant medication management of students with attention deficit hyperactivity disorder: What educators need to know. *Teacher Education and Special Education, 20*, 170–178.

Schunk, D. H. (1996). Goal and self-evaluative influences during children's cognitive skill learning. *American Educational Research Journal, 33*, 359–382.

Schweitzer, J. B., & Sulzer-Azaroff, B. (1995). Self-control in boys with attention-deficit hyperactivity disorder: Effects of added stimulation and time. *Journal of Child Psychology and Psychiatry, 36*, 671–686.

Scott, T. J. (1970). The use of music to reduce hyperactivity in children. *American Journal of Orthopsychiatry, 40*, 677–680.

Seibert, S., & Gruenfeld, L. (1992). Masculinity, femininity, and behavior in groups. *Small Group Research, 23*, 95–112.

Semrud-Clikeman, M., Nielsen, K. H., Clinton, A., Sylvester, L., Parle, N., & Connor, R. (1999). An intervention approach for children with teacher- and parent-identified attentional difficulties. *Journal of Learning Disabilities, 32*, 581–590.

Senf, G. (1986). LD research and sociological and scientific perspective. In J. K. Torgesen & B. Y. L. Wong (Eds.), Psychological and educational perspectives on learning disabilities (pp. 27–53). San Diego: Academic Press.

Sergeant, J. A. (2000). The cognitive-energetic model: An approach to attention deficit hyperactivity disorder. *Neuroscience Biobehavioral Review, 24*, 7–12.

Sergeant, J. A., Geurts, H., Huijbregts, S., Scheres, A., & Oosterlaan, J. (2003). The top and bottom of ADHD: A neuropsychological perspective. *Neuroscience and Biobehavioral Review, 27*, 583–592.

Sergeant, J. A., & Scholten, C. A. (1985). On resource strategy limitations in hyperactivity: Cognitive impulsivity reconsidered. *Journal of Child Psychology and Psychiatry, 26*, 97–110.

Settle, S. A., & Milich, R. (1999). Social persistence following failure in boys and girls with LD. *Journal of Learning Disabilities, 32*, 201–212.

Shaffer, R. J., Jacokes, L. E., Cassily, J. F., Greenspan, S. I., Tuchman, R. F., & Stemmer, P. J. (2001). Effect of interactive metronome rhythmicity training on children with ADHD. *American Journal of Occupational Therapy, 55*, 155–162.

Share, D. L., & Silva, P. A. (2003). Gender bias in IQ-discrepancy and post-discrepancy definitions of reading disability. *Journal of Learning Disabilities, 36*, 155–162.

Shaw, G., & Brown, G. (1999). Arousal, time estimation, and time use in attention-disordered children. *Developmental Neuropsychology, 16*, 227–242.

Shaywitz, S. E., Fletcher, J. M., & Shaywitz, B. A. (1994). Issues in the definition and classification of attention deficit disorder. Special issue: ADD and its relationship to spoken and written language. *Topics in Language Disorders, 14*, 1–25.

Shaywitz, S. E., & Shaywitz, B. A. (1988). Attention deficit disorder: Current perspectives. In J. F. Kavanagh & J. T. J. Truss (Eds.), *Learning disabilities: Proceedings of a national conference* (pp. 369–567). Parkton, MD: York Press.

Shaywitz, S. E., & Shaywitz, B. A. (1991). Introduction to the special series on attention deficit disorder. *Journal of Learning Disabilities, 24,* 68.

Shaywitz, S. E., Shaywitz, B. A., Fletcher, J. M., & Escobar, M. D. (1990). Prevalence of reading disability in boys and girls. *Journal of the American Medical Association, 264,* 998–1002.

Shea, C. (1994). "Invisible" maladies: Students who say they have learning disabilities encounter skepticism. *The Chronicle of Higher Education, 40*(2), 53–55.

Shelton, T. L., & Barkley, R. A. (1994). Critical issues in the assessment of attention deficit disorders in children. *Topics in Language Disorders, 14*(4), 26–41.

Shimabukuro, P., Prater, M. A., Jenkins, A., & Edelen-Smith, P. (1999). The effects of self-monitoring of academic performance of students with learning disabilities and ADD/ADHD. *Education and Treatment of Children, 22,* 1–10.

Shimabukuro, P., & Serena, M. (1999). The effects of self-monitoring of academic performance of students with learning disabilities and ADD/ADHD. *Education and Treatment of Children, 22,* 1–10.

Shirey, L. L., & Reynolds, R. E. (1988). Effect of interest on attention and learning. *Journal of Educational Psychology, 80,* 159–166.

Shroyer, C., & Zentall, S. S. (1986). Effects of rate, nonrelevant information, and repetition on the listening comprehension of hyperactive children. *Journal of Special Education, 20,* 231–239.

Silvia, P. J. (2002). Self-awareness and emotional intensity: Cognition and emotional intensity. *Cognition and Emotion, 16,* 195–216.

Singer, H. S., Brown, J., Quaskey, S., Rosenberg, S., Mellits, E. D., & Denckla, M. B. (1995). The treatment of attention-deficit hyperactivity disorder in Tourette's syndrome: A double-blind placebo controlled study with clonidine and desipramine. *Pediatrics, 95,* 74–81.

Singh, S. D., Ellis, C. R., Winston, A. S., Singh, N. N., Leung, J. P., & Oswald, D. P. (1998). Recognition of facial expressions of emotion by children with attention-deficit hyperactivity disorder. *Behavior Modification, 22,* 128–142.

Slate, S. E., Meyer, T. L., Burns W. J., & Montgomery, D. D. (1998). Computerized cognitive training for severely emotionally disturbed children with ADHD. *Behavior Modification, 22,* 415–437.

Slavin, R. E. (1987). *Cooperative learning: Student teams.* Washington, DC: NEA Professional Library.

Slavin, R. E. (1991). Are cooperative learning and "untracking" harmful to the gifted? *Educational Leadership, 48,* 68–71.

Slusarek, M., Velling, S., Bunk, D., & Eggers, C. (2001). Motivational effects on inhibitory control in children with ADHD. *Journal of the American Academy of Psychiatry, 40,* 355–363.

Smelter, R. W., Rasch, B. W., Fleming, J., Nazos, P., & Baranowski, S. (1996). Is attention deficit disorder becoming a desired diagnosis? *Phi Delta Kappan, 77, 429–432.*

Smith, R. M., Salend, S. J., & Ryan, S. (2001). Watch your language: Closing or opening the special education curtain. *Teaching Exceptional Children, 33,* 18–23.

Snyder, S. (1995). Movie portrayals of juvenile delinquents: Part II—sociology and psychology. *Adolescence, 30,* 324–337.

Solanto, M. V. (1990). The effects of reinforcement and response cost on a delayed-response task in children with Attention-Deficit Hyperactivity Disorder—A research note. *Journal of Child Psychology and Psychiatry and Allied Disciplines, 31,* 803–808.

Sonuga-Barke, E. J. S. (2001). Parent-based therapies for preschool ADHD: A randomized controlled trial with a community sample. *Journal of the American Academy of Child and Adolescent Psychiatry, 40,* 402–408.

Sonuga-Barke, E. J. S. (2002). Interval length and time-use by children with AD/HD: A comparison of four models. *Journal of Abnormal Child Psychology, 30,* 257–264.

Sonuga-Barke, E. J. S., & Goldfoot, M. T. (1995). The effect of child hyperactivity on mothers expectations for development. *Child Care Health and Development, 21,* 17–29.

Sonuga-Barke, E. J. S., de Houwer, J., de Ruiter, K., Ajzenstzen, M., & Holland, S. (2004). AD/HD and the capture of attention by briefly exposed delay-related cues: Evidence from a conditioning paradigm. *Journal of Child Psychology and Psychiatry, 45*, 274–283.

Sonuga-Barke, E. J. S., Houlberg, K., & Hall, M. (1994). When is "impulsiveness" not impulsive? The case of hyperactive children's cognitive style, 35, 1247–1253.

Sonuga-Barke, E. J. S., Williams, E., Hall, M., & Saxton, T. (1996). Hyperactivity and delay aversion III: The effect on cognitive style of imposing delay after errors. *Journal of Child Psychology and Psychiatry, 37*, 189–194.

Sprague, R. L., & Sleator, E. K. (1977). Methylphenidate in hyperkinetic children: Differences in dose effects on learning and social behavior. *Science, 198*, 1274–1276.

Stage, S. A., Abbott, R. D., Jenkins, J. R., & Berninger, V. W. (2003). Predicting response to early reading intervention from verbal IQ, reading-related language abilities, attention ratings, and verbal IQ-word reading discrepancy: Failure to validate discrepancy method. *Journal of Learning Disabilities, 36*, 24.

Stahl, N. D., & Clarizio, H. F. (1999). Conduct disorder and comorbidity. *Psychology in the Schools, 36*, 41–50.

Stanovich, K. (1988). The right and wrong places to look for the cognitive locus of reading disability. *Annals of Dyslexia, 38*, 157–177.

Stanovich, K. (1993). The construct validity of discrepancy definitions in learning disabilities. In G. R. Lyon (Ed.), *Better understanding learning disabilities: New views from research and their implications for education and public policy.* (pp. 273–308). Baltimore, MD: Paul H. Brookes Publishing Co.

Steinkamp, M. W. (1980). Relationships between environmental distractions and task performance of hyperactive and normal children. *Journal of Learning Disabilities, 13*, 209–214.

Sternberg, R. J. (1985). *Beyond IQ.* Cambridge: Cambridge University Press.

Stevens, L. J., Zentall, S. S., Deck, J. L., Abate, M. L., Watkins, B. A., Lipp, S. R., et al. (1995). Essential fatty acid metabolism in boys with attention-deficit hyperactivity disorders. *American Journal of Clinical Nutrition, 62*, 761–768.

Stevenson, H. W. (1992). Learning from Asian schools. Scientific American, 267, 70–76.

Stipek, D., & MacIver, D. (1989). Developmental changes in children's assessment of intellectual competence. *Child Development, 60*, 521–538.

Stormont, M., & Zentall, S. S. (1999). Assessment of setting in the behavioral ratings of preschoolers with and without high levels of activity. *Psychology in the Schools, 36*, 109–115.

Stormont, M., Zentall, S. S., Beyda, S., Javorsky, T., & Belfiore, P. (2000). Playground contexts for aggression for preschoolers with hyperactivity. *Journal of Behavioral Education, 10*, 37–48.

Stormont-Spurgin, M., & Zentall, S. S. (1995). Contributing factors in the manifestation of aggression in preschoolers with hyperactivity. *Journal of Child Psychology and Psychiatry, 36*, 491–509.

Stormont-Spurgin, M., & Zentall, S. S. (1996). Child-rearing practices associated with aggression in youth with and without ADHD: An exploratory study. *International Journal of Disability, Development, and Education, 43*, 135–146.

Strain, P. S., Cooke, T. P., & Apolloni, T. (1976). Role of peers in modifying classmates social behavior—Review. *Journal of Special Education, 10*, 351–356.

Strauss, A. A., & Lehtinen, L. E. (1947). *Psychopathology and education of the brain injured child.* New York: Grun and Stratton.

Streett, B. E. (1995, Fall). Attention-deficit hyperactivity disorder and conduct disorder. *The Counselor*, pp. 23–26.

Stuss, D., & Benson, D. F. (1984). *Cognition and memory.* In E. Perecman (Ed.), *The frontal lobes revisited* (pp. 141–158). New York: IRBN Press.

Sullivan, M. A., & O'Leary, S. G. (1990). Maintenance following reward and cost token programs. *Behavior Therapy, 21*, 139–149.

Swanson, J. M., McBurnett, K., Christian, D. L., & Wigal, T. (1995). Stimulant medication and treatment of children with ADHD. In T. H. Ollendick & R. J. Prinz (Eds.), *Advances in Clinical Child Psychology* (Vol. 17, pp. 265–322). New York: Plenum Press.

Swartz, J. L., & Martin, W. E., Jr. (1997). *Applied Ecological Psychology for Schools Within Communities: Assessment and Intervention.* Hillsdale, NJ: Lawrence Erlbaum Associates, Inc.

Tabassam, W., & Grainger, J. (2002). Self-concept, attributional style and self-efficacy beliefs of students with learning disabilities with and without attention deficit hyperactivity disorder. *Journal of Learning Disabilities, 25,* 141–151.

Tannock, R. (1997). Television, videogames, and ADHD: Challenging a popular belief. *The ADHD Report, 5,* 3–7.

Tannock, R., & Martinussen, R. (2001). Reconceptualizing ADHD. *Educational Leadership, 59,* 20–25.

Tannock, R., Martinussen, R., & Frijters, J. (2000). Naming speed performance and stimulant effects indicate effortful, semantic processing deficits in attention deficit/hyperactivity disorder. *Journal of Abnormal Child Psychology 28,* 237–252.

Tannock, R., Purvis, K. L., & Schachar, R. J. (1993). Narrative abilities in children with attention deficit disorder and normal peers. *Journal of Abnormal Child Psychology, 21,* 103–117.

Tannock, R., Schachar, R. J., & Logan, G. D. (1993). Does methylphenidate induce overfocusing in hyperactive children? *Journal of Clinical Child Psychology, 22,* 28–41.

Tant, J. L., & Douglas, V. I. (1982). Problem solving in hyperactive, normal and reading-disabled boys. *Journal of Abnormal Child Psychology, 10,* 285–306.

Taylor, A. F., Kuo, F. E., & Sullivan, W. C. (2001). Coping with ADD: The surprising connection to green play settings. *Environment and Behavior, 33,* 54–77.

Teicher, M. H., Ito, Y., Glod, C. A., & Barber, N. I. (1996). Objective measurement of hyperactivity and attentional problems in ADHD. *Journal of the American Academy of Child and Adolescent Psychiatry, 35,* 334–342.

Thomas, D. R., Becker, W. C., & Armstrong, M. (1968). Production and elimination of disruptive classroom behavior by systematically varying teacher's behavior. *Journal of Applied Behavior Analysis, 1,* 35–45.

Topolski, T. D., Edwards, T. C., Patrick, D. L., Varley, P., Way, M. E., Buesching, D. P. (2004). Quality of life of adolescent males with ADHD. *Journal of Attention Disorders, 7,* 163–173.

Torgesen, J. K. (2000). Individual differences in response to early interventions in reading: The lingering problem of treatment resisters. *Learning Disabilities Research and Practice, 15,* 55–64.

Traub, S. H., & Little, C. (Eds.). (1994). *Theories of deviance* (4th ed.). Itasca, IL: Peacock.

Tremblay, R. E. (2000). The origins of youth violence. *Isuma, 1*(2), 19–24.

Tripp, G., & Alsop, B. (1999). Sensitivity to reward frequency in boys with attention deficit hyperactivity disorder. *Journal of Clinical Child Psychology, 28,* 366–375.

Tseng, M. H., Henderson, A., Chow, S. M. K., & Yao, G. (2004). Relationship between motor proficiency, attention, impulse, and activity in children with ADHD. *Developmental Medicine and Child Neurology, 46,* 381–388.

Udvari-Solner, A. (1994). A decision-making model for curricular adaptations in cooperative groups. In J. S. Thousand, R. A. Villa, & A. I. Nevin (Eds.), *Creativity and collaborative learning* (pp. 56–77). Baltimore: Paul H. Brookes Publishing Co.

Umbreit, J. (1995). Functional assessment and intervention in a regular classroom setting for the disruptive behavior of a student with attention deficit hyperactivity disorder. *Behavioral Disorders, 20,* 267–278.

U.S. Department of Education. (1991). Thirteenth annual report to Congress on the implementation of the Individuals with Disabilities Education Act. Washington, DC: Author.

U.S. Department of Education (2002). Twenty-fourth annual report to Congress on the implementation of the Individuals with Disabilities Education Act. Washington, DC: Author.

U.S. General Accounting Office. (2001). *Student discipline: Individuals with Disabilities Education Act.* Washington, DC: Author.

Van Acker, R., Grant, S. H., & Henry, D. (1996). Teacher and student behavior as a function of risk for aggression. *Education and Treatment of Children, 19,* 316–334.

van der Meere, J., & Sergeant, J. (1988). Focused attention in pervasively hyperactive children. *Journal of Abnormal Child Psychology, 16,* 627–639.

van der Meere, J. J., Shalev, R., Borger, N. A., & Gross-Tsur, V. (1995). Sustained attention activation and MPH in ADHD: A research note. *Journal of Child Psychology and Psychiatry, 36,* 697–703.

van der Meere, J., & Stemerkink, N. (1999). The development of state regulation in normal children: An indirect comparison with children with ADHD. *Developmental Neuropsychology, 16,* 213–225.

Van Houten, R., Nau, P. A., MacKenzie-Keating, S., Sameoto, D., & Colavecchia, J. B. (1982). An analysis of some variables influencing the effectiveness of reprimands. *Journal of Applied Behavior Analysis, 15,* 65–83.

Varni, J. W., & Henker, B. (1979). Self-regulation approach to the treatment of three hyperactive boys. *Child Behavior Therapy, 1,* 171–192.

Vaughn, S., Levy, S., Coleman, M., & Boss, C. S. (2002). Reading instruction for students with LD and EBD, a synthesis. *Journal of Special Education, 36,* 2–13.

Velting, O. N., & Whitehurst, G. J. (1997). Inattentive-hyperactivity and reading achievement in children from low-income families: A longitudinal model. *Journal of Abnormal Child Psychology, 25,* 321–331.

Vernon, M., Coley, J., Hafer, J., & Dubois, J. (1980). Using sign language to remediate severe reading problems. *Journal of Learning Disabilities,* 13, 215–218.

Vitaro, F., Tremblay, R. E., Gagnon, C., & Pelletier, D. (1994). Predictive accuracy of behavioral and sociometric assessments of high-risk kindergarten children. *Journal of Clinical Child Psychology, 23,* 272–282.

Voelker, S. L., Carter, R. A., Sprague, D. J., Gdowski, J. M., & Lachar, D. (1989). Developmental trends in memory and metamemory in children with attention deficit disorder. *Journal of Pediatric Psychology, 14,* 75–88.

Waddell, K. J. (1984). The self-concept and social adaptation of hyperactive children in adolescence. *Journal of Clinical Child Psychology, 13,* 50–55.

Wahler, R. G. (1975). Some structural aspects of deviant child behavior. *Journal of Applied Behavior Analysis, 8,* 27–42.

Walker, B. C. (1980). The relative effects of painting and gross-motor activities on the intrinsic locus-of-control of hyperactivity in learning disabled elementary school pupils. *Studies in Art Education, 21,* 13–21.

Walker, H. M., & Sprague, J. R. (1999). Longitudinal research and functional behavioral assessment issues. *Behavior Disorders, 24,* 335–337.

Wallander, J. L. (1988). The relationship between attention problems in childhood and antisocial behaviour in eleven year old children in Dunedin, New Zealand. *Journal of Child Psychology and Psychiatry, 29,* 53–62.

Warner-Rogers, J., Taylor, A., Taylor, E., & Sandberg, S. (2000). Inattentive behavior in childhood. *Journal of Learning Disabilities, 33,* 520–537.

Waschbusch, D. A., Pelham, W. E., Jennings, J. R., Greiner, A. R., Tarter, R. E., & Moss, H. B. (2002). Reactive aggression in boys with disruptive behavior disorders: Behavior, physiology, and affect. *Journal of Abnormal Child Psychology, 30,* 641–656.

Wasson, A. S. (1980). Stimulus-seeking, perceived school environment, and school misbehavior. *Adolescence, 15,* 603–607.

Wasson, A. S. (1981). Susceptibility to boredom and deviant behavior at school. *Psychological Reports, 48,* 901–902.

Webb, N. M. (1992). Testing a theoretical model of student interaction and learning in small groups. In R. Hertz-Lazarowitz & N. Miller (Eds.), *Interaction in cooperative groups: The theoretical anatomy of group learning* (pp. 102–119). New York: Cambridge University Press.

Webster, E. R. (1998). *Learning Efficiency Test-II manual.* Novato, CA: Academic Therapy Publications.

Webster, E. R., Hall, W. C., Brown, B. M., & Bolen, M. L. (1996). Memory modality differences in children with attention deficit hyperactivity disorder with and without learning disabilities. *Psychology in the Schools, 33,* 193–201.

Wehby, J. H., Symons, F. J., & Canale, J. A. (1998). Teaching practices in classrooms for students with emotional and behavioral disorders: Discrepancies between recommendations and observations. *Behavioral Disorders, 24*(1), 51–56.

Weiler, M. D., Bernstein, J. H., Bellinger, D., & Waber, D. P. (2002). Information processing deficits in children with attention-deficit/hyperactivity disorder, inattentive subtype, and children with reading disability. *Journal of Learning Disabilities, 35,* 448–461.

Weingartner, H., Rapoport, J. L., Buchsbaum, M. S., Bunney W. E., Jr., Ebert, M. H., Mikkelsen, E. J., et al. (1980). Cognitive processes in normal and hyperactive children and their response to amphetamine treatment. *Journal of Abnormal Psychology, 89*, 25–37.

Weiss, G., & Hechtman, L. T. (1993). *Hyperactive children grown up* (2nd ed.). New York: Guilford Press.

Wells, K. C. (2001). Comprehensive versus matched psychosocial treatment in the MTA study: Conceptual and empirical issues. *Journal of Clinical Child Psychology, 30*, 131–135.

Wendt, M. S. (2000). The effect of an activity program designed with intense physical exercise on the behavior of attention deficit hyperactivity disorder. *Dissertation Abstracts International; 61* (2-A), 500. University Microfilms International (UMI No. 9964398)

Whalen, C. K. (1989). Attention deficit and hyperactivity disorders. In *Handbook of child psychopathology* (2nd ed., pp. 131–160). New York: Plenum Press.

Whalen, C. K. (2001). ADHD treatment in the 21st century: Pushing the envelope. *Journal of Clinical Child Psychology, 30*, 136–140.

Whalen, C. K., & Henker, B. (1985). The social worlds of hyperactive (ADDH) children. *Clinical Psychology Review, 5*, 447–478.

Whalen, C. K., & Henker, B. (1991). Therapies for hyperactive children: Comparisons, combinations, and compromises. *Journal of Consulting and Clinical Psychology, 59*, 126–137.

Whalen, C. K., Henker, B., Collins, B. E., McAuliffe, S., & Vaux, A. (1979). Peer interaction in a structured communication task: Comparisons of normal and hyperactive boys and of methylphenidate (ritalin) and placebo effects. *Child Development, 50*, 388–401.

Whaley-Klahn, M. A., & Loney, J. (1977). A multivariate study of the relationship of parental management to self-esteem and initial drug response in hyperkinetic/MBD boys. *Psychology in the Schools, 14*, 485–492.

Whinnery, K. W., Fuchs, D., & Fuchs, L. S. (1991). General, special, and remedial teachers' acceptance of behavioral and instructional strategies for mainstreaming students with mild handicaps. *Remedial and Special Education, 12*, 6–17.

Wilens, T. E., Biederman, J., & Spencer, T. J. (2002). Attention deficit/hyperactivity disorder across the lifespan. *Annual Review of Medicine, 53*, 113–131.

Willcutt, E. G., & Pennington, B. F. (2000). Comorbidity of reading disability and attention-deficit/hyperactivity disorder: Differences by gender and sybtype. *Journal of Learning Disabilities, 33*, 179–191.

Willcutt, E. G., Pennington, B. F., Boada, R., Ogline, J. S., Tunich, R. A., Chhabildas, N. A., et al. (2001). A comparison of the cognitive deficits in reading disability and attention-deficit/hyperactivity disorder. *Journal of Abnormal Psychology, 110*, 157–172.

Willcutt, E. G., Pennington, B. F., & DeFries, J. C. (2000). Etiology of inattention and hyperactivity/impulsivity in a community sample of twins with learning disabilities. *Journal of Abnormal Child Psychololgy, 28*, 149–159.

Willerman, L. (1973). Activity level and hyperactivity in twins. *Child Development, 44*, 288–293.

Williams, C. A., & Forehand, R. (1984). An examination of predictor variables for child compliance and noncompliance. *Journal of Abnormal Child Psychology, 12*, 491–504.

Witt, J. C., Elliott, S. N., & Martens, B. K. (1984). Acceptability of behavioral interventions used in classrooms: The influence of amount of teacher time, severity of behavior problem, and type of intervention. *Behavior Disorders, 9*, 95–104.

Witzel, B. S., & Mercer, C. D. (2003). Using rewards to teach students with disabilities. *Remedial and Special Education, 24*, 88–96.

Wohlwill, J. F., & Heft, H. (1987). The physical environment and the development of the child. In D. Stokols & I. Altman (Eds.), *Handbook of Environmental Psychology* (Vol. 1, pp. 281–328).

Wolraich, M. L., Hannah, J. N., Baumgaertel, A., & Feurer, I. D. (1998). Examination of DSM-IV criteria for attention deficit/hyperactivity disorder in a county-wide sample. *Journal of Developmental and Behavioral Pediatrics, 19*, 162–168.

Wolraich, M. L., Hannah, J. N., Pinnock, T. J., Baumgaertel, A., & Brown, J. (1996). Comparison of diagnostic criteria for attention deficit hyperactivity disorder in a county-wide sample.

Journal of the American Academy of Child and Adolescent Psychiatry, 35, 319–324.

Wolraich, M. L., Lindgren, S., Stromquist, A., Milich, R., Davis, C., & Watson, D. (1990). Stimulant medication use by primary care physicians in the treatment of attention-deficit hyperactivity disorder. *Pediatrics, 86,* 95–101.

Woltersdorf, M. A. (1992). Videotape self-modeling in the treatment of attention-deficit hyperactivity disorder. *Child and Family Behavior Therapy, 14,* 53–73.

Wong, B. (1979). The role of theory in learning disabilities research: Part II. A selective review of current theories of learning and reading disabilities. *Journal of Learning Disabilities, 12,* 649–658.

Wong, B. Y. L. (1986). Problems and issues in definition of LD. In J. K. Torgesen, & B. Y. L. Wong (Eds.), Psychological and educational perspectives on learning disabilities (pp. 3–26) San Diego: Academic Press.

Woodcock, R. W., & Johnson, M. B. (1989). *Woodcock-Johnson Psycho-Educational Battery—Revised.* Allen, TX: DLM Teaching Resources.

Woodward, L., Taylor, E., & Dowdney, L. (1998). The parenting and family functioning of children with hyperactivity. *Journal of Child Psychology and Psychiatry, 39,* 161–169.

Worland, J., North-Jones, M., & Stern, J. A. (1973). Performance and activity of hyperactive and normal boys as a function of distraction and reward. *Journal of Abnormal Child Psychology, 1,* 363–377.

Worthington, L. A., Wortham, J., Patterson, D. A., & Smith, C. (1998). Project facilitate: An overview of an inservice education program for parents and educators. *Teacher and Special Education, 20,* 123–132.

Wu, S., Pink, W., Crain, R., & Moles, O. (1982). Student suspension: A critical reappraisal. *Urban Review, 14,* 245–303.

Xin, Y. P. (1999). The effects of instruction in solving mathematical word problems with students with learning problems: A meta-analysis. *Journal of Special Education, 32,* 207–225.

Zagar, R., & Bowers, N. D. (1983). The effect of time of day on problem solving and classroom behavior.*Psychology in the Schools, 20,* 337–345.

Zajonc, R. B. (1965). Social facilitation. *Science, 149,* 269–274.

Zakay, D. (1992). The role of attention in children's time perception. *Journal of Experimental Child Psychology, 54,* 355–371.

Zametkin, A. J., Liebenauer, I. I., Fitzgerald, G. A., King, A. C., Minkunas, D. V., Herscovitch P., et al. (1993). Brain metabolism in teenagers with attention-deficit hyperactivity disorder. *Archives of General Psychiatry, 50,* 333–340.

Zametkin, A. J., Nordahl, T. E., Gross, M., King, A. C., Semple, W. E., Rumsey, J., et al. (1990). Cerebral glucose metabolism in adults with hyperactivity of childhood onset. *New England Journal of Medicine, 323,* 1361–1366.

Zentall, S. S. (1975). Optimal stimulation as theoretical basis of hyperactivity. *American Journal of Orthopsychiatry, 45,* 549–563.

Zentall, S. S. (1980). Behavioral comparisons of hyperactive and normally active children in natural settings. *Journal of Abnormal Child Psychology, 8,* 93–109.

Zentall, S. S. (1983). Effects of psychotropic drugs on the behavior of preacademic children: A review. *Topics in Early Childhood Special Education, 3,* 29–39.

Zentall, S. S. (1984). Context effects in the behavioral ratings of hyperactive children. *Journal of Abnormal Child Psychology, 12,* 345–352.

Zentall, S. S. (1985a). A context for hyperactivity. In K. D. Gadow (Ed.), *Advances in learning and behavioral disabilities* (Vol. 4, pp. 273–343). Greenwich, CT: JAI Press.

Zentall, S. S. (1985b). Stimulus-control factors in search performance of hyperactive children. *Journal of Learning Disabilities, 18,* 480–485.

Zentall, S. S. (1986a). Assessment of emotionally disturbed preschoolers. *Diagnostique, 11,* 154–179.

Zentall, S. S. (1986b). Effects of color stimulation on performance and activity of hyperactive and nonhyperactive children. *Journal of Abnormal Child Psychology, 8,* 93–109.

Zentall, S. (1988). Production deficiencies in elicited language but not in spontaneous verbalizations of hyperactive children. *Journal of Abnormal Child Psychology, 16,* 657–673.

Zentall, S. S. (1989a). Attentional cuing in spelling tasks for hyperactive and comparison regular classroom children. *Journal of Special Education, 23,* 83–93.

Zentall, S. S. (1989b). Self-control training with hyperactive and impulsive children. In J. N. Hughes & R. J. Hall (Eds.), *Handbook of cognitive behavioral approaches in educational settings* (pp. 305–346). New York: Guilford Press.

Zentall, S. S. (1990). Fact-retrieval automatization and math problem solving by learning disabled, attention-disordered, and normal adolescents. *Journal of Educational Psychology, 82,* 856–865.

Zentall, S. S. (1993). Research on the educational implications of attention deficit hyperactivity disorder. *Exceptional Children, 60,* 143–153.

Zentall, S. S. (1995). Modifying classroom tasks and environments. In S. Goldstein (Ed.), *Understanding and managing children's classroom behavior* (pp. 356–374). New York: Wiley.

Zentall, S. S., & Dwyer, A. M. (1988). Color effects on the impulsivity and activity of hyperactive children. *Journal of School Psychology, 27,* 165–174.

Zentall, S. S., Falkenberg, S. D., & Smith, L. B. (1985). Effects of color stimulation on the copying performance of attention-problem adolescents. *Journal of Abnormal Child Psychology, 13,* 501–511.

Zentall, S. S., & Ferkis, M. A. (1993). Mathematical problem-solving for ADHD children with and without learning disabilities. *Learning Disability Quarterly, 16,* 6–18.

Zentall, S. S., & Gohs, D. E. (1984). Hyperactive and comparison children's response to detailed vs. global cues in communication tasks. *Learning Disability Quarterly, 7,* 77–87.

Zentall, S. S., Gohs, D. E., & Culatta, B. (1983). Language and activity of hyperactive and comparison preschoolers during listening tasks. *Exceptional Children, 50,* 255–266.

Zentall, S. S., & Goldstein, S. (1999). *Seven steps to homework success: A family guide for solving common homework problems.* New York: Specialty Press.

Zentall, S. S., Grskovic, J., Javorsky, J., & Hall, A. M. (2000). Effects of noninformational color on reading test performance of students with attention deficit hyperactivity disorder (ADHD). *Diagnostique, 25,* 129–146.

Zentall, S. S., Hall, A. M., & Lee, D. L. (1998). Attentional focus of students with hyperactivity during a word-search task. *Journal of Abnormal Child Psychology, 26,* 335–343.

Zentall, S. S., Harper, G., & Stormont-Spurgin, M. (1993). Children with hyperactivity and their organizational abilities. *Journal of Educational Research, 60,* 143–153.

Zentall, S. S., & Javorsky, J. (1995) Functional and clinical assessment of ADHD: Implications of DSM-IV in the schools. *Journal of Psychoeducational Assessment: ADHD Special Monograph,* 22–41.

Zentall, S. S., & Javorsky, J. (2005). *Inservice education for teachers of students with ADHD.* Manuscript submitted for publication.

Zentall, S. S., Javorsky, J., & Cassady, J. C. (2001). Social comprehension of children with hyperactivity. *Journal of Attention Disorders, 5,* 11–24.

Zentall, S. S., & Kruczek, T. (1988). The attraction of color for active attention problem children. *Exceptional Children, 54,* 357–362.

Zentall, S. S., Kuester, D., & Craig, B. (2006). *Behavior and goals of students with and without ADHD during cooperative problem solving.* Manuscript in preparation.

Zentall, S. S., & Leib, S. (1985). Structured tasks: Effects on activity and performance of hyperactive and normal children. *Journal of Educational Research, 79,* 91–95.

Zentall, S. S., & Meyer, M. (1987). Self-regulation of stimulation for ADD-H children during reading and vigilance task performance. *Journal of Abnormal Child Psychology, 15,* 519–536.

Zentall, S. S., Moon, S., Hall, A. M., & Grskovic, J. (2001). Learning and motivational characteristics of boys with giftedness and/or attention deficit/hyperactivity disorder. *Exceptional Children, 67,* 499–519.

Zentall, S. S., & Shaw, J. H. (1980). Effects of classroom noise on performance and activity of second-grade hyperactive and control children. *Journal of Educational Psychology, 72,* 830–840.

Zentall, S. S., & Smith, Y. N. (1992). Assessment and validation of the learning and behavioral style preferences of hyperactive and comparison children. *Learning and Individual Differences, 4,* 25–41.

Zentall, S. S., & Smith, Y. N. (1993). Mathematical performance and behavior of children with hyperactivity, with and without coexisting aggression. *Behavior Research and Therapy, 31,* 701–710.

Zentall, S. S., Smith, Y. N., Lee, Y. B., & Wieczorek, C. (1994). Mathematical outcomes of attention-deficit hyperactivity disorder. *Journal of Learning Disabilities, 27,* 510–519.

Zentall, S. S., & Stormont-Spurgin, M. L. (1995). Educator preferences of accommodations for students with attention deficit hyperactivity disorder. *Teacher Education and Special Education, 18,* 115–123.

Zentall, S. S., & Zentall, T. R. (1976). Activity and task performance of hyperactive children as a function of environmental stimulation. *Journal of Consulting and Clinical Psychology, 44,* 693–697.

Zentall, S. S., & Zentall, T. R. (1983). Optimal stimulation: A model of disordered activity and performance in normal and deviant children. *Psychological Bulletin, 94,* 446–471.

Zentall, S. S., Zentall, T. R., & Barack, R. C. (1978). Distraction as a function of within-task stimulation for hyperactive and normal children. *Journal of Learning Disabilities, 11,* 540–548.

Zentall, S. S., Zentall, T. R., & Booth, M. E. (1978). Within-task stimulation: Effects on activity and spelling performance in hyperactive and normal children. *Journal of Educational Research, 71,* 223–230.

Zimmerman, B. J. (2000). Attaining self-regulation: A social cognitive perspective. In *Handbook of self-regulation.* Academic Press.

Zimmerman, B. J. (2001). Attaining self-regulation: A social cognitive perspective. In M. Boekaeris, P. R. Pintrich, & M. Zeidner (Eds.), *Handbook of self-regulation* (pp. 13–41). San Diego, CA: Academic Press.

Name Index

Subject Index